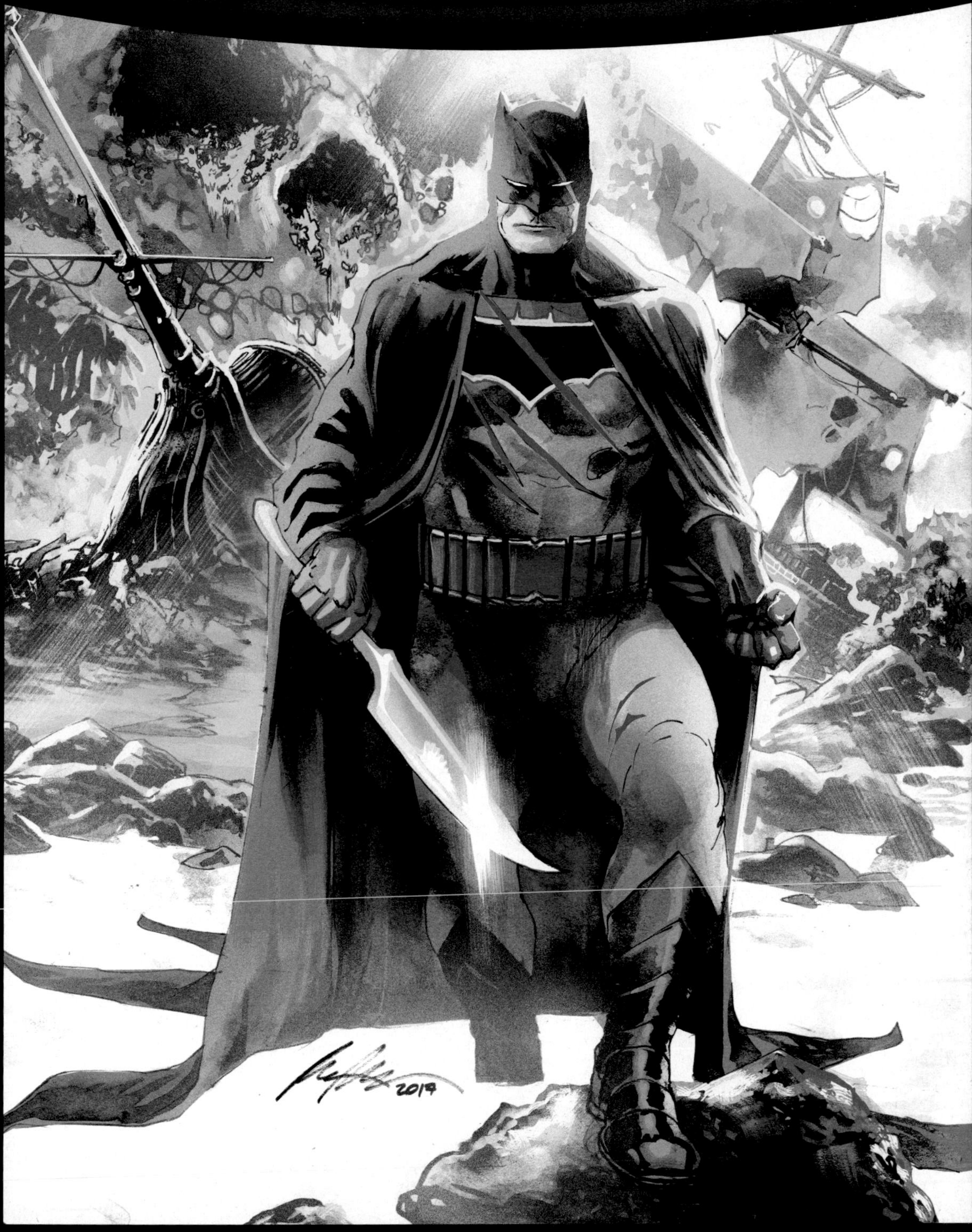

ALL-STAR BATMAN

VOL.3 THE FIRST ALLY

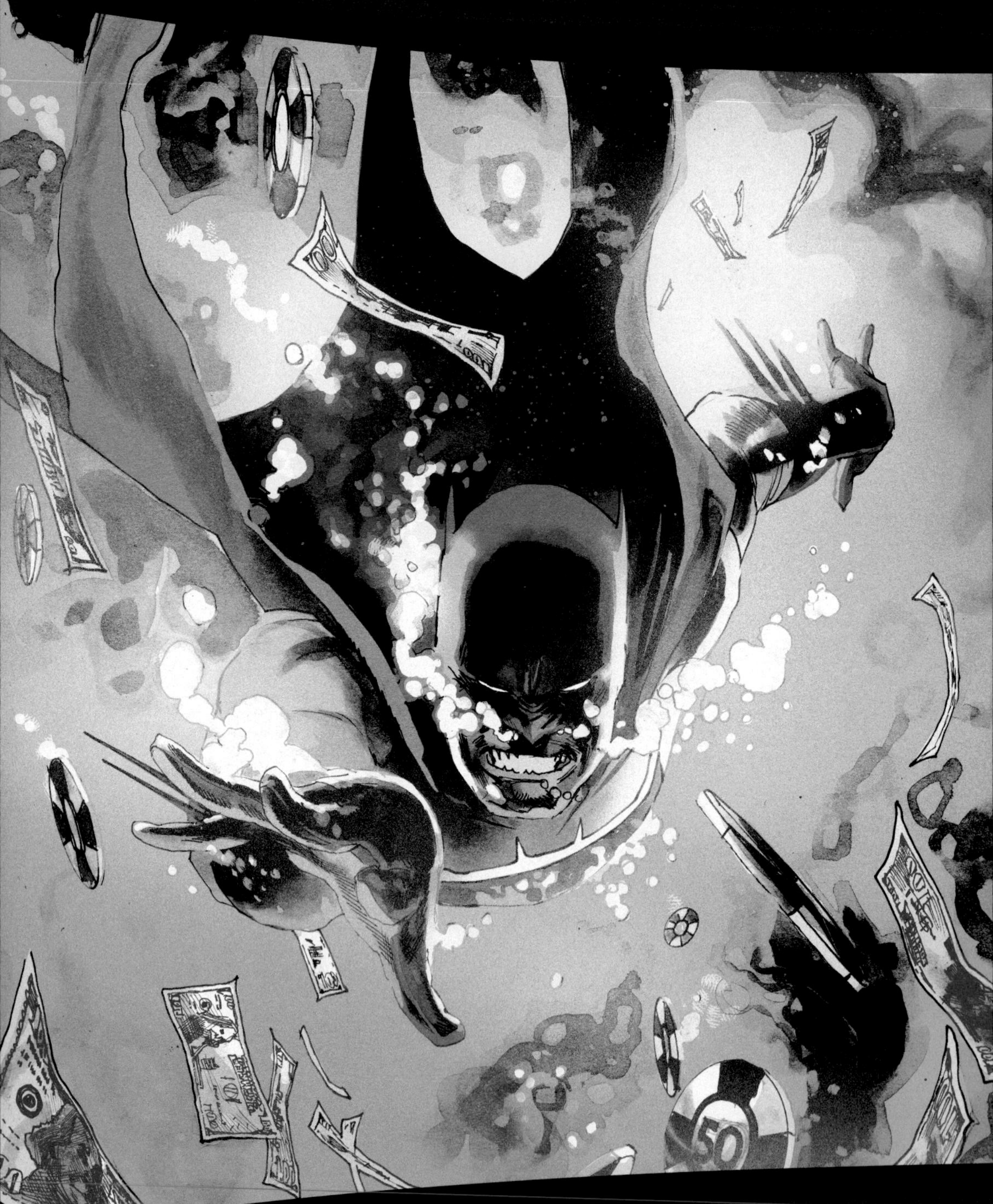

ALL-STAR BATMAN

VOL.3 THE FIRST ALLY

SCOTT SNYDER
RAFAEL ALBUQUERQUE
RAFAEL SCAVONE
writers

RAFAEL ALBUQUERQUE
SEBASTIAN FIUMARA
artists

JORDIE BELLAIRE
TRISH MULVIHILL
CRIS PETER
LEE LOUGHRIDGE
colorists

STEVE WANDS
DEZI SIENTY
letterers

RAFAEL ALBUQUERQUE
collection cover artist

BATMAN created by **BOB KANE** with **BILL FINGER**

MARK DOYLE Editor - Original Series ✳ **REBECCA TAYLOR** Associate Editor - Original Series ✳ **DAVE WIELGOSZ** Assistant Editor - Original Series
JEB WOODARD Group Editor - Collected Editions ✳ **ROBIN WILDMAN** Editor - Collected Edition
STEVE COOK Design Director - Books ✳ **DAMIAN RYLAND** Publication Design

BOB HARRAS Senior VP - Editor-in-Chief, DC Comics
PAT McCALLUM Executive Editor, DC Comics

DIANE NELSON President ✳ **DAN DiDIO** Publisher ✳ **JIM LEE** Publisher ✳ **GEOFF JOHNS** President & Chief Creative Officer
AMIT DESAI Executive VP - Business & Marketing Strategy, Direct to Consumer & Global Franchise Management
SAM ADES Senior VP & General Manager, Digital Services ✳ **BOBBIE CHASE** VP & Executive Editor, Young Reader & Talent Development
MARK CHIARELLO Senior VP - Art, Design & Collected Editions ✳ **JOHN CUNNINGHAM** Senior VP - Sales & Trade Marketing
ANNE DePIES Senior VP - Business Strategy, Finance & Administration ✳ **DON FALLETTI** VP - Manufacturing Operations
LAWRENCE GANEM VP - Editorial Administration & Talent Relations ✳ **ALISON GILL** Senior VP - Manufacturing & Operations
HANK KANALZ Senior VP - Editorial Strategy & Administration ✳ **JAY KOGAN** VP - Legal Affairs ✳ **JACK MAHAN** VP - Business Affairs
NICK J. NAPOLITANO VP - Manufacturing Administration ✳ **EDDIE SCANNELL** VP - Consumer Marketing
COURTNEY SIMMONS Senior VP - Publicity & Communications ✳ **JIM (SKI) SOKOLOWSKI** VP - Comic Book Specialty Sales & Trade Marketing
NANCY SPEARS VP - Mass, Book, Digital Sales & Trade Marketing ✳ **MICHELE R. WELLS** VP - Content Strategy

ALL-STAR BATMAN VOL. 3: THE FIRST ALLY

DC Comics, 2900 West Alameda Ave., Burbank, CA 91505
Printed by LSC Communications, Kendallville, IN, USA. 8/10/18. First Printing.
ISBN: 978-1-4012-8430-5

Library of Congress Cataloging-in-Publication Data is available.

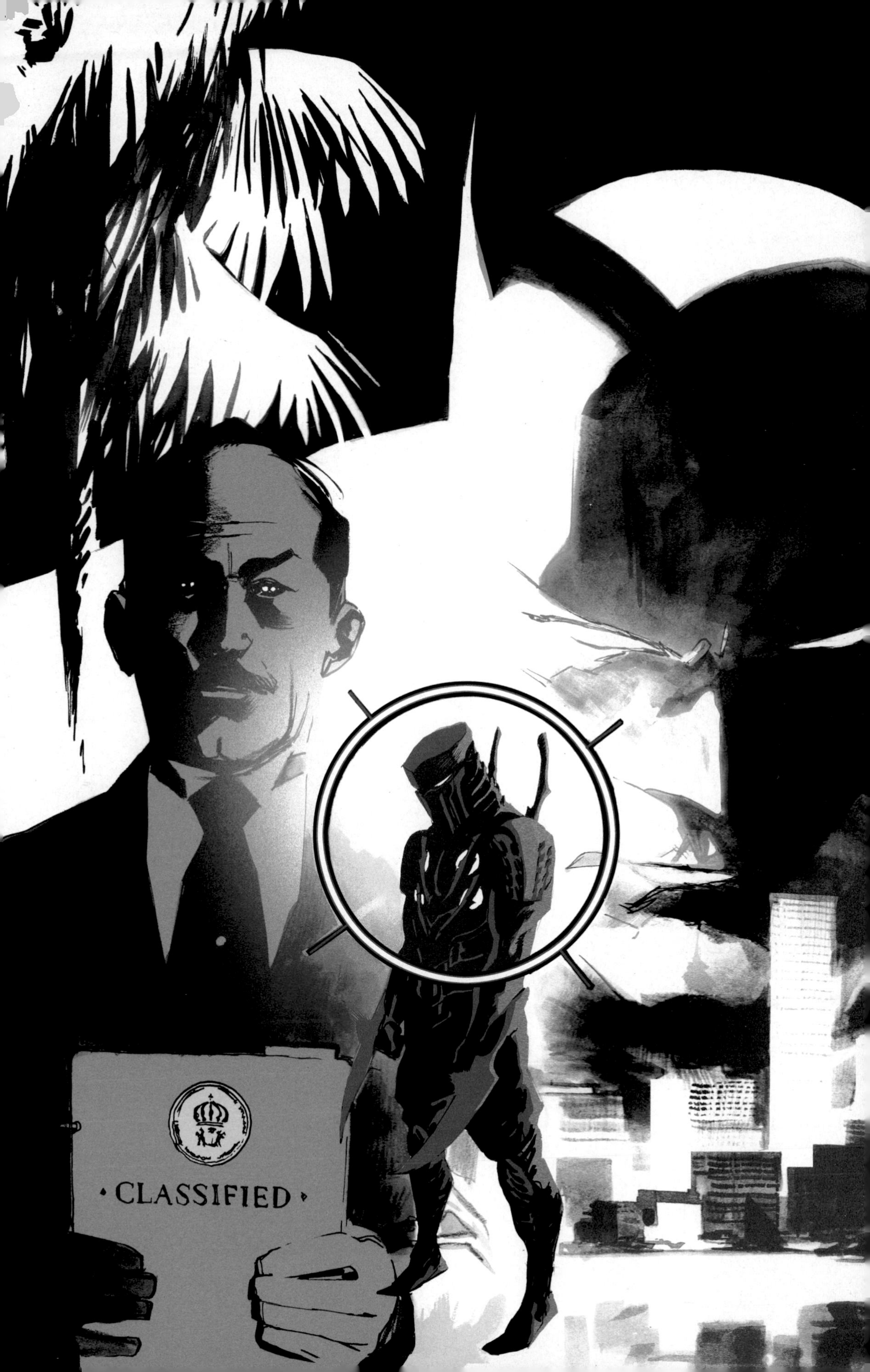
CLASSIFIED

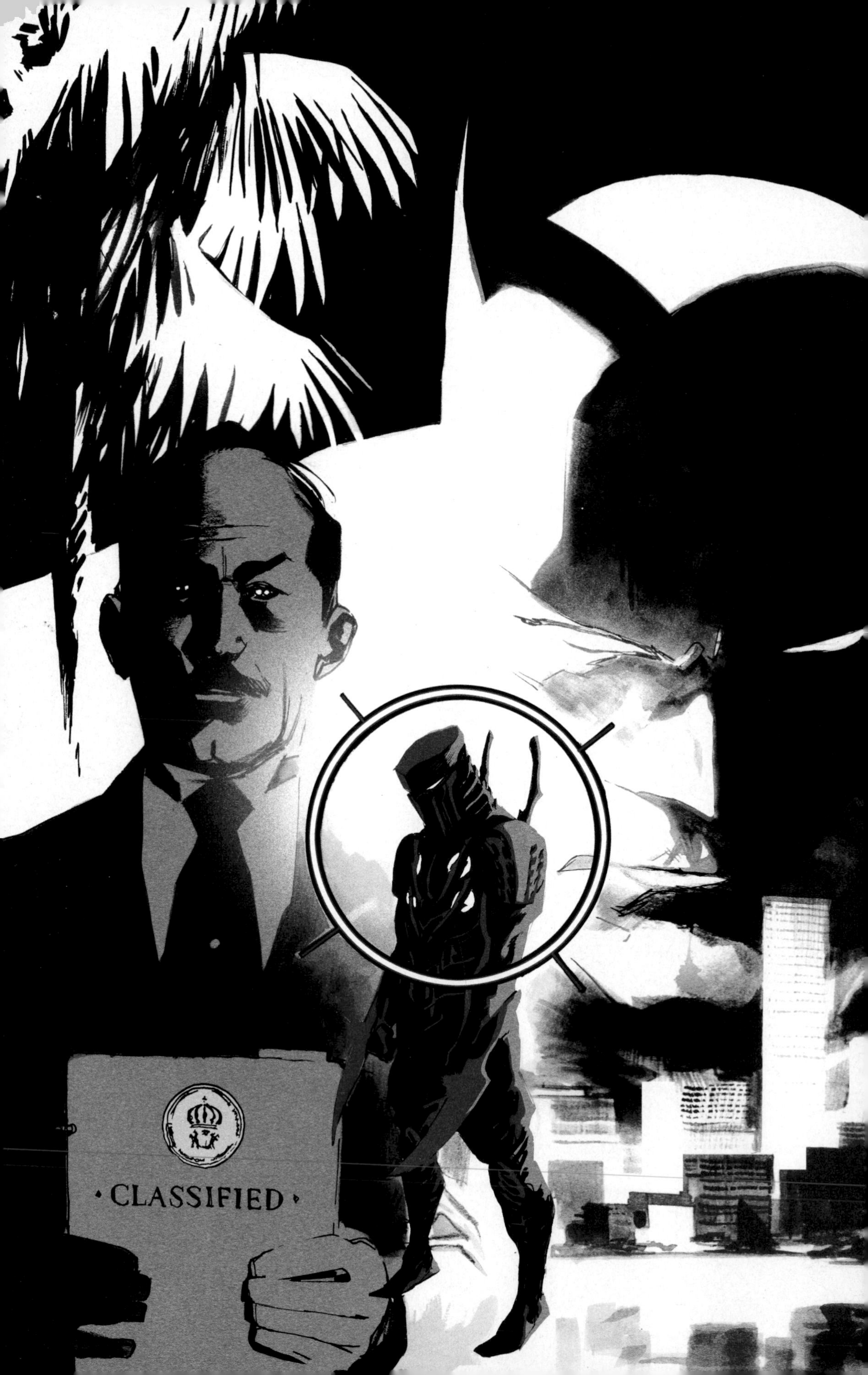
CLASSIFIED

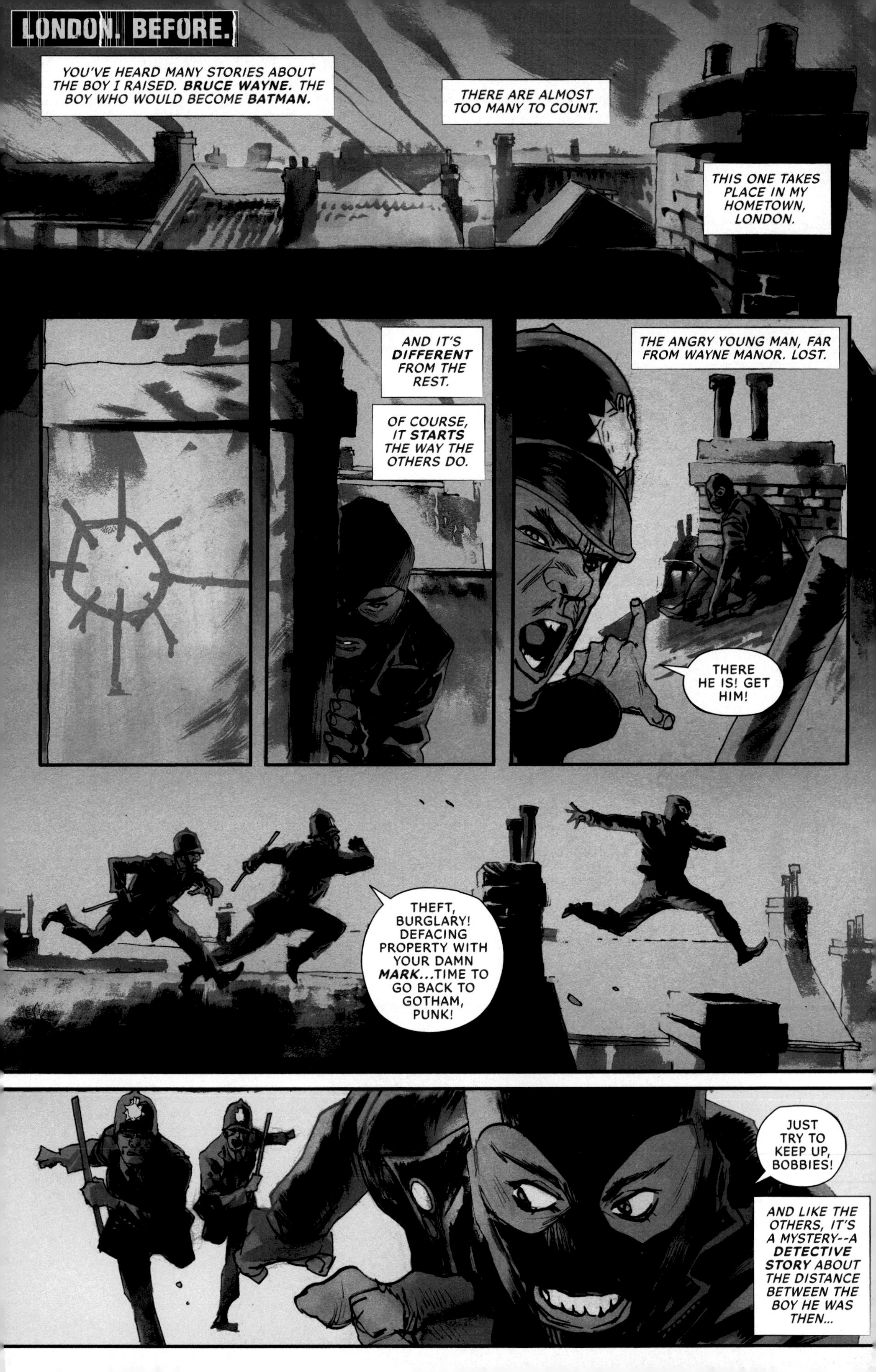
LONDON. BEFORE.
YOU'VE HEARD MANY STORIES ABOUT THE BOY I RAISED. **BRUCE WAYNE.** THE BOY WHO WOULD BECOME **BATMAN.**
THERE ARE ALMOST TOO MANY TO COUNT.
THIS ONE TAKES PLACE IN MY HOMETOWN, LONDON.
AND IT'S **DIFFERENT** FROM THE REST.
OF COURSE, IT **STARTS** THE WAY THE OTHERS DO.
THE ANGRY YOUNG MAN, FAR FROM WAYNE MANOR. LOST.
THERE HE IS! GET HIM!
THEFT, BURGLARY! DEFACING PROPERTY WITH YOUR DAMN ***MARK...*** TIME TO GO BACK TO GOTHAM, PUNK!
JUST TRY TO KEEP UP, BOBBIES!
AND LIKE THE OTHERS, IT'S A MYSTERY--A **DETECTIVE STORY** ABOUT THE DISTANCE BETWEEN THE BOY HE WAS THEN...

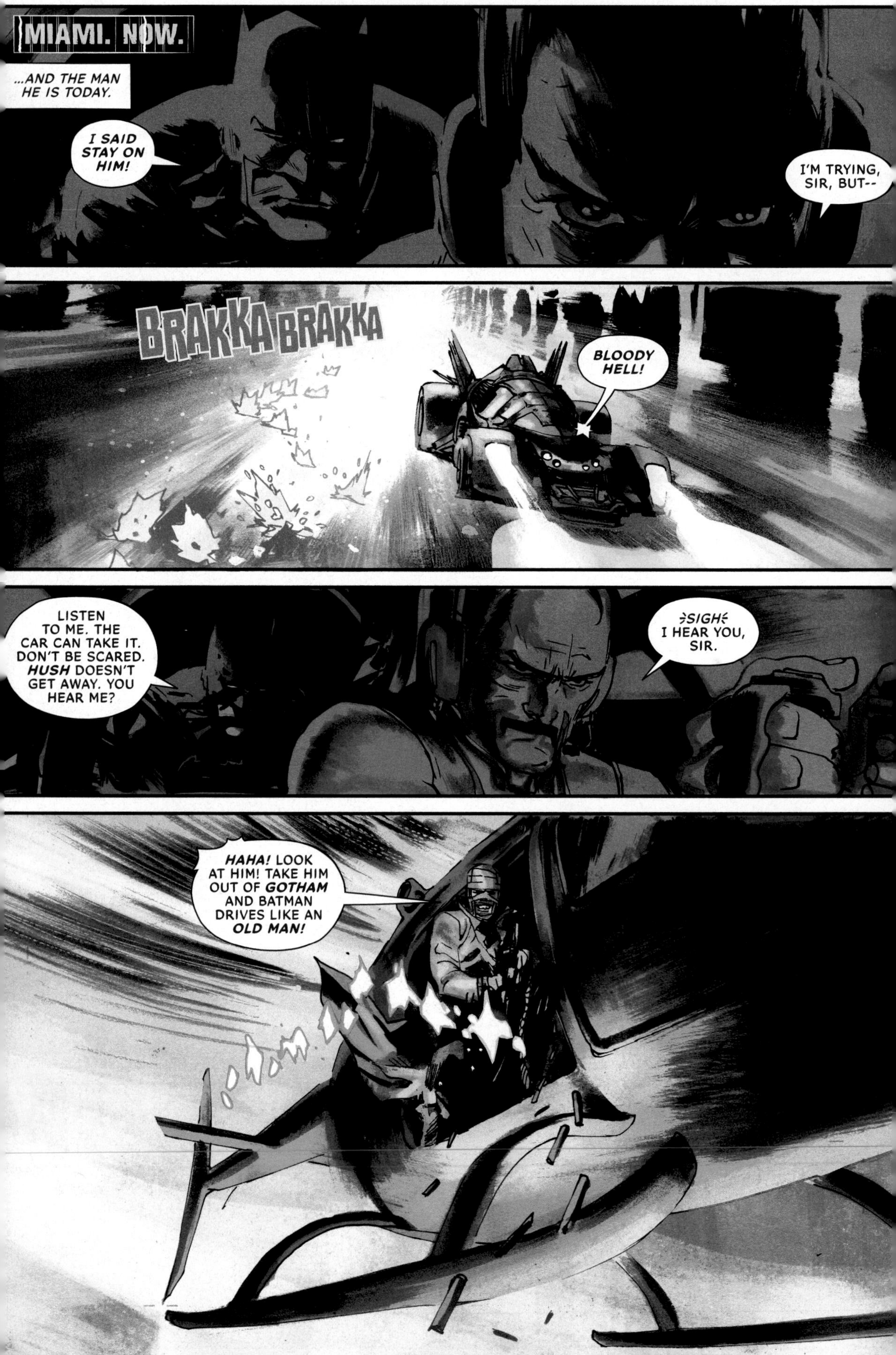
MIAMI. NOW.
...AND THE MAN HE IS TODAY.
I SAID STAY ON HIM!
I'M TRYING, SIR, BUT--
BRAKKA BRAKKA
BLOODY HELL!
LISTEN TO ME. THE CAR CAN TAKE IT. DON'T BE SCARED. HUSH DOESN'T GET AWAY. YOU HEAR ME?
SIGH I HEAR YOU, SIR.
HAHA! LOOK AT HIM! TAKE HIM OUT OF GOTHAM AND BATMAN DRIVES LIKE AN OLD MAN!

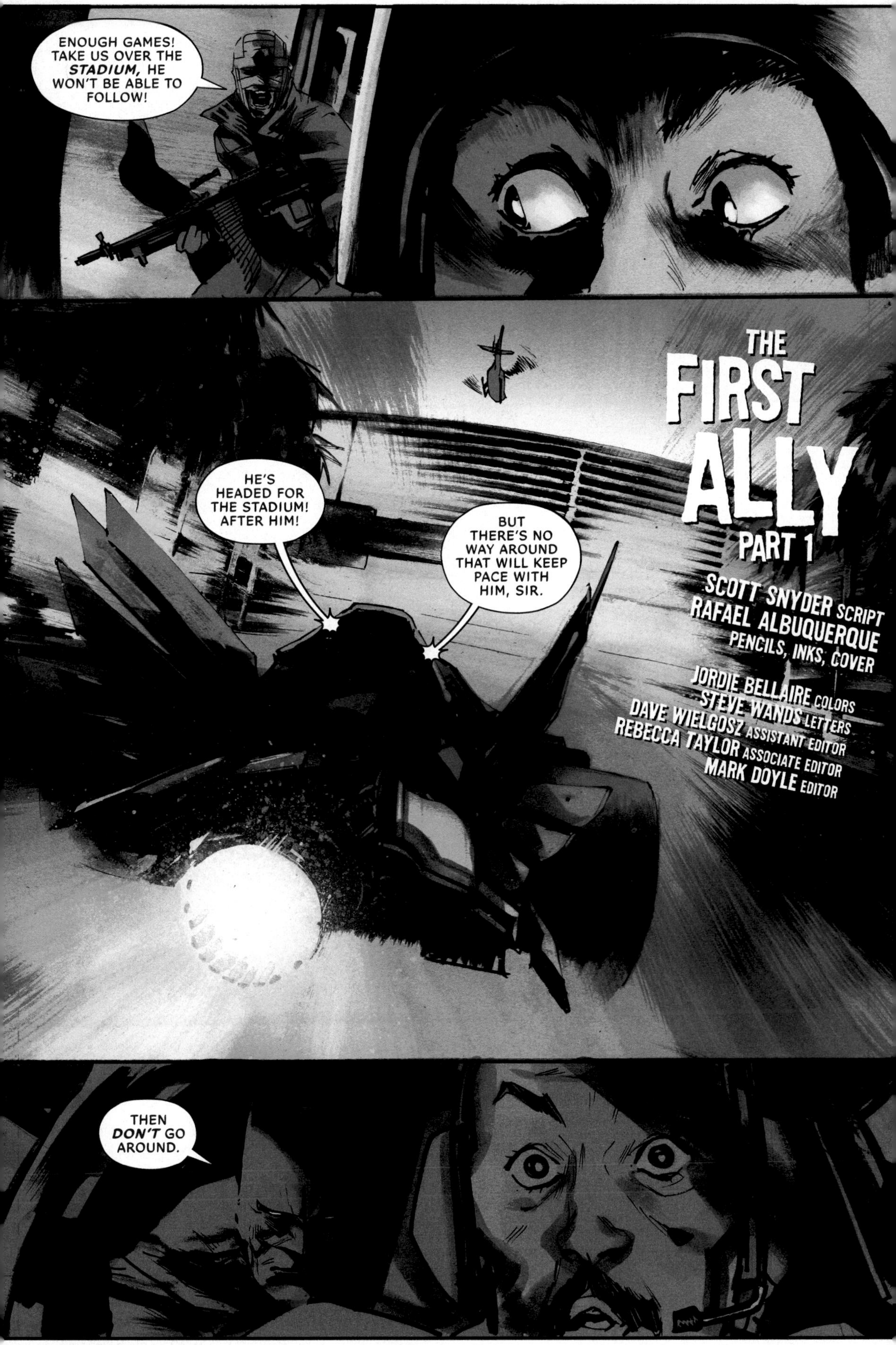
ENOUGH GAMES! TAKE US OVER THE *STADIUM,* HE WON'T BE ABLE TO FOLLOW!
THE FIRST ALLY PART 1
SCOTT SNYDER SCRIPT
RAFAEL ALBUQUERQUE PENCILS, INKS, COVER
JORDIE BELLAIRE COLORS
STEVE WANDS LETTERS
DAVE WIELGOSZ ASSISTANT EDITOR
REBECCA TAYLOR ASSOCIATE EDITOR
MARK DOYLE EDITOR
HE'S HEADED FOR THE STADIUM! AFTER HIM!
BUT THERE'S NO WAY AROUND THAT WILL KEEP PACE WITH HIM, SIR.
THEN *DON'T* GO AROUND.

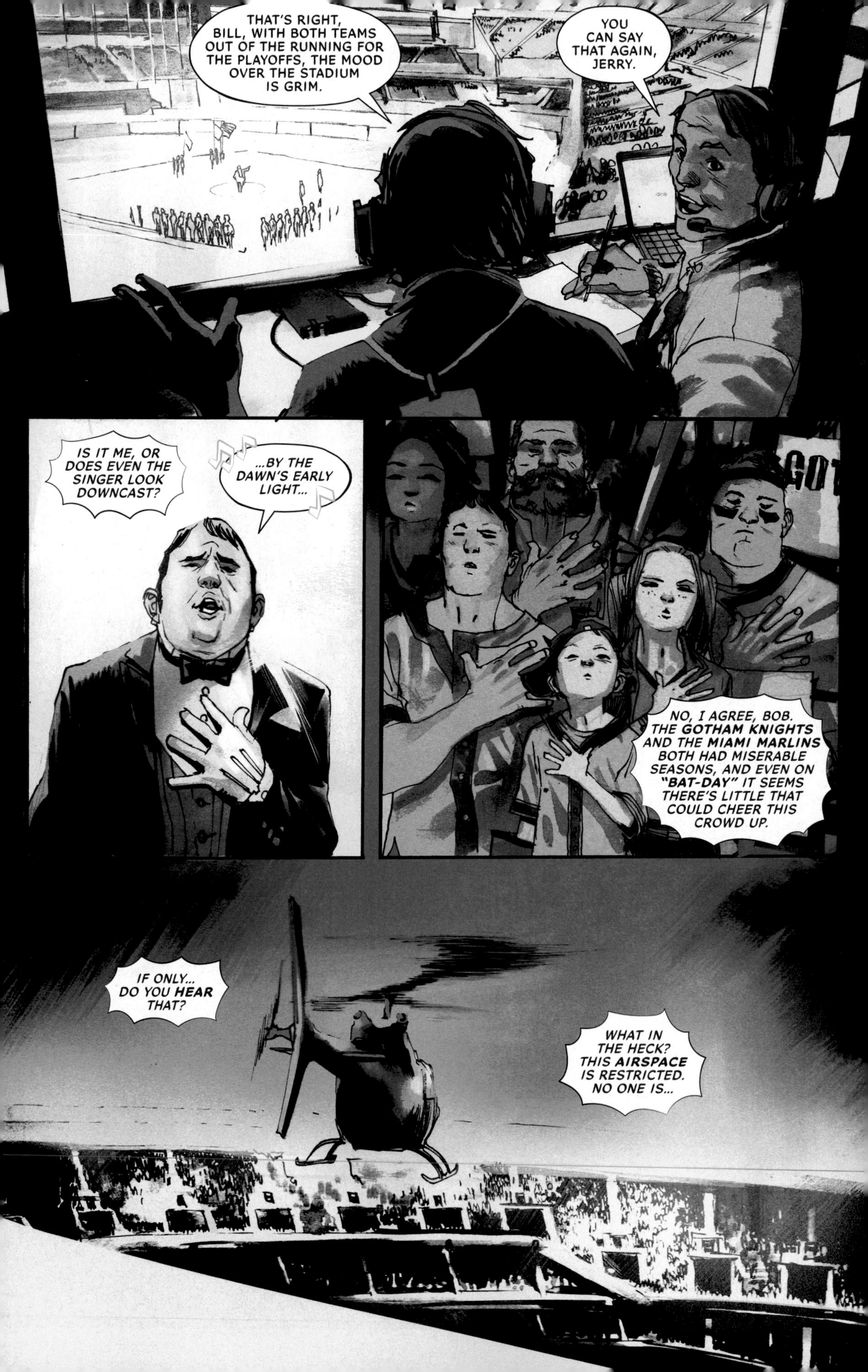
THAT'S RIGHT, BILL, WITH BOTH TEAMS OUT OF THE RUNNING FOR THE PLAYOFFS, THE MOOD OVER THE STADIUM IS GRIM.
YOU CAN SAY THAT AGAIN, JERRY.
IS IT ME, OR DOES EVEN THE SINGER LOOK DOWNCAST?
...BY THE DAWN'S EARLY LIGHT...
NO, I AGREE, BOB. THE GOTHAM KNIGHTS AND THE MIAMI MARLINS BOTH HAD MISERABLE SEASONS, AND EVEN ON "BAT-DAY" IT SEEMS THERE'S LITTLE THAT COULD CHEER THIS CROWD UP.
IF ONLY... DO YOU HEAR THAT?
WHAT IN THE HECK? THIS AIRSPACE IS RESTRICTED. NO ONE IS...

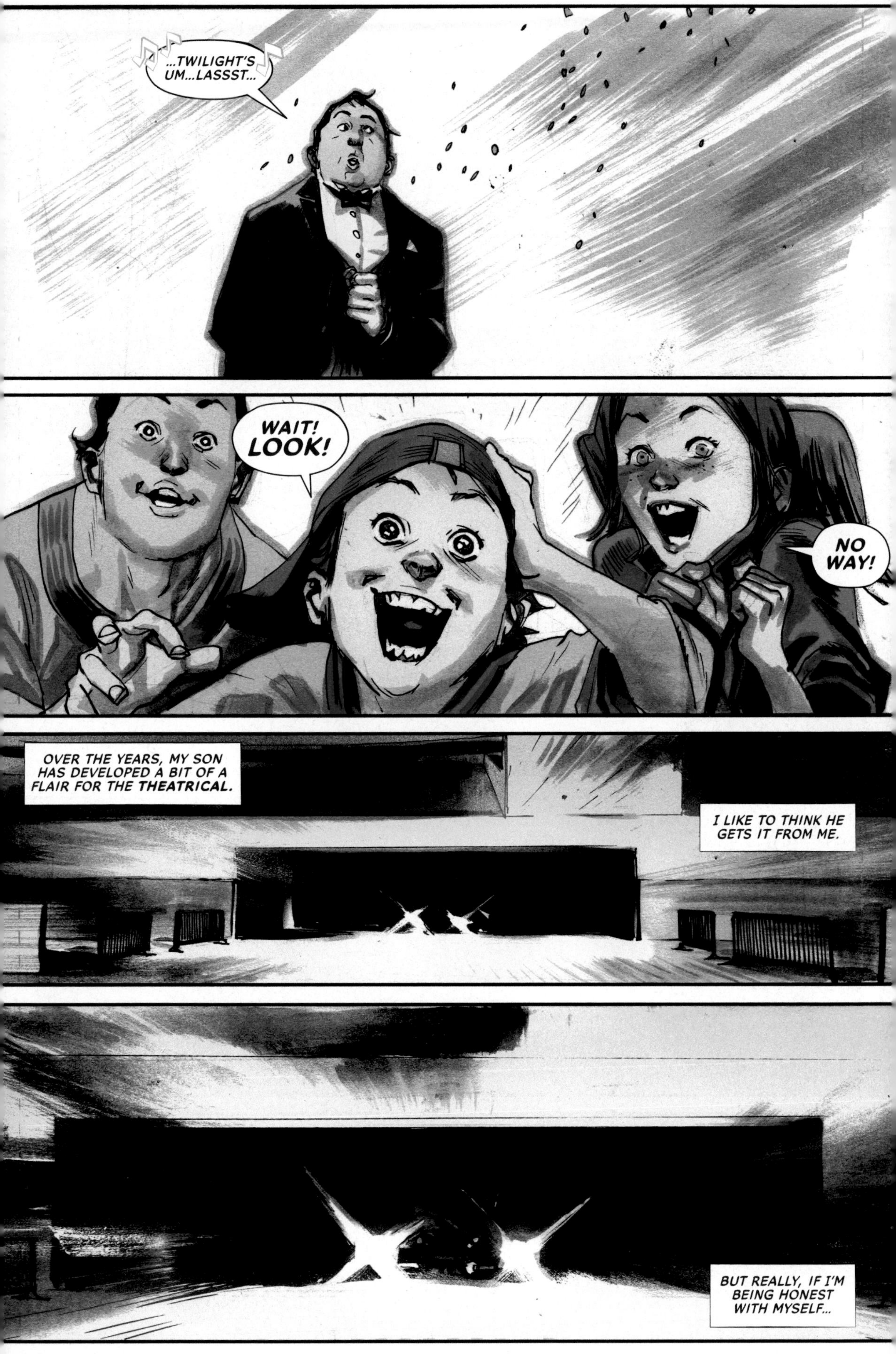
...TWILIGHT'S UM...LASSST...
WAIT! LOOK!
NO WAY!
OVER THE YEARS, MY SON HAS DEVELOPED A BIT OF A FLAIR FOR THE THEATRICAL.
I LIKE TO THINK HE GETS IT FROM ME.
BUT REALLY, IF I'M BEING HONEST WITH MYSELF...

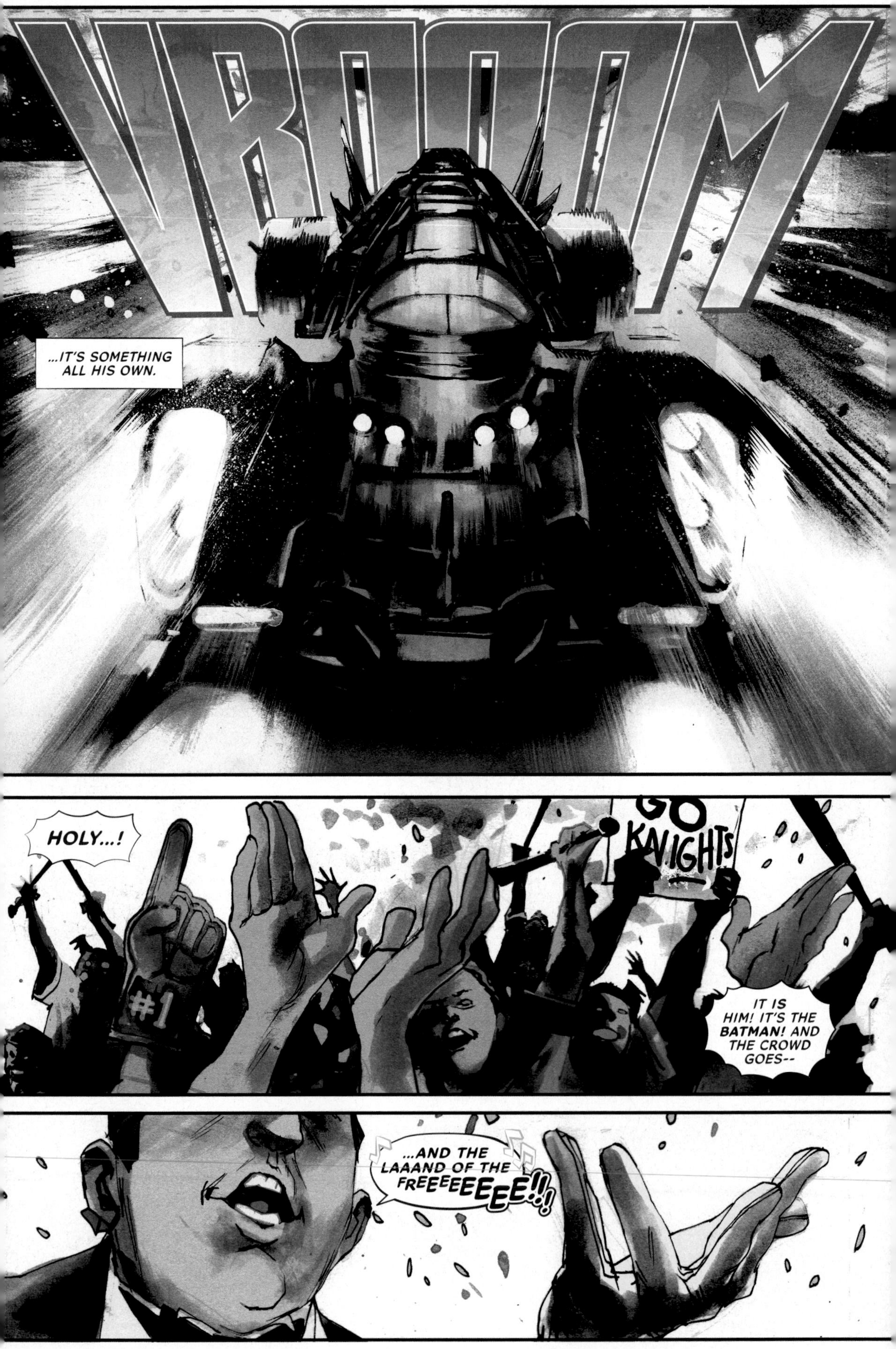
VROOM
...IT'S SOMETHING ALL HIS OWN.
HOLY...!
GO KNIGHTS
#1
IT IS HIM! IT'S THE BATMAN! AND THE CROWD GOES--
...AND THE LAAAND OF THE FREEEEEEEEE!!!

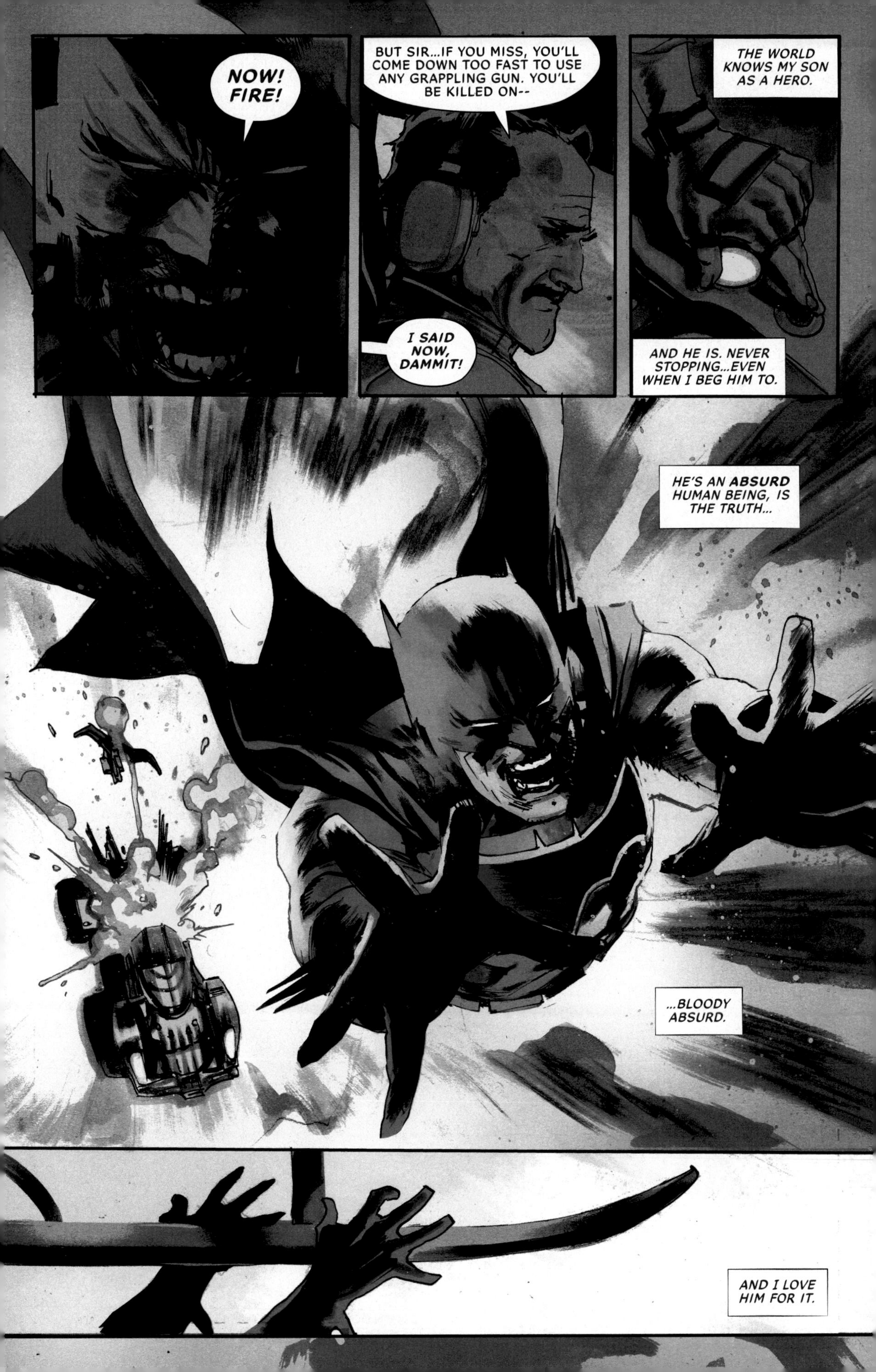
NOW! FIRE!
BUT SIR...IF YOU MISS, YOU'LL COME DOWN TOO FAST TO USE ANY GRAPPLING GUN. YOU'LL BE KILLED ON--
I SAID NOW, DAMMIT!
THE WORLD KNOWS MY SON AS A HERO.
AND HE IS. NEVER STOPPING...EVEN WHEN I BEG HIM TO.
HE'S AN ABSURD HUMAN BEING, IS THE TRUTH...
...BLOODY ABSURD.
AND I LOVE HIM FOR IT.

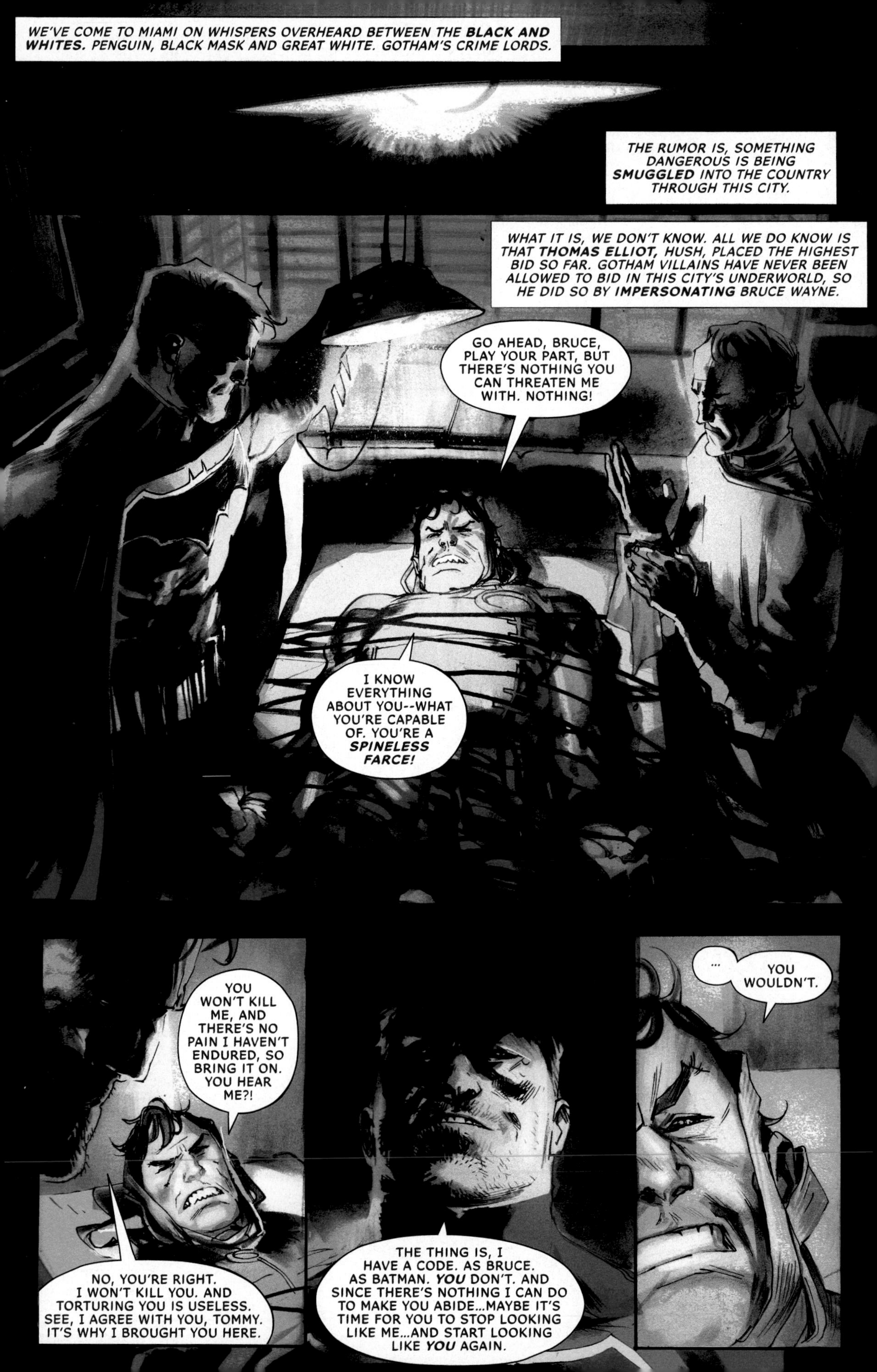
WE'VE COME TO MIAMI ON WHISPERS OVERHEARD BETWEEN THE **BLACK AND WHITES.** PENGUIN, BLACK MASK AND GREAT WHITE. GOTHAM'S CRIME LORDS.
THE RUMOR IS, SOMETHING DANGEROUS IS BEING **SMUGGLED** INTO THE COUNTRY THROUGH THIS CITY.
WHAT IT IS, WE DON'T KNOW. ALL WE DO KNOW IS THAT **THOMAS ELLIOT,** HUSH, PLACED THE HIGHEST BID SO FAR. GOTHAM VILLAINS HAVE NEVER BEEN ALLOWED TO BID IN THIS CITY'S UNDERWORLD, SO HE DID SO BY **IMPERSONATING** BRUCE WAYNE.
GO AHEAD, BRUCE, PLAY YOUR PART, BUT THERE'S NOTHING YOU CAN THREATEN ME WITH. NOTHING!
I KNOW EVERYTHING ABOUT YOU--WHAT YOU'RE CAPABLE OF. YOU'RE A ***SPINELESS FARCE!***
YOU WON'T KILL ME, AND THERE'S NO PAIN I HAVEN'T ENDURED, SO BRING IT ON. YOU HEAR ME?!
NO, YOU'RE RIGHT. I WON'T KILL YOU. AND TORTURING YOU IS USELESS. SEE, I AGREE WITH YOU, TOMMY. IT'S WHY I BROUGHT YOU HERE.
THE THING IS, I HAVE A CODE. AS BRUCE. AS BATMAN. ***YOU*** DON'T. AND SINCE THERE'S NOTHING I CAN DO TO MAKE YOU ABIDE...MAYBE IT'S TIME FOR YOU TO STOP LOOKING LIKE ME...AND START LOOKING LIKE ***YOU*** AGAIN.
...
YOU WOULDN'T.

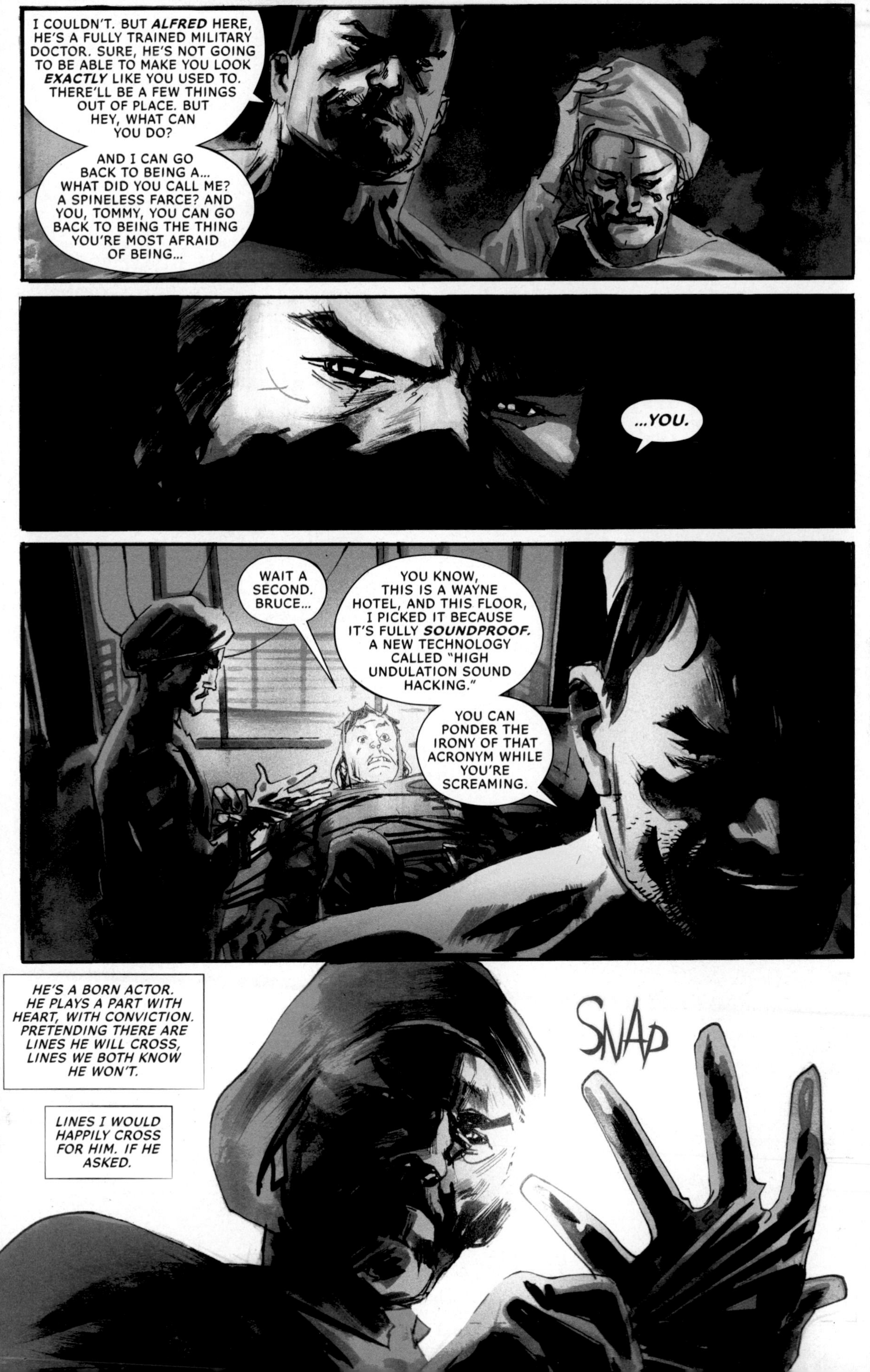
I COULDN'T. BUT ALFRED HERE, HE'S A FULLY TRAINED MILITARY DOCTOR. SURE, HE'S NOT GOING TO BE ABLE TO MAKE YOU LOOK EXACTLY LIKE YOU USED TO. THERE'LL BE A FEW THINGS OUT OF PLACE. BUT HEY, WHAT CAN YOU DO?
AND I CAN GO BACK TO BEING A... WHAT DID YOU CALL ME? A SPINELESS FARCE? AND YOU, TOMMY, YOU CAN GO BACK TO BEING THE THING YOU'RE MOST AFRAID OF BEING...
...YOU.
WAIT A SECOND. BRUCE...
YOU KNOW, THIS IS A WAYNE HOTEL, AND THIS FLOOR, I PICKED IT BECAUSE IT'S FULLY SOUNDPROOF. A NEW TECHNOLOGY CALLED "HIGH UNDULATION SOUND HACKING."
YOU CAN PONDER THE IRONY OF THAT ACRONYM WHILE YOU'RE SCREAMING.
HE'S A BORN ACTOR. HE PLAYS A PART WITH HEART, WITH CONVICTION. PRETENDING THERE ARE LINES HE WILL CROSS, LINES WE BOTH KNOW HE WON'T.
LINES I WOULD HAPPILY CROSS FOR HIM. IF HE ASKED.
SNAP

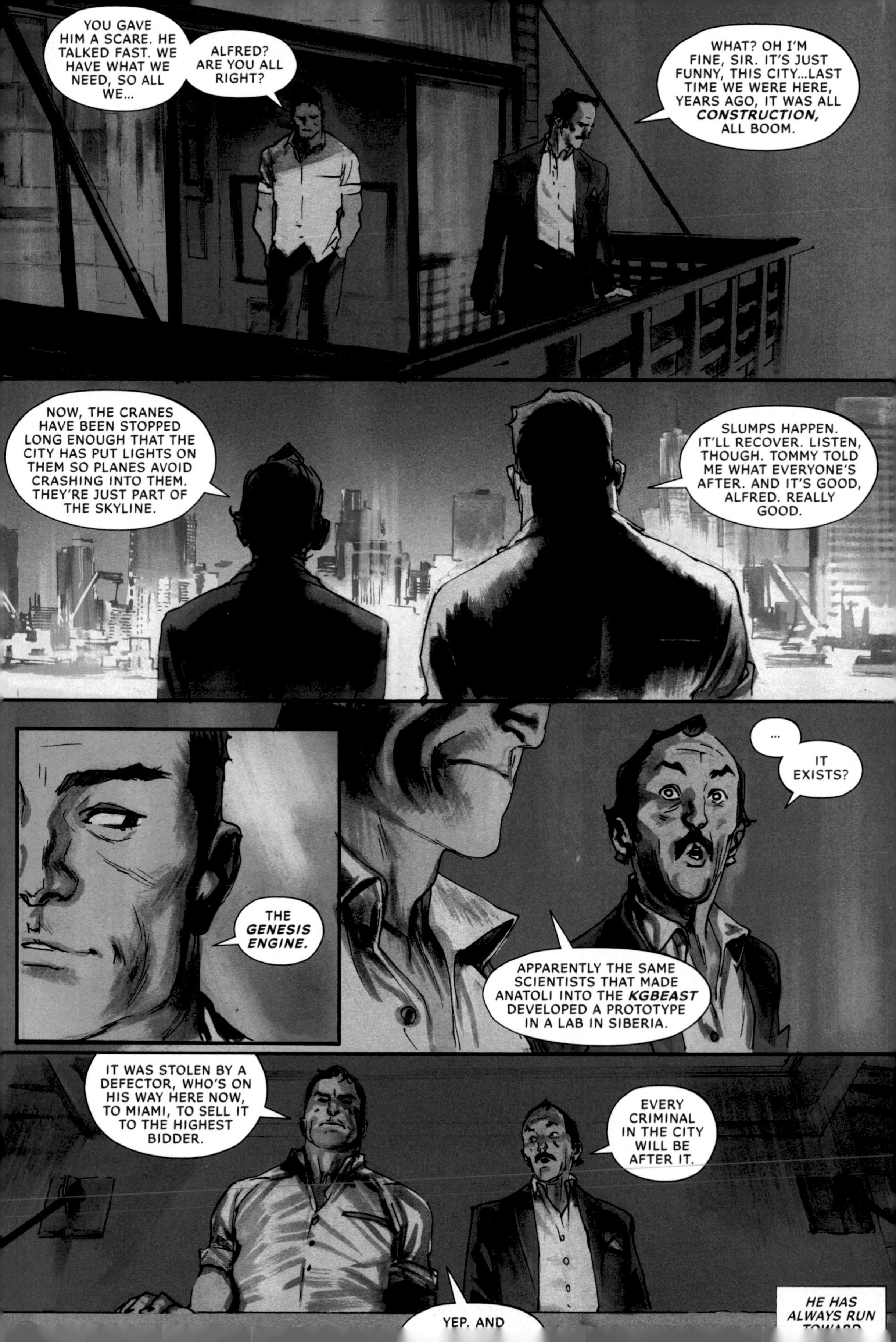
YOU GAVE HIM A SCARE. HE TALKED FAST. WE HAVE WHAT WE NEED, SO ALL WE...
ALFRED? ARE YOU ALL RIGHT?
WHAT? OH I'M FINE, SIR. IT'S JUST FUNNY, THIS CITY...LAST TIME WE WERE HERE, YEARS AGO, IT WAS ALL *CONSTRUCTION,* ALL BOOM.
NOW, THE CRANES HAVE BEEN STOPPED LONG ENOUGH THAT THE CITY HAS PUT LIGHTS ON THEM SO PLANES AVOID CRASHING INTO THEM. THEY'RE JUST PART OF THE SKYLINE.
SLUMPS HAPPEN. IT'LL RECOVER. LISTEN, THOUGH. TOMMY TOLD ME WHAT EVERYONE'S AFTER. AND IT'S GOOD, ALFRED. REALLY GOOD.
THE *GENESIS ENGINE.*
...
IT EXISTS?
APPARENTLY THE SAME SCIENTISTS THAT MADE ANATOLI INTO THE *KGBEAST* DEVELOPED A PROTOTYPE IN A LAB IN SIBERIA.
IT WAS STOLEN BY A DEFECTOR, WHO'S ON HIS WAY HERE NOW, TO MIAMI, TO SELL IT TO THE HIGHEST BIDDER.
EVERY CRIMINAL IN THE CITY WILL BE AFTER IT.
YEP. AND
HE HAS ALWAYS RUN

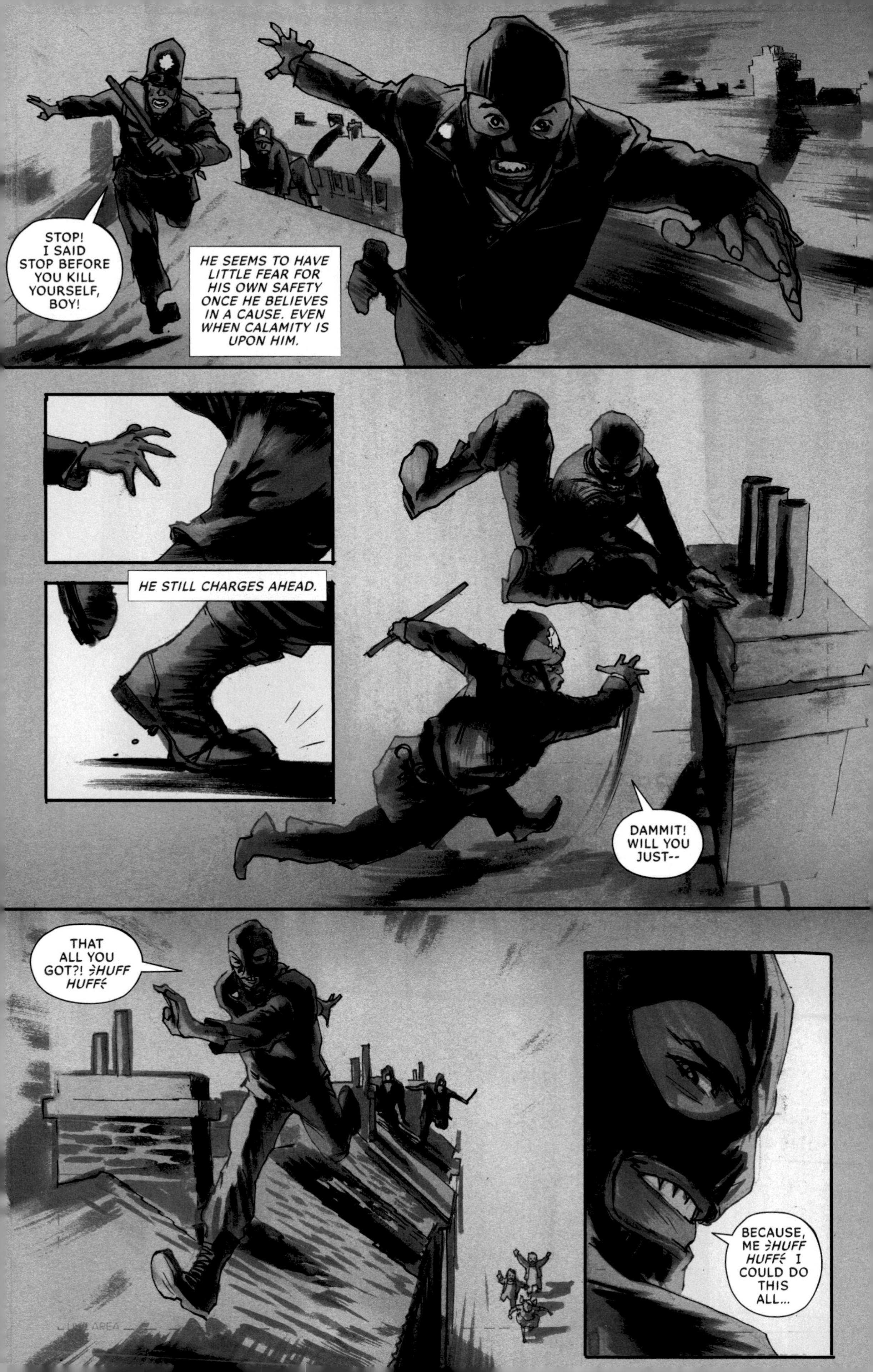
STOP! I SAID STOP BEFORE YOU KILL YOURSELF, BOY!
HE SEEMS TO HAVE LITTLE FEAR FOR HIS OWN SAFETY ONCE HE BELIEVES IN A CAUSE. EVEN WHEN CALAMITY IS UPON HIM.
HE STILL CHARGES AHEAD.
DAMMIT! WILL YOU JUST--
THAT ALL YOU GOT?! *HUFF HUFF*
BECAUSE, ME *HUFF HUFF* I COULD DO THIS ALL...

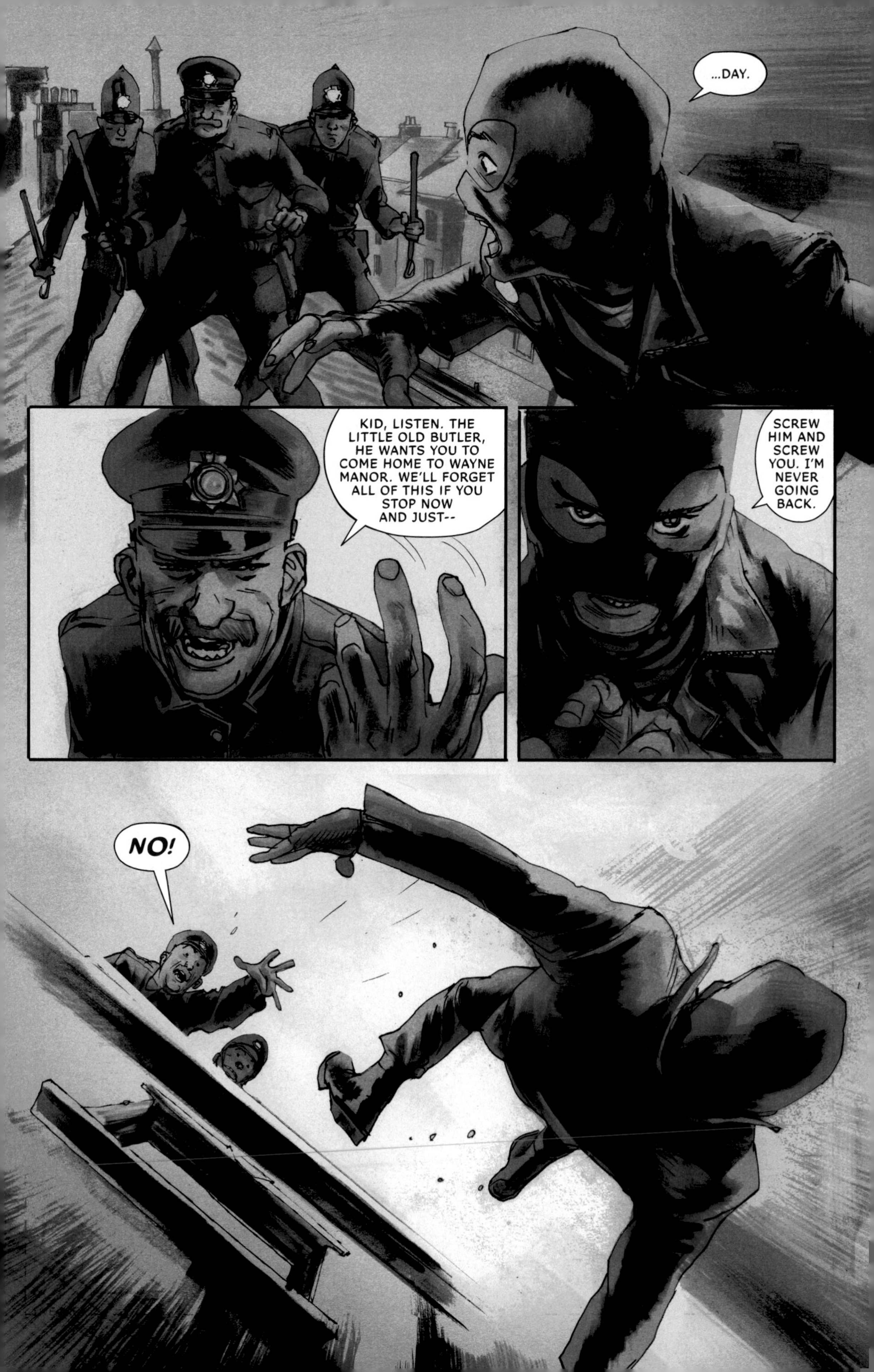
...DAY.
KID, LISTEN. THE LITTLE OLD BUTLER, HE WANTS YOU TO COME HOME TO WAYNE MANOR. WE'LL FORGET ALL OF THIS IF YOU STOP NOW AND JUST--
SCREW HIM AND SCREW YOU. I'M NEVER GOING BACK.
NO!

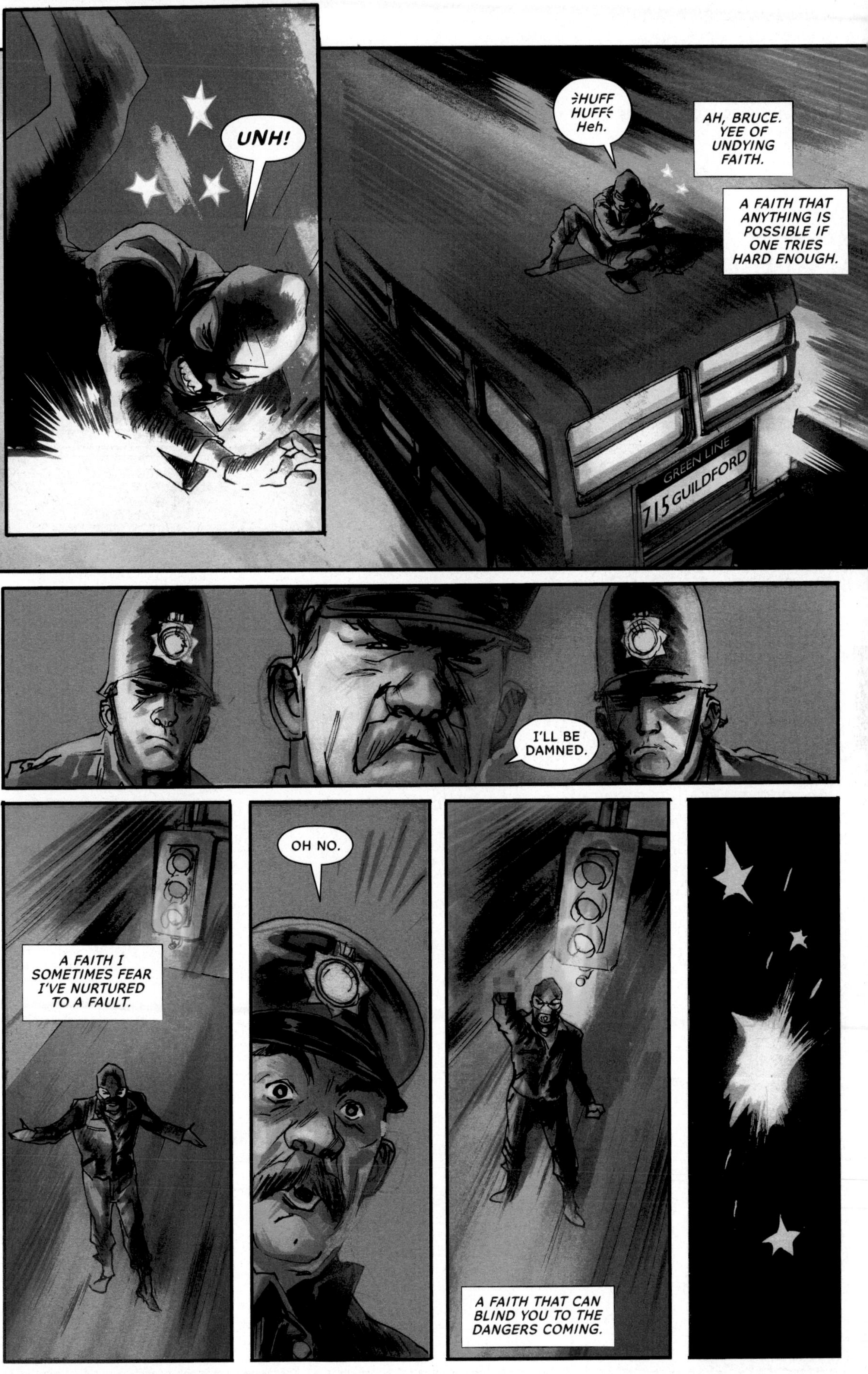
UNH!
HUFF HUFF Heh.
AH, BRUCE. YEE OF UNDYING FAITH.
A FAITH THAT ANYTHING IS POSSIBLE IF ONE TRIES HARD ENOUGH.
GREEN LINE
715 GUILDFORD
I'LL BE DAMNED.
A FAITH I SOMETIMES FEAR I'VE NURTURED TO A FAULT.
OH NO.
A FAITH THAT CAN BLIND YOU TO THE DANGERS COMING.

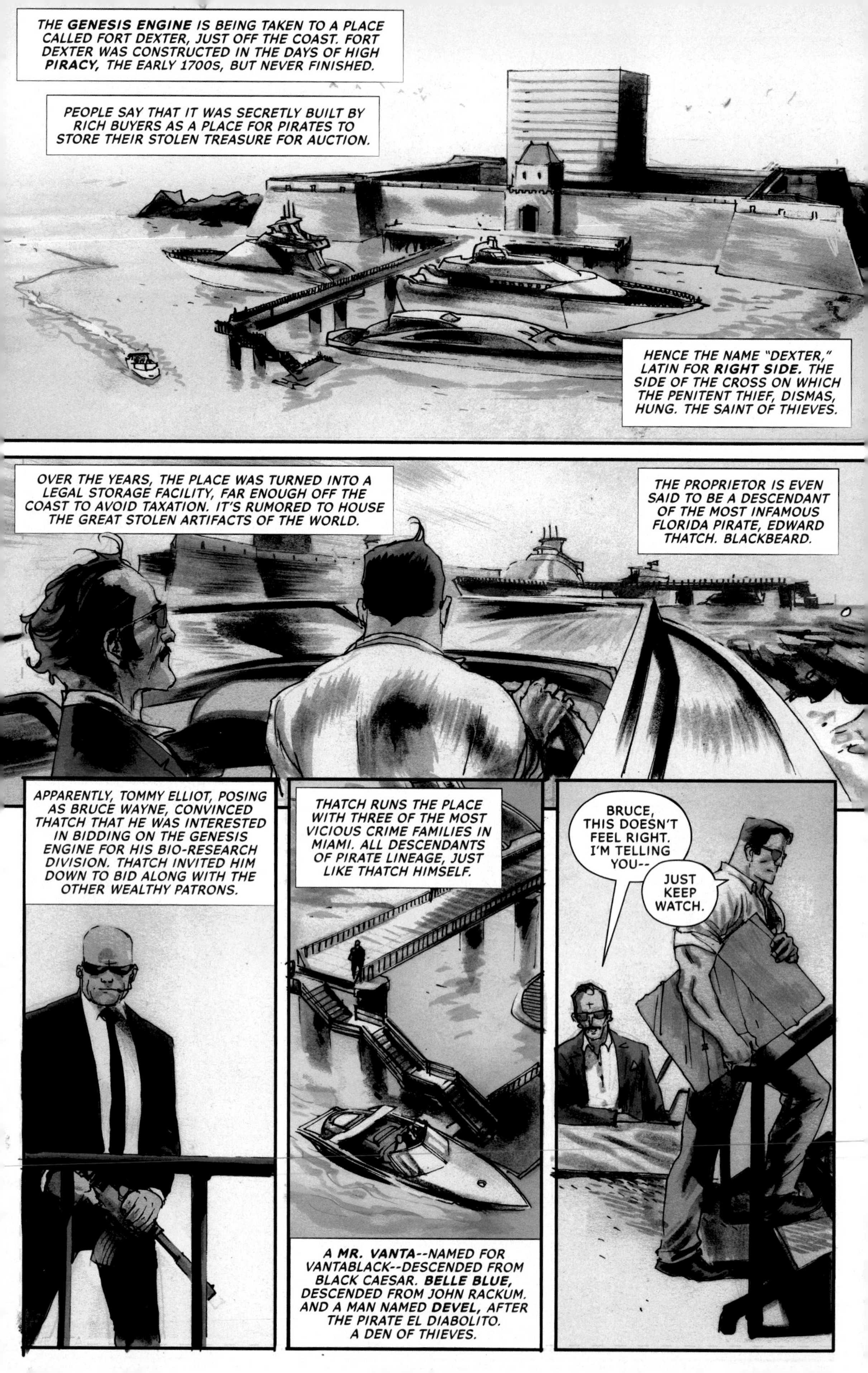
THE **GENESIS ENGINE** IS BEING TAKEN TO A PLACE CALLED FORT DEXTER, JUST OFF THE COAST. FORT DEXTER WAS CONSTRUCTED IN THE DAYS OF HIGH **PIRACY,** THE EARLY 1700S, BUT NEVER FINISHED.
PEOPLE SAY THAT IT WAS SECRETLY BUILT BY RICH BUYERS AS A PLACE FOR PIRATES TO STORE THEIR STOLEN TREASURE FOR AUCTION.
HENCE THE NAME "DEXTER," LATIN FOR **RIGHT SIDE.** THE SIDE OF THE CROSS ON WHICH THE PENITENT THIEF, DISMAS, HUNG. THE SAINT OF THIEVES.
OVER THE YEARS, THE PLACE WAS TURNED INTO A LEGAL STORAGE FACILITY, FAR ENOUGH OFF THE COAST TO AVOID TAXATION. IT'S RUMORED TO HOUSE THE GREAT STOLEN ARTIFACTS OF THE WORLD.
THE PROPRIETOR IS EVEN SAID TO BE A DESCENDANT OF THE MOST INFAMOUS FLORIDA PIRATE, EDWARD THATCH. BLACKBEARD.
APPARENTLY, TOMMY ELLIOT, POSING AS BRUCE WAYNE, CONVINCED THATCH THAT HE WAS INTERESTED IN BIDDING ON THE GENESIS ENGINE FOR HIS BIO-RESEARCH DIVISION. THATCH INVITED HIM DOWN TO BID ALONG WITH THE OTHER WEALTHY PATRONS.
THATCH RUNS THE PLACE WITH THREE OF THE MOST VICIOUS CRIME FAMILIES IN MIAMI. ALL DESCENDANTS OF PIRATE LINEAGE, JUST LIKE THATCH HIMSELF.
A **MR. VANTA**--NAMED FOR VANTABLACK--DESCENDED FROM BLACK CAESAR. **BELLE BLUE,** DESCENDED FROM JOHN RACKUM. AND A MAN NAMED **DEVEL,** AFTER THE PIRATE EL DIABOLITO. A DEN OF THIEVES.
BRUCE, THIS DOESN'T FEEL RIGHT. I'M TELLING YOU--
JUST KEEP WATCH.

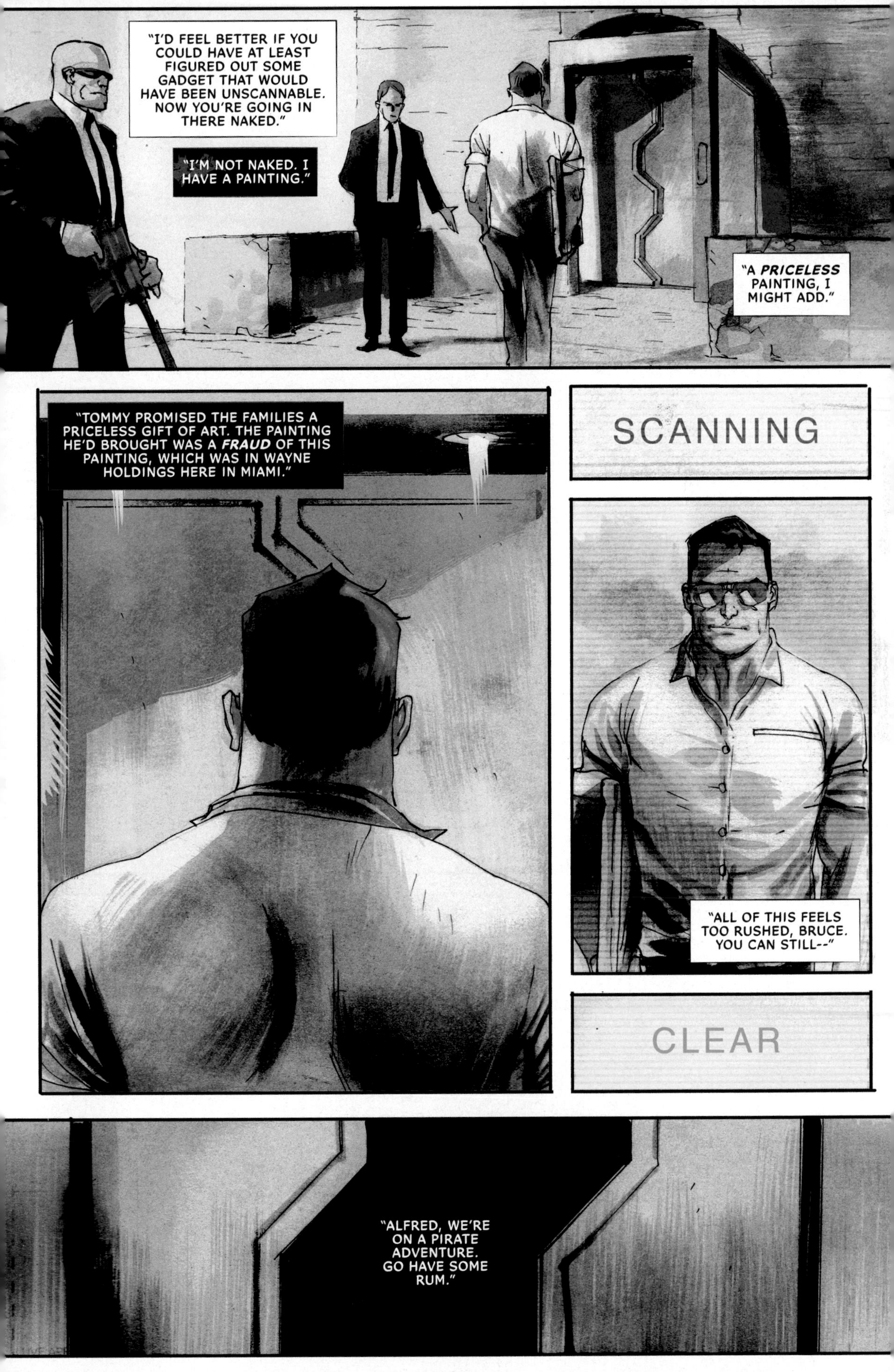
"I'D FEEL BETTER IF YOU COULD HAVE AT LEAST FIGURED OUT SOME GADGET THAT WOULD HAVE BEEN UNSCANNABLE. NOW YOU'RE GOING IN THERE NAKED."
"I'M NOT NAKED. I HAVE A PAINTING."
"A *PRICELESS* PAINTING, I MIGHT ADD."
"TOMMY PROMISED THE FAMILIES A PRICELESS GIFT OF ART. THE PAINTING HE'D BROUGHT WAS A *FRAUD* OF THIS PAINTING, WHICH WAS IN WAYNE HOLDINGS HERE IN MIAMI."
SCANNING
"ALL OF THIS FEELS TOO RUSHED, BRUCE. YOU CAN STILL--"
CLEAR
"ALFRED, WE'RE ON A PIRATE ADVENTURE. GO HAVE SOME RUM."

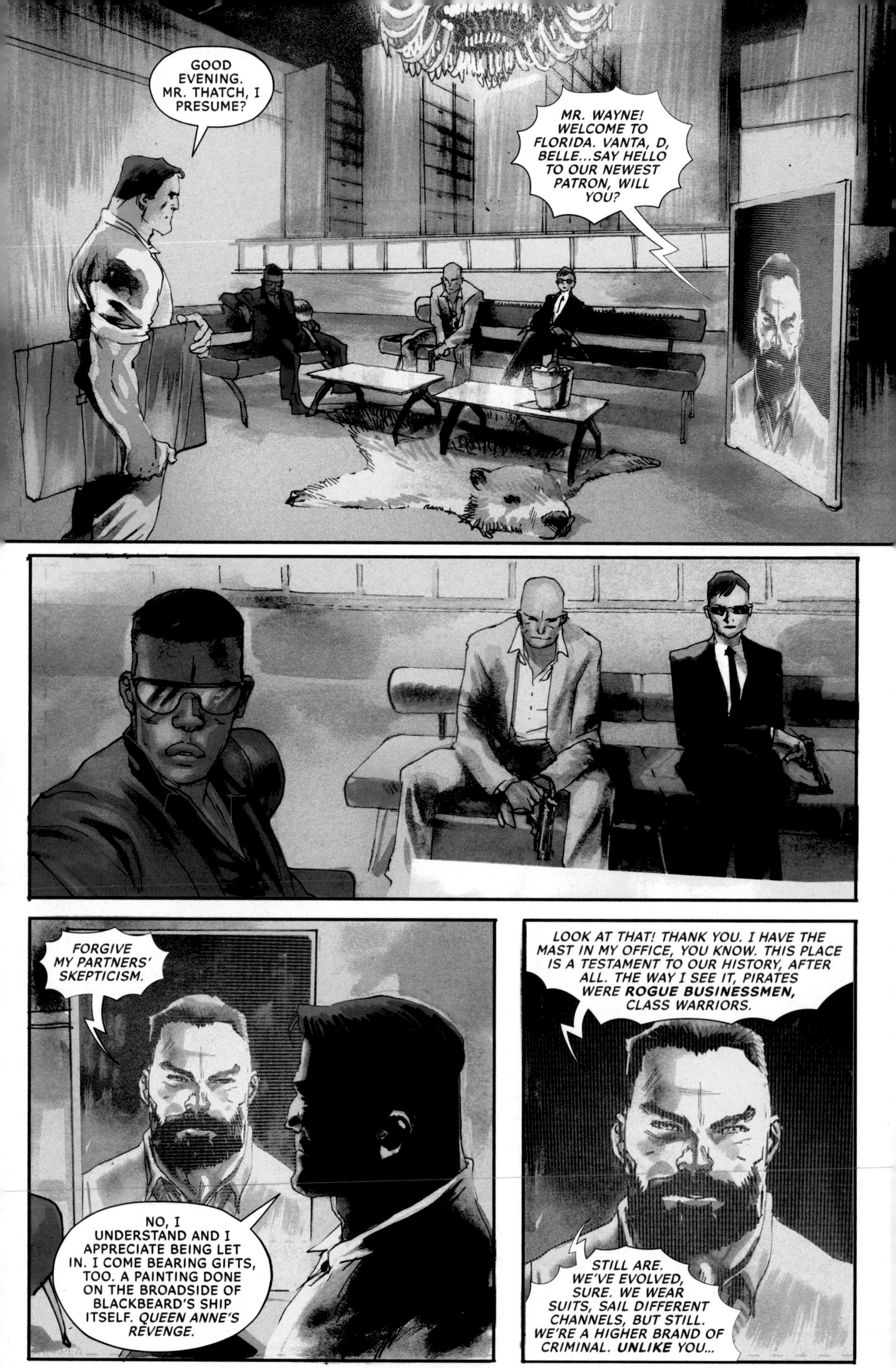
GOOD EVENING. MR. THATCH, I PRESUME?
MR. WAYNE! WELCOME TO FLORIDA. VANTA, D, BELLE...SAY HELLO TO OUR NEWEST PATRON, WILL YOU?
FORGIVE MY PARTNERS' SKEPTICISM.
NO, I UNDERSTAND AND I APPRECIATE BEING LET IN. I COME BEARING GIFTS, TOO. A PAINTING DONE ON THE BROADSIDE OF BLACKBEARD'S SHIP ITSELF. *QUEEN ANNE'S REVENGE.*
LOOK AT THAT! THANK YOU. I HAVE THE MAST IN MY OFFICE, YOU KNOW. THIS PLACE IS A TESTAMENT TO OUR HISTORY, AFTER ALL. THE WAY I SEE IT, PIRATES WERE ***ROGUE BUSINESSMEN,*** *CLASS WARRIORS.*
STILL ARE. WE'VE EVOLVED, SURE. WE WEAR SUITS, SAIL DIFFERENT CHANNELS, BUT STILL. WE'RE A HIGHER BRAND OF CRIMINAL. **UNLIKE** YOU...

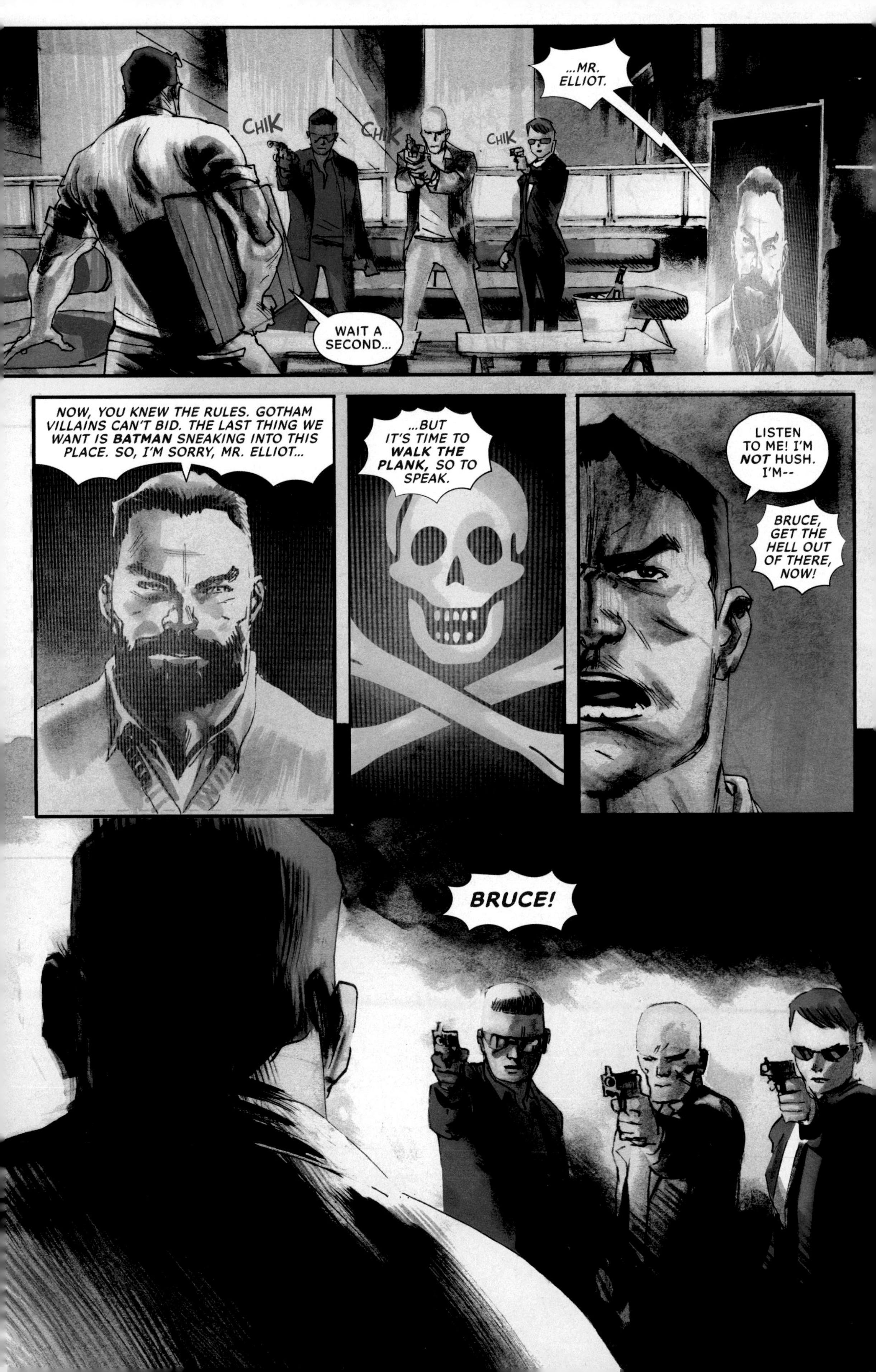

CHIK
CHIK
CHIK
...MR. ELLIOT.
WAIT A SECOND...
NOW, YOU KNEW THE RULES. GOTHAM VILLAINS CAN'T BID. THE LAST THING WE WANT IS BATMAN SNEAKING INTO THIS PLACE. SO, I'M SORRY, MR. ELLIOT...
...BUT IT'S TIME TO WALK THE PLANK, SO TO SPEAK.
LISTEN TO ME! I'M NOT HUSH. I'M--
BRUCE, GET THE HELL OUT OF THERE, NOW!
BRUCE!

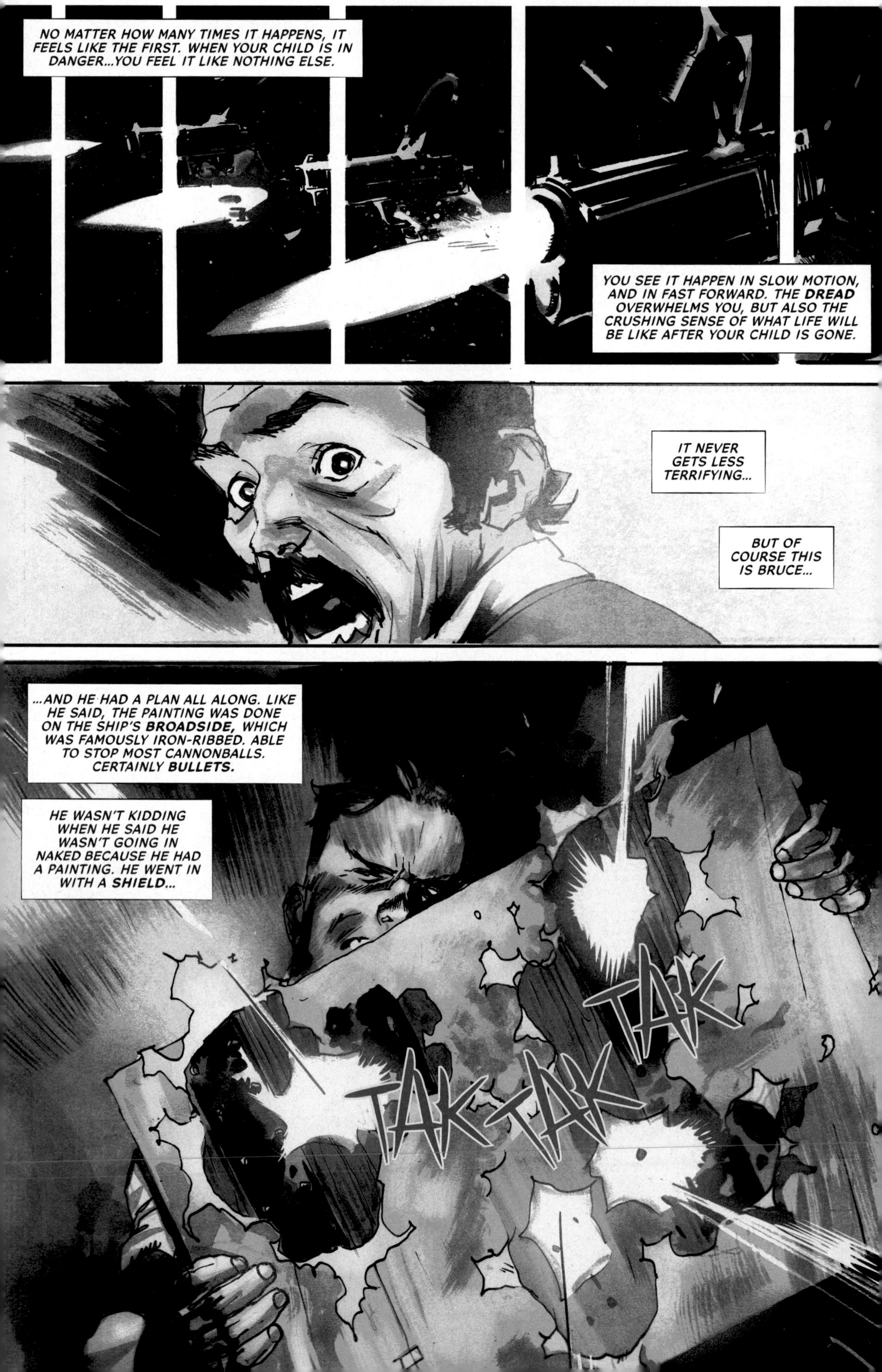
NO MATTER HOW MANY TIMES IT HAPPENS, IT FEELS LIKE THE FIRST. WHEN YOUR CHILD IS IN DANGER...YOU FEEL IT LIKE NOTHING ELSE.
YOU SEE IT HAPPEN IN SLOW MOTION, AND IN FAST FORWARD. THE DREAD OVERWHELMS YOU, BUT ALSO THE CRUSHING SENSE OF WHAT LIFE WILL BE LIKE AFTER YOUR CHILD IS GONE.
IT NEVER GETS LESS TERRIFYING...
BUT OF COURSE THIS IS BRUCE...
...AND HE HAD A PLAN ALL ALONG. LIKE HE SAID, THE PAINTING WAS DONE ON THE SHIP'S BROADSIDE, WHICH WAS FAMOUSLY IRON-RIBBED. ABLE TO STOP MOST CANNONBALLS. CERTAINLY BULLETS.
HE WASN'T KIDDING WHEN HE SAID HE WASN'T GOING IN NAKED BECAUSE HE HAD A PAINTING. HE WENT IN WITH A SHIELD...
TAK TAK TAK

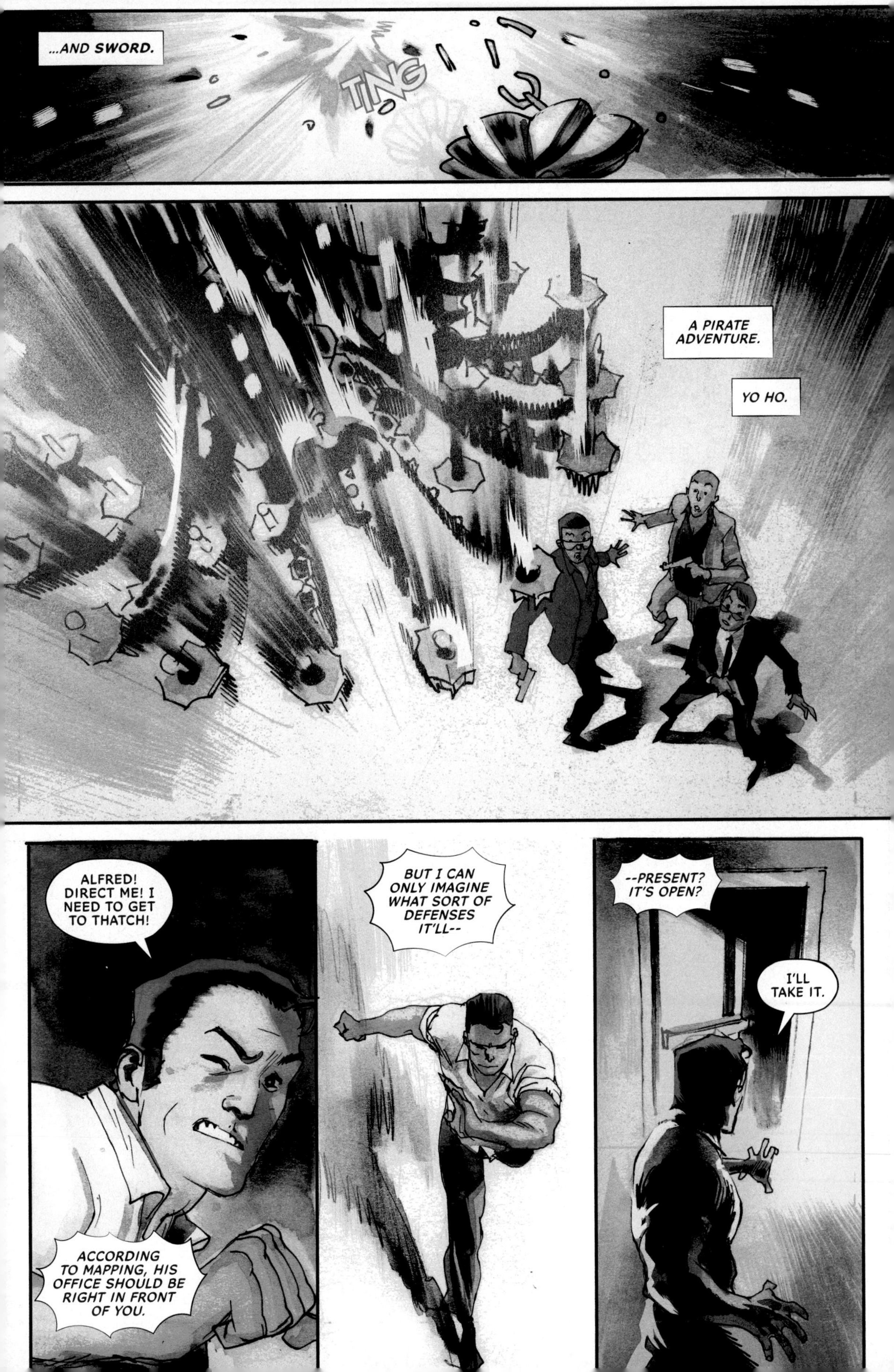
...AND SWORD.
TING
A PIRATE ADVENTURE.
YO HO.
ALFRED! DIRECT ME! I NEED TO GET TO THATCH!
ACCORDING TO MAPPING, HIS OFFICE SHOULD BE RIGHT IN FRONT OF YOU.
BUT I CAN ONLY IMAGINE WHAT SORT OF DEFENSES IT'LL--
--PRESENT? IT'S OPEN?
I'LL TAKE IT.

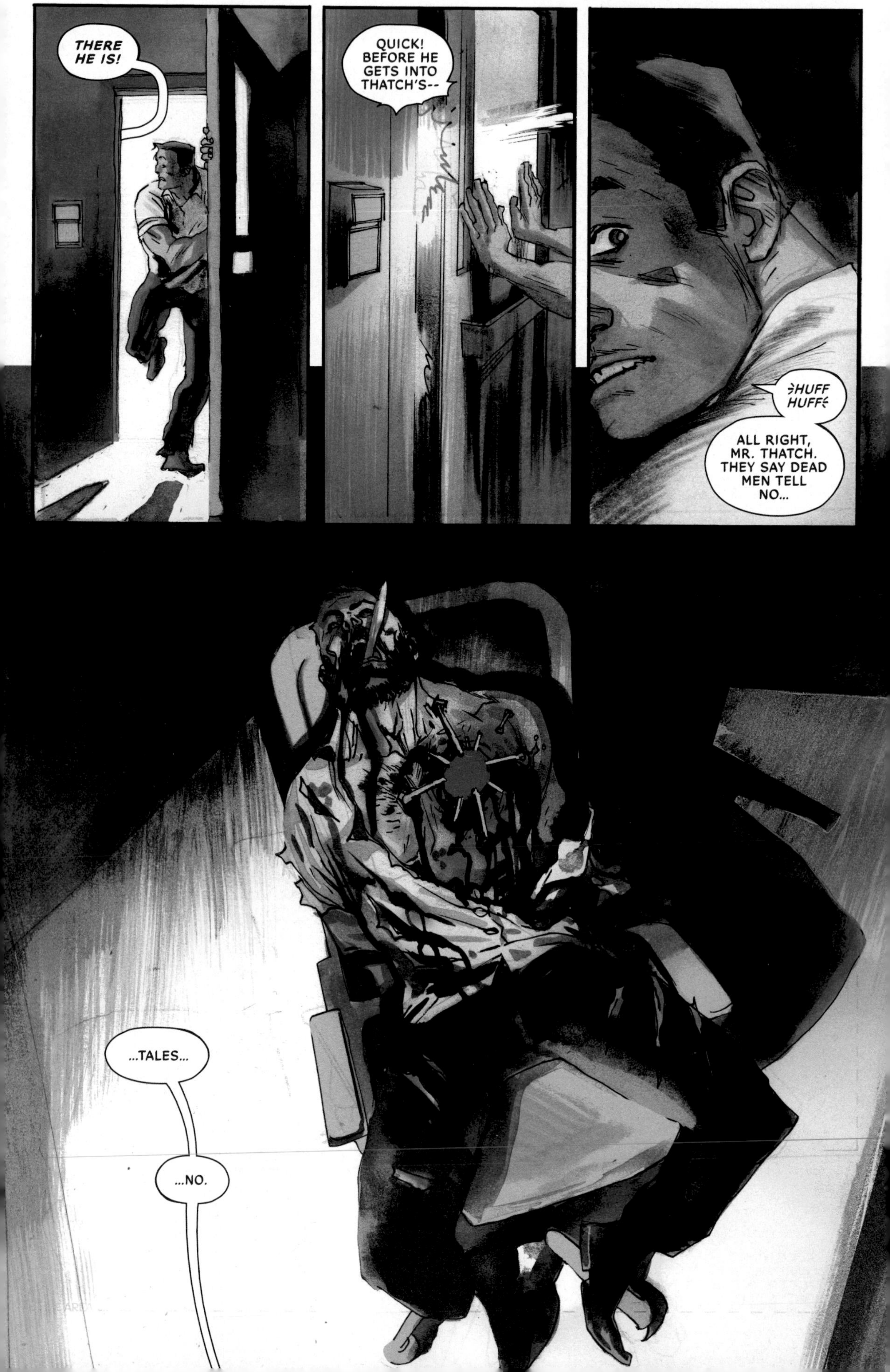
THERE HE IS!
QUICK! BEFORE HE GETS INTO THATCH'S--
HUFF HUFF
ALL RIGHT, MR. THATCH. THEY SAY DEAD MEN TELL NO...
...TALES...
...NO.

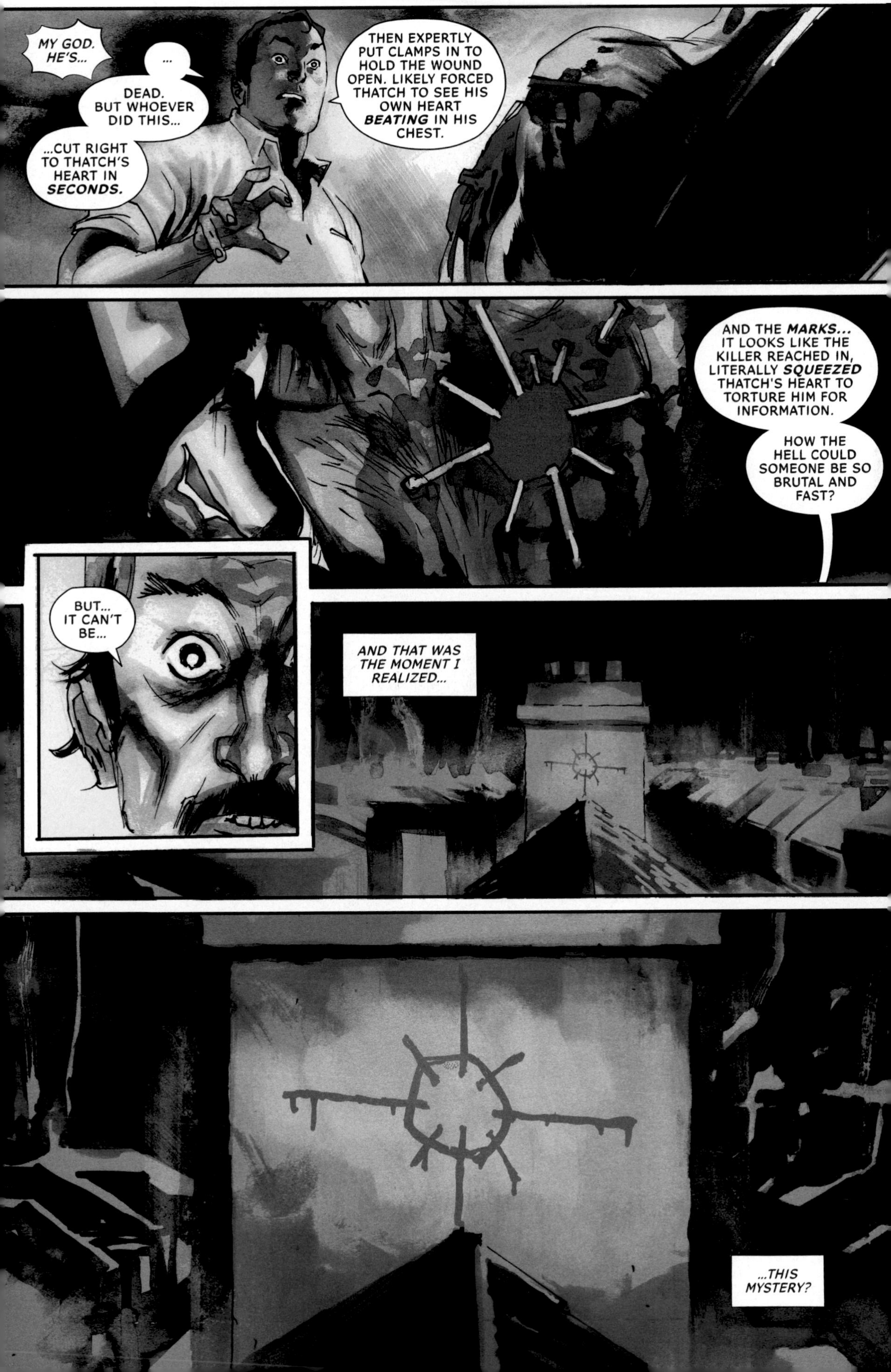
MY GOD. HE'S...
...
DEAD. BUT WHOEVER DID THIS...
...CUT RIGHT TO THATCH'S HEART IN SECONDS.
THEN EXPERTLY PUT CLAMPS IN TO HOLD THE WOUND OPEN. LIKELY FORCED THATCH TO SEE HIS OWN HEART BEATING IN HIS CHEST.
AND THE MARKS... IT LOOKS LIKE THE KILLER REACHED IN, LITERALLY SQUEEZED THATCH'S HEART TO TORTURE HIM FOR INFORMATION.
HOW THE HELL COULD SOMEONE BE SO BRUTAL AND FAST?
BUT... IT CAN'T BE...
AND THAT WAS THE MOMENT I REALIZED...
...THIS MYSTERY?

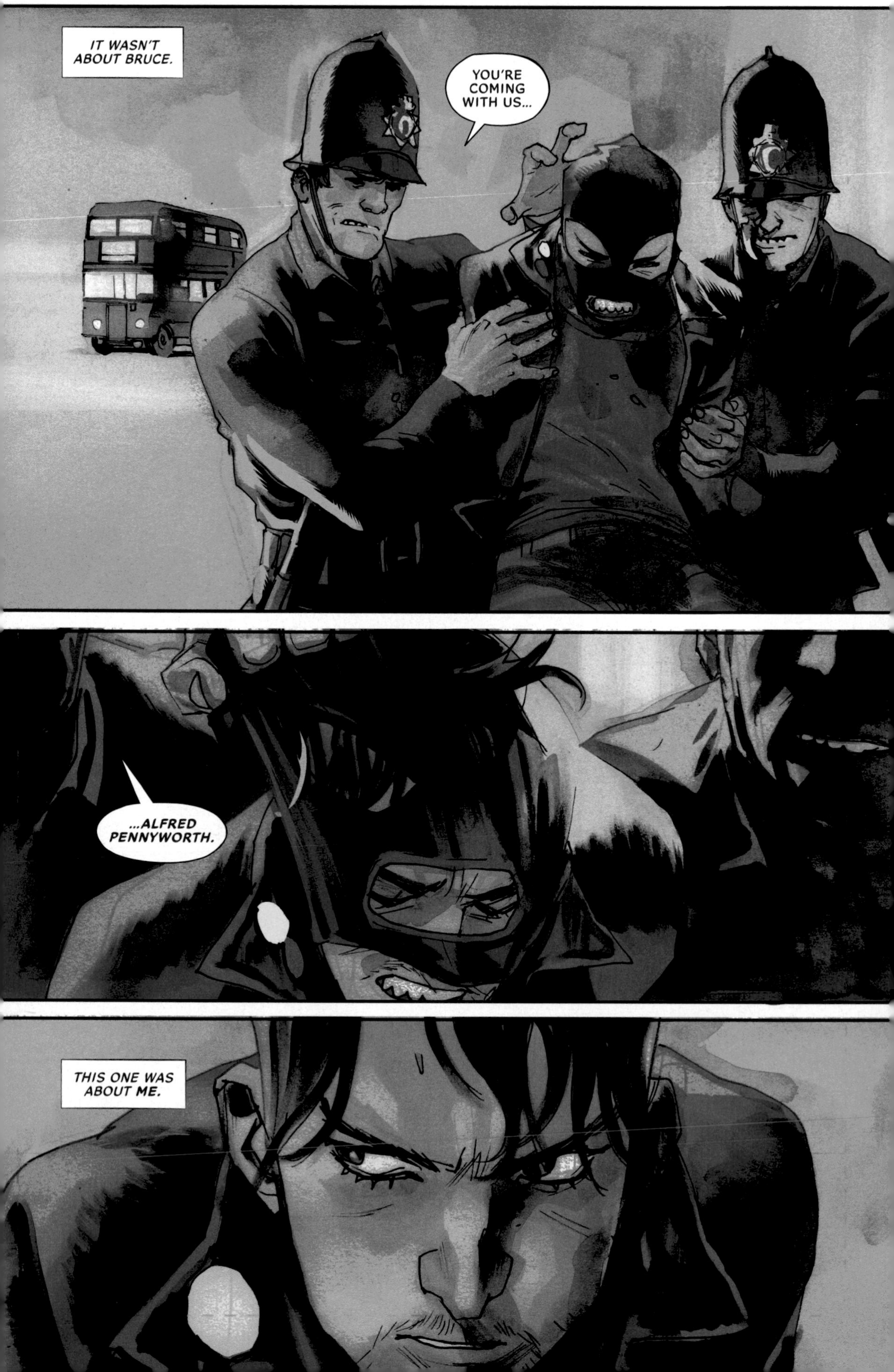
IT WASN'T ABOUT BRUCE.
YOU'RE COMING WITH US...
...ALFRED PENNYWORTH.
THIS ONE WAS ABOUT ME.

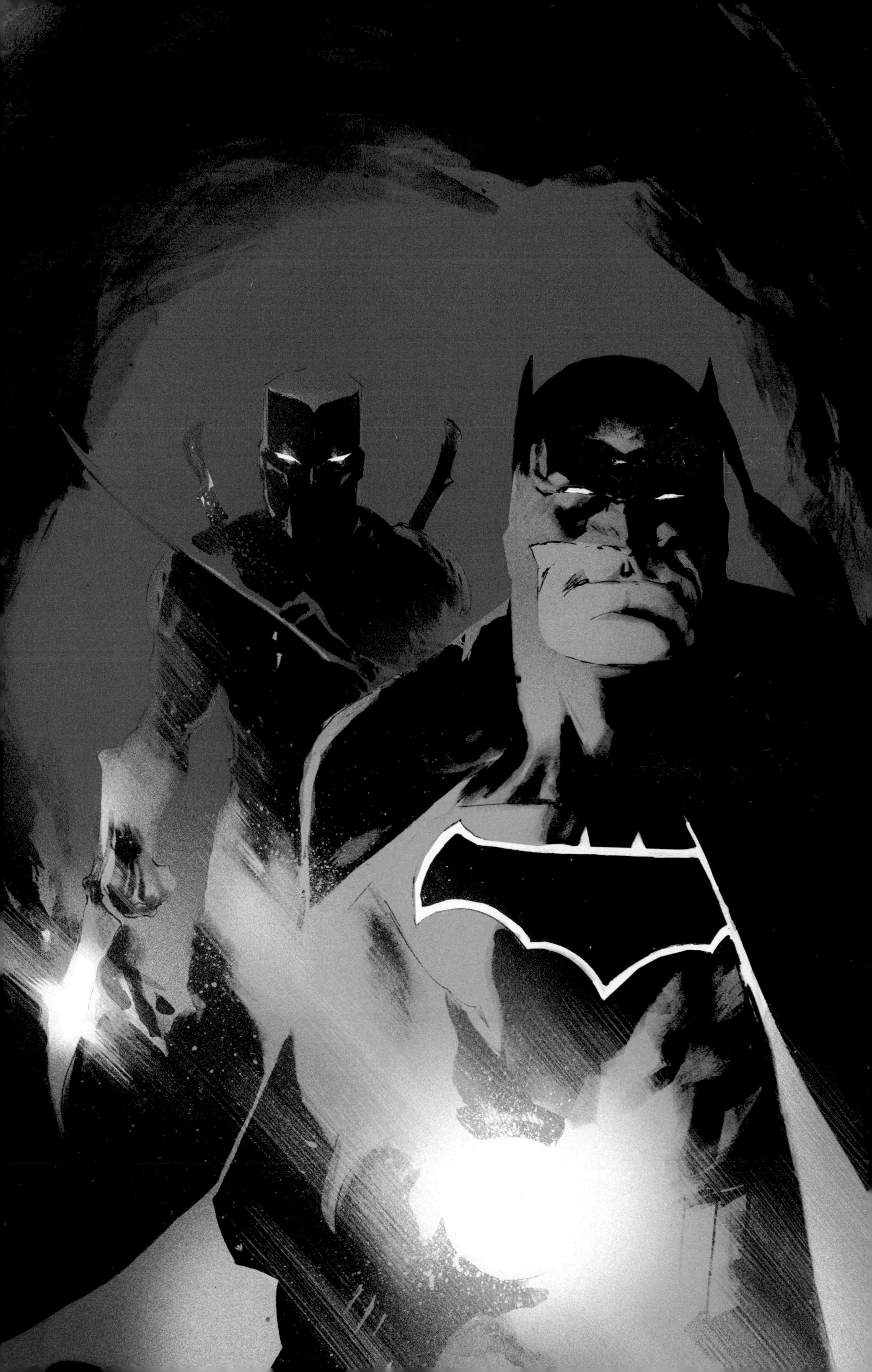

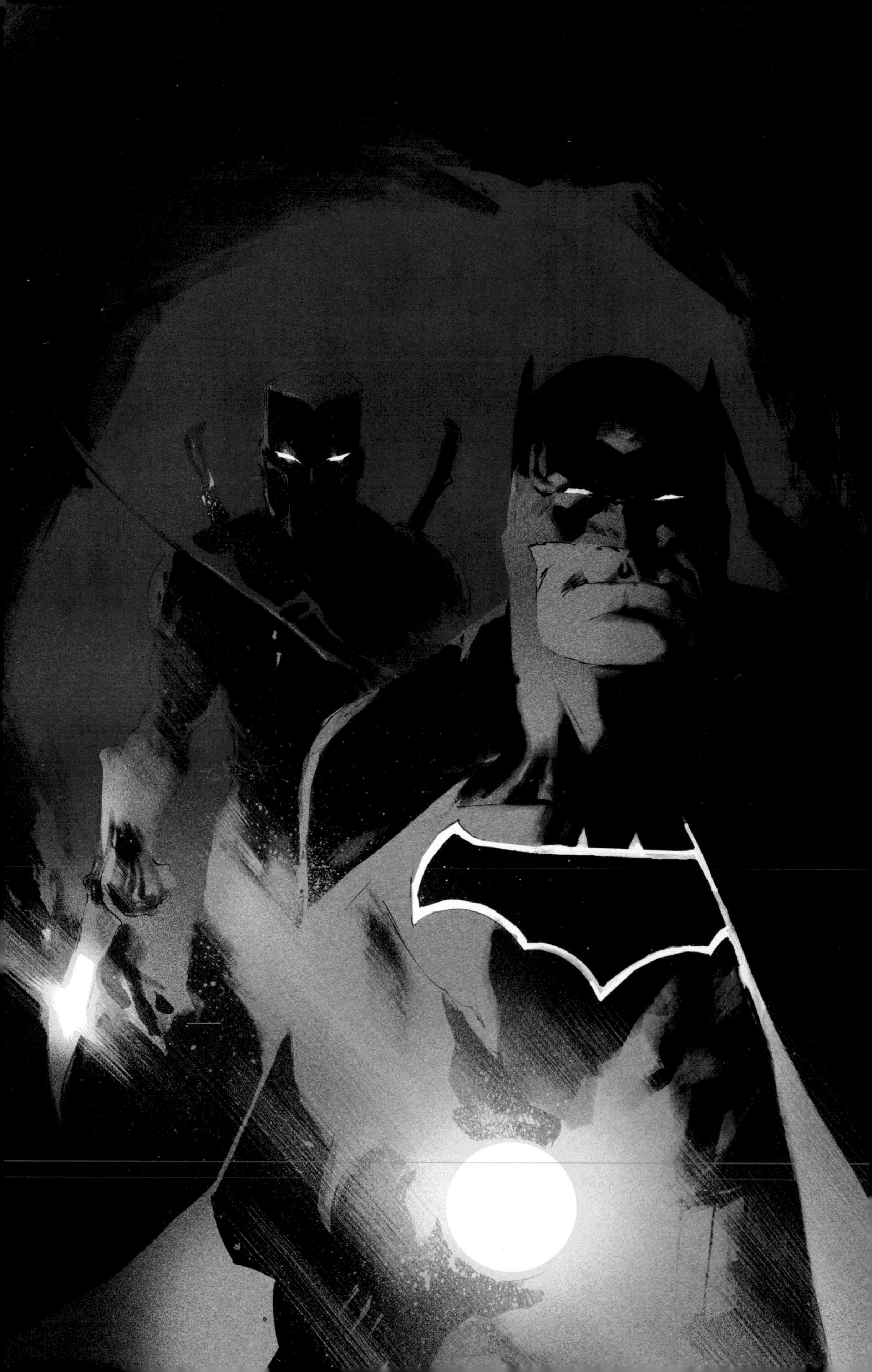

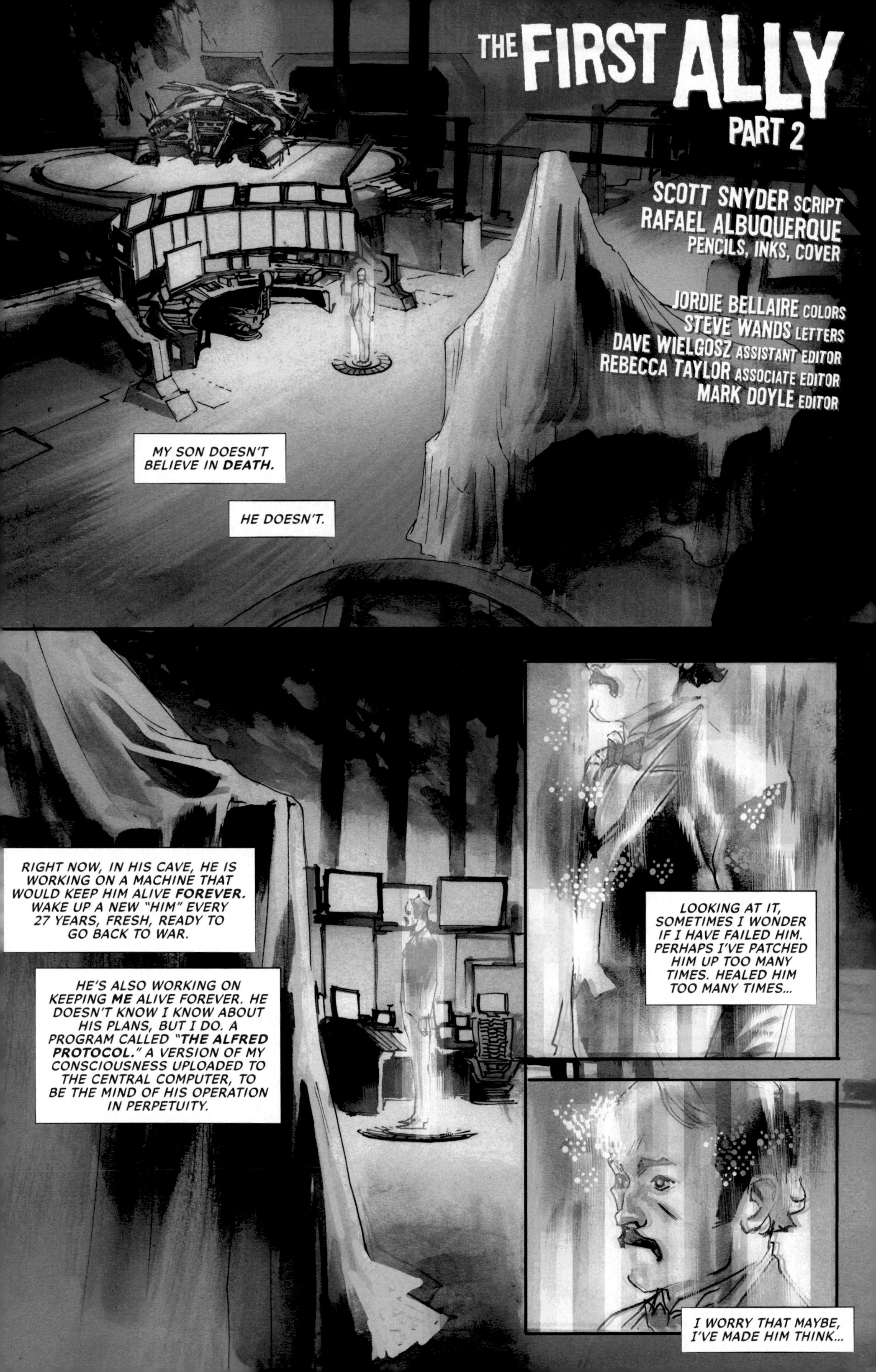
THE FIRST ALLY
PART 2
SCOTT SNYDER SCRIPT
RAFAEL ALBUQUERQUE PENCILS, INKS, COVER
JORDIE BELLAIRE COLORS
STEVE WANDS LETTERS
DAVE WIELGOSZ ASSISTANT EDITOR
REBECCA TAYLOR ASSOCIATE EDITOR
MARK DOYLE EDITOR
MY SON DOESN'T BELIEVE IN DEATH.
HE DOESN'T.
RIGHT NOW, IN HIS CAVE, HE IS WORKING ON A MACHINE THAT WOULD KEEP HIM ALIVE FOREVER. WAKE UP A NEW "HIM" EVERY 27 YEARS, FRESH, READY TO GO BACK TO WAR.
HE'S ALSO WORKING ON KEEPING ME ALIVE FOREVER. HE DOESN'T KNOW I KNOW ABOUT HIS PLANS, BUT I DO. A PROGRAM CALLED "THE ALFRED PROTOCOL." A VERSION OF MY CONSCIOUSNESS UPLOADED TO THE CENTRAL COMPUTER, TO BE THE MIND OF HIS OPERATION IN PERPETUITY.
LOOKING AT IT, SOMETIMES I WONDER IF I HAVE FAILED HIM. PERHAPS I'VE PATCHED HIM UP TOO MANY TIMES. HEALED HIM TOO MANY TIMES...
I WORRY THAT MAYBE, I'VE MADE HIM THINK...

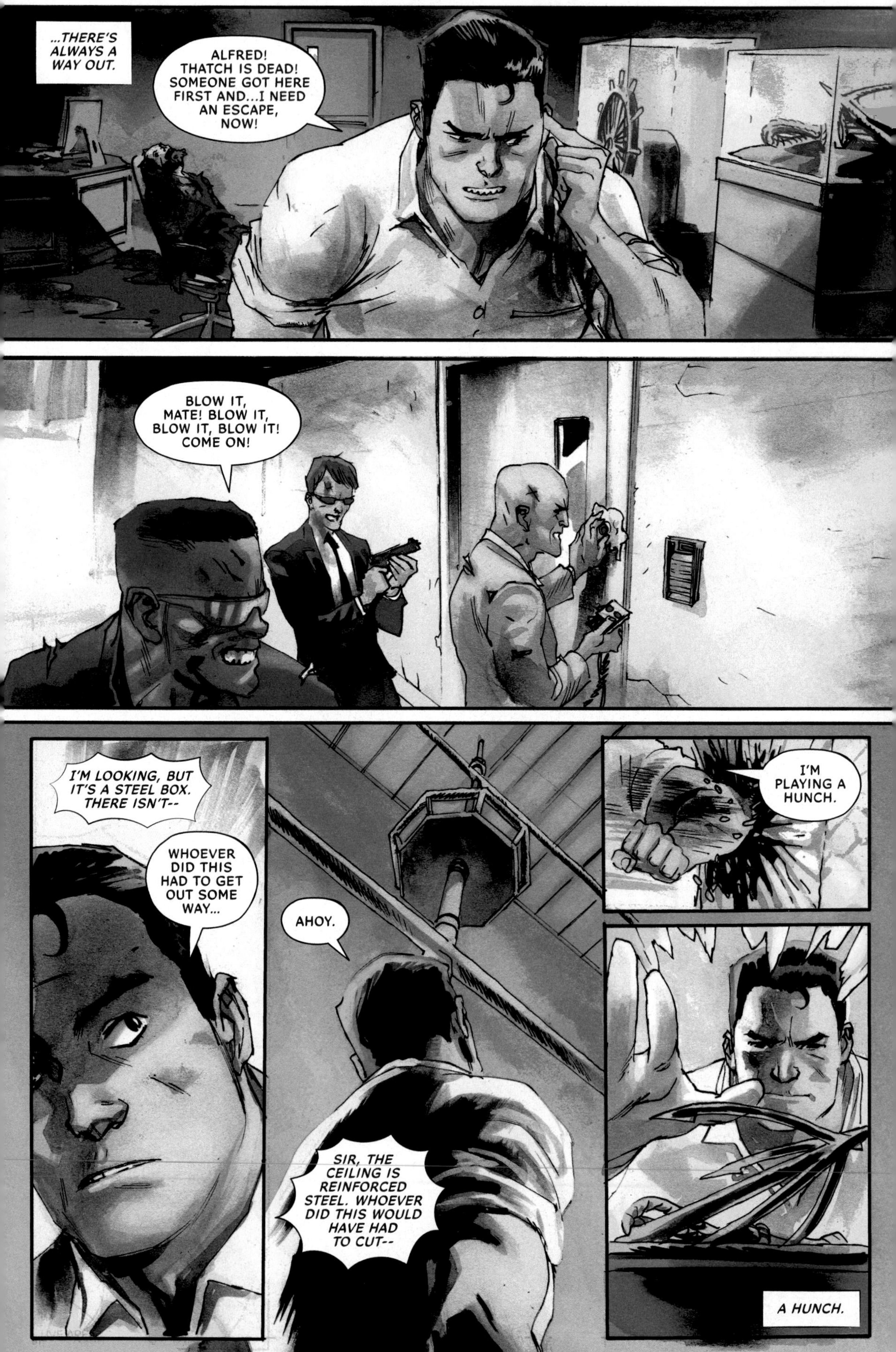
...THERE'S ALWAYS A WAY OUT.
ALFRED! THATCH IS DEAD! SOMEONE GOT HERE FIRST AND...I NEED AN ESCAPE, NOW!
BLOW IT, MATE! BLOW IT, BLOW IT, BLOW IT! COME ON!
I'M LOOKING, BUT IT'S A STEEL BOX. THERE ISN'T--
WHOEVER DID THIS HAD TO GET OUT SOME WAY...
AHOY.
SIR, THE CEILING IS REINFORCED STEEL. WHOEVER DID THIS WOULD HAVE HAD TO CUT--
I'M PLAYING A HUNCH.
A HUNCH.

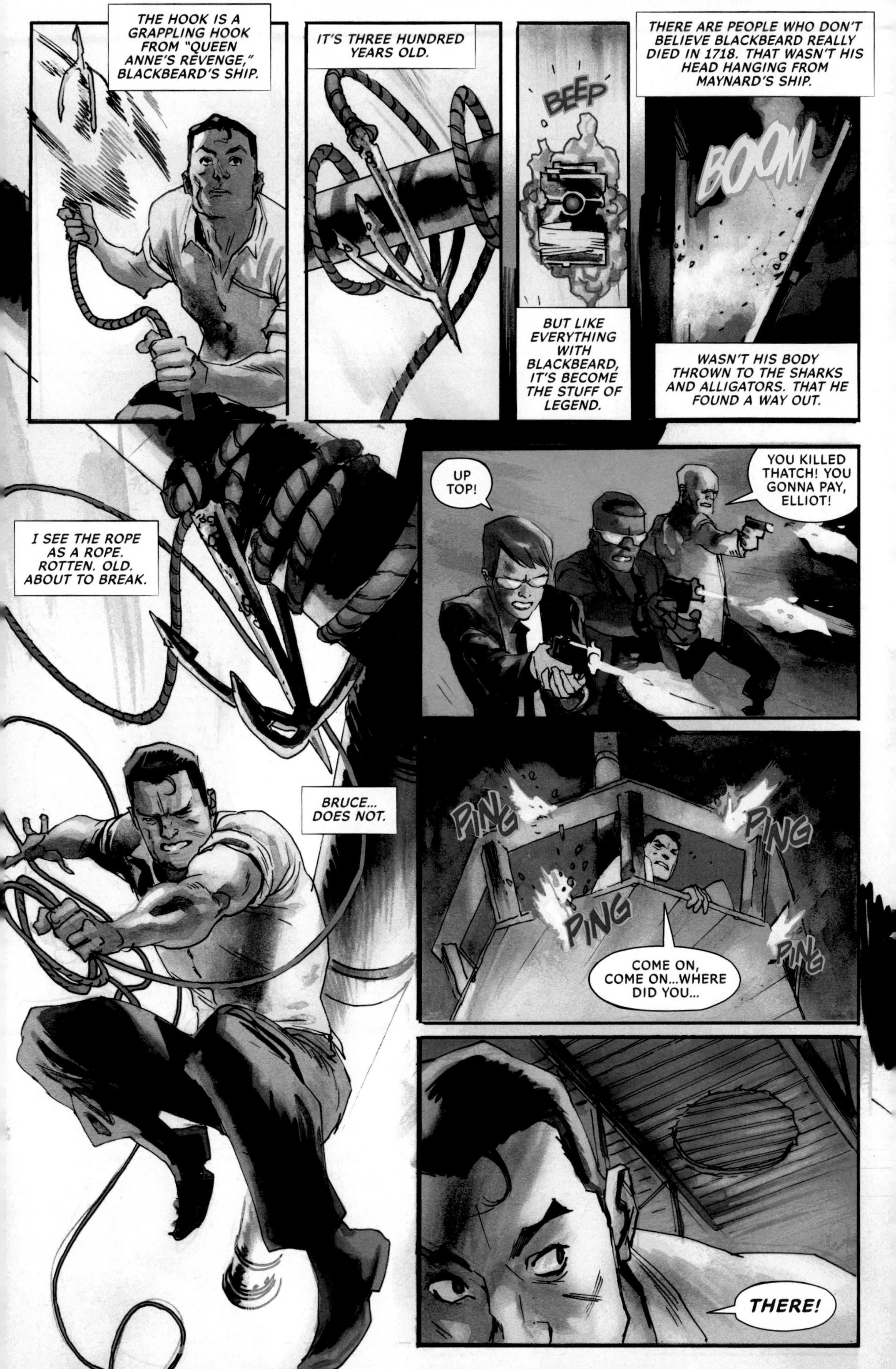
THE HOOK IS A GRAPPLING HOOK FROM "QUEEN ANNE'S REVENGE," BLACKBEARD'S SHIP.
IT'S THREE HUNDRED YEARS OLD.
BEEP
BUT LIKE EVERYTHING WITH BLACKBEARD, IT'S BECOME THE STUFF OF LEGEND.
THERE ARE PEOPLE WHO DON'T BELIEVE BLACKBEARD REALLY DIED IN 1718. THAT WASN'T HIS HEAD HANGING FROM MAYNARD'S SHIP.
BOOM
WASN'T HIS BODY THROWN TO THE SHARKS AND ALLIGATORS. THAT HE FOUND A WAY OUT.
I SEE THE ROPE AS A ROPE. ROTTEN. OLD. ABOUT TO BREAK.
BRUCE... DOES NOT.
UP TOP!
YOU KILLED THATCH! YOU GONNA PAY, ELLIOT!
PING
PING
PING
PING
COME ON, COME ON...WHERE DID YOU...
THERE!

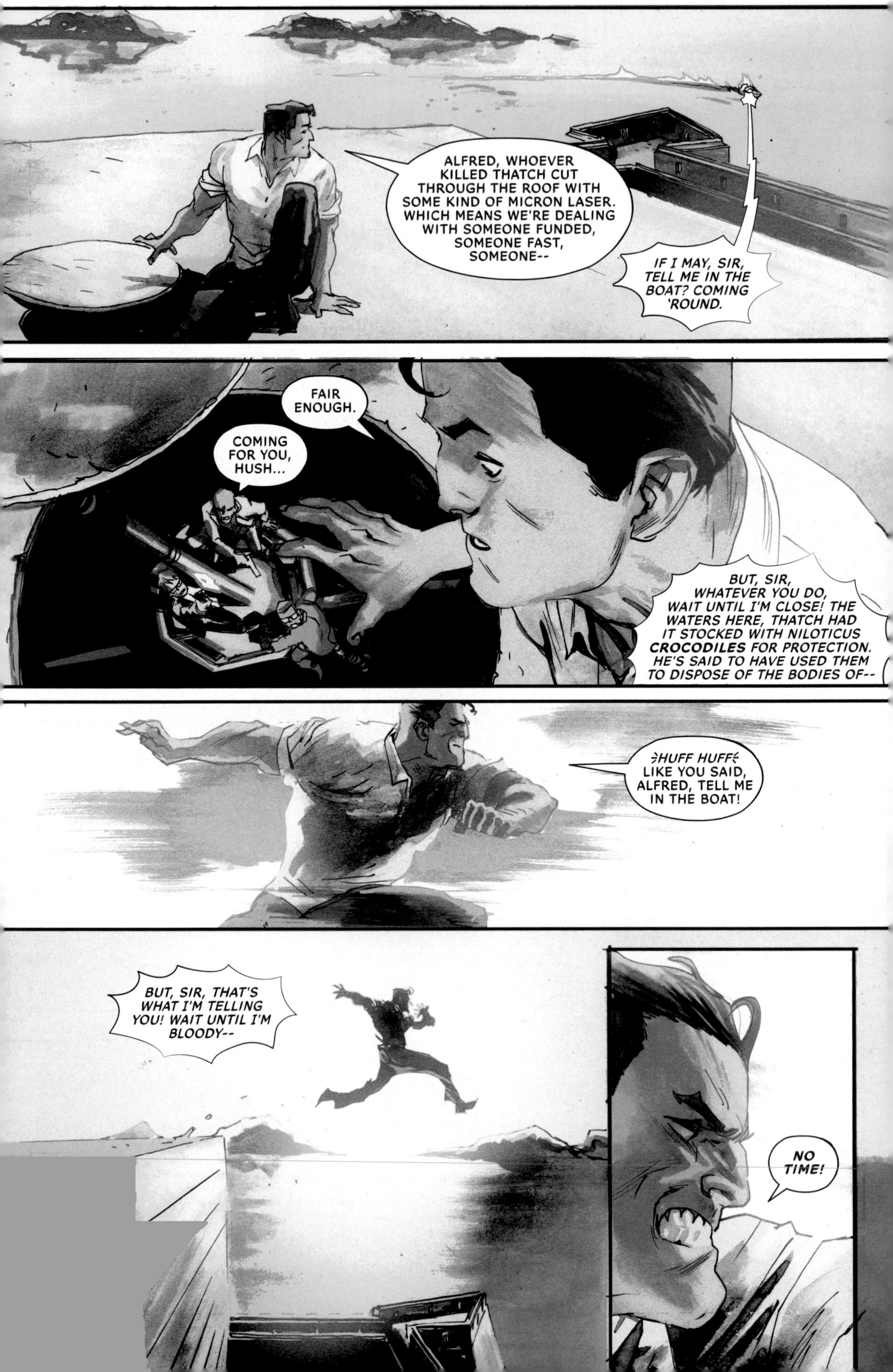
ALFRED, WHOEVER KILLED THATCH CUT THROUGH THE ROOF WITH SOME KIND OF MICRON LASER. WHICH MEANS WE'RE DEALING WITH SOMEONE FUNDED, SOMEONE FAST, SOMEONE--
IF I MAY, SIR, TELL ME IN THE BOAT? COMING 'ROUND.
FAIR ENOUGH.
COMING FOR YOU, HUSH...
BUT, SIR, WHATEVER YOU DO, WAIT UNTIL I'M CLOSE! THE WATERS HERE, THATCH HAD IT STOCKED WITH NILOTICUS CROCODILES FOR PROTECTION. HE'S SAID TO HAVE USED THEM TO DISPOSE OF THE BODIES OF--
HUFF HUFF LIKE YOU SAID, ALFRED, TELL ME IN THE BOAT!
BUT, SIR, THAT'S WHAT I'M TELLING YOU! WAIT UNTIL I'M BLOODY--
NO TIME!

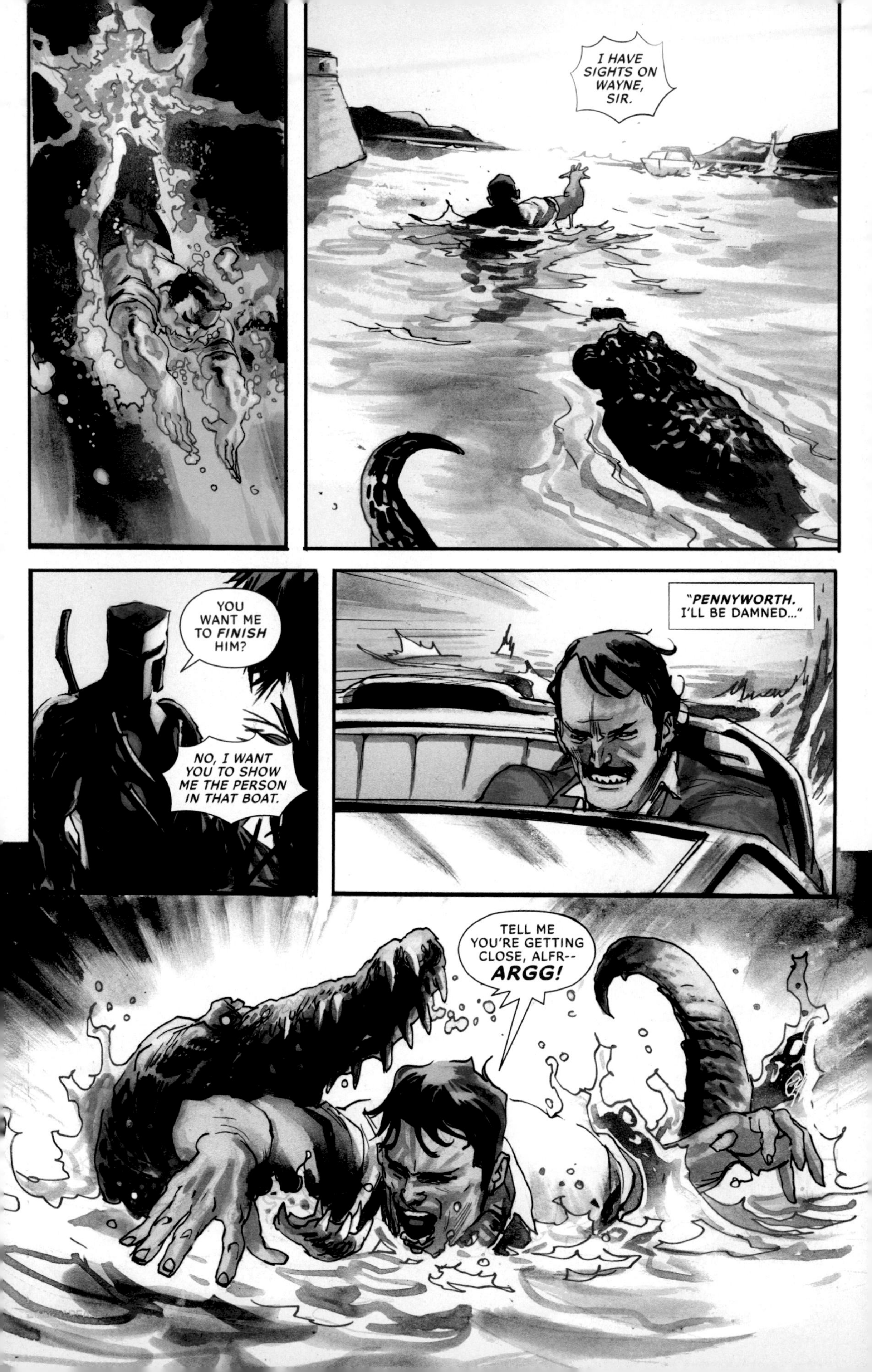
I HAVE SIGHTS ON WAYNE, SIR.
YOU WANT ME TO *FINISH* HIM?
NO, I WANT YOU TO SHOW ME THE PERSON IN THAT BOAT.
"*PENNYWORTH.* I'LL BE DAMNED..."
TELL ME YOU'RE GETTING CLOSE, ALFR-- ***ARGG!***

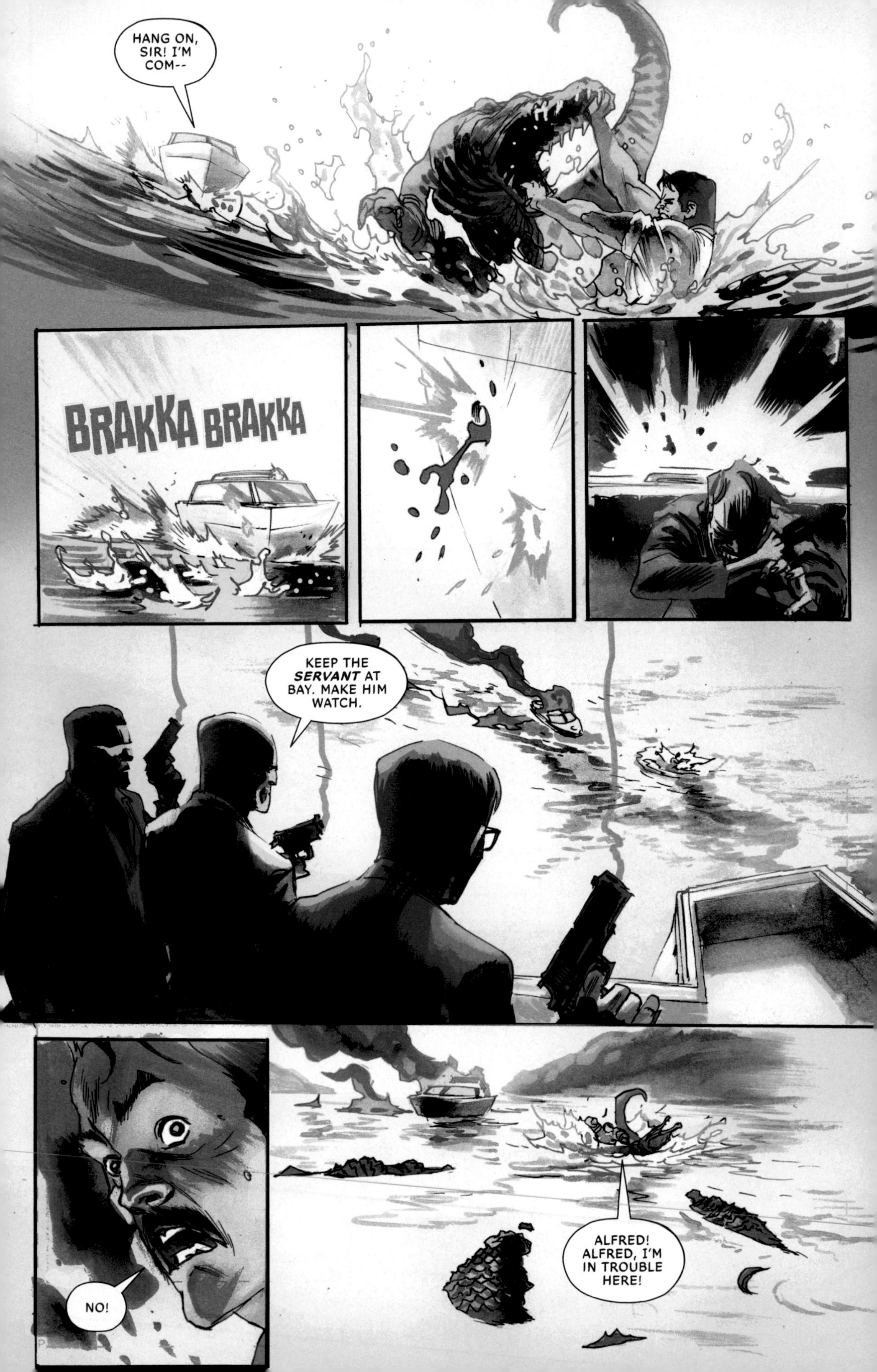
HANG ON, SIR! I'M COM--
BRAKKA BRAKKA
KEEP THE SERVANT AT BAY. MAKE HIM WATCH.
NO!
ALFRED! ALFRED, I'M IN TROUBLE HERE!

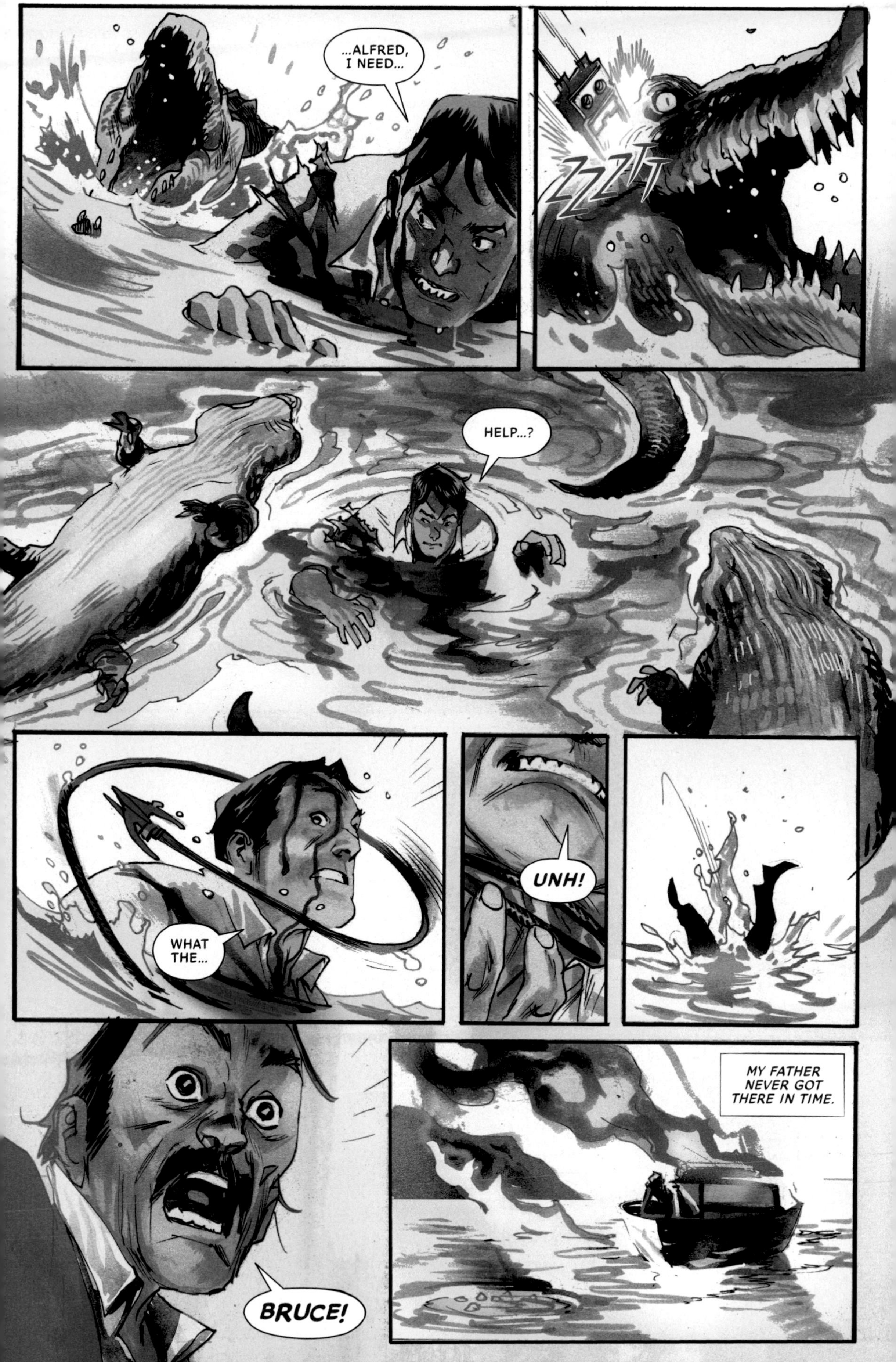

...ALFRED, I NEED...
ZZZTT
HELP...?
WHAT THE...
UNH!
BRUCE!
MY FATHER NEVER GOT THERE IN TIME.

THAT WAS TRUE FROM A YOUNG AGE FOR ME.

I WOULD ASK MY MOTHER WHY. WHY DID HE CARE MORE ABOUT A FAMILY THOUSANDS OF MILES AWAY THAN OURS, BUT SHE ALWAYS JUST TOLD ME NOT TO TALK BADLY ABOUT HIM.

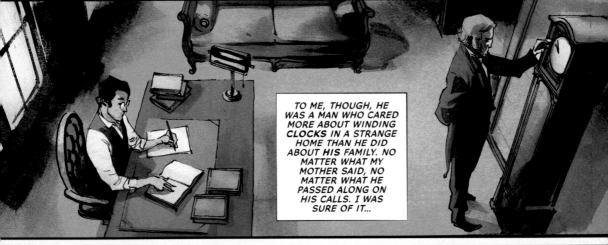

TO ME, THOUGH, HE WAS A MAN WHO CARED MORE ABOUT WINDING *CLOCKS* IN A STRANGE HOME THAN HE DID ABOUT *HIS* FAMILY. NO MATTER WHAT MY MOTHER SAID, NO MATTER WHAT HE PASSED ALONG ON HIS CALLS. I WAS SURE OF IT...

HE WASN'T THERE TO *PROTECT* US. NOT MY MOTHER. NOT *ME*. I LEARNED NOTHING FROM HIM. WHEN I WAS DISCOVERING LOVE?

HE WAS WINDING THEIR CLOCKS.

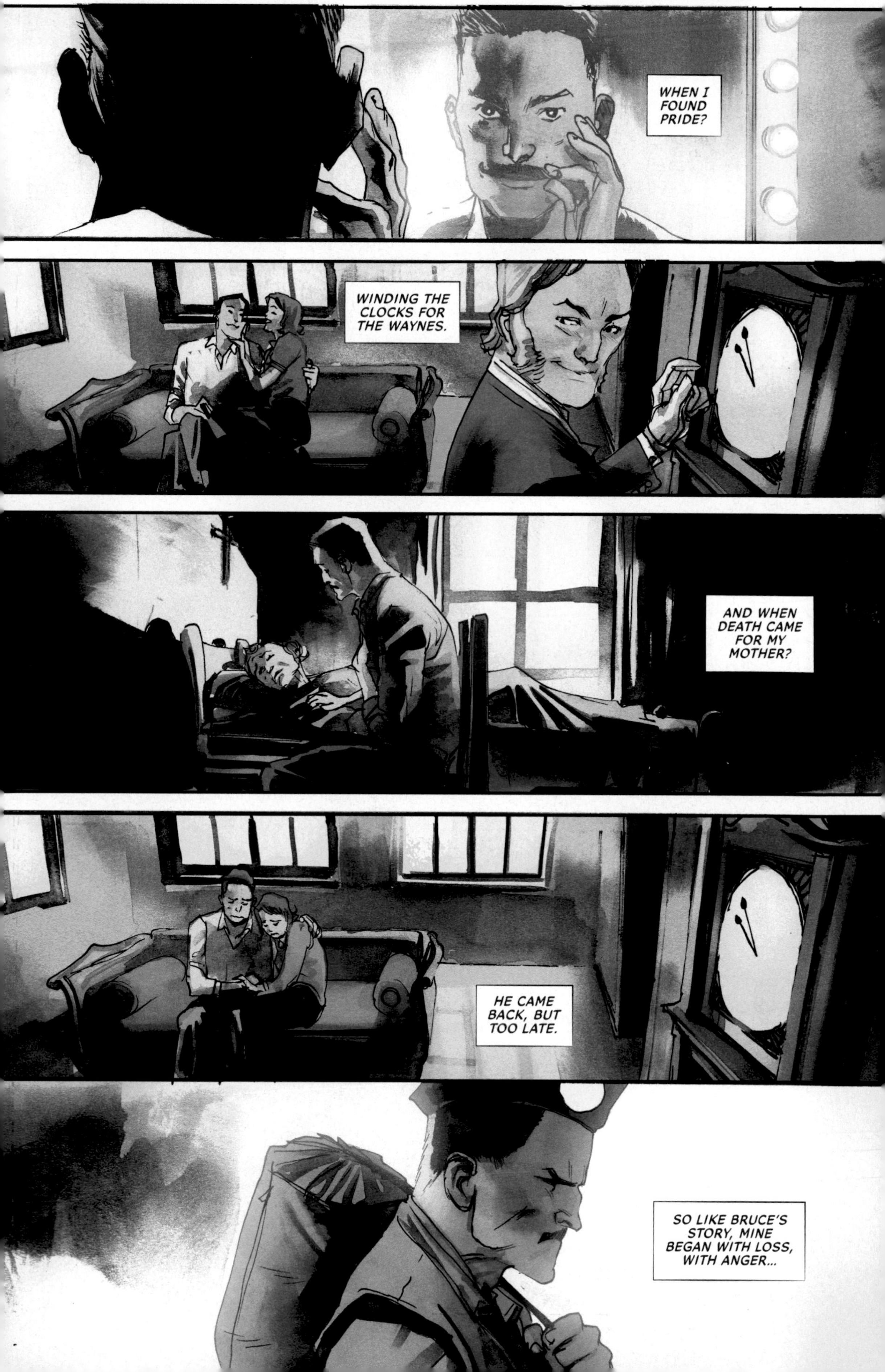
WHEN I FOUND PRIDE?
WINDING THE CLOCKS FOR THE WAYNES.
AND WHEN DEATH CAME FOR MY MOTHER?
HE CAME BACK, BUT TOO LATE.
SO LIKE BRUCE'S STORY, MINE BEGAN WITH LOSS, WITH ANGER...

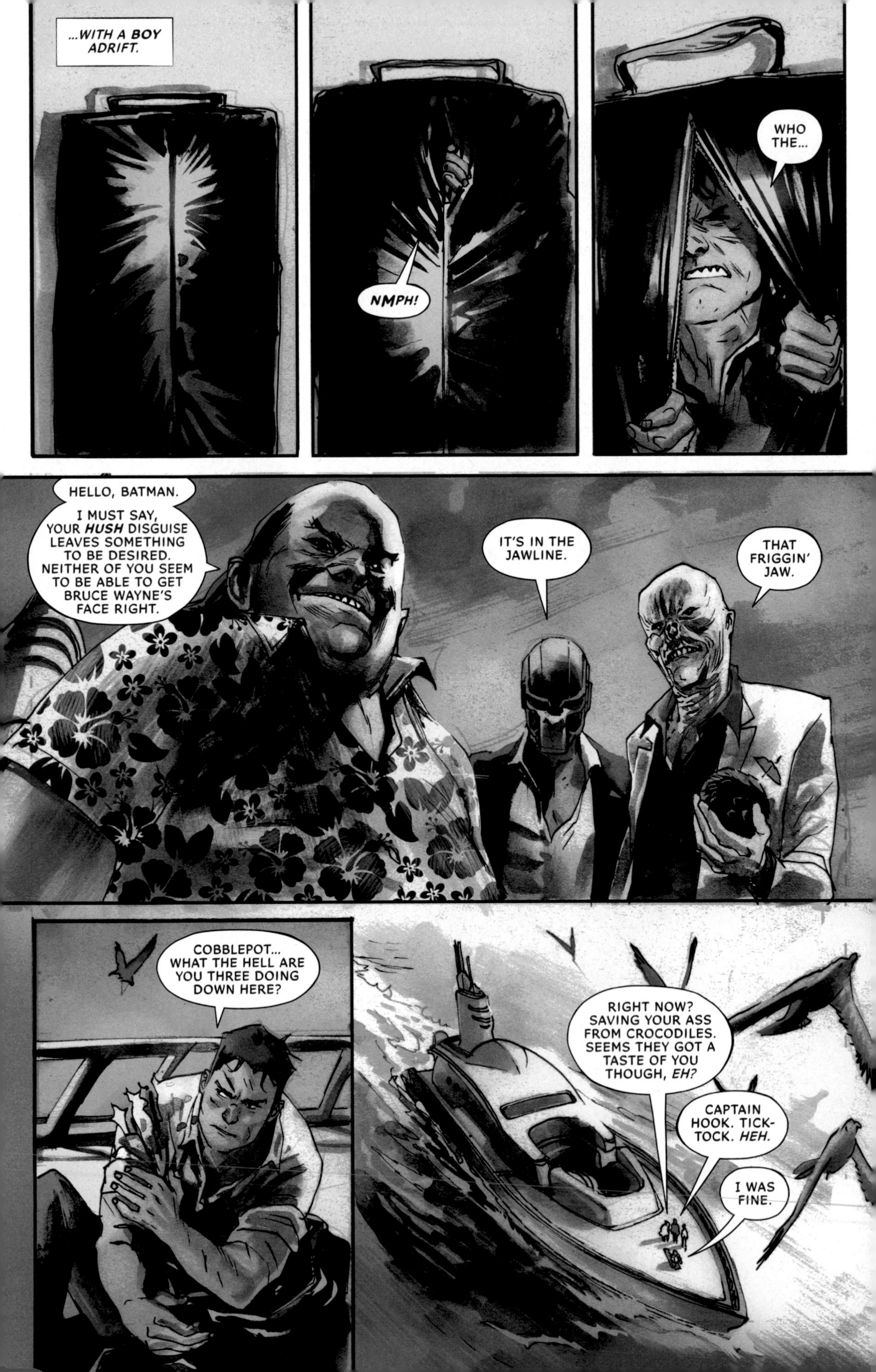
...WITH A BOY ADRIFT.
NMPH!
WHO THE...
HELLO, BATMAN.
I MUST SAY, YOUR HUSH DISGUISE LEAVES SOMETHING TO BE DESIRED. NEITHER OF YOU SEEM TO BE ABLE TO GET BRUCE WAYNE'S FACE RIGHT.
IT'S IN THE JAWLINE.
THAT FRIGGIN' JAW.
COBBLEPOT... WHAT THE HELL ARE YOU THREE DOING DOWN HERE?
RIGHT NOW? SAVING YOUR ASS FROM CROCODILES. SEEMS THEY GOT A TASTE OF YOU THOUGH, EH?
CAPTAIN HOOK. TICK-TOCK. HEH.
I WAS FINE.

AW, OF COURSE YOU WERE. HERE, YOU HAVE A *TOOTH* IN YOUR SHOULDER.

NOW LET ME ASK YOU A QUESTION, BATMAN. DO YOU KNOW WHAT THE *GENESIS ENGINE* IS?

DO *YOU?*

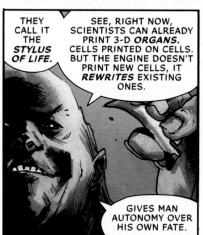

THEY CALL IT THE *STYLUS OF LIFE.*

SEE, RIGHT NOW, SCIENTISTS CAN ALREADY PRINT 3-D *ORGANS.* CELLS PRINTED ON CELLS. BUT THE ENGINE DOESN'T PRINT NEW CELLS, IT *REWRITES* EXISTING ONES.

GIVES MAN AUTONOMY OVER HIS OWN FATE.

MORE THAN THAT, IT'S A *WEAPON.* THE KEEPER CAN WRITE ANYTHING HE OR SHE WANTS INTO EXISTENCE THROUGH LIVING TISSUE. WE'RE TALKING HUMAN *MONSTERS,* ANYTHING.

NOW YOU'RE SPEAKING MY LANGUAGE.

AND HERE I WONDERED WHY YOU THREE WERE AFTER IT.

WE'RE AFTER IT TO *DESTROY* IT. HUSH WANTED IT TO MAKE HIMSELF BRUCE WAYNE, ONCE AND FOR ALL. NEAR-SIGHTED FOOL.

BUT IN THE *WRONG* HANDS, IT COULD BE USED TO CREATE WHOLE ARMIES OF NIGHTMARES. NOW, WE'LL HELP YOU GET IT, IF YOU PROMISE TO *DESTROY* IT.

HELP ME HOW?

IT WAS SUPPOSED TO ARRIVE AT *DEXTER* BY LAND. THIS TIME, THE RENDEZVOUS POINT IS AT *SEA.* WE KNOW THE *COORDINATES.*

APPARENTLY THERE'S SOMEONE AFTER THE ENGINE THAT HAS THE DELIVERY BOY SPOOKED.

REAL SPOOKED.

THEN WE HAVE NOTHING LEFT TO TALK ABOUT.

AND MY BRUCE WAYNE? IT'S *PERFECT.*

WHAT DO YOU KNOW ABOUT HIM?

NOTHING.

WHEN BRUCE SETS HIS MIND TO SOMETHING, THERE'S NO DISSUADING HIM...

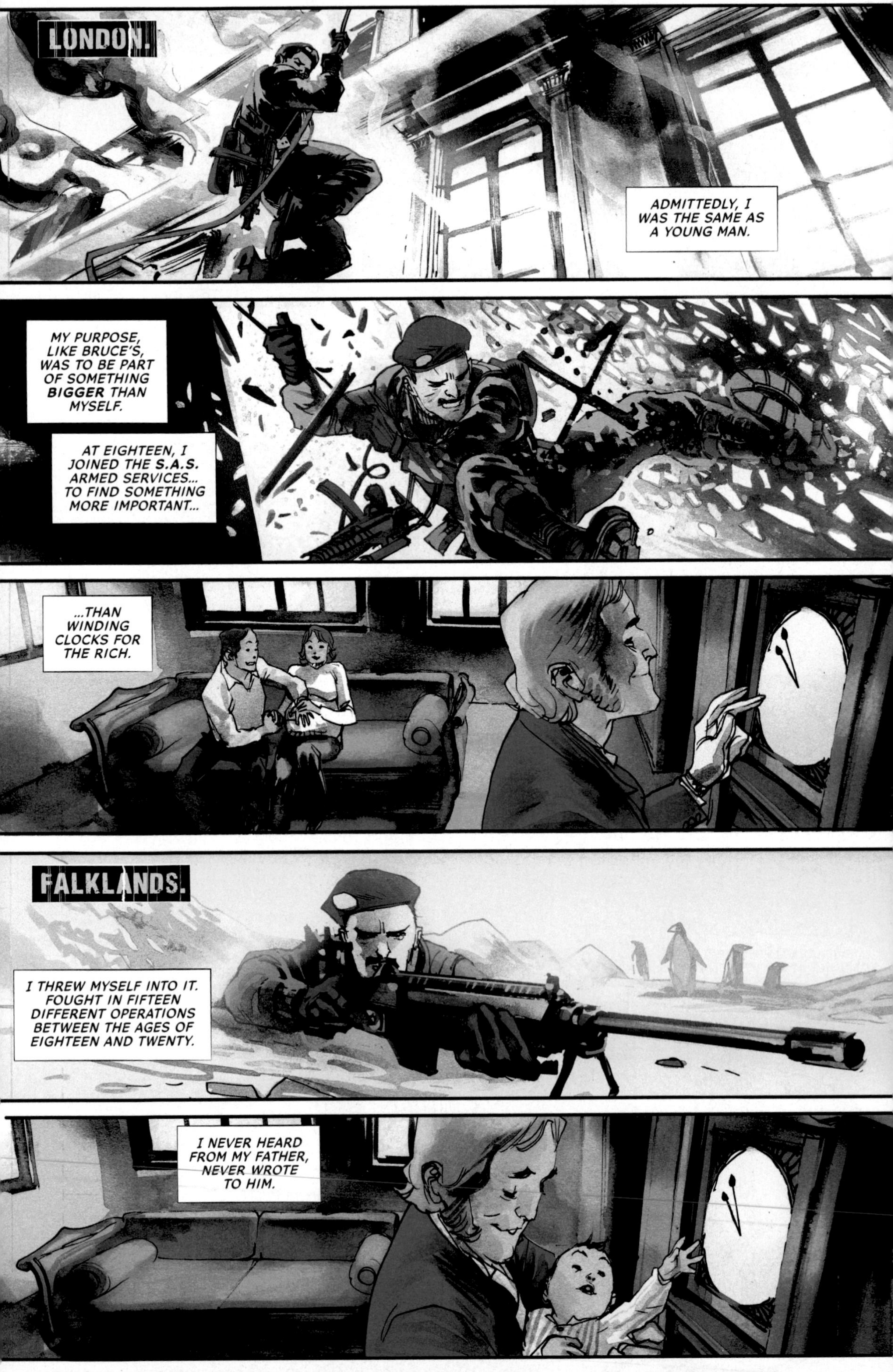
LONDON.
ADMITTEDLY, I WAS THE SAME AS A YOUNG MAN.
MY PURPOSE, LIKE BRUCE'S, WAS TO BE PART OF SOMETHING **BIGGER** THAN MYSELF.
AT EIGHTEEN, I JOINED THE **S.A.S.** ARMED SERVICES... TO FIND SOMETHING MORE IMPORTANT...
...THAN WINDING CLOCKS FOR THE RICH.
FALKLANDS.
I THREW MYSELF INTO IT. FOUGHT IN FIFTEEN DIFFERENT OPERATIONS BETWEEN THE AGES OF EIGHTEEN AND TWENTY.
I NEVER HEARD FROM MY FATHER, NEVER WROTE TO HIM.

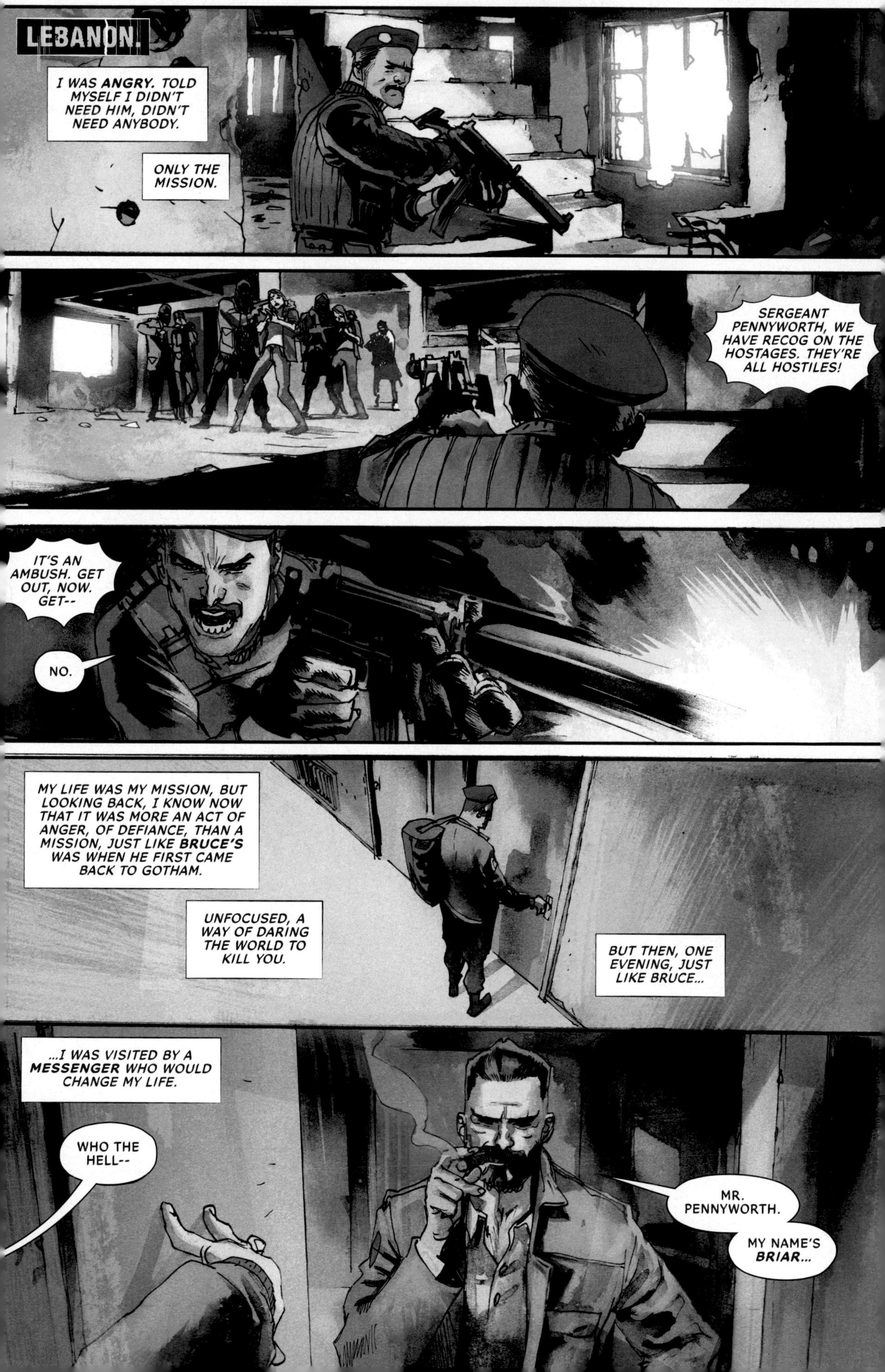
LEBANON.
I WAS ANGRY. TOLD MYSELF I DIDN'T NEED HIM, DIDN'T NEED ANYBODY.
ONLY THE MISSION.
SERGEANT PENNYWORTH, WE HAVE RECOG ON THE HOSTAGES. THEY'RE ALL HOSTILES!
IT'S AN AMBUSH. GET OUT, NOW. GET--
NO.
MY LIFE WAS MY MISSION, BUT LOOKING BACK, I KNOW NOW THAT IT WAS MORE AN ACT OF ANGER, OF DEFIANCE, THAN A MISSION, JUST LIKE BRUCE'S WAS WHEN HE FIRST CAME BACK TO GOTHAM.
UNFOCUSED, A WAY OF DARING THE WORLD TO KILL YOU.
BUT THEN, ONE EVENING, JUST LIKE BRUCE...
...I WAS VISITED BY A MESSENGER WHO WOULD CHANGE MY LIFE.
WHO THE HELL--
MR. PENNYWORTH.
MY NAME'S BRIAR...

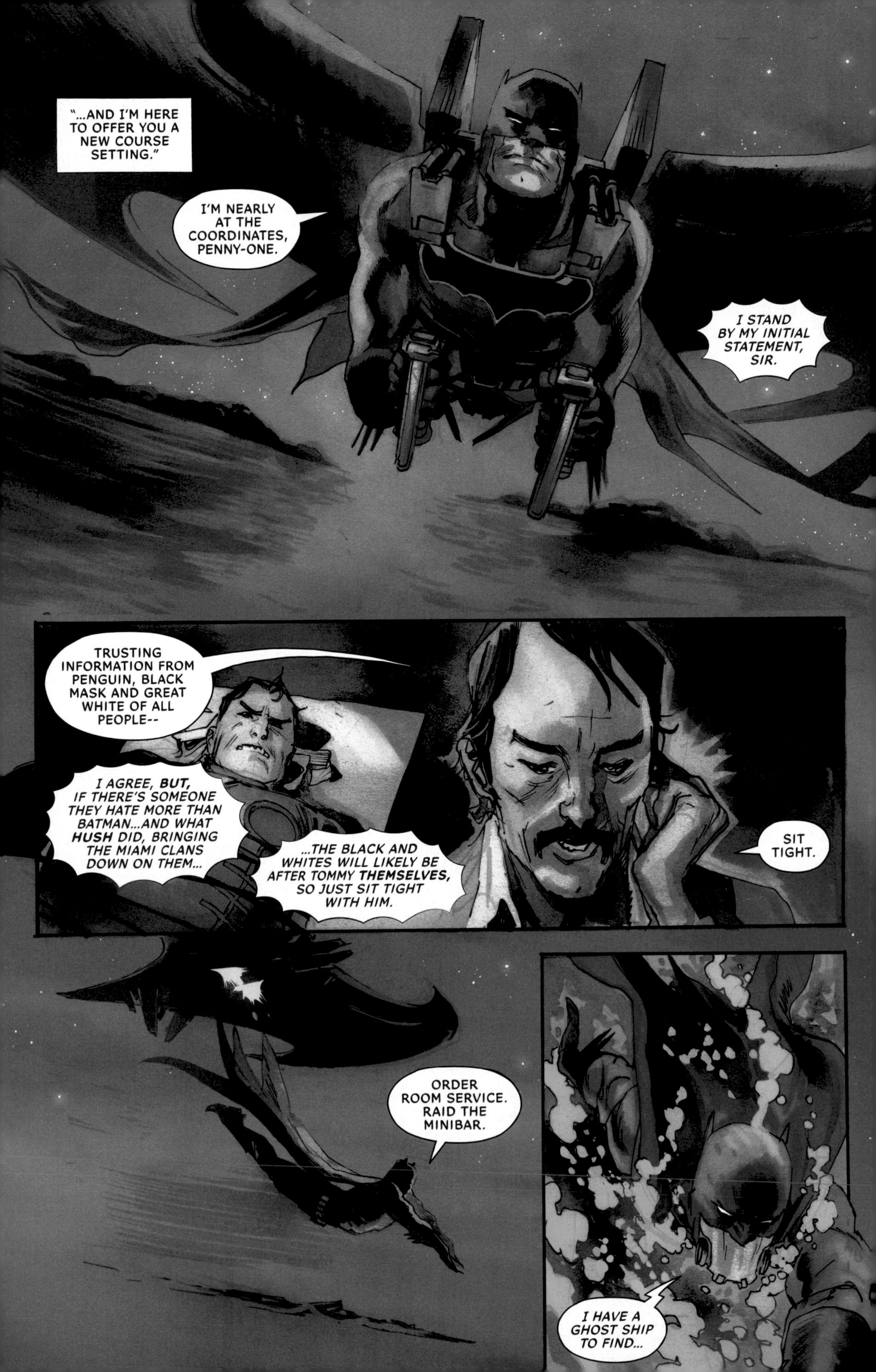
"...AND I'M HERE TO OFFER YOU A NEW COURSE SETTING."
I'M NEARLY AT THE COORDINATES, PENNY-ONE.
I STAND BY MY INITIAL STATEMENT, SIR.
TRUSTING INFORMATION FROM PENGUIN, BLACK MASK AND GREAT WHITE OF ALL PEOPLE--
I AGREE, BUT, IF THERE'S SOMEONE THEY HATE MORE THAN BATMAN...AND WHAT HUSH DID, BRINGING THE MIAMI CLANS DOWN ON THEM...
...THE BLACK AND WHITES WILL LIKELY BE AFTER TOMMY THEMSELVES, SO JUST SIT TIGHT WITH HIM.
SIT TIGHT.
ORDER ROOM SERVICE. RAID THE MINIBAR.
I HAVE A GHOST SHIP TO FIND...

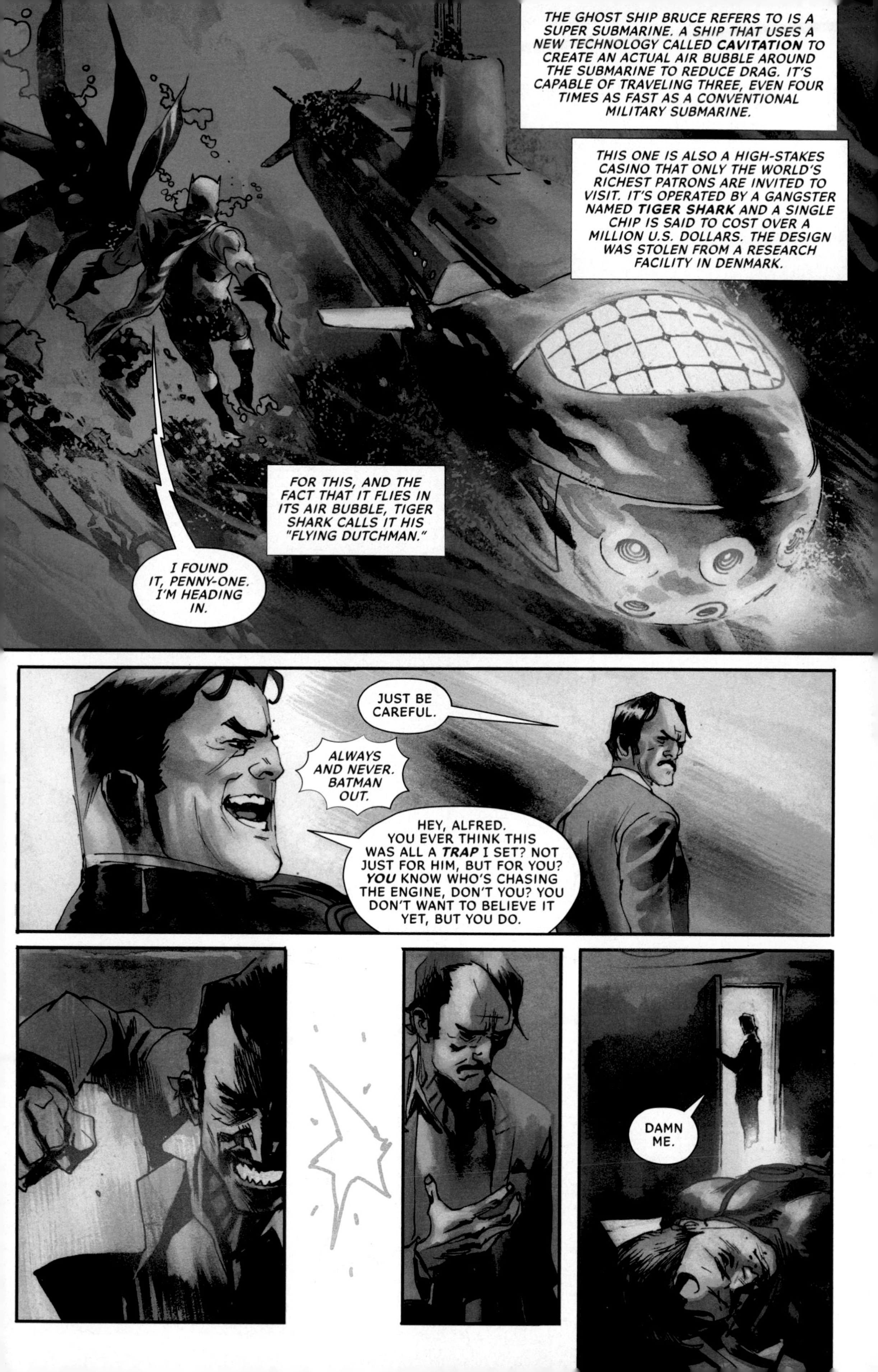
THE GHOST SHIP BRUCE REFERS TO IS A SUPER SUBMARINE. A SHIP THAT USES A NEW TECHNOLOGY CALLED **CAVITATION** TO CREATE AN ACTUAL AIR BUBBLE AROUND THE SUBMARINE TO REDUCE DRAG. IT'S CAPABLE OF TRAVELING THREE, EVEN FOUR TIMES AS FAST AS A CONVENTIONAL MILITARY SUBMARINE.
THIS ONE IS ALSO A HIGH-STAKES CASINO THAT ONLY THE WORLD'S RICHEST PATRONS ARE INVITED TO VISIT. IT'S OPERATED BY A GANGSTER NAMED **TIGER SHARK** AND A SINGLE CHIP IS SAID TO COST OVER A MILLION U.S. DOLLARS. THE DESIGN WAS STOLEN FROM A RESEARCH FACILITY IN DENMARK.
FOR THIS, AND THE FACT THAT IT FLIES IN ITS AIR BUBBLE, TIGER SHARK CALLS IT HIS "FLYING DUTCHMAN."
I FOUND IT, PENNY-ONE. I'M HEADING IN.
JUST BE CAREFUL.
ALWAYS AND NEVER. BATMAN OUT.
HEY, ALFRED. YOU EVER THINK THIS WAS ALL A ***TRAP*** I SET? NOT JUST FOR HIM, BUT FOR YOU? ***YOU*** KNOW WHO'S CHASING THE ENGINE, DON'T YOU? YOU DON'T WANT TO BELIEVE IT YET, BUT YOU DO.
DAMN ME.

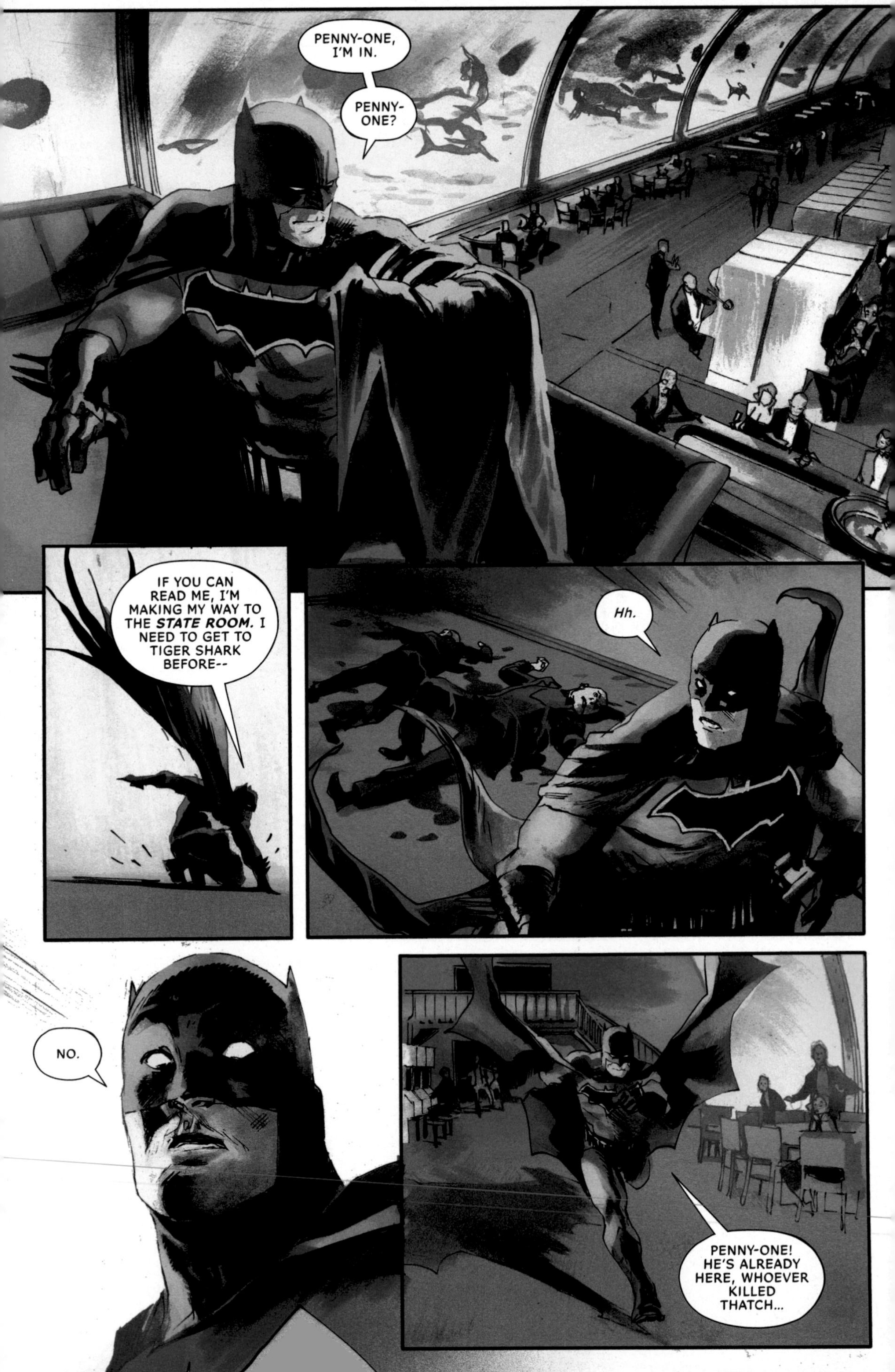
PENNY-ONE, I'M IN.
PENNY-ONE?
IF YOU CAN READ ME, I'M MAKING MY WAY TO THE *STATE ROOM.* I NEED TO GET TO TIGER SHARK BEFORE--
Hh.
NO.
PENNY-ONE! HE'S ALREADY HERE, WHOEVER KILLED THATCH...

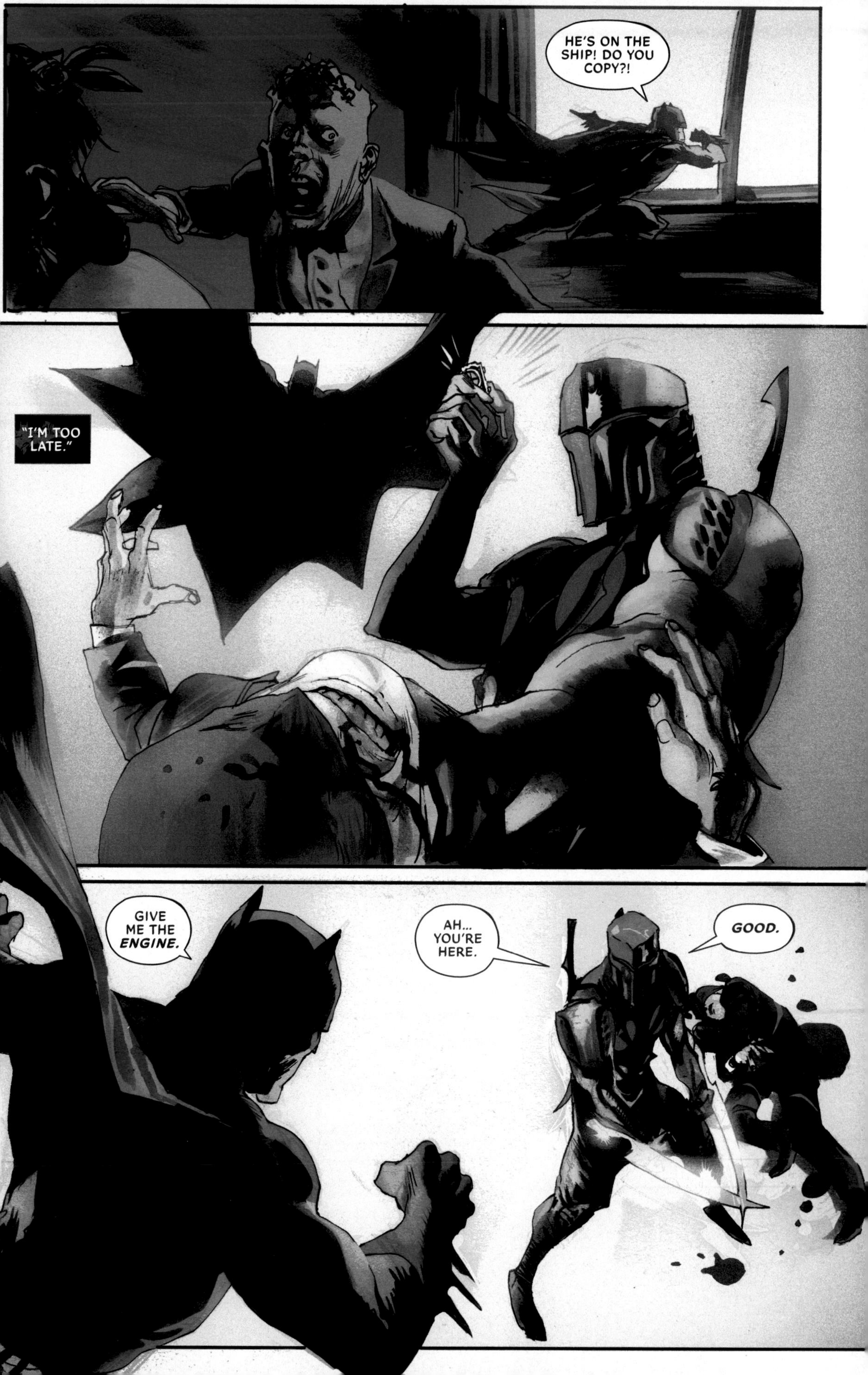
HE'S ON THE SHIP! DO YOU COPY?!
"I'M TOO LATE."
GIVE ME THE *ENGINE.*
AH... YOU'RE HERE.
GOOD.

THIS ENDS NOW.

I WON'T LET YOU GET AWAY.

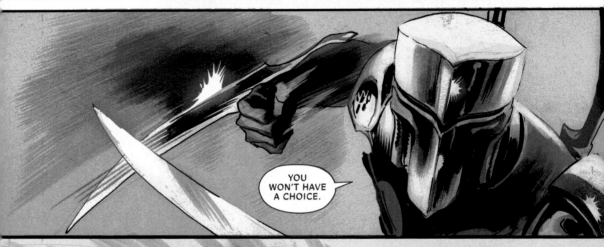

YOU WON'T HAVE A CHOICE.

CRRAAACK

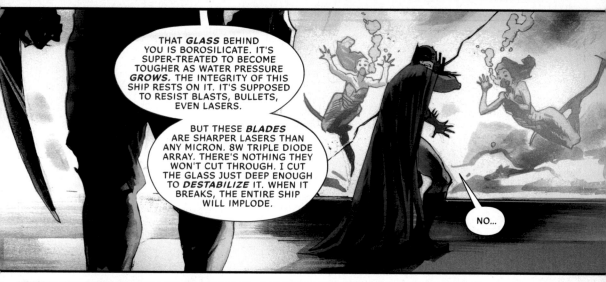

THAT *GLASS* BEHIND YOU IS BOROSILICATE. IT'S SUPER-TREATED TO BECOME TOUGHER AS WATER PRESSURE *GROWS.* THE INTEGRITY OF THIS SHIP RESTS ON IT. IT'S SUPPOSED TO RESIST BLASTS, BULLETS, EVEN LASERS.

BUT THESE *BLADES* ARE SHARPER LASERS THAN ANY MICRON. 8W TRIPLE DIODE ARRAY. THERE'S NOTHING THEY WON'T CUT THROUGH. I CUT THE GLASS JUST DEEP ENOUGH TO *DESTABILIZE* IT. WHEN IT BREAKS, THE ENTIRE SHIP WILL IMPLODE.

NO...

I'M SURE YOUR MIND IS RACING TO THE DIFFERENT TOOLS IN YOUR BELT THAT COULD HELP YOU NOW...PERHAPS YOU CAN SEAL THE GLASS IN TIME.

BUT WITH YOUR SUBSCAPULAR ARTERY CUT OPEN, YOU'LL ONLY STAY CONSCIOUS FOR A MATTER OF SECONDS.

ARRGH!

YOU HAVE THE GENESIS ENGINE?

YES.

THEN BLOW THE SHIP AND GET OUT OF THERE.

UNDER-STOOD.

THIS ISN'T ABOUT YOU, BATMAN. THE IDEA HERE WAS TO CREATE WHAT WOULD LOOK LIKE AN ACCIDENT.

TO THE REST OF THE WORLD, THE GENESIS ENGINE WOULD BE NOTHING MORE THAN ANOTHER SUNKEN TREASURE.

JUST LIKE YOU.

"WHO ARE YOU? DO I KNOW YOU?"

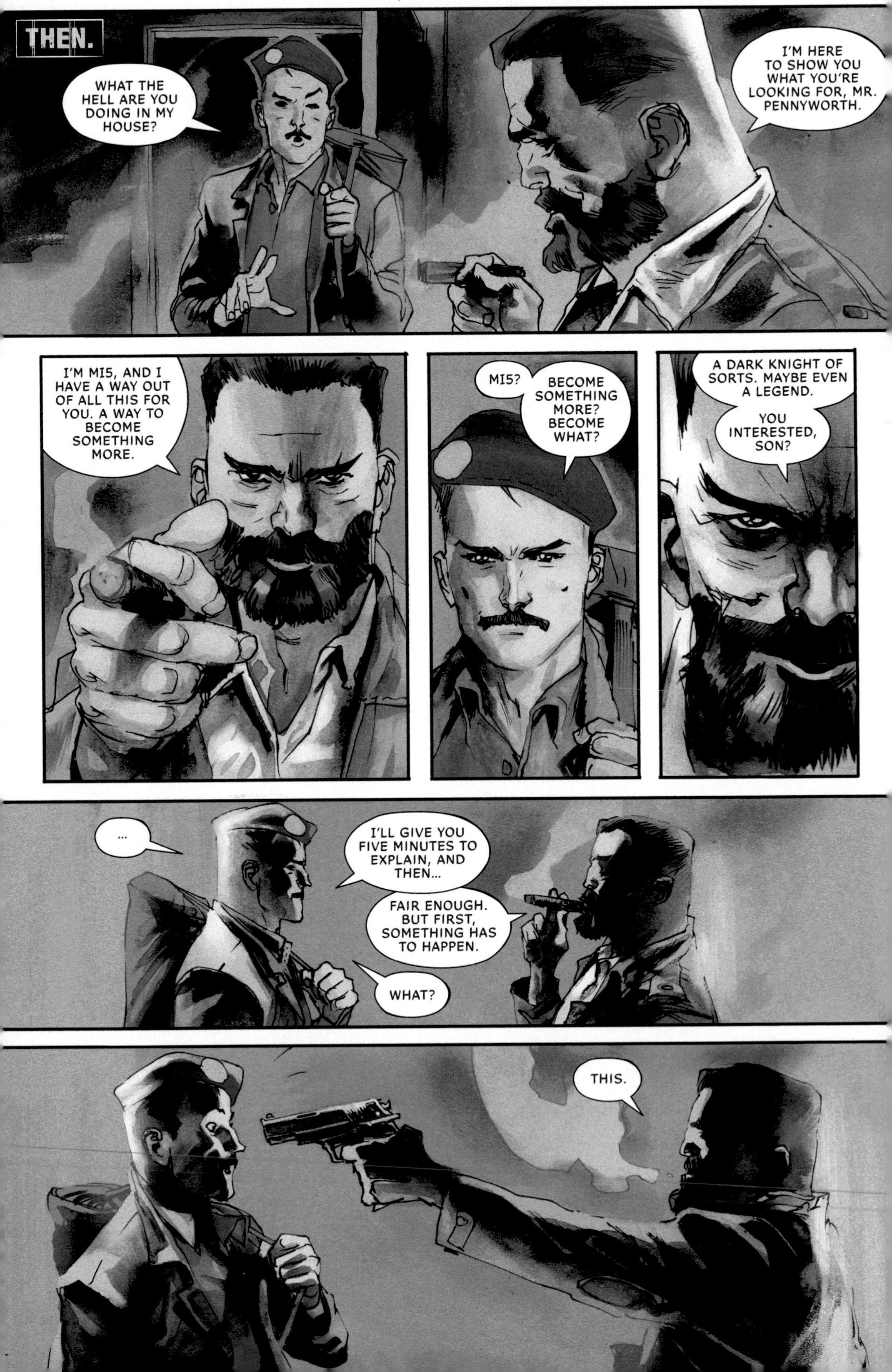
THEN.
WHAT THE HELL ARE YOU DOING IN MY HOUSE?
I'M HERE TO SHOW YOU WHAT YOU'RE LOOKING FOR, MR. PENNYWORTH.
I'M MI5, AND I HAVE A WAY OUT OF ALL THIS FOR YOU. A WAY TO BECOME SOMETHING MORE.
MI5?
BECOME SOMETHING MORE? BECOME WHAT?
A DARK KNIGHT OF SORTS. MAYBE EVEN A LEGEND.
YOU INTERESTED, SON?
...
I'LL GIVE YOU FIVE MINUTES TO EXPLAIN, AND THEN...
FAIR ENOUGH. BUT FIRST, SOMETHING HAS TO HAPPEN.
WHAT?
THIS.

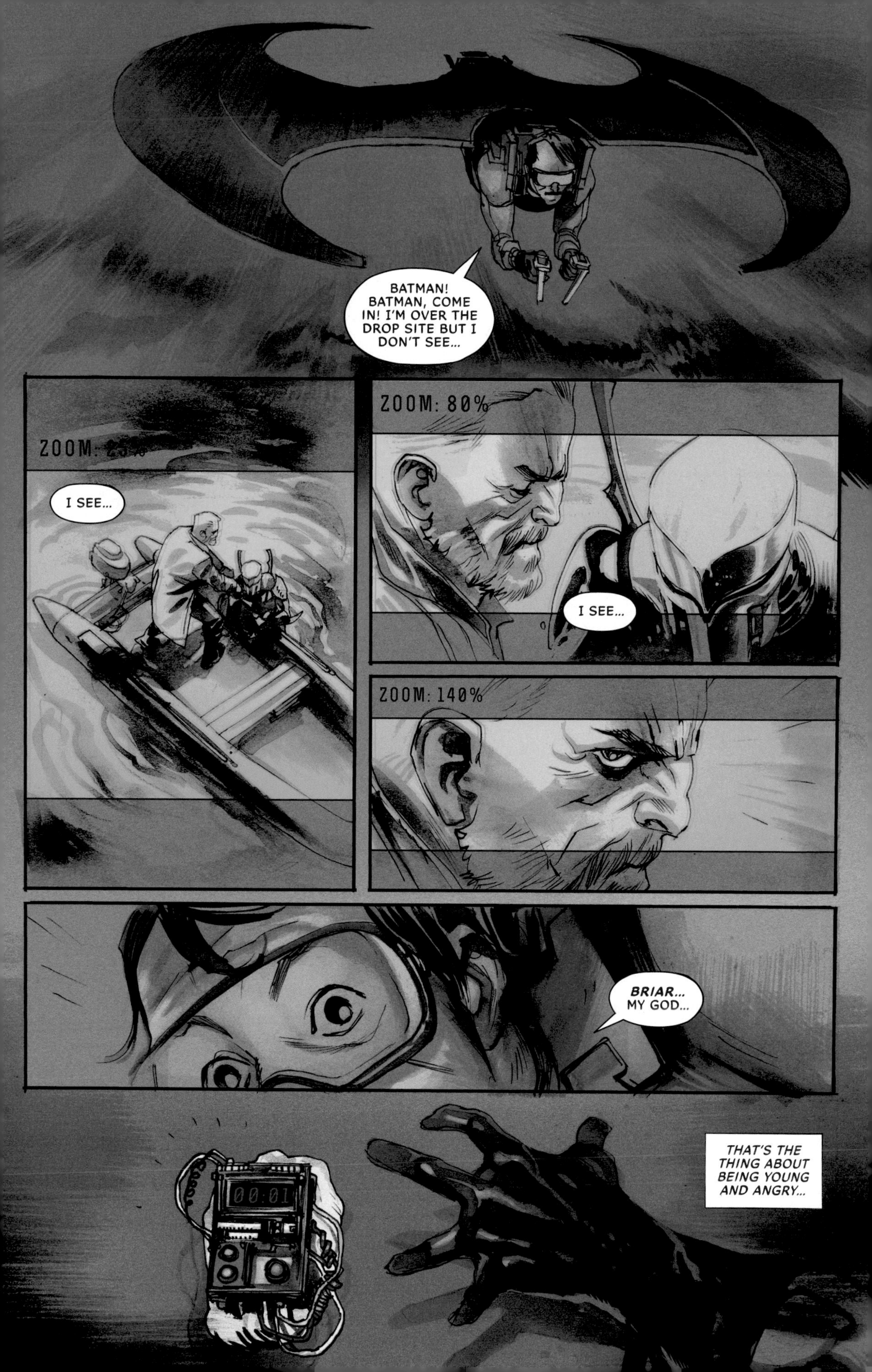
BATMAN! BATMAN, COME IN! I'M OVER THE DROP SITE BUT I DON'T SEE...
ZOOM: 25%
I SEE...
ZOOM: 80%
I SEE...
ZOOM: 140%
BRIAR... MY GOD...
00:01
THAT'S THE THING ABOUT BEING YOUNG AND ANGRY...

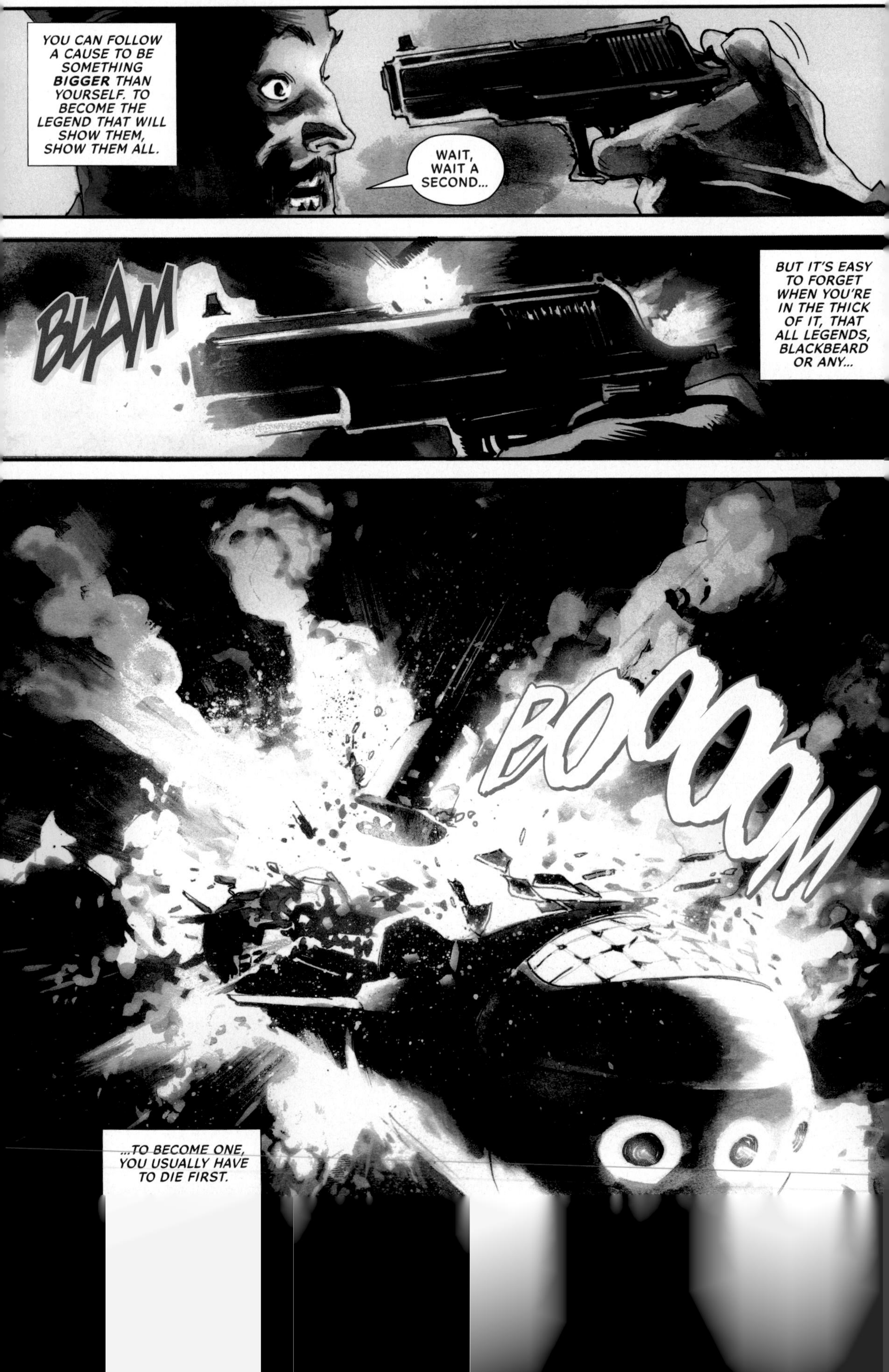

YOU CAN FOLLOW A CAUSE TO BE SOMETHING **BIGGER** THAN YOURSELF. TO BECOME THE LEGEND THAT WILL SHOW THEM, SHOW THEM ALL.
WAIT, WAIT A SECOND...
BLAM
BUT IT'S EASY TO FORGET WHEN YOU'RE IN THE THICK OF IT, THAT ALL LEGENDS, BLACKBEARD OR ANY...
BOOOOOM
...TO BECOME ONE, YOU USUALLY HAVE TO DIE FIRST.

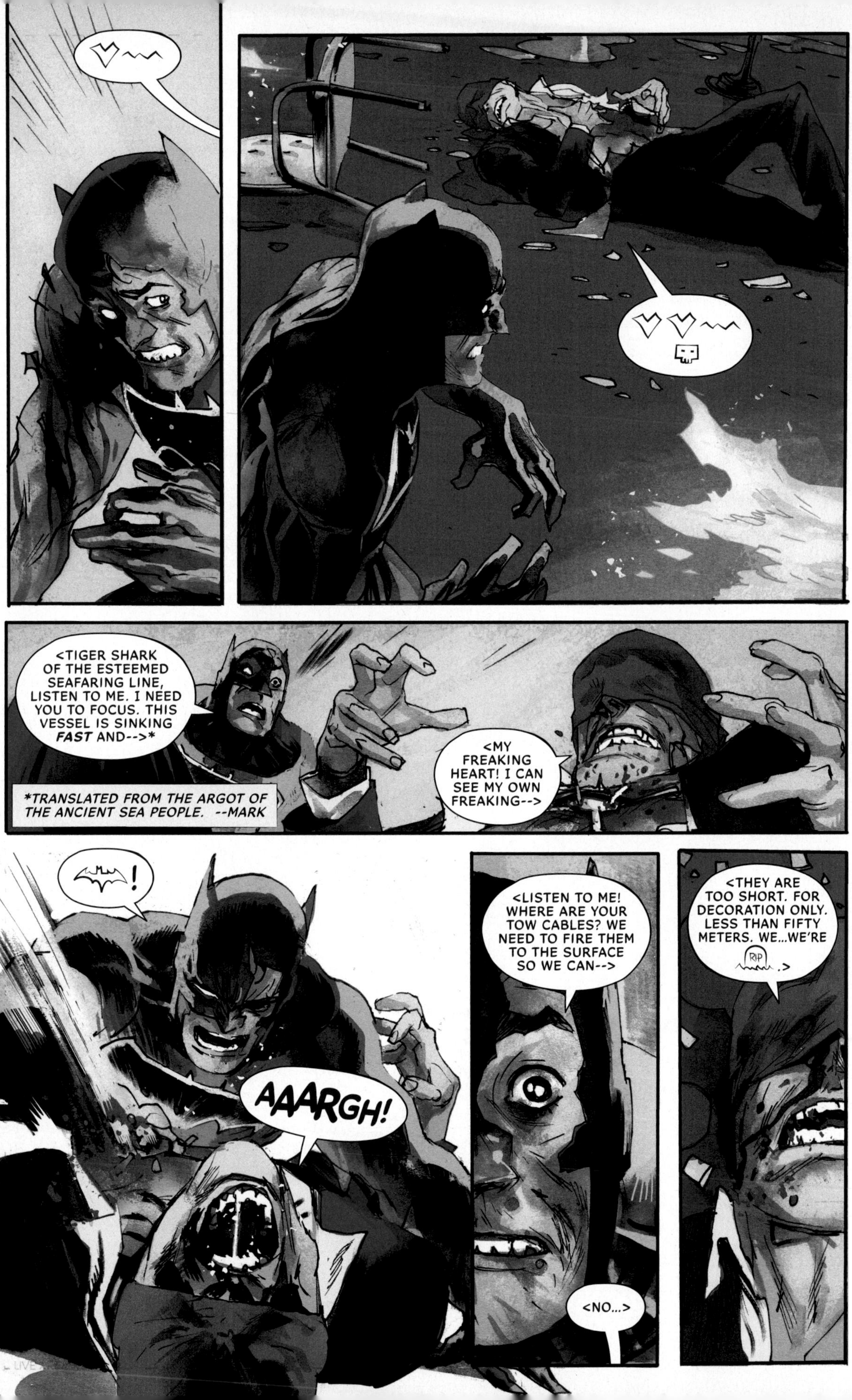
<TIGER SHARK OF THE ESTEEMED SEAFARING LINE, LISTEN TO ME. I NEED YOU TO FOCUS. THIS VESSEL IS SINKING *FAST* AND-->*
*TRANSLATED FROM THE ARGOT OF THE ANCIENT SEA PEOPLE. --MARK
<MY FREAKING HEART! I CAN SEE MY OWN FREAKING-->
!
AAARGH!
<LISTEN TO ME! WHERE ARE YOUR TOW CABLES? WE NEED TO FIRE THEM TO THE SURFACE SO WE CAN-->
<NO...>
<THEY ARE TOO SHORT. FOR DECORATION ONLY. LESS THAN FIFTY METERS. WE...WE'RE
RIP
.>

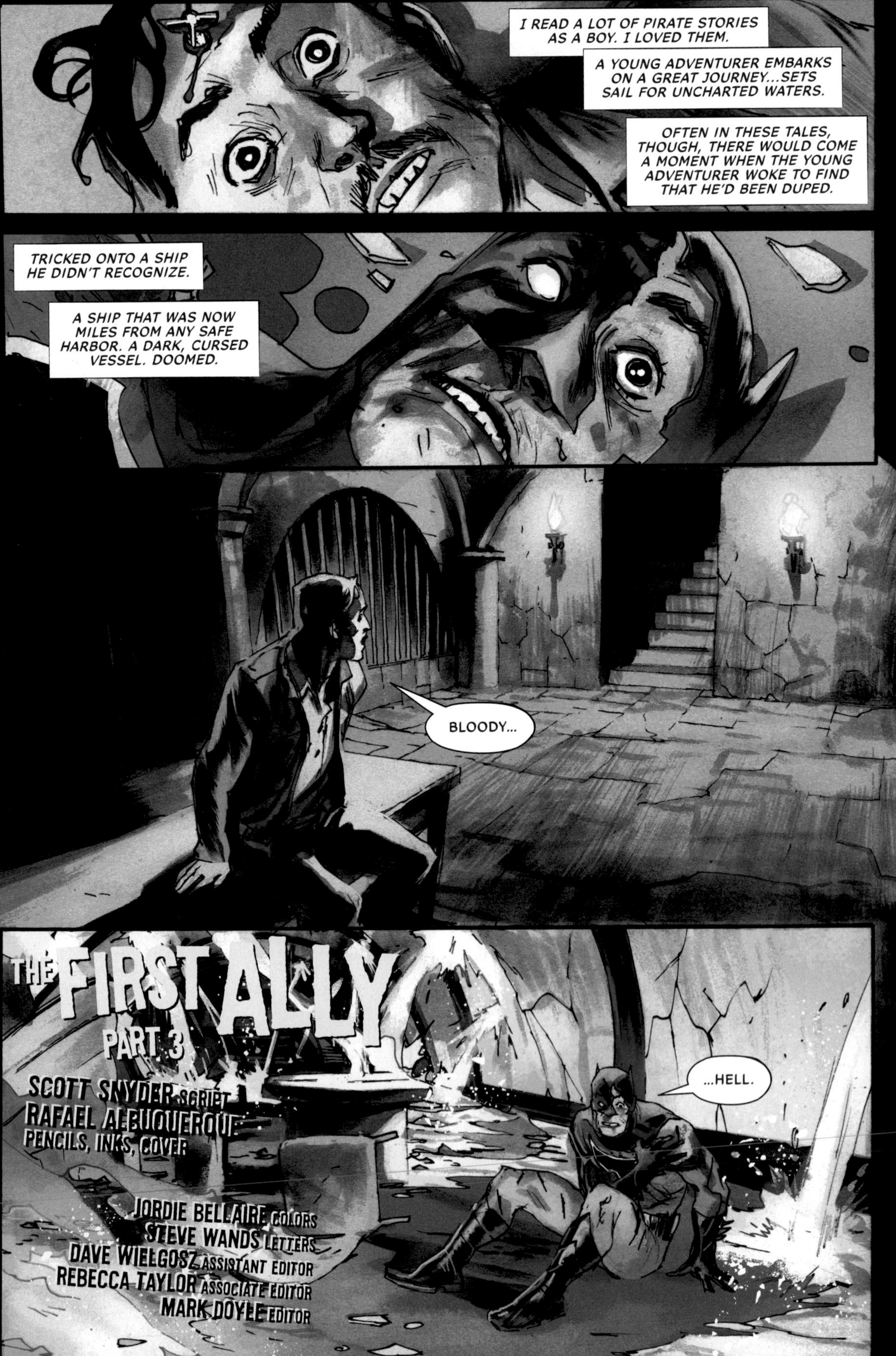

I READ A LOT OF PIRATE STORIES AS A BOY. I LOVED THEM.
A YOUNG ADVENTURER EMBARKS ON A GREAT JOURNEY...SETS SAIL FOR UNCHARTED WATERS.
OFTEN IN THESE TALES, THOUGH, THERE WOULD COME A MOMENT WHEN THE YOUNG ADVENTURER WOKE TO FIND THAT HE'D BEEN DUPED.
TRICKED ONTO A SHIP HE DIDN'T RECOGNIZE.
A SHIP THAT WAS NOW MILES FROM ANY SAFE HARBOR. A DARK, CURSED VESSEL. DOOMED.
BLOODY...
THE FIRST ALLY
PART 3
SCOTT SNYDER SCRIPT
RAFAEL ALBUQUERQUE PENCILS, INKS, COVER
JORDIE BELLAIRE COLORS
STEVE WANDS LETTERS
DAVE WIELGOSZ ASSISTANT EDITOR
REBECCA TAYLOR ASSOCIATE EDITOR
MARK DOYLE EDITOR
...HELL.

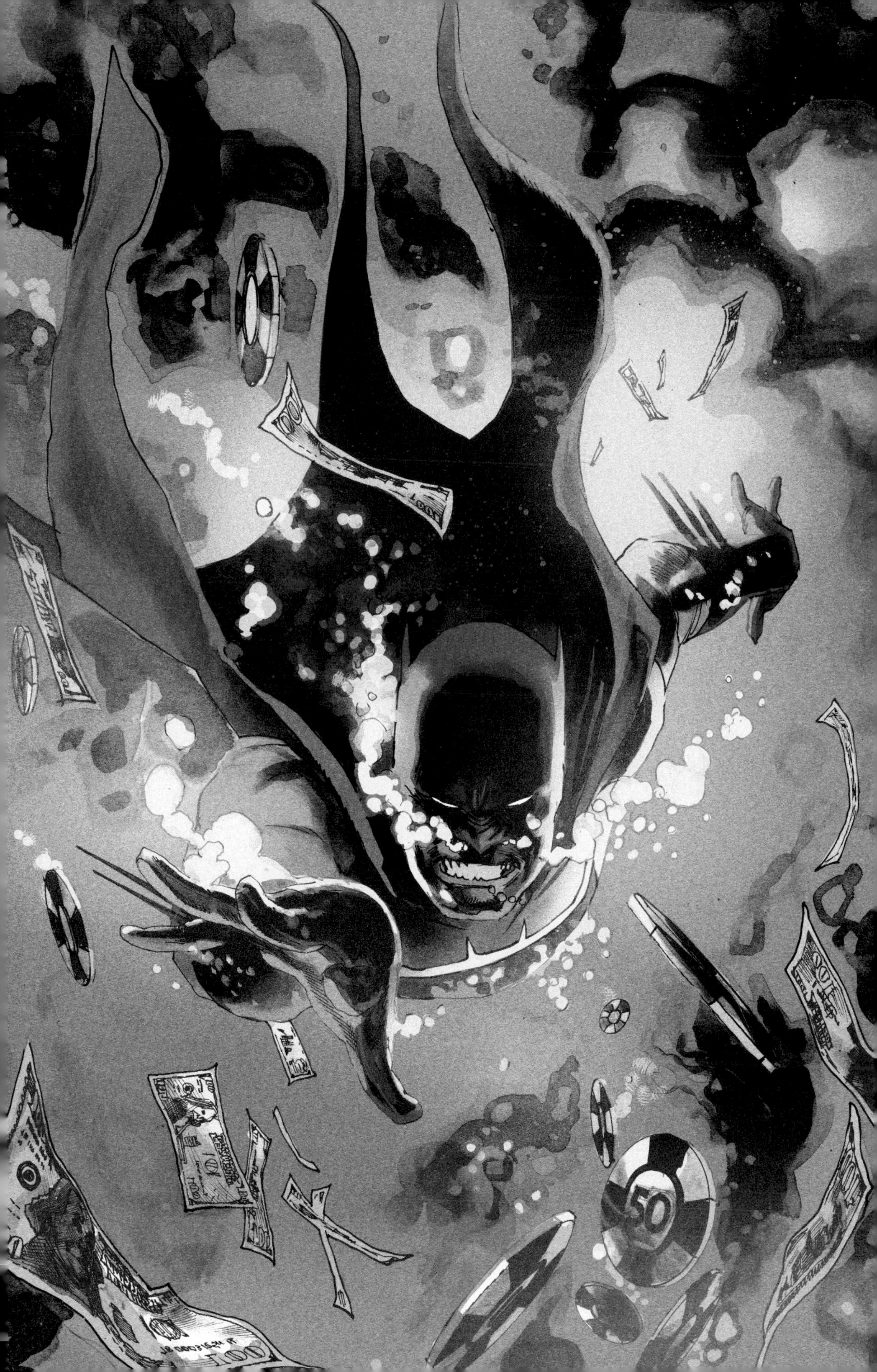
50

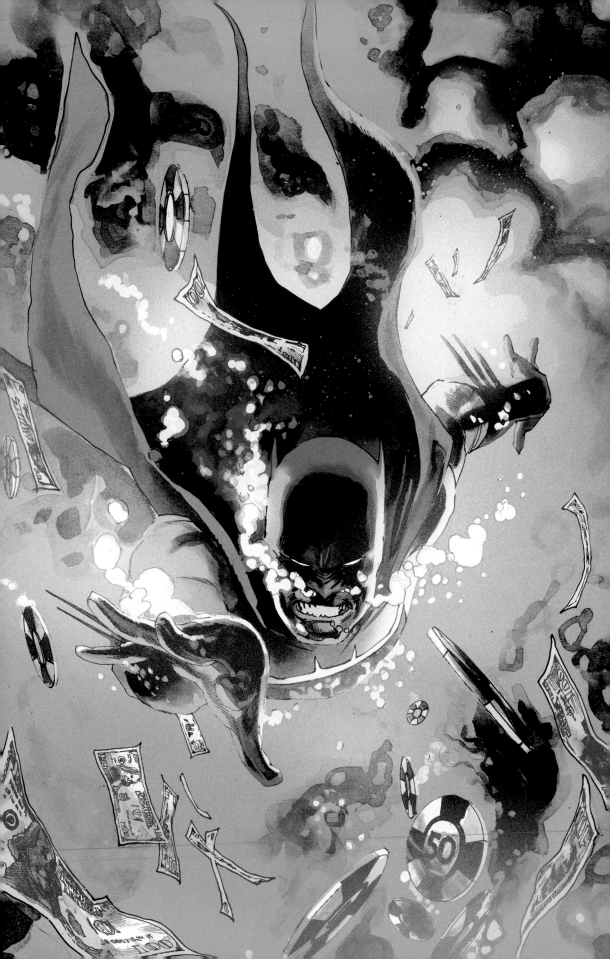

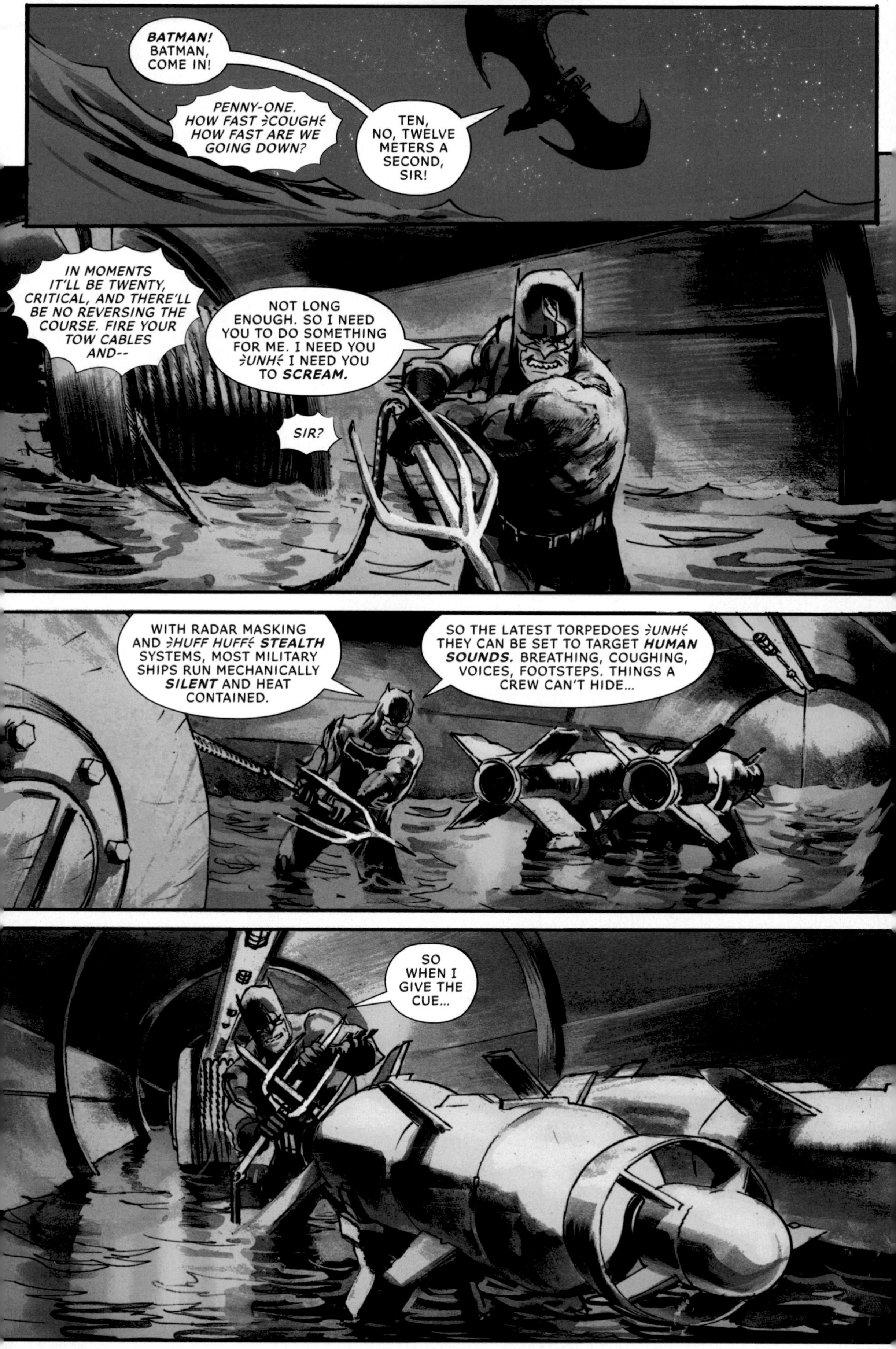
BATMAN! BATMAN, COME IN!
PENNY-ONE. HOW FAST ⋺COUGH⋲ HOW FAST ARE WE GOING DOWN?
TEN, NO, TWELVE METERS A SECOND, SIR!
IN MOMENTS IT'LL BE TWENTY, CRITICAL, AND THERE'LL BE NO REVERSING THE COURSE. FIRE YOUR TOW CABLES AND--
NOT LONG ENOUGH. SO I NEED YOU TO DO SOMETHING FOR ME. I NEED YOU ⋺UNH⋲ I NEED YOU TO SCREAM.
SIR?
WITH RADAR MASKING AND ⋺HUFF HUFF⋲ STEALTH SYSTEMS, MOST MILITARY SHIPS RUN MECHANICALLY SILENT AND HEAT CONTAINED.
SO THE LATEST TORPEDOES ⋺UNH⋲ THEY CAN BE SET TO TARGET HUMAN SOUNDS. BREATHING, COUGHING, VOICES, FOOTSTEPS. THINGS A CREW CAN'T HIDE...
SO WHEN I GIVE THE CUE...

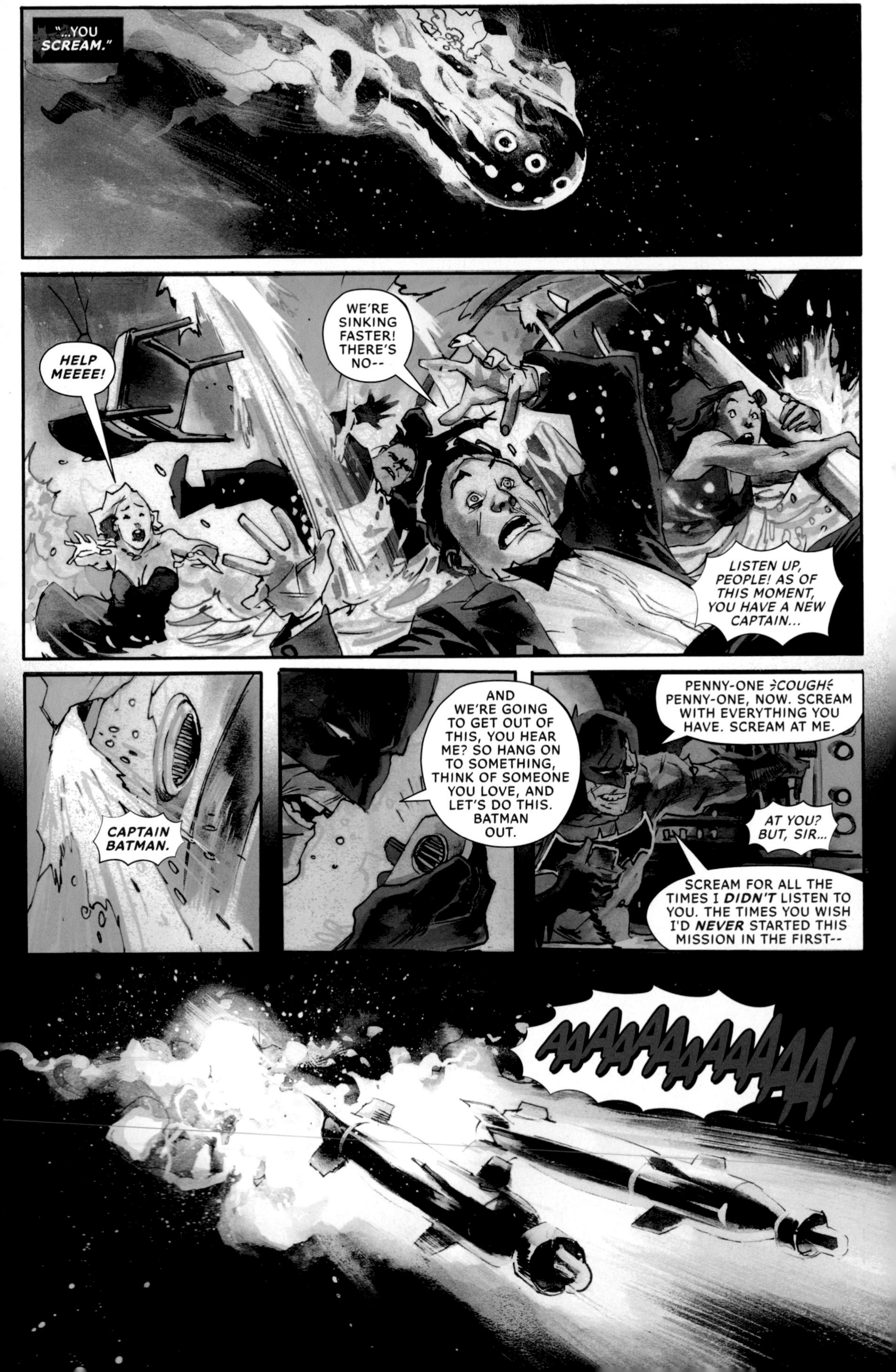
"...YOU SCREAM."
HELP MEEEE!
WE'RE SINKING FASTER! THERE'S NO--
LISTEN UP, PEOPLE! AS OF THIS MOMENT, YOU HAVE A NEW CAPTAIN...
CAPTAIN BATMAN.
AND WE'RE GOING TO GET OUT OF THIS, YOU HEAR ME? SO HANG ON TO SOMETHING, THINK OF SOMEONE YOU LOVE, AND LET'S DO THIS. BATMAN OUT.
PENNY-ONE *COUGH* PENNY-ONE, NOW. SCREAM WITH EVERYTHING YOU HAVE. SCREAM AT ME.
AT YOU? BUT, SIR...
SCREAM FOR ALL THE TIMES I DIDN'T LISTEN TO YOU. THE TIMES YOU WISH I'D NEVER STARTED THIS MISSION IN THE FIRST--
AAAAAAAAAAAAAA!

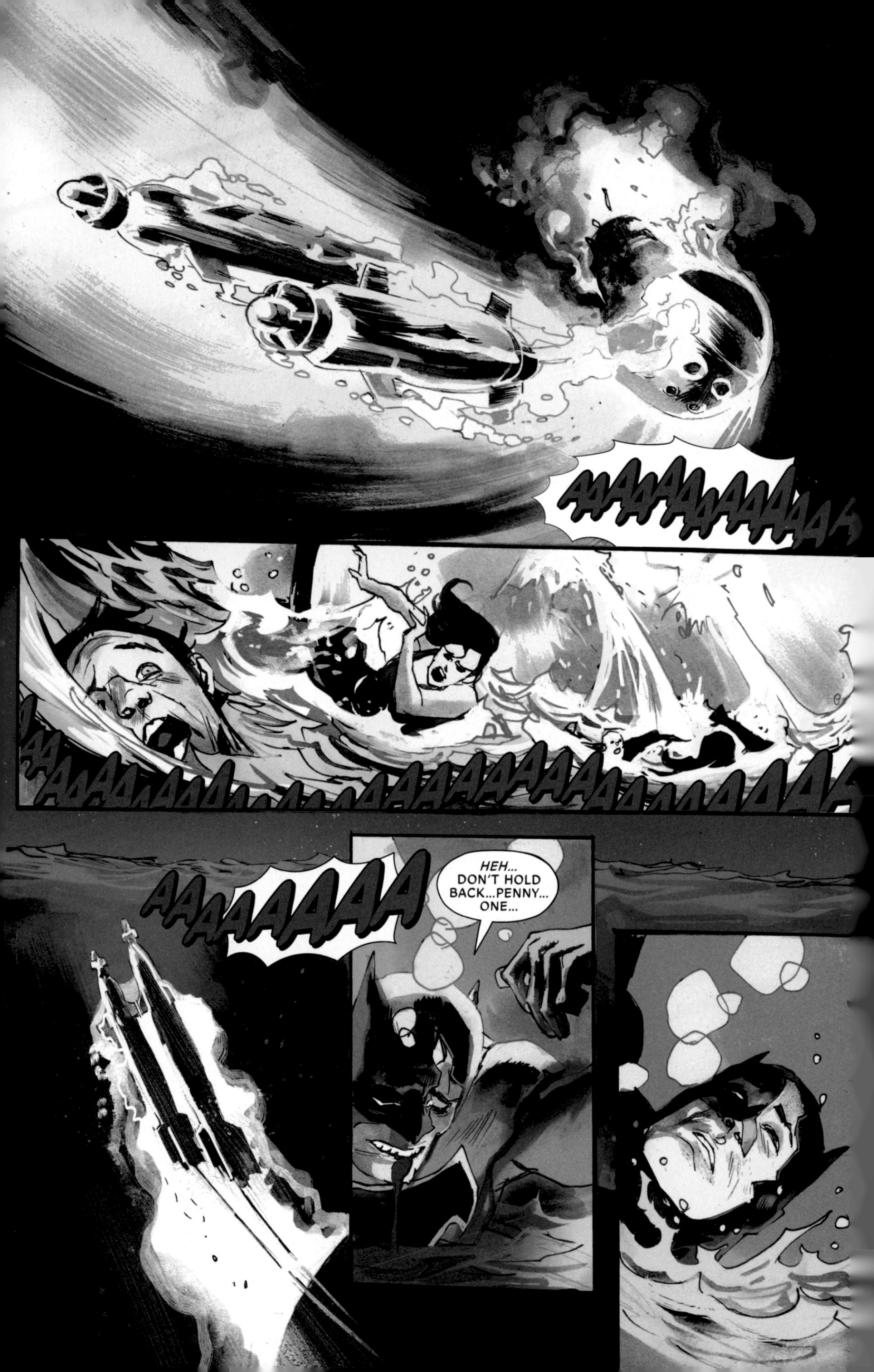
AAAAAAAAAAAAAA
AAAAAAAAAAAAAAAAAAAAAAAAAAAAAAAA
AAAAAAAA
HEH... DON'T HOLD BACK...PENNY... ONE...

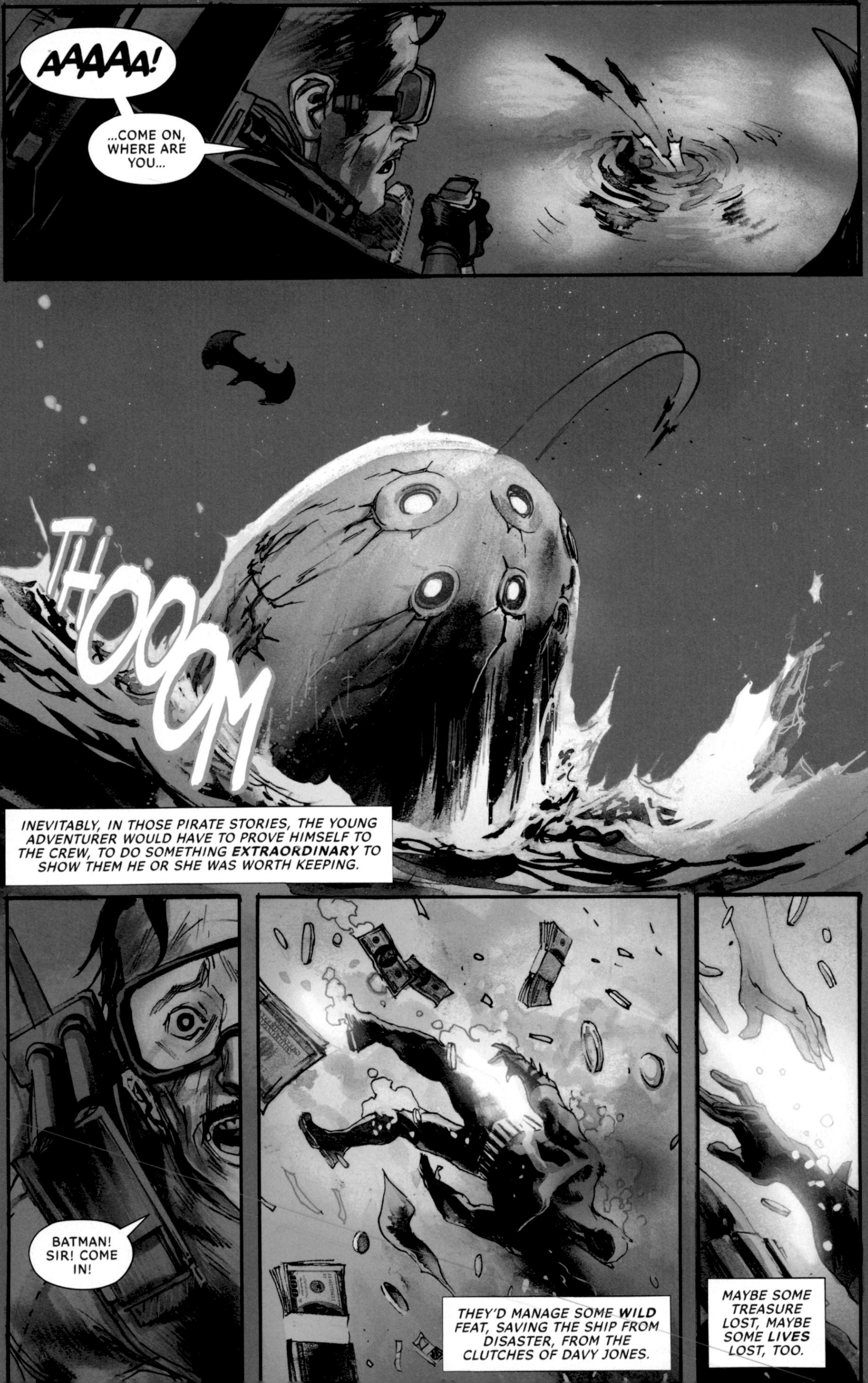
AAAAA!
...COME ON, WHERE ARE YOU...
THOOOOM
INEVITABLY, IN THOSE PIRATE STORIES, THE YOUNG ADVENTURER WOULD HAVE TO PROVE HIMSELF TO THE CREW, TO DO SOMETHING EXTRAORDINARY TO SHOW THEM HE OR SHE WAS WORTH KEEPING.
BATMAN! SIR! COME IN!
THEY'D MANAGE SOME WILD FEAT, SAVING THE SHIP FROM DISASTER, FROM THE CLUTCHES OF DAVY JONES.
MAYBE SOME TREASURE LOST, MAYBE SOME LIVES LOST, TOO.

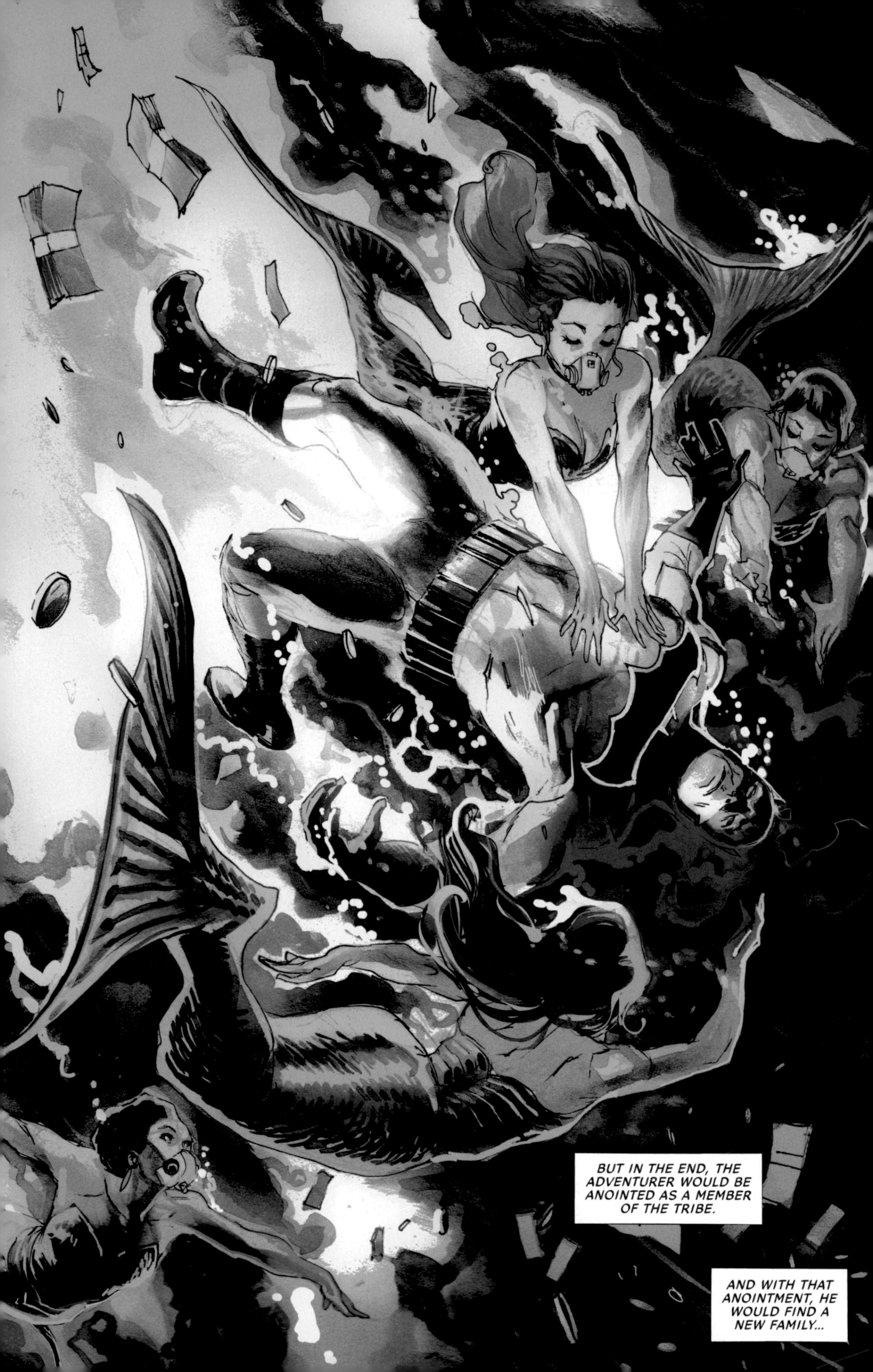
BUT IN THE END, THE ADVENTURER WOULD BE ANOINTED AS A MEMBER OF THE TRIBE.
AND WITH THAT ANOINTMENT, HE WOULD FIND A NEW FAMILY...

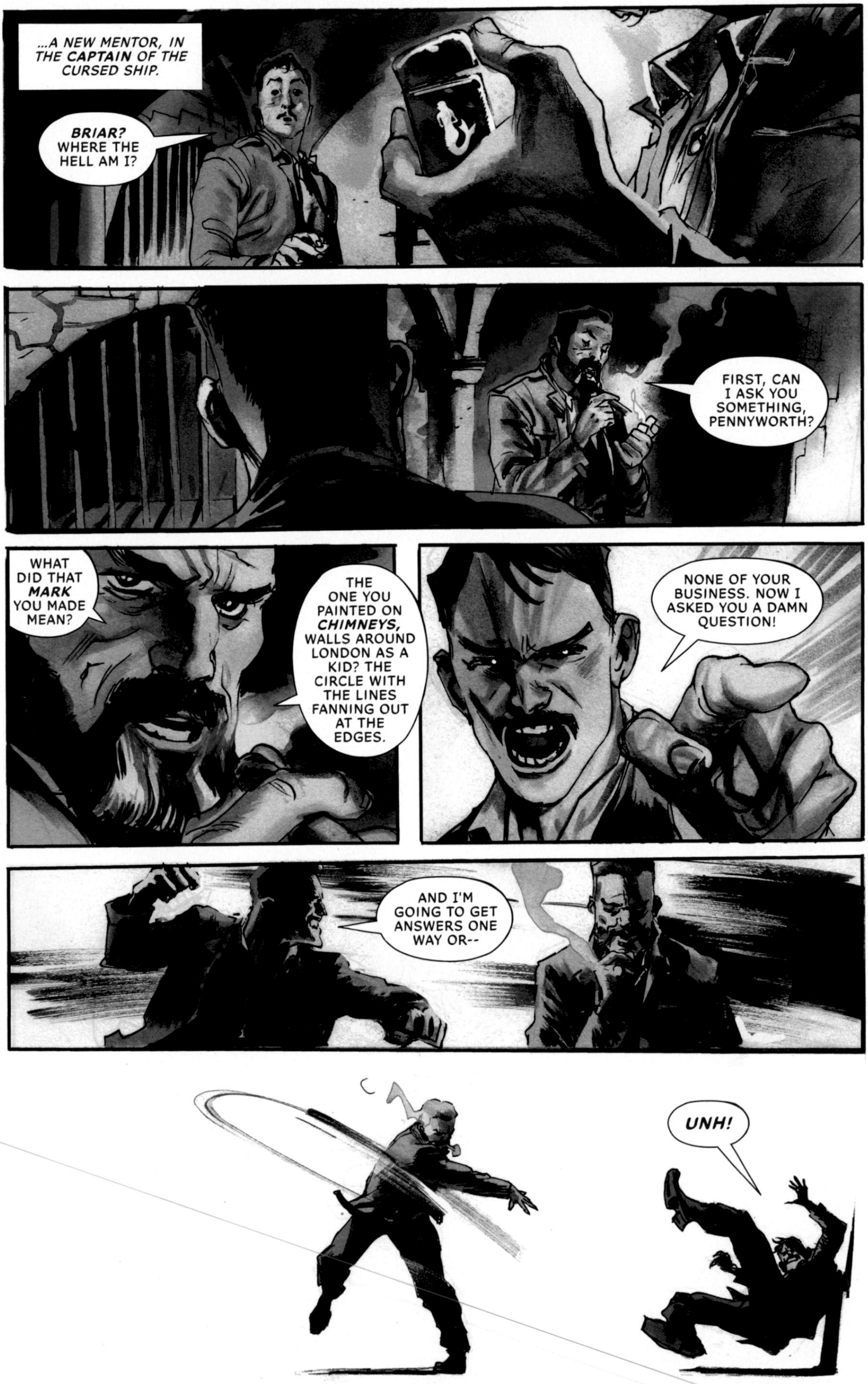
...A NEW MENTOR, IN THE CAPTAIN OF THE CURSED SHIP.
BRIAR? WHERE THE HELL AM I?
FIRST, CAN I ASK YOU SOMETHING, PENNYWORTH?
WHAT DID THAT MARK YOU MADE MEAN?
THE ONE YOU PAINTED ON CHIMNEYS, WALLS AROUND LONDON AS A KID? THE CIRCLE WITH THE LINES FANNING OUT AT THE EDGES.
NONE OF YOUR BUSINESS. NOW I ASKED YOU A DAMN QUESTION!
AND I'M GOING TO GET ANSWERS ONE WAY OR--
UNH!

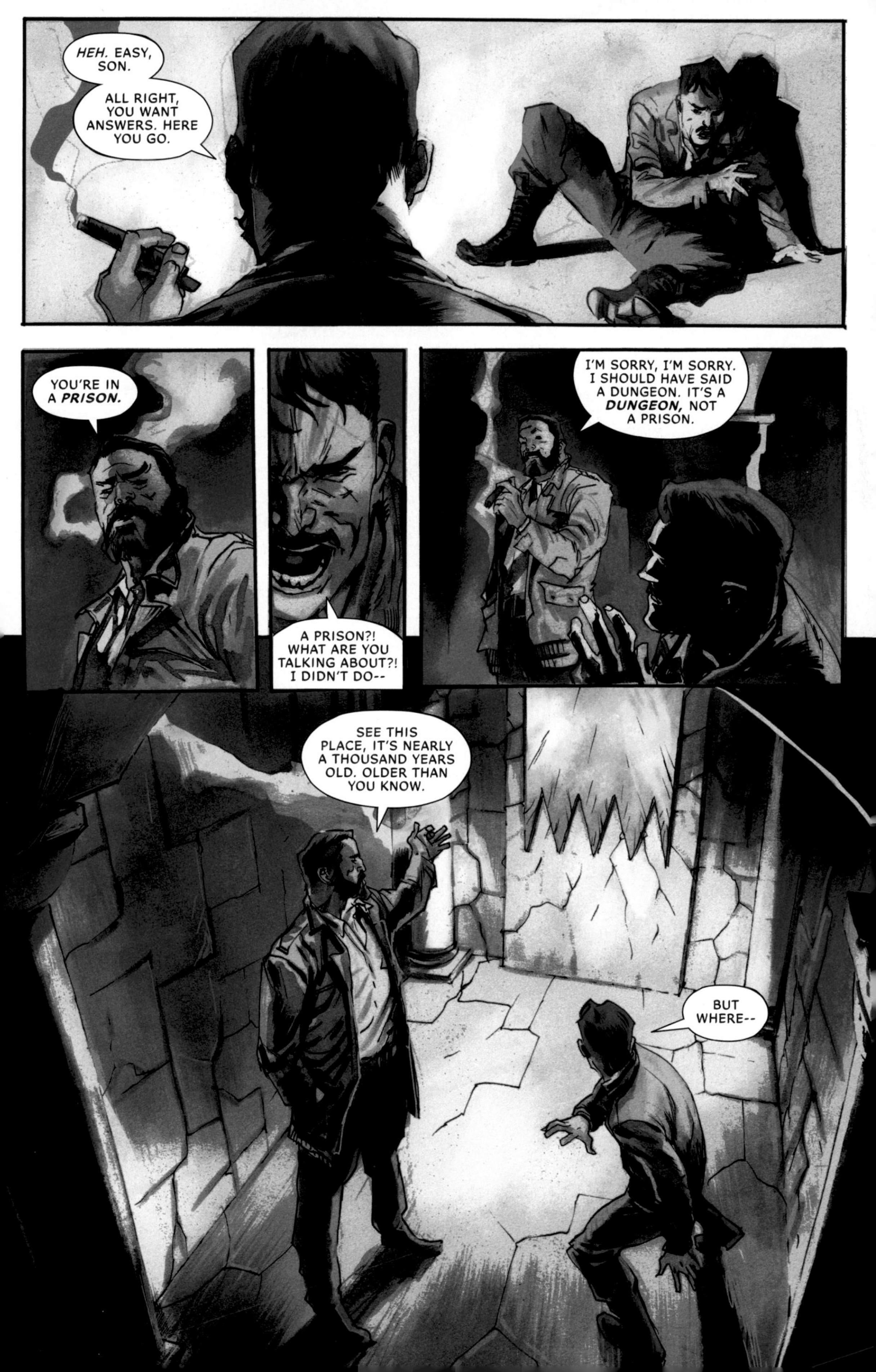

HEH. EASY, SON.
ALL RIGHT, YOU WANT ANSWERS. HERE YOU GO.
YOU'RE IN A ***PRISON.***
A PRISON?! WHAT ARE YOU TALKING ABOUT?! I DIDN'T DO--
I'M SORRY, I'M SORRY. I SHOULD HAVE SAID A DUNGEON. IT'S A ***DUNGEON,*** NOT A PRISON.
SEE THIS PLACE, IT'S NEARLY A THOUSAND YEARS OLD. OLDER THAN YOU KNOW.
BUT WHERE--

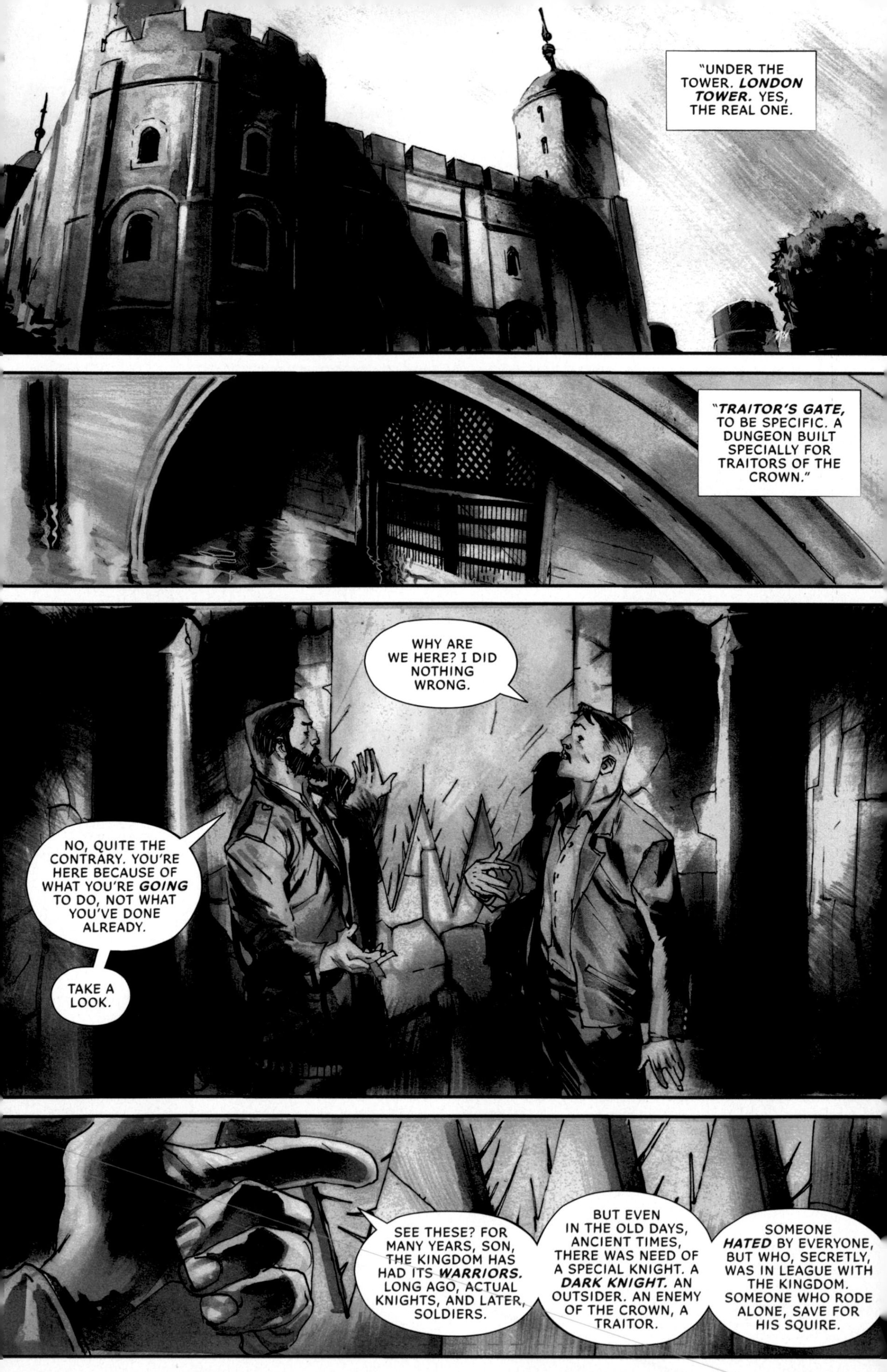
"UNDER THE TOWER. *LONDON TOWER.* YES, THE REAL ONE.
"*TRAITOR'S GATE,* TO BE SPECIFIC. A DUNGEON BUILT SPECIALLY FOR TRAITORS OF THE CROWN."
WHY ARE WE HERE? I DID NOTHING WRONG.
NO, QUITE THE CONTRARY. YOU'RE HERE BECAUSE OF WHAT YOU'RE *GOING* TO DO, NOT WHAT YOU'VE DONE ALREADY.
TAKE A LOOK.
SEE THESE? FOR MANY YEARS, SON, THE KINGDOM HAS HAD ITS *WARRIORS.* LONG AGO, ACTUAL KNIGHTS, AND LATER, SOLDIERS.
BUT EVEN IN THE OLD DAYS, ANCIENT TIMES, THERE WAS NEED OF A SPECIAL KNIGHT. A *DARK KNIGHT.* AN OUTSIDER. AN ENEMY OF THE CROWN, A TRAITOR.
SOMEONE *HATED* BY EVERYONE, BUT WHO, SECRETLY, WAS IN LEAGUE WITH THE KINGDOM. SOMEONE WHO RODE ALONE, SAVE FOR HIS SQUIRE.

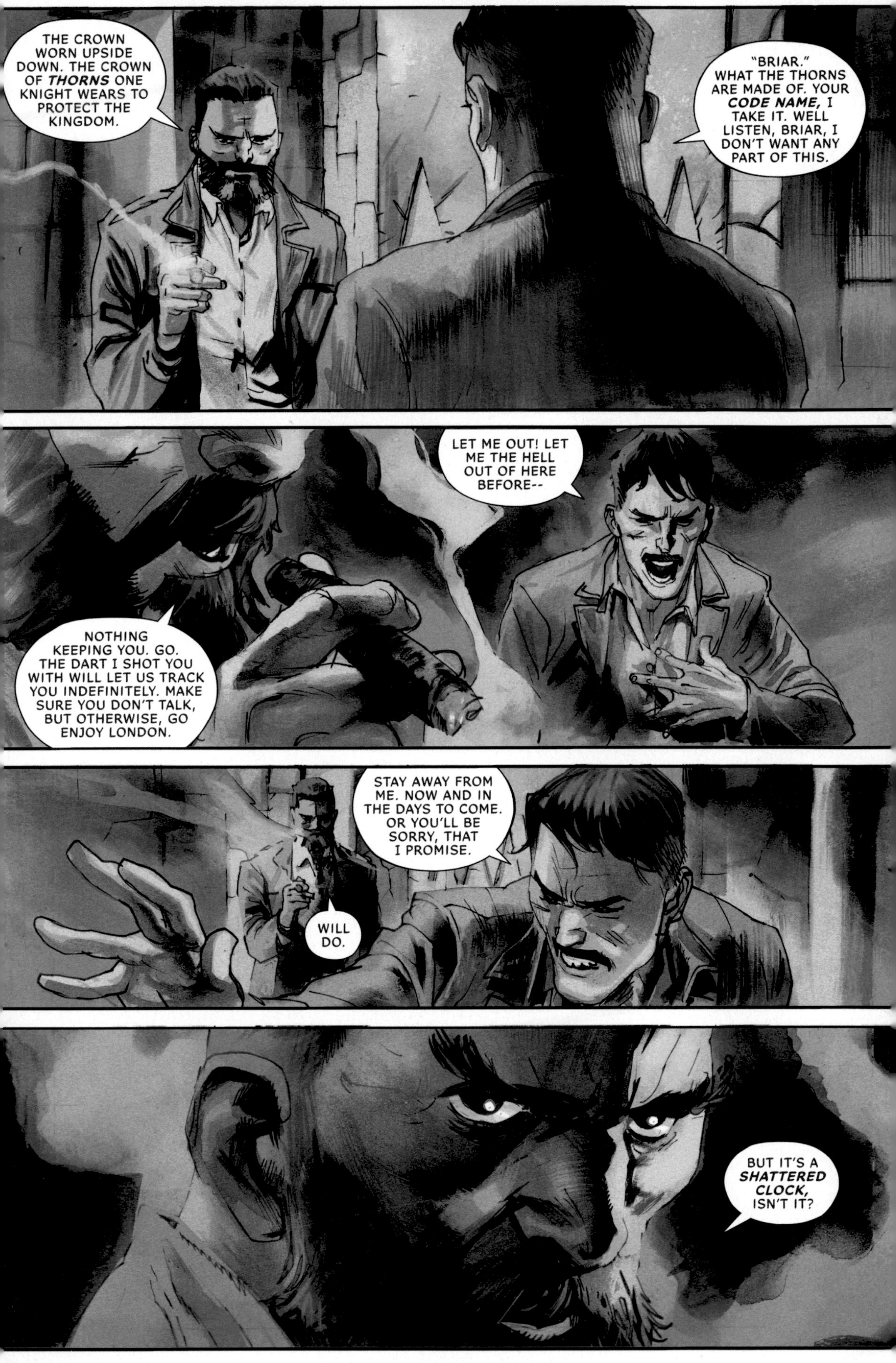
THE CROWN WORN UPSIDE DOWN. THE CROWN OF ***THORNS*** ONE KNIGHT WEARS TO PROTECT THE KINGDOM.
"BRIAR." WHAT THE THORNS ARE MADE OF. YOUR ***CODE NAME,*** I TAKE IT. WELL LISTEN, BRIAR, I DON'T WANT ANY PART OF THIS.
LET ME OUT! LET ME THE HELL OUT OF HERE BEFORE--
NOTHING KEEPING YOU. GO. THE DART I SHOT YOU WITH WILL LET US TRACK YOU INDEFINITELY. MAKE SURE YOU DON'T TALK, BUT OTHERWISE, GO ENJOY LONDON.
STAY AWAY FROM ME. NOW AND IN THE DAYS TO COME. OR YOU'LL BE SORRY, THAT I PROMISE.
WILL DO.
BUT IT'S A ***SHATTERED CLOCK,*** ISN'T IT?

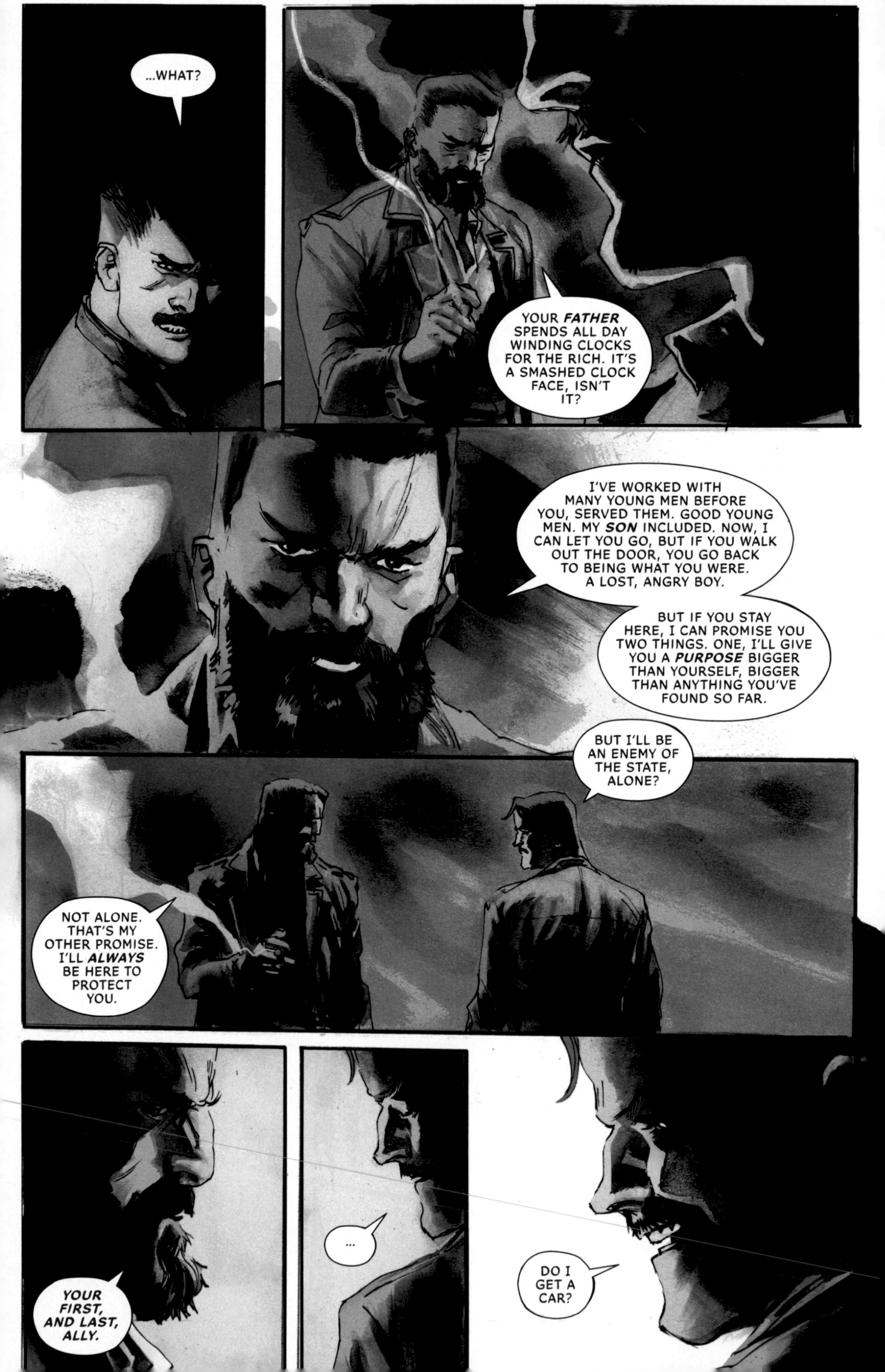
...WHAT?
YOUR FATHER SPENDS ALL DAY WINDING CLOCKS FOR THE RICH. IT'S A SMASHED CLOCK FACE, ISN'T IT?
I'VE WORKED WITH MANY YOUNG MEN BEFORE YOU, SERVED THEM. GOOD YOUNG MEN. MY SON INCLUDED. NOW, I CAN LET YOU GO, BUT IF YOU WALK OUT THE DOOR, YOU GO BACK TO BEING WHAT YOU WERE. A LOST, ANGRY BOY.
BUT IF YOU STAY HERE, I CAN PROMISE YOU TWO THINGS. ONE, I'LL GIVE YOU A PURPOSE BIGGER THAN YOURSELF, BIGGER THAN ANYTHING YOU'VE FOUND SO FAR.
BUT I'LL BE AN ENEMY OF THE STATE, ALONE?
NOT ALONE. THAT'S MY OTHER PROMISE. I'LL ALWAYS BE HERE TO PROTECT YOU.
YOUR FIRST, AND LAST, ALLY.
...
DO I GET A CAR?

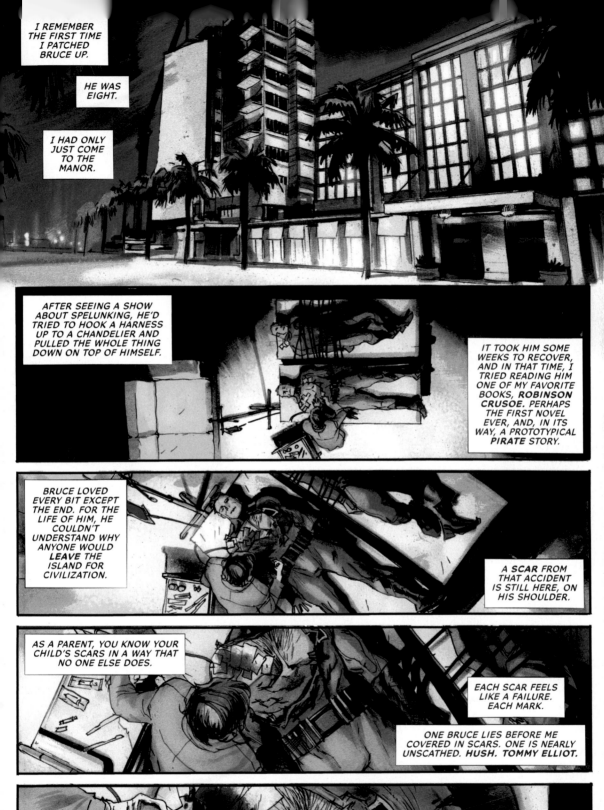

I REMEMBER THE FIRST TIME I PATCHED BRUCE UP.

HE WAS EIGHT.

I HAD ONLY JUST COME TO THE MANOR.

AFTER SEEING A SHOW ABOUT SPELUNKING, HE'D TRIED TO HOOK A HARNESS UP TO A CHANDELIER AND PULLED THE WHOLE THING DOWN ON TOP OF HIMSELF.

IT TOOK HIM SOME WEEKS TO RECOVER, AND IN THAT TIME, I TRIED READING HIM ONE OF MY FAVORITE BOOKS, *ROBINSON CRUSOE*. PERHAPS THE FIRST NOVEL EVER, AND, IN ITS WAY, A PROTOTYPICAL *PIRATE* STORY.

BRUCE LOVED EVERY BIT EXCEPT THE END. FOR THE LIFE OF HIM, HE COULDN'T UNDERSTAND WHY ANYONE WOULD *LEAVE* THE ISLAND FOR CIVILIZATION.

A *SCAR* FROM THAT ACCIDENT IS STILL HERE, ON HIS SHOULDER.

AS A PARENT, YOU KNOW YOUR CHILD'S SCARS IN A WAY THAT NO ONE ELSE DOES.

EACH SCAR FEELS LIKE A FAILURE. EACH MARK.

ONE BRUCE LIES BEFORE ME COVERED IN SCARS. ONE IS NEARLY UNSCATHED. *HUSH. TOMMY ELLIOT.*

AND YET THERE IS PRIDE IN THESE SCARS, TOO. HE SURVIVED.

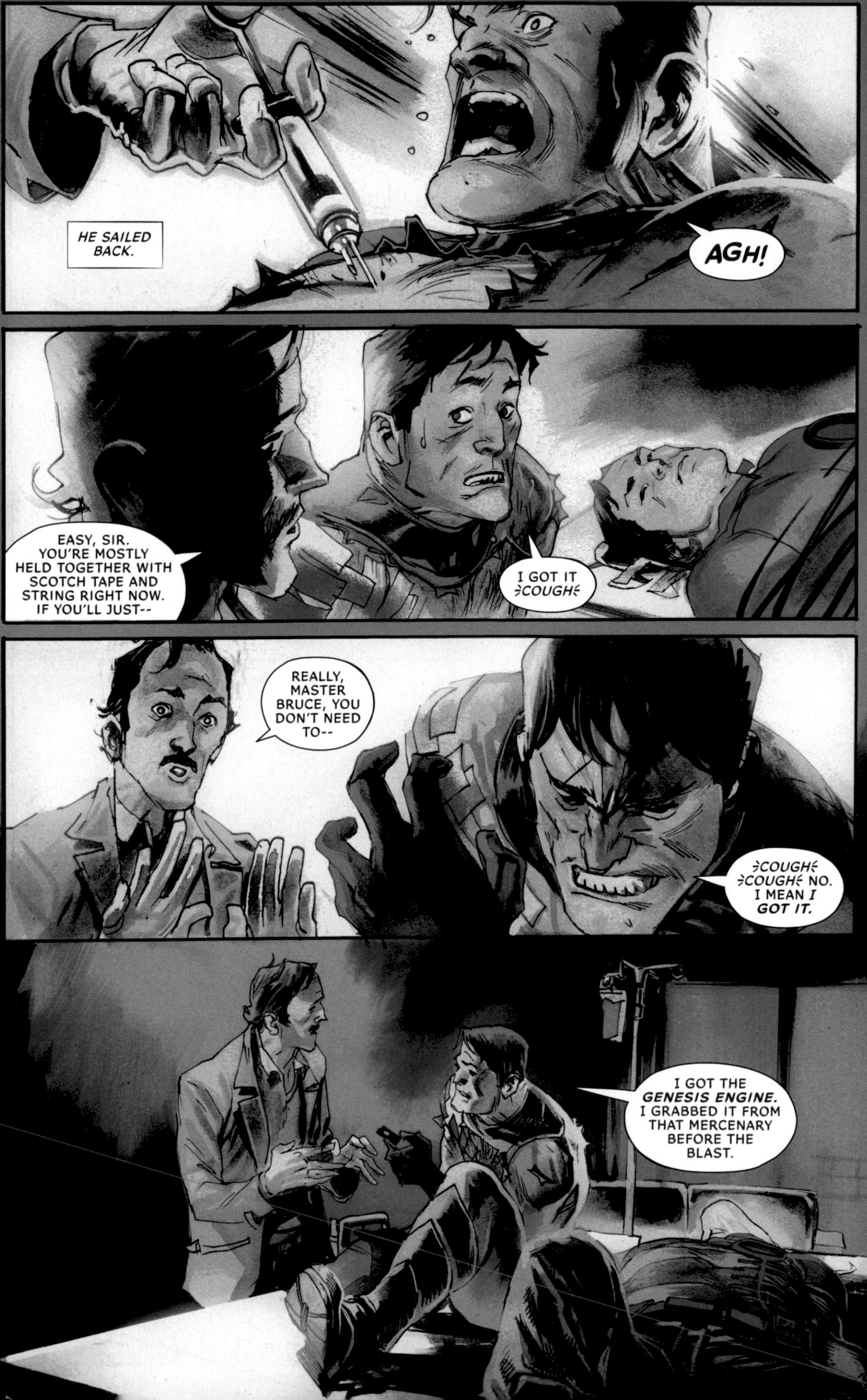

HE SAILED BACK.
AGH!
EASY, SIR. YOU'RE MOSTLY HELD TOGETHER WITH SCOTCH TAPE AND STRING RIGHT NOW. IF YOU'LL JUST--
I GOT IT *COUGH*
REALLY, MASTER BRUCE, YOU DON'T NEED TO--
COUGH *COUGH* NO. I MEAN *I GOT IT.*
I GOT THE *GENESIS ENGINE.* I GRABBED IT FROM THAT MERCENARY BEFORE THE BLAST.

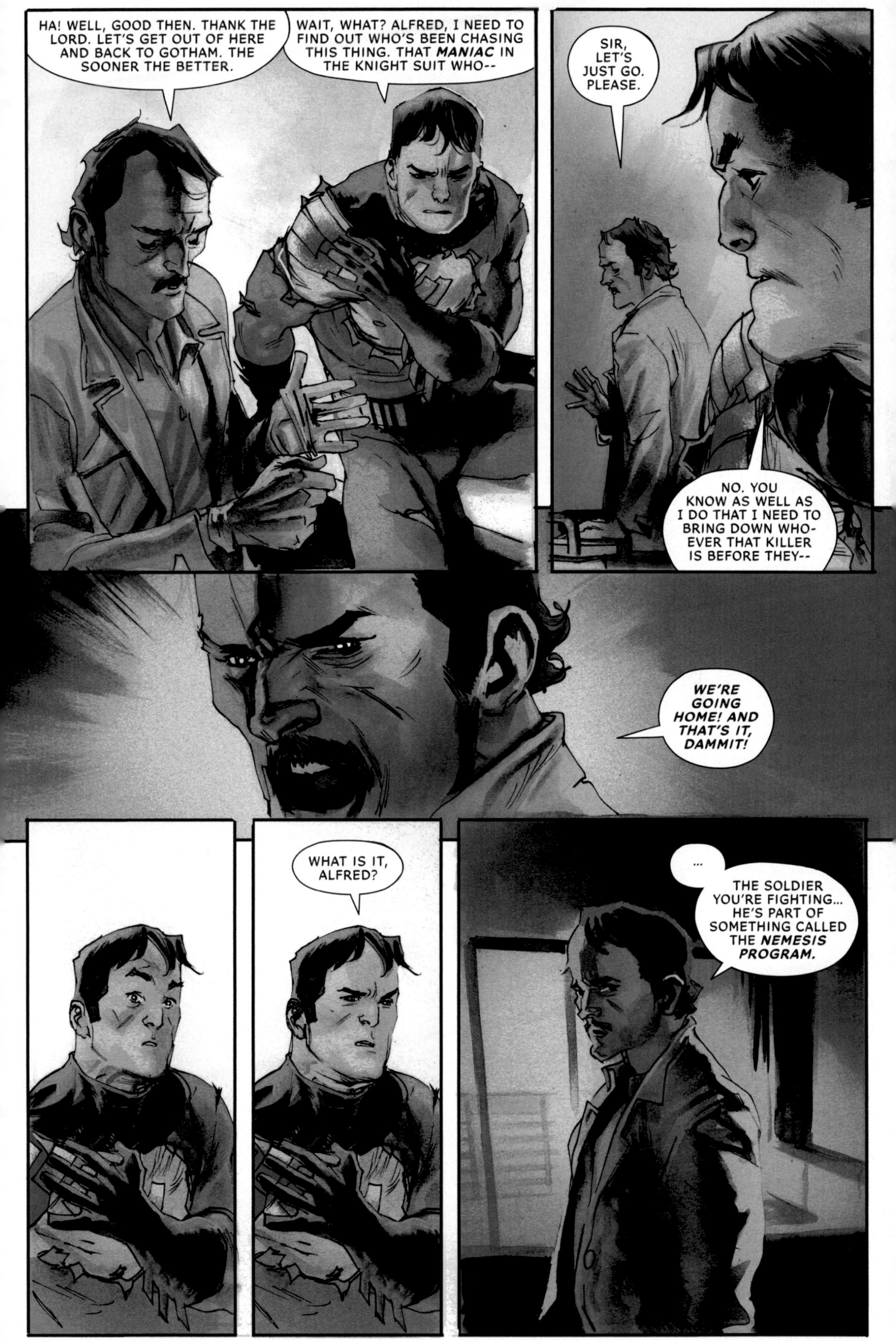
HA! WELL, GOOD THEN. THANK THE LORD. LET'S GET OUT OF HERE AND BACK TO GOTHAM. THE SOONER THE BETTER.
WAIT, WHAT? ALFRED, I NEED TO FIND OUT WHO'S BEEN CHASING THIS THING. THAT *MANIAC* IN THE KNIGHT SUIT WHO--
SIR, LET'S JUST GO. PLEASE.
NO. YOU KNOW AS WELL AS I DO THAT I NEED TO BRING DOWN WHO-EVER THAT KILLER IS BEFORE THEY--
WE'RE GOING HOME! AND THAT'S IT, DAMMIT!
WHAT IS IT, ALFRED?
...
THE SOLDIER YOU'RE FIGHTING... HE'S PART OF SOMETHING CALLED THE *NEMESIS PROGRAM.*

"BRUCE, WHEN I WAS YOUNG, SERVING IN THE MILITARY, I WAS GIVEN AN OFFER TO BE PART OF SOMETHING BIGGER.

"AN MI5 PROGRAM THAT WAS...OFF THE BOOKS. A *BLACK LEDGER* INITIATIVE. A SINGLE SOLDIER, AN ERRANT KNIGHT.

"THE TRAINING WOULD LAST A YEAR. THE MAN WHO RAN THE PROGRAM WAS NAMED BRIAR, AND IN MANY WAYS, HE BECAME TO ME WHAT I HAVE BEEN TO YOU.

"A *MENTOR* OF SORTS, THE VOICE IN MY EAR IN THE FIELD.

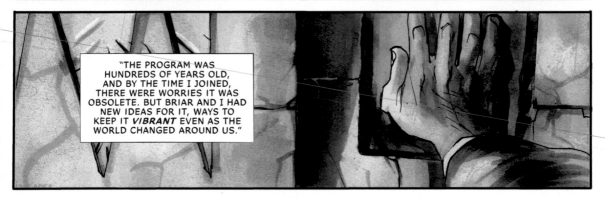

"THE PROGRAM WAS HUNDREDS OF YEARS OLD, AND BY THE TIME I JOINED, THERE WERE WORRIES IT WAS OBSOLETE. BUT BRIAR AND I HAD NEW IDEAS FOR IT, WAYS TO KEEP IT *VIBRANT* EVEN AS THE WORLD CHANGED AROUND US."

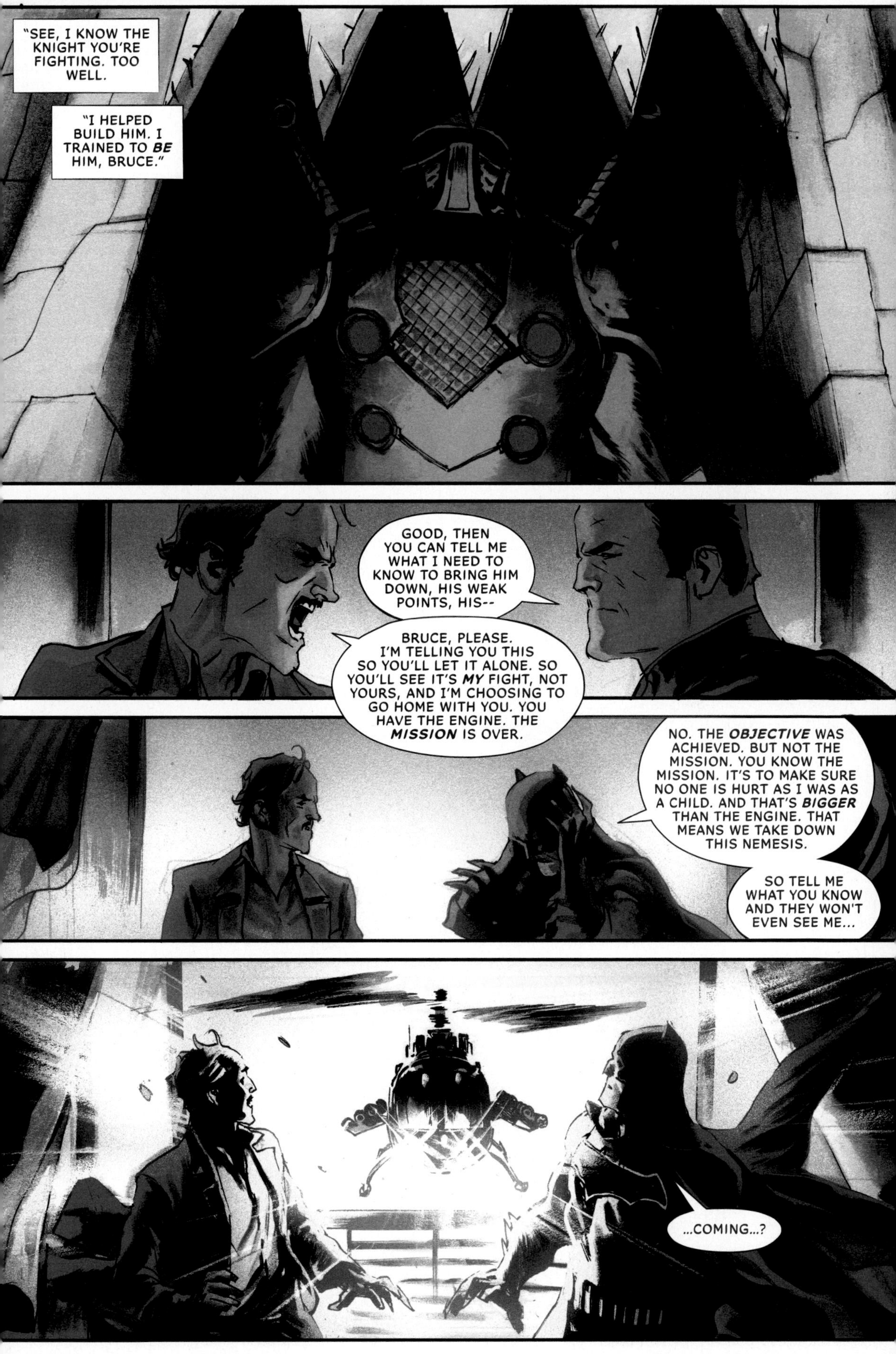
"SEE, I KNOW THE KNIGHT YOU'RE FIGHTING. TOO WELL.
"I HELPED BUILD HIM. I TRAINED TO *BE* HIM, BRUCE."
GOOD, THEN YOU CAN TELL ME WHAT I NEED TO KNOW TO BRING HIM DOWN, HIS WEAK POINTS, HIS--
BRUCE, PLEASE. I'M TELLING YOU THIS SO YOU'LL LET IT ALONE. SO YOU'LL SEE IT'S *MY* FIGHT, NOT YOURS, AND I'M CHOOSING TO GO HOME WITH YOU. YOU HAVE THE ENGINE. THE *MISSION* IS OVER.
NO. THE *OBJECTIVE* WAS ACHIEVED. BUT NOT THE MISSION. YOU KNOW THE MISSION. IT'S TO MAKE SURE NO ONE IS HURT AS I WAS AS A CHILD. AND THAT'S *BIGGER* THAN THE ENGINE. THAT MEANS WE TAKE DOWN THIS NEMESIS.
SO TELL ME WHAT YOU KNOW AND THEY WON'T EVEN SEE ME...
...COMING...?

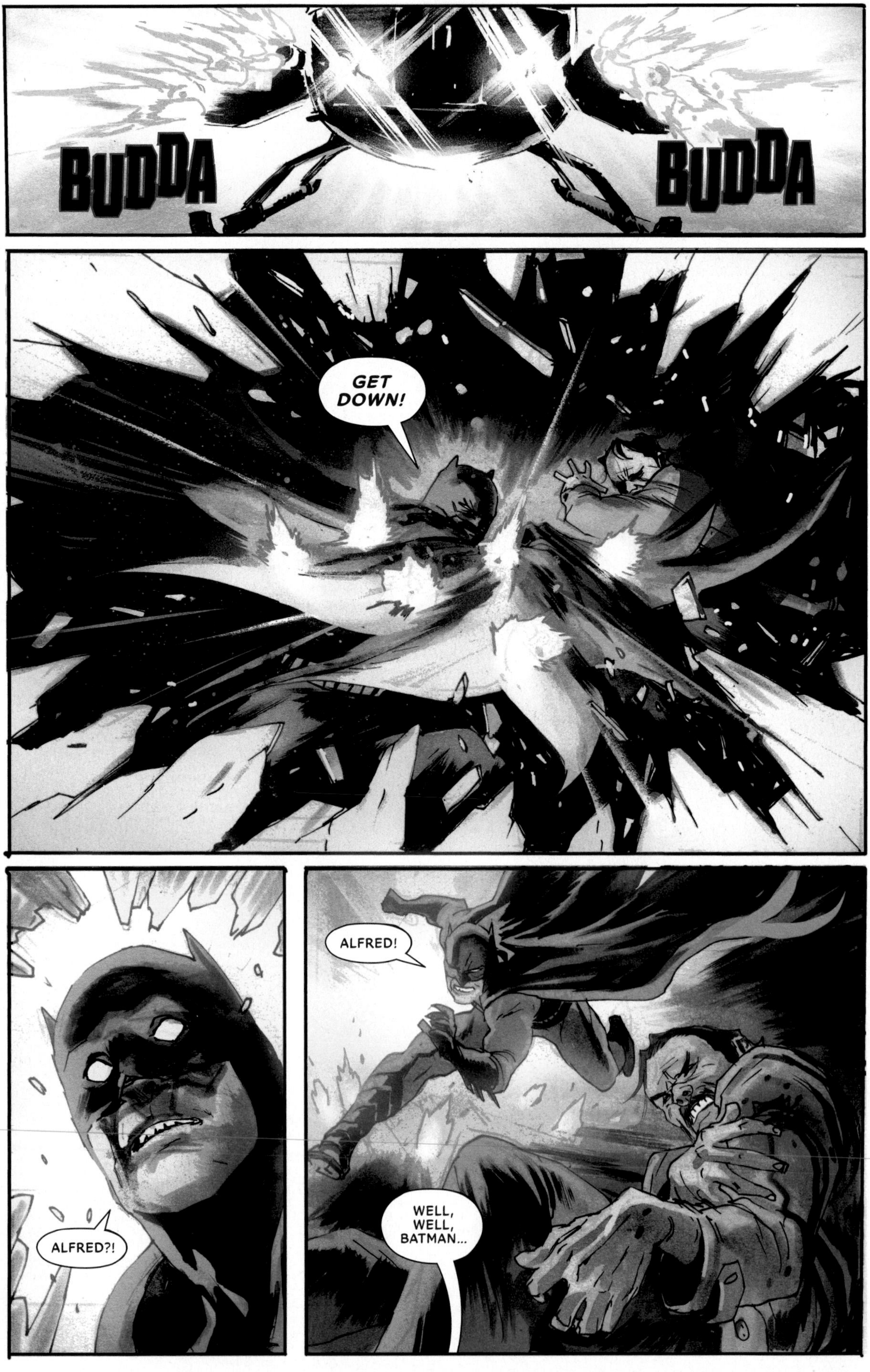
BUDDA
BUDDA
GET DOWN!
ALFRED?!
ALFRED!
WELL, WELL, BATMAN...

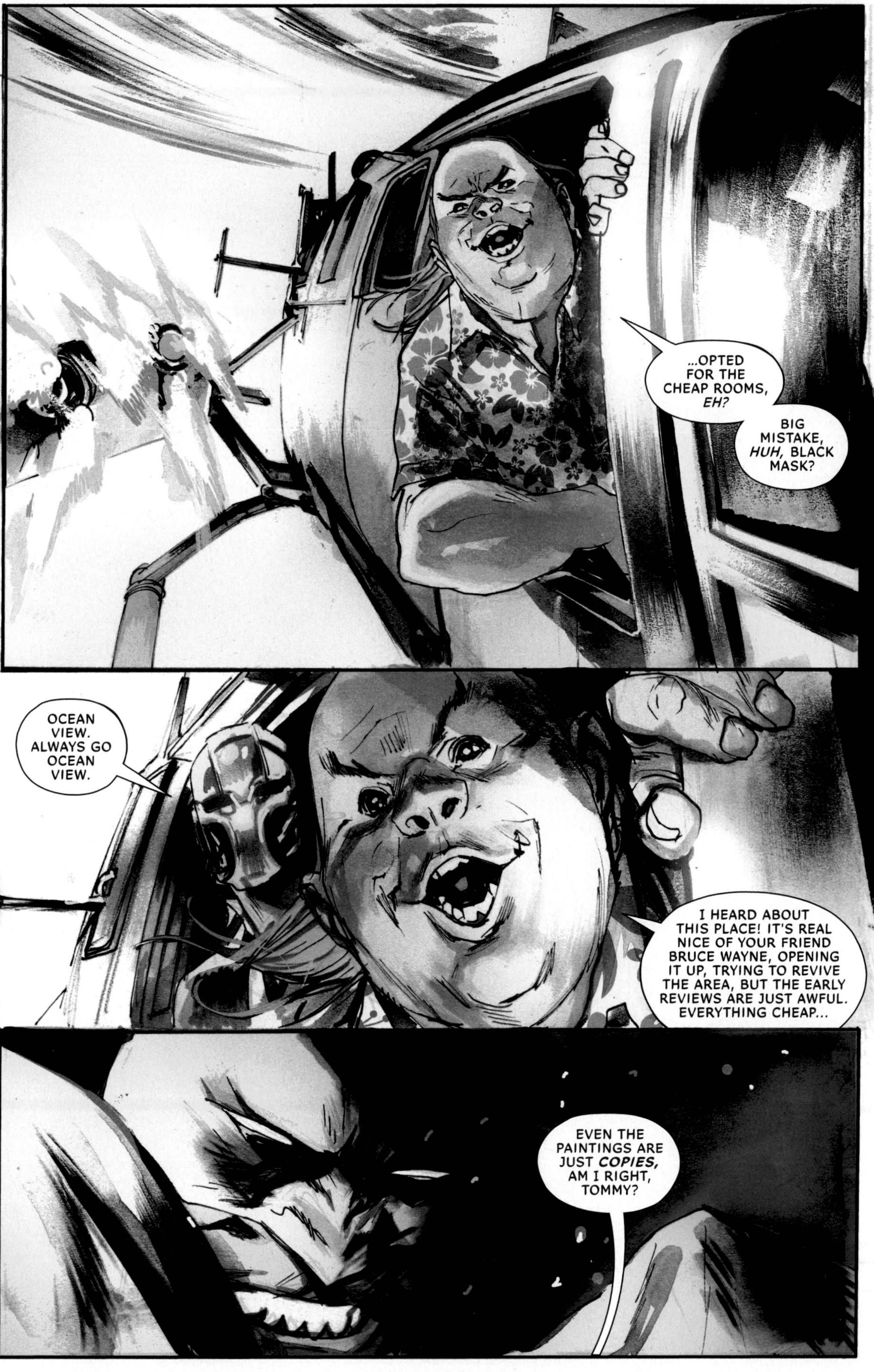
...OPTED FOR THE CHEAP ROOMS, *EH?*
BIG MISTAKE, *HUH,* BLACK MASK?
OCEAN VIEW. ALWAYS GO OCEAN VIEW.
I HEARD ABOUT THIS PLACE! IT'S REAL NICE OF YOUR FRIEND BRUCE WAYNE, OPENING IT UP, TRYING TO REVIVE THE AREA, BUT THE EARLY REVIEWS ARE JUST AWFUL. EVERYTHING CHEAP...
EVEN THE PAINTINGS ARE JUST *COPIES,* AM I RIGHT, TOMMY?

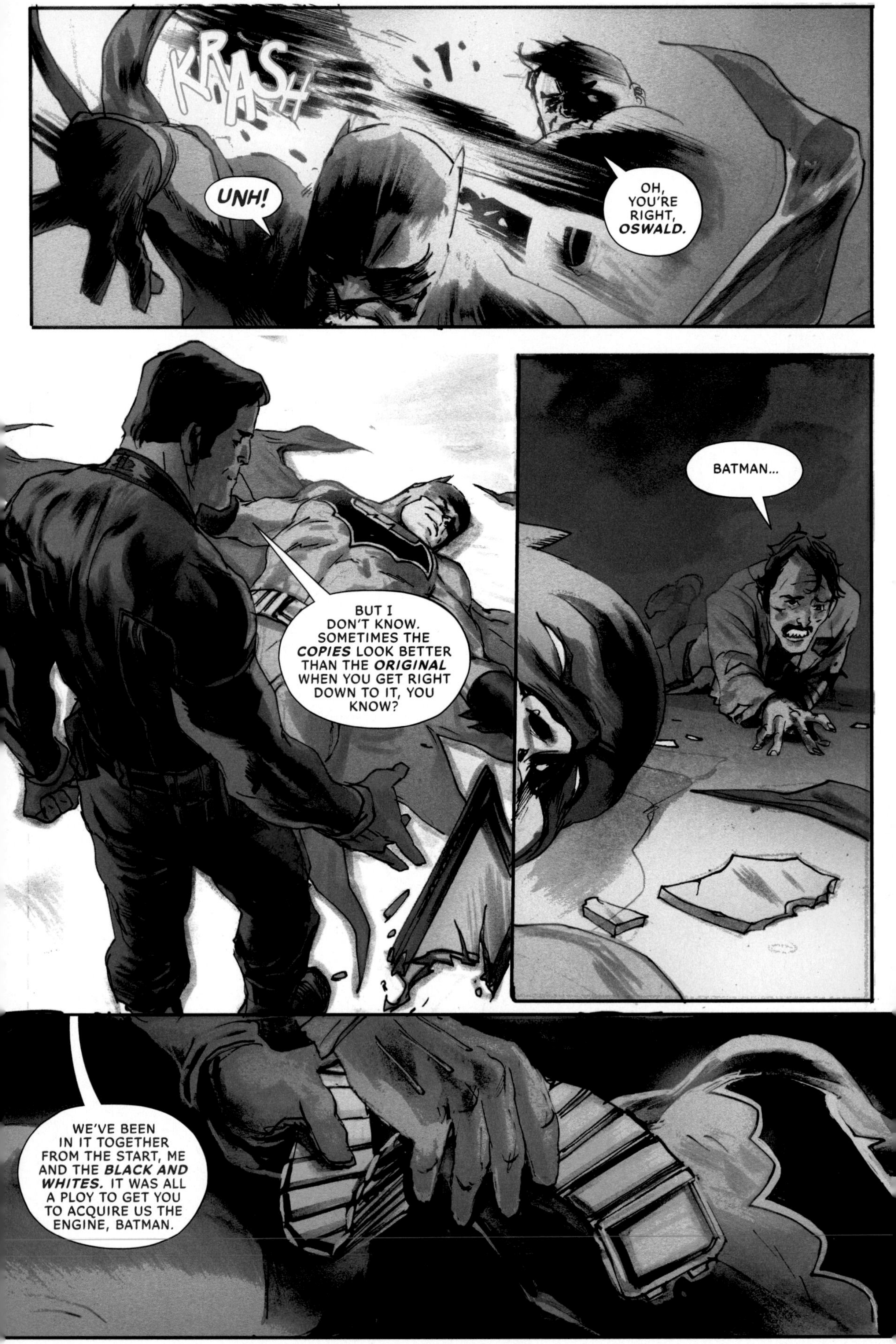
KRASH
UNH!
OH, YOU'RE RIGHT, OSWALD.
BUT I DON'T KNOW. SOMETIMES THE COPIES LOOK BETTER THAN THE ORIGINAL WHEN YOU GET RIGHT DOWN TO IT, YOU KNOW?
BATMAN...
WE'VE BEEN IN IT TOGETHER FROM THE START, ME AND THE BLACK AND WHITES. IT WAS ALL A PLOY TO GET YOU TO ACQUIRE US THE ENGINE, BATMAN.

NOW WE HAVE IT AND CAN HEAD BACK TO GOTHAM AND LEAVE YOU TO YOUR SUNNY HOLIDAY.

YOU CAN STAY HERE, AT YOUR *FRIEND'S* SINKING SHIP OF A HOTEL. HELL, YOU AND BRUCE WAYNE, YOU'RE SO CLOSE YOU MIGHT AS WELL BE *CO-CAPTAINS* OF THIS PLACE, AM I RIGHT?

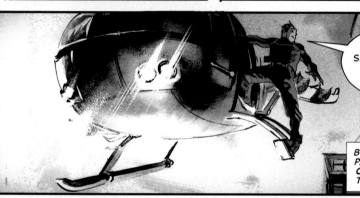

AND YOU KNOW WHAT THEY SAY...CAPTAIN ALWAYS GOES *DOWN* WITH HIS SHIP, DOESN'T HE, BATMAN?

PIRATE STORIES--WHY DID I LOVE THEM AS A BOY? BECAUSE AT HEART THEY'RE ABOUT CHILDREN WHO *REBEL* AGAINST THEIR PARENTS TO CREATE NEW LIVES FOR THEMSELVES. THEY'RE STORIES OF DEFIANCE.

BUT THE TRICK IS, WHEN YOU LOOK AT THEM AS A PARENT, YOU SEE, THEY'RE ACTUALLY WRITTEN AS *CAUTIONARY* TALES. THE CHILD COMES HOME IN THE END, JUST BEFORE DOOM STRIKES THE SHIP.

BUT THIS TALE, BRUCE, THE ONE I'VE HELPED MAKE FOR YOU, BATMAN...I WORRY IT HAS GONE ON TOO LONG... THAT I'VE KEPT IT GOING WITH YOU LONG PAST ITS NATURAL END.

LET HER RIP, FELLAS.

THAT'S WHAT I WAS SCREAMING ABOUT WHEN YOU WERE ON THAT WRECKED SUBMARINE. NOT THE WAYS YOU'VE FAILED *ME* BUT THE WAYS I MAY HAVE FAILED *YOU.*

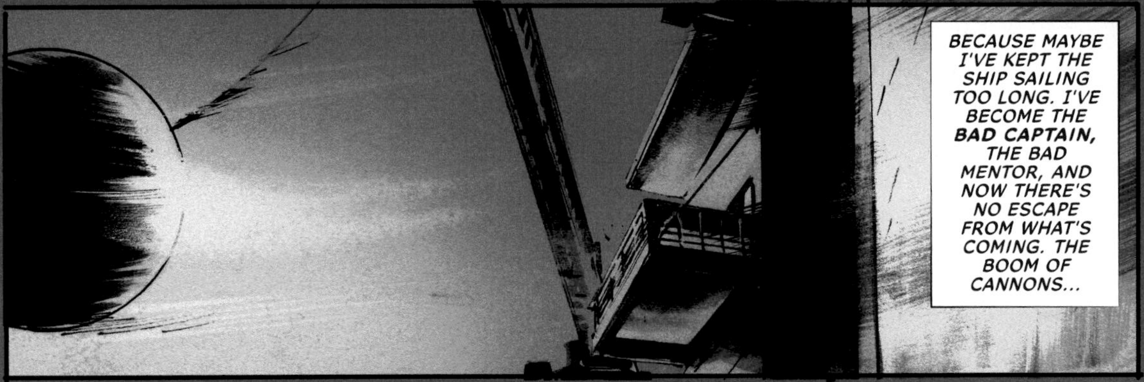
BECAUSE MAYBE I'VE KEPT THE SHIP SAILING TOO LONG. I'VE BECOME THE **BAD CAPTAIN,** THE BAD MENTOR, AND NOW THERE'S NO ESCAPE FROM WHAT'S COMING. THE BOOM OF CANNONS...

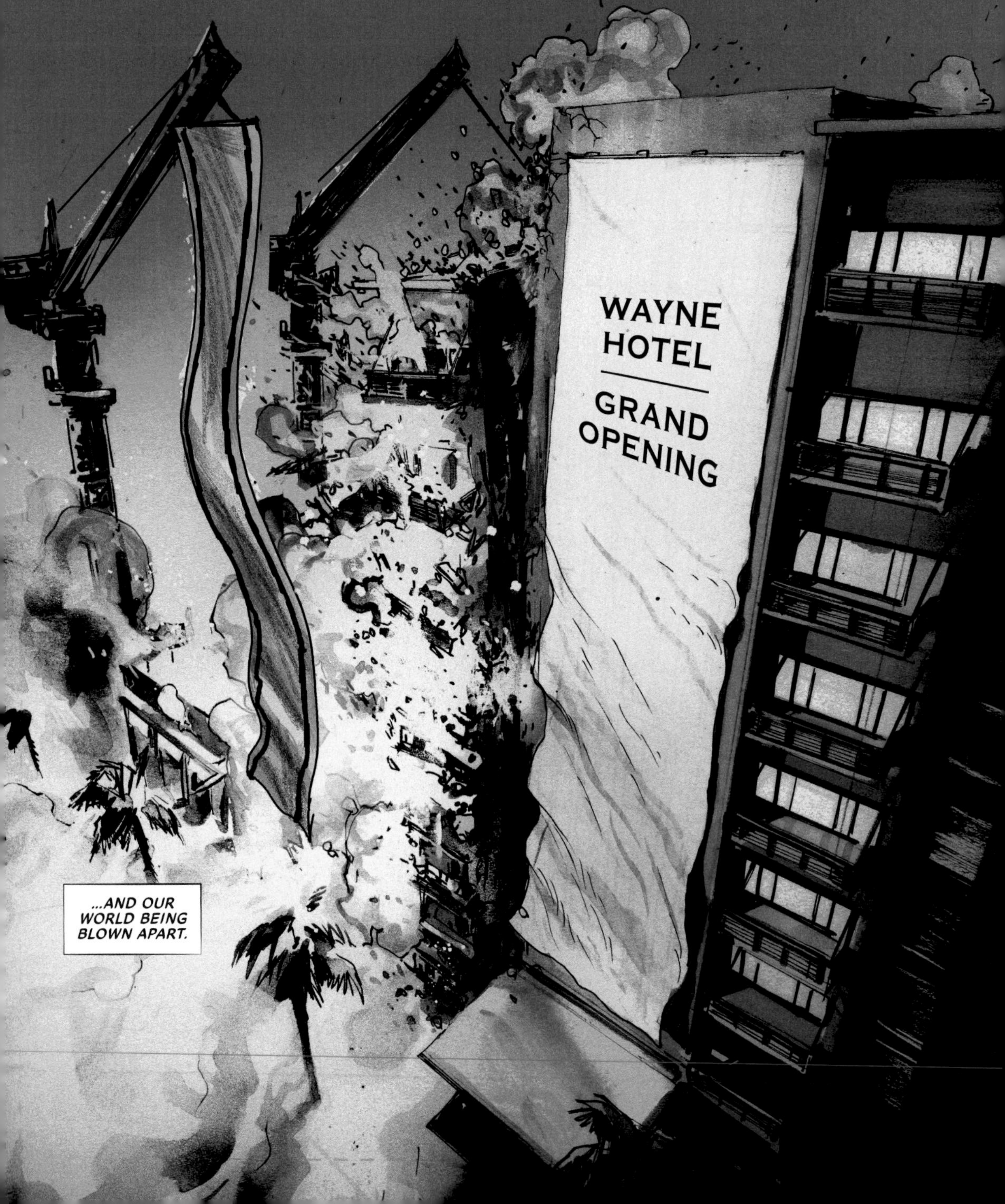
WAYNE HOTEL
GRAND OPENING
...AND OUR WORLD BEING BLOWN APART.

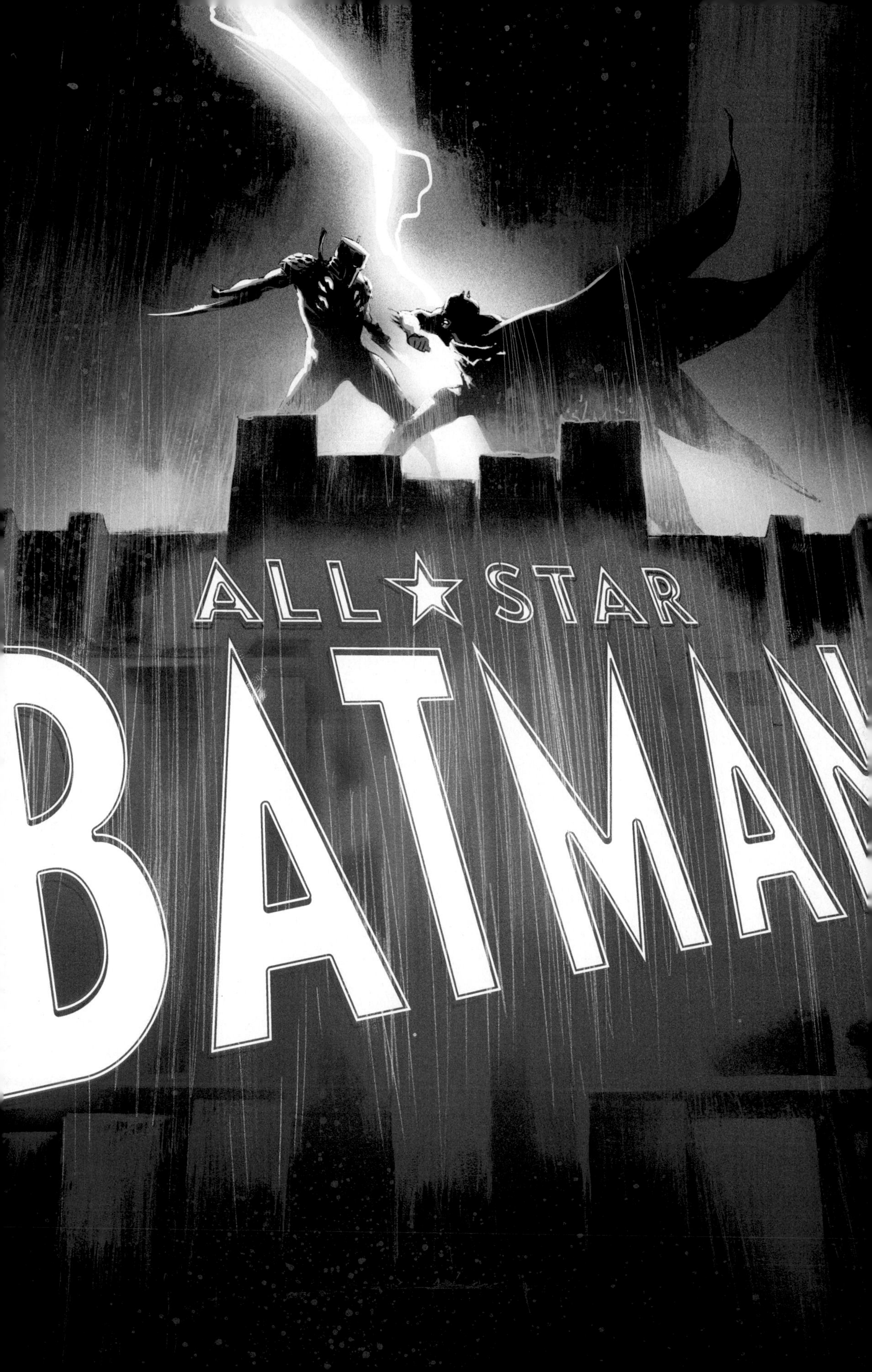
ALL STAR
BATMAN

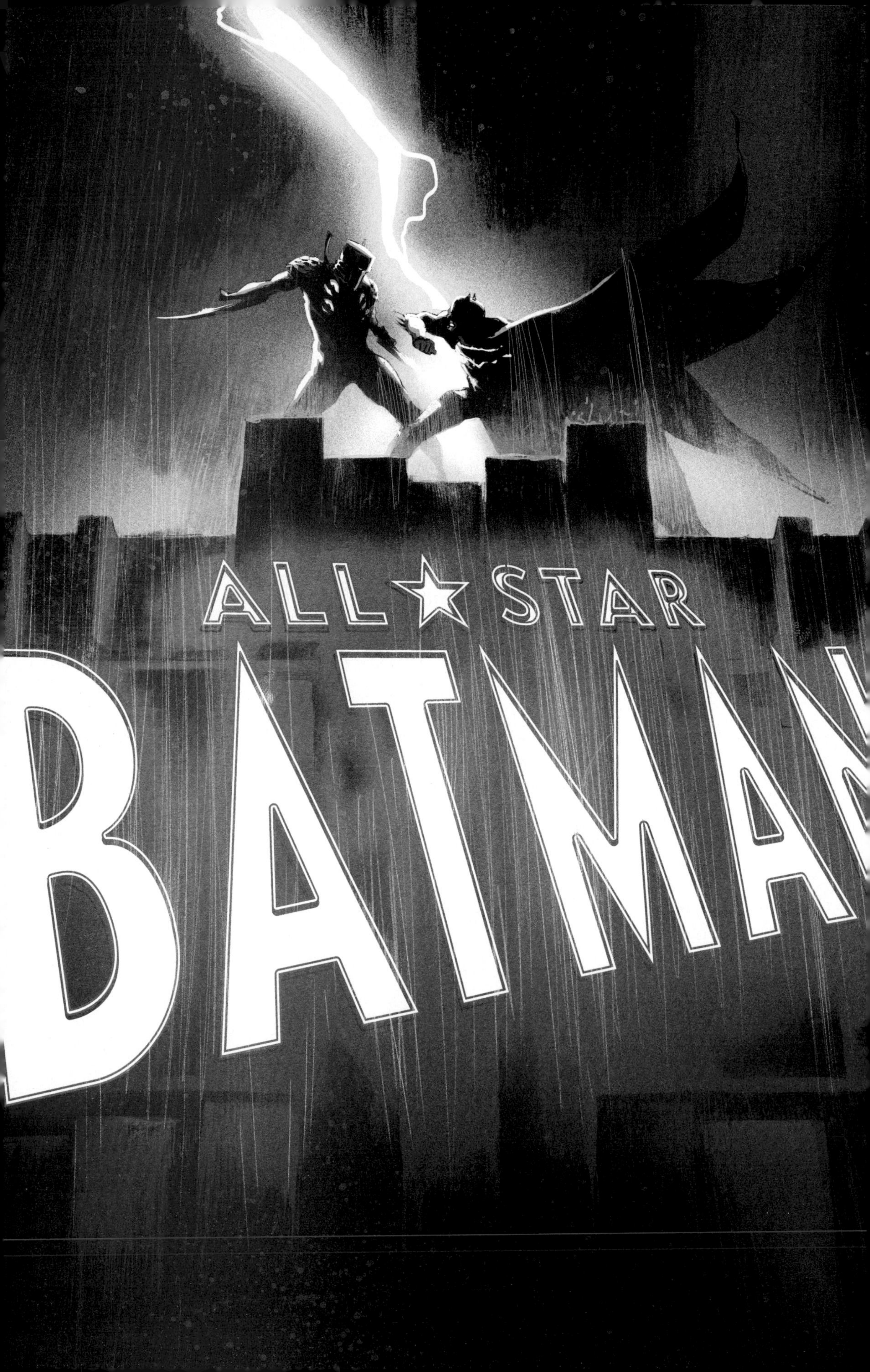
ALL STAR
BATMAN

HE'D BE FINE WITHOUT ME.

THAT'S WHAT I TELL MYSELF LATE AT NIGHT. IN A COUPLE YEARS, HE'D COME TO HIS SENSES. STOP ALL THIS.

ON--YOUR-- KNEES, NOW!

¿HUFF HUFF¿

YOU'VE-- GONE. **TOO-- FAR**, BATMAN. MOVE. AND-- WE. OPEN-- FIRE.

PENNY-ONE. IF YOU CAN HEAR THIS, I NEED YOU. I'M GOING FOR IT, FOR MY--

BUDDA **BUDDA** **BUDDA**

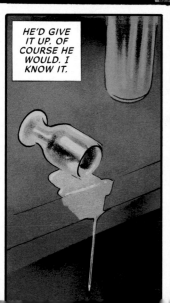

HE'D GIVE IT UP. OF COURSE HE WOULD. I KNOW IT.

SANTA CLARA, CUBA.

IT'S WHY I BOUGHT AN APARTMENT IN CUBA THE FIRST WEEK HE WAS BATMAN. BECAUSE SOME PART OF ME KNOWS THAT WHEN I DO IT, WHEN I QUIT, HE WILL QUIT, TOO. HE'LL RETIRE.

AND WE COULD GET OFF THIS CURSED SHIP TOGETHER... BEFORE IT **SINKS**.

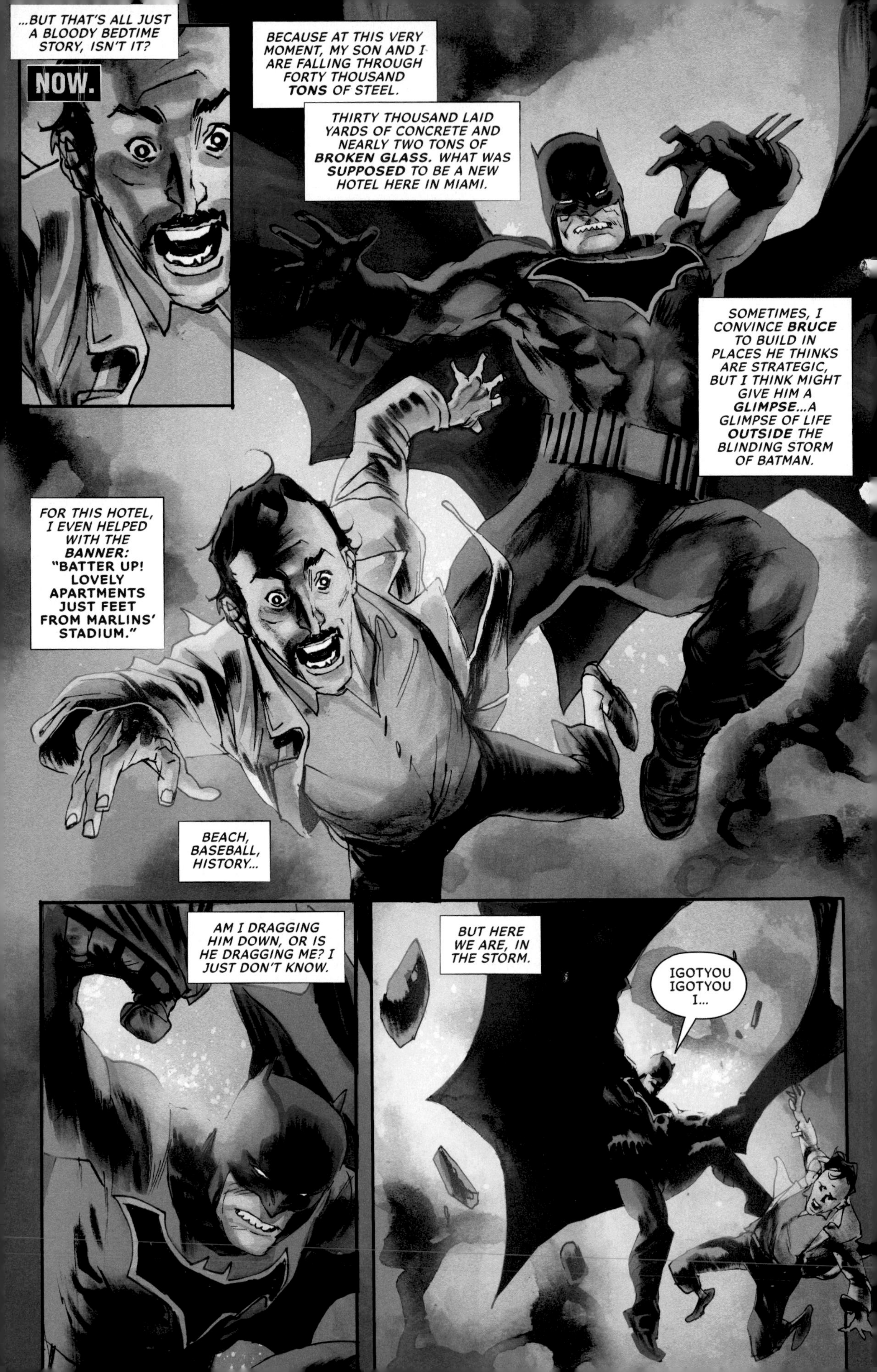
...BUT THAT'S ALL JUST A BLOODY BEDTIME STORY, ISN'T IT?
NOW.
BECAUSE AT THIS VERY MOMENT, MY SON AND I ARE FALLING THROUGH FORTY THOUSAND TONS OF STEEL.
THIRTY THOUSAND LAID YARDS OF CONCRETE AND NEARLY TWO TONS OF BROKEN GLASS. WHAT WAS SUPPOSED TO BE A NEW HOTEL HERE IN MIAMI.
SOMETIMES, I CONVINCE BRUCE TO BUILD IN PLACES HE THINKS ARE STRATEGIC, BUT I THINK MIGHT GIVE HIM A GLIMPSE...A GLIMPSE OF LIFE OUTSIDE THE BLINDING STORM OF BATMAN.
FOR THIS HOTEL, I EVEN HELPED WITH THE BANNER: "BATTER UP! LOVELY APARTMENTS JUST FEET FROM MARLINS' STADIUM."
BEACH, BASEBALL, HISTORY...
AM I DRAGGING HIM DOWN, OR IS HE DRAGGING ME? I JUST DON'T KNOW.
BUT HERE WE ARE, IN THE STORM.
IGOTYOU IGOTYOU I...

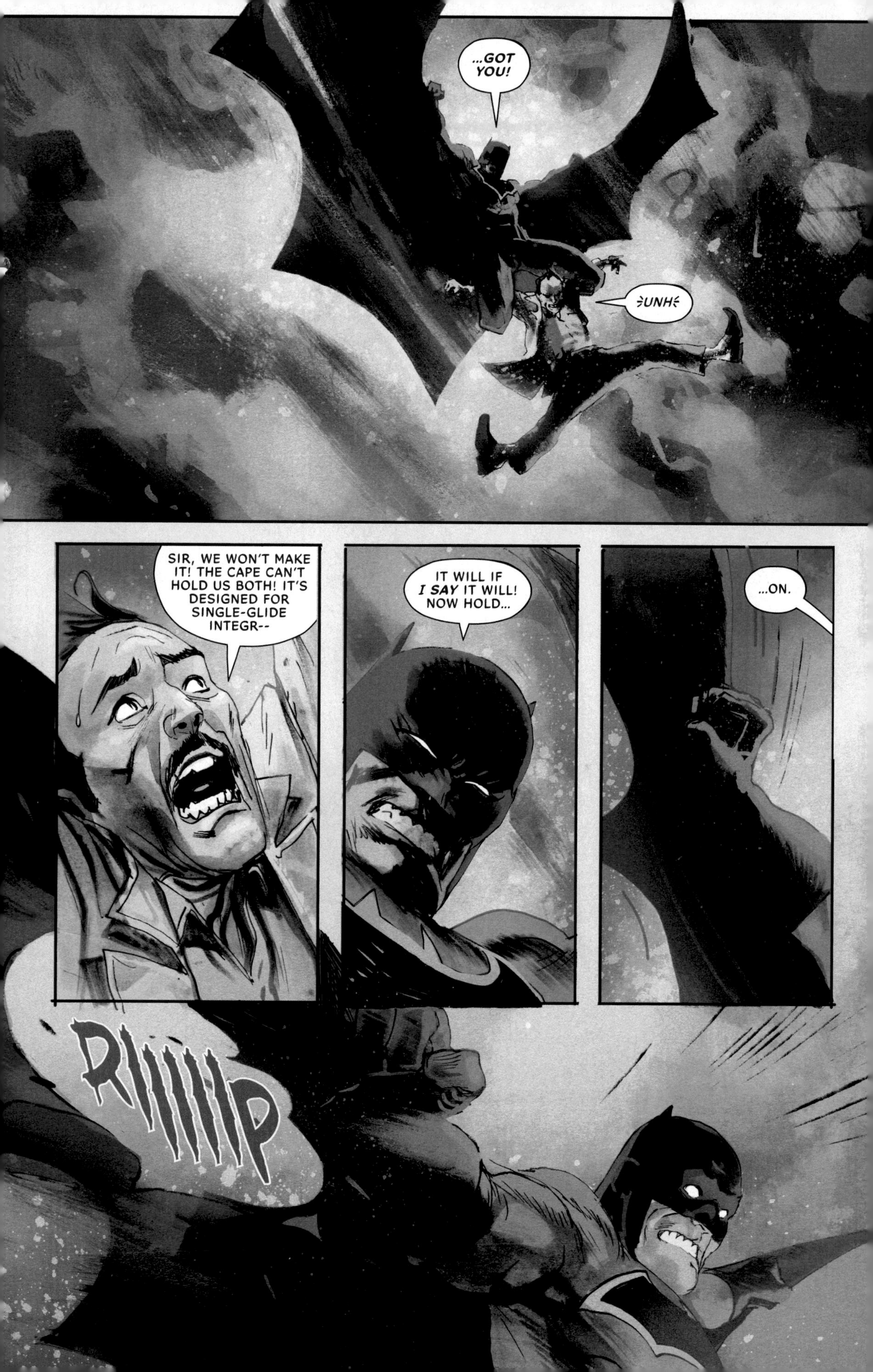
...GOT YOU!
UNH
SIR, WE WON'T MAKE IT! THE CAPE CAN'T HOLD US BOTH! IT'S DESIGNED FOR SINGLE-GLIDE INTEGR--
IT WILL IF *I SAY* IT WILL! NOW HOLD...
...ON.
RIIIIIP

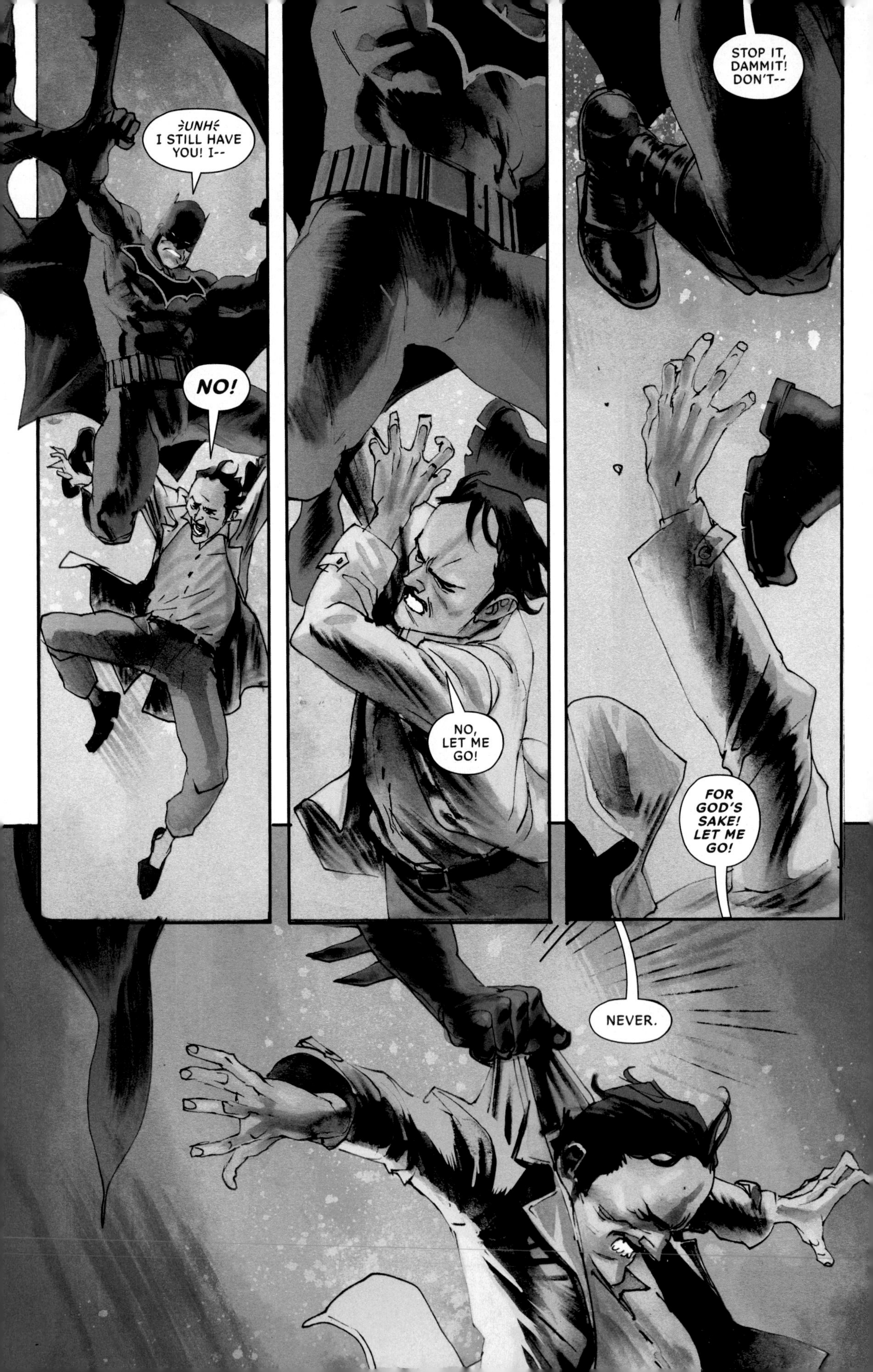

»UNH«
I STILL HAVE YOU! I--
NO!
NO, LET ME GO!
STOP IT, DAMMIT! DON'T--
FOR GOD'S SAKE! LET ME GO!
NEVER.

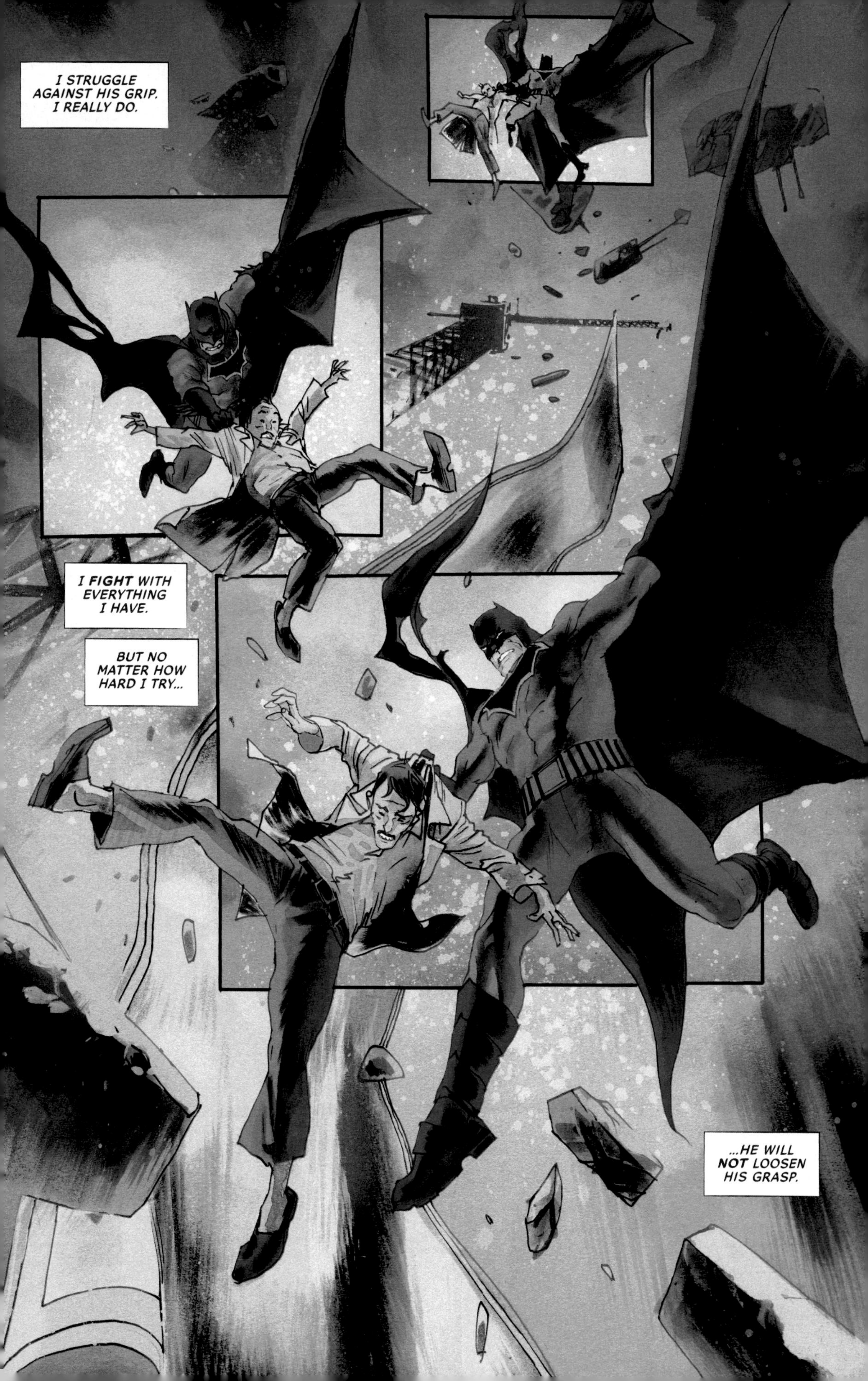
I STRUGGLE AGAINST HIS GRIP. I REALLY DO.
I **FIGHT** WITH EVERYTHING I HAVE.
BUT NO MATTER HOW HARD I TRY...
...HE WILL **NOT** LOOSEN HIS GRASP.

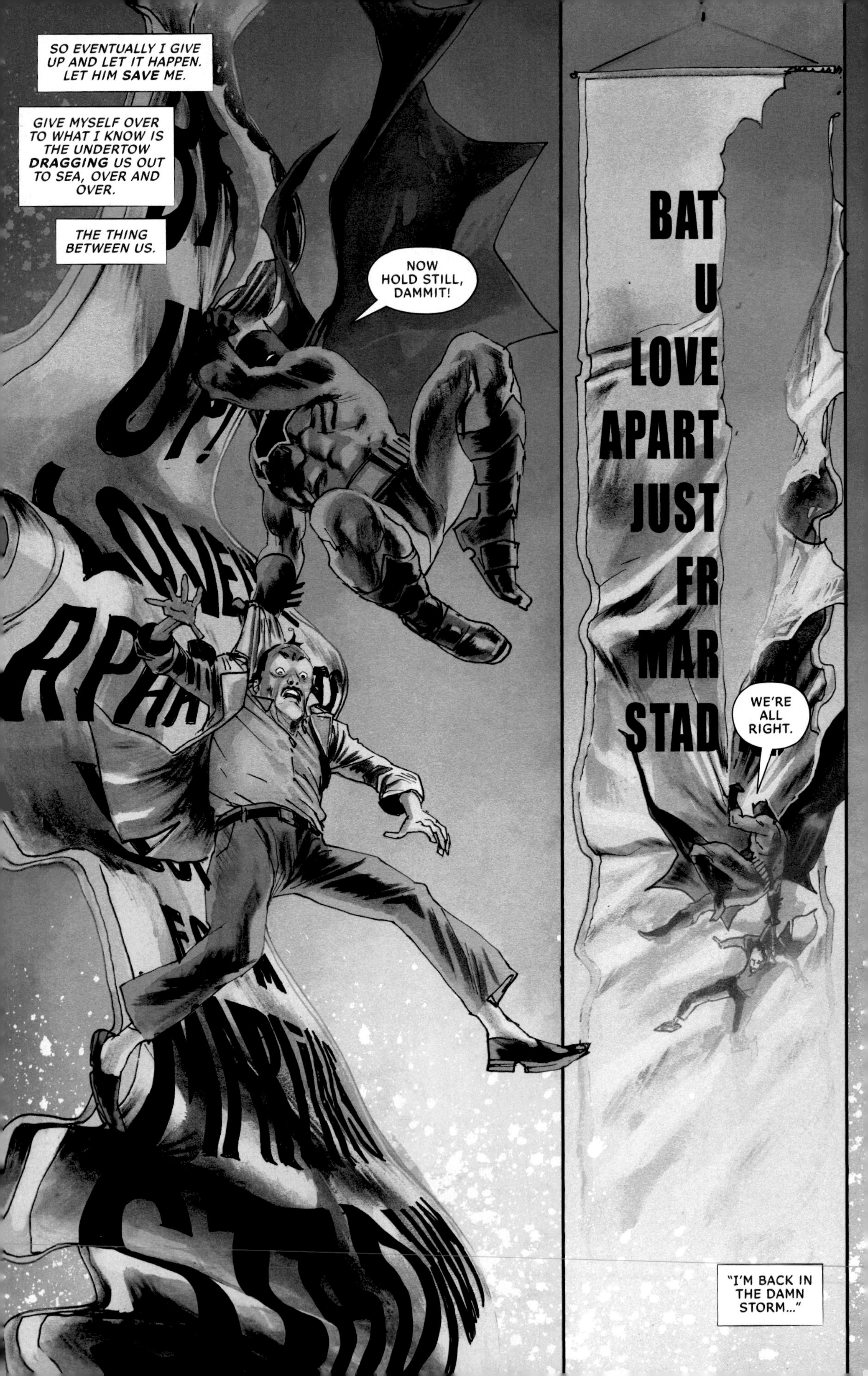
SO EVENTUALLY I GIVE UP AND LET IT HAPPEN. LET HIM **SAVE** ME.
GIVE MYSELF OVER TO WHAT I KNOW IS THE UNDERTOW **DRAGGING** US OUT TO SEA, OVER AND OVER.
THE THING BETWEEN US.
NOW HOLD STILL, DAMMIT!
BAT
U
LOVE
APART
JUST
FR
MAR
STAD
WE'RE ALL RIGHT.
"I'M BACK IN THE DAMN STORM..."

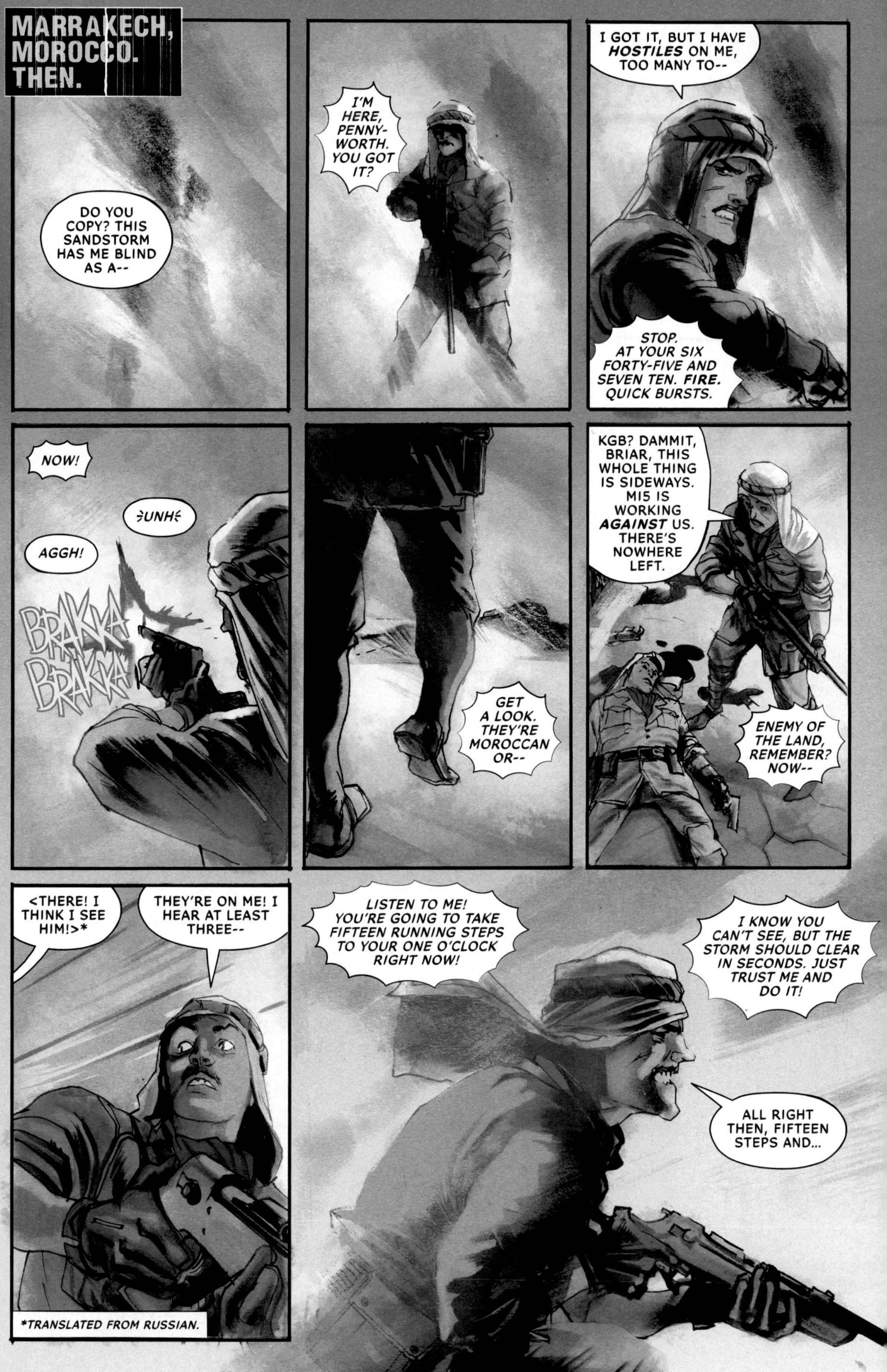
MARRAKECH, MOROCCO. THEN.
DO YOU COPY? THIS SANDSTORM HAS ME BLIND AS A--
I'M HERE, PENNY-WORTH. YOU GOT IT?
I GOT IT, BUT I HAVE HOSTILES ON ME, TOO MANY TO--
STOP. AT YOUR SIX FORTY-FIVE AND SEVEN TEN. FIRE. QUICK BURSTS.
NOW!
UNH
AGGH!
BRAKKA BRAKKA
GET A LOOK. THEY'RE MOROCCAN OR--
KGB? DAMMIT, BRIAR, THIS WHOLE THING IS SIDEWAYS. MI5 IS WORKING AGAINST US. THERE'S NOWHERE LEFT.
ENEMY OF THE LAND, REMEMBER? NOW--
<THERE! I THINK I SEE HIM!>*
THEY'RE ON ME! I HEAR AT LEAST THREE--
LISTEN TO ME! YOU'RE GOING TO TAKE FIFTEEN RUNNING STEPS TO YOUR ONE O'CLOCK RIGHT NOW!
I KNOW YOU CAN'T SEE, BUT THE STORM SHOULD CLEAR IN SECONDS. JUST TRUST ME AND DO IT!
ALL RIGHT THEN, FIFTEEN STEPS AND...
*TRANSLATED FROM RUSSIAN.

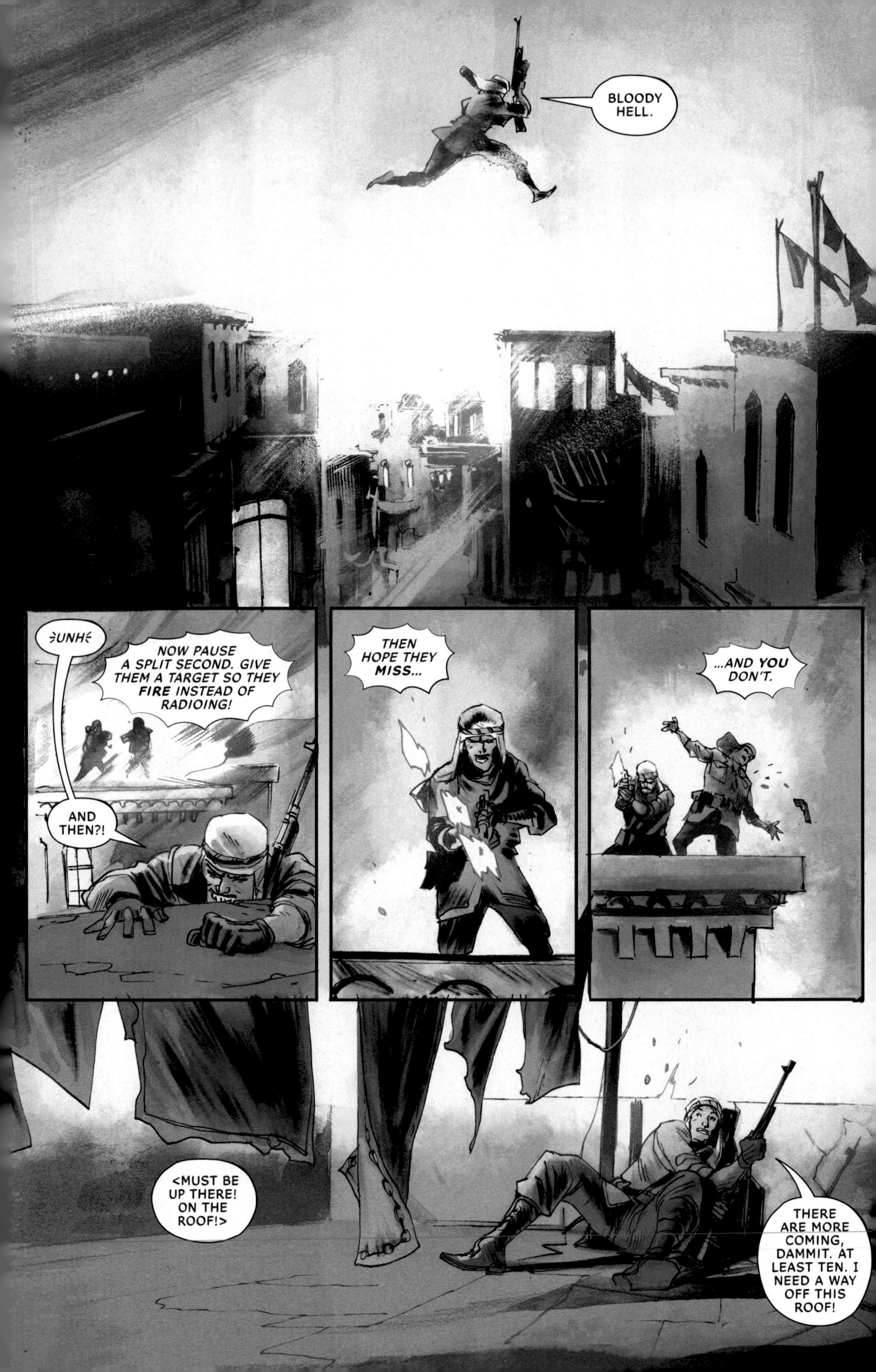
BLOODY HELL.
UNH
NOW PAUSE A SPLIT SECOND. GIVE THEM A TARGET SO THEY FIRE INSTEAD OF RADIOING!
AND THEN?!
THEN HOPE THEY MISS...
...AND YOU DON'T.
<MUST BE UP THERE! ON THE ROOF!>
THERE ARE MORE COMING, DAMMIT. AT LEAST TEN. I NEED A WAY OFF THIS ROOF!

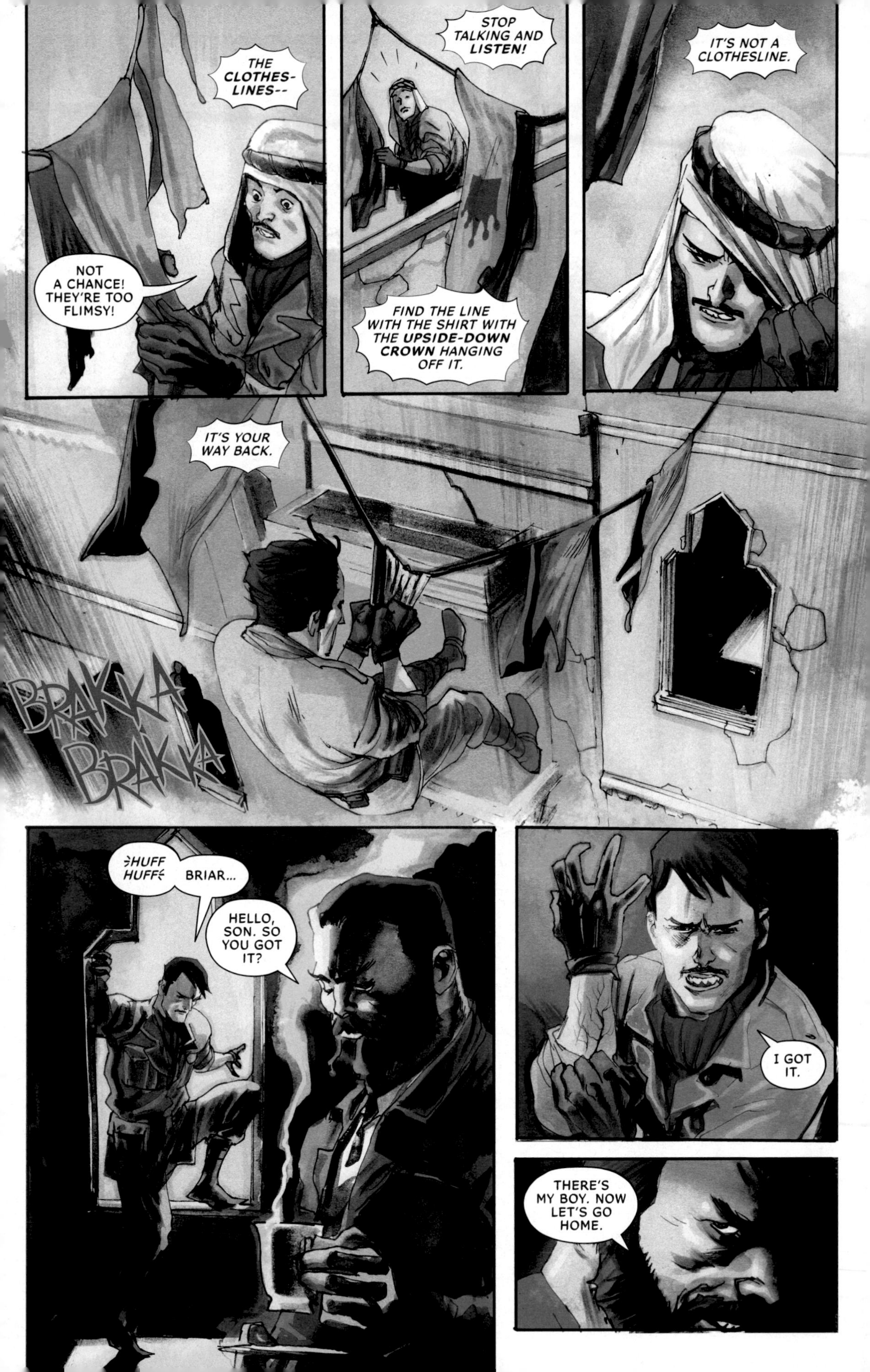
THE CLOTHES-LINES--
NOT A CHANCE! THEY'RE TOO FLIMSY!
STOP TALKING AND LISTEN!
FIND THE LINE WITH THE SHIRT WITH THE UPSIDE-DOWN CROWN HANGING OFF IT.
IT'S NOT A CLOTHESLINE.
IT'S YOUR WAY BACK.
BRAKKA BRAKKA
HUFF HUFF
BRIAR...
HELLO, SON. SO YOU GOT IT?
I GOT IT.
THERE'S MY BOY. NOW LET'S GO HOME.

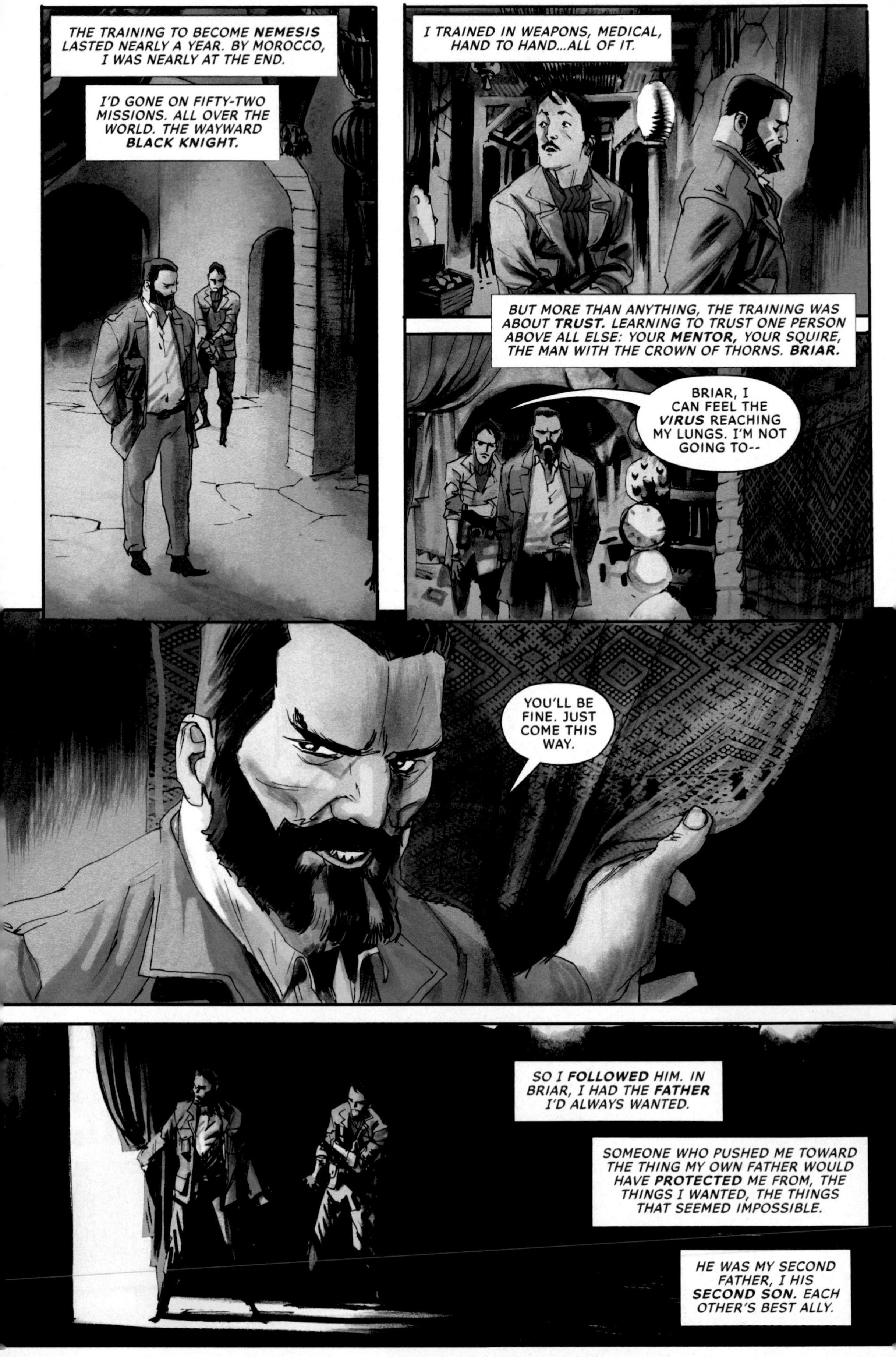
THE TRAINING TO BECOME NEMESIS LASTED NEARLY A YEAR. BY MOROCCO, I WAS NEARLY AT THE END.
I'D GONE ON FIFTY-TWO MISSIONS. ALL OVER THE WORLD. THE WAYWARD BLACK KNIGHT.
I TRAINED IN WEAPONS, MEDICAL, HAND TO HAND...ALL OF IT.
BUT MORE THAN ANYTHING, THE TRAINING WAS ABOUT TRUST. LEARNING TO TRUST ONE PERSON ABOVE ALL ELSE: YOUR MENTOR, YOUR SQUIRE, THE MAN WITH THE CROWN OF THORNS. BRIAR.
BRIAR, I CAN FEEL THE VIRUS REACHING MY LUNGS. I'M NOT GOING TO--
YOU'LL BE FINE. JUST COME THIS WAY.
SO I FOLLOWED HIM. IN BRIAR, I HAD THE FATHER I'D ALWAYS WANTED.
SOMEONE WHO PUSHED ME TOWARD THE THING MY OWN FATHER WOULD HAVE PROTECTED ME FROM, THE THINGS I WANTED, THE THINGS THAT SEEMED IMPOSSIBLE.
HE WAS MY SECOND FATHER, I HIS SECOND SON. EACH OTHER'S BEST ALLY.

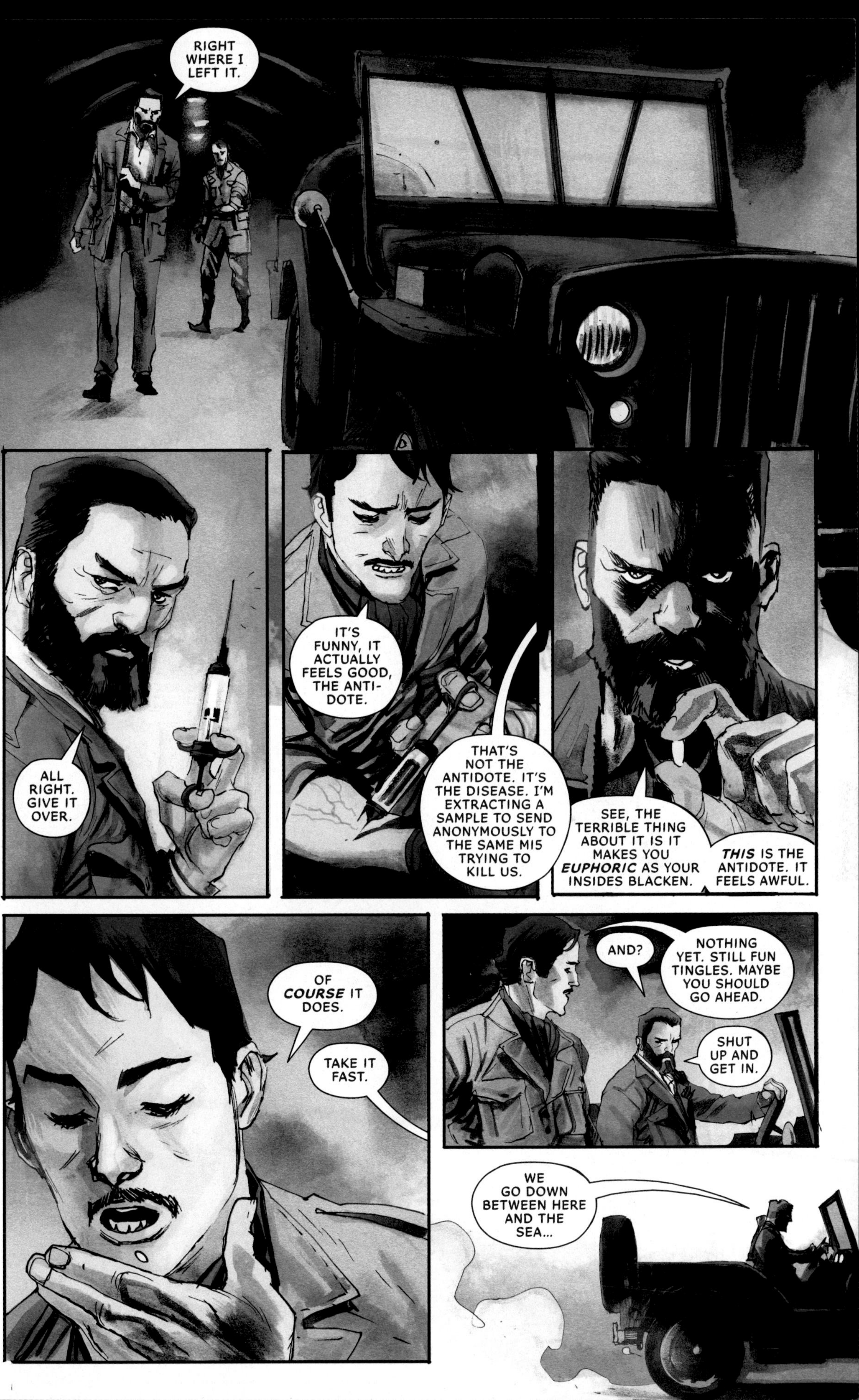
RIGHT WHERE I LEFT IT.
ALL RIGHT. GIVE IT OVER.
IT'S FUNNY, IT ACTUALLY FEELS GOOD, THE ANTI-DOTE.
THAT'S NOT THE ANTIDOTE. IT'S THE DISEASE. I'M EXTRACTING A SAMPLE TO SEND ANONYMOUSLY TO THE SAME MI5 TRYING TO KILL US.
SEE, THE TERRIBLE THING ABOUT IT IS IT MAKES YOU EUPHORIC AS YOUR INSIDES BLACKEN.
THIS IS THE ANTIDOTE. IT FEELS AWFUL.
OF COURSE IT DOES.
TAKE IT FAST.
AND?
NOTHING YET. STILL FUN TINGLES. MAYBE YOU SHOULD GO AHEAD.
SHUT UP AND GET IN.
WE GO DOWN BETWEEN HERE AND THE SEA...

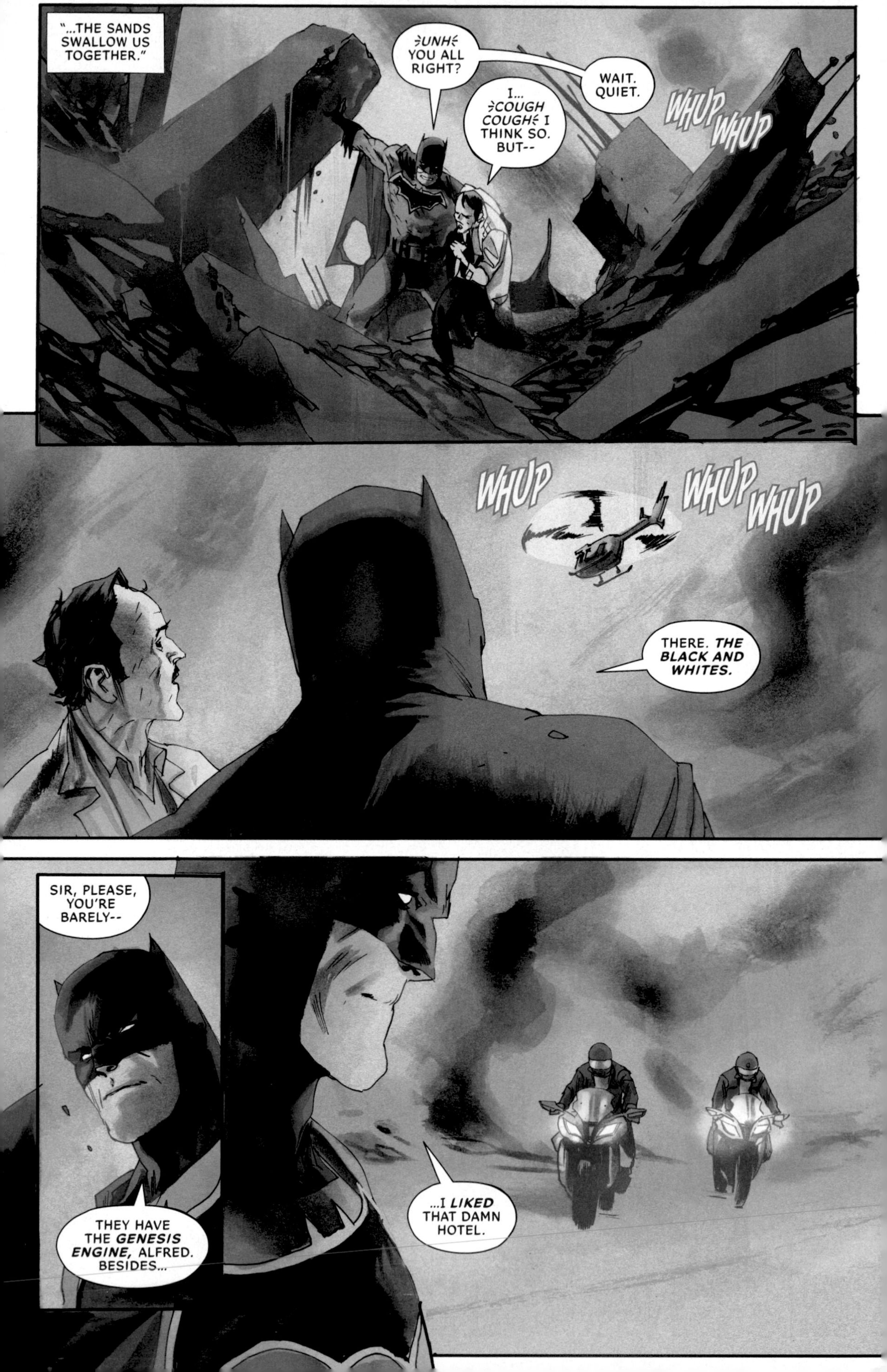
"...THE SANDS SWALLOW US TOGETHER."
UNH YOU ALL RIGHT?
I... COUGH COUGH I THINK SO. BUT--
WAIT. QUIET.
WHUP WHUP
WHUP
WHUP WHUP
THERE. THE BLACK AND WHITES.
SIR, PLEASE, YOU'RE BARELY--
THEY HAVE THE GENESIS ENGINE, ALFRED. BESIDES...
...I LIKED THAT DAMN HOTEL.

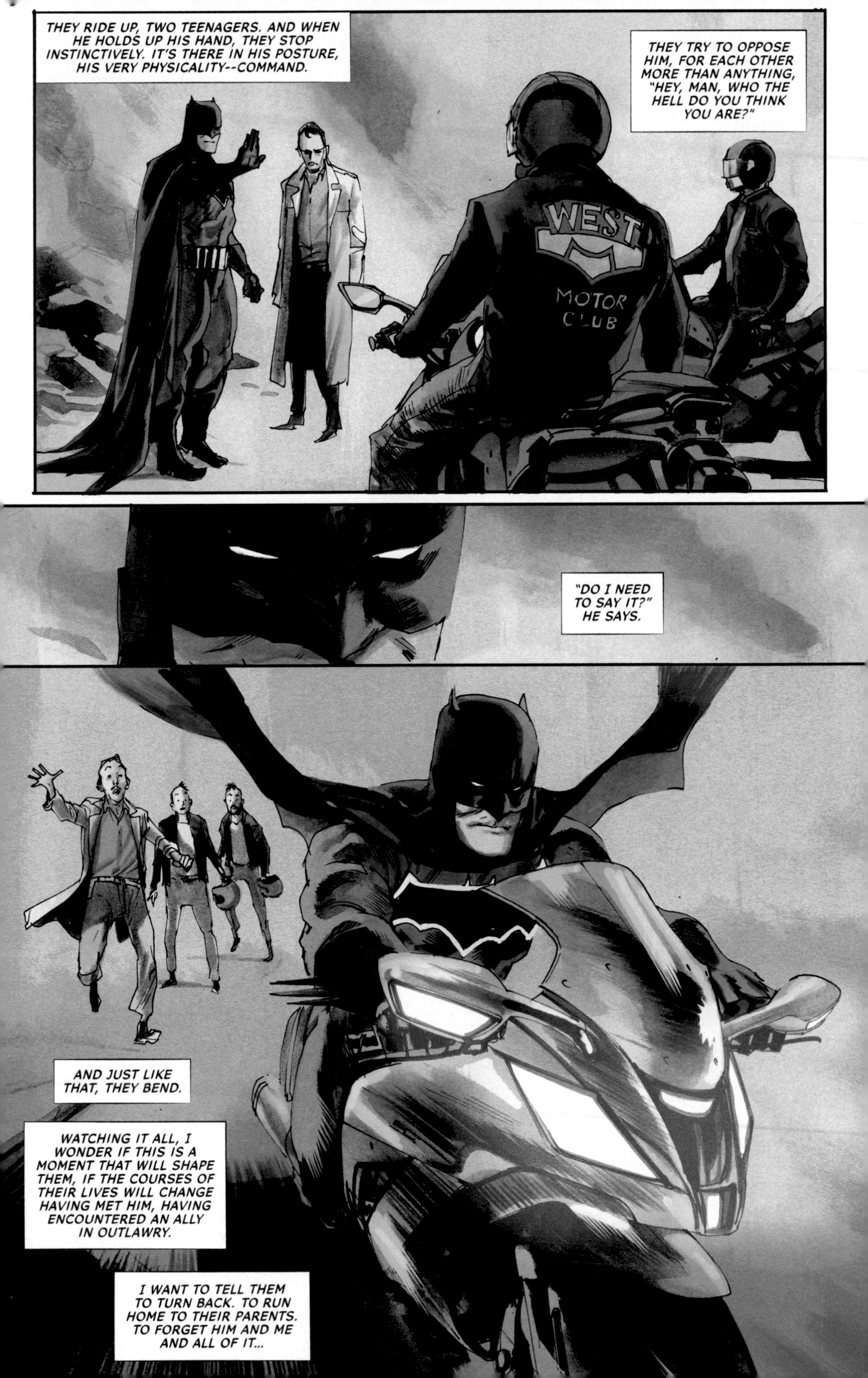
THEY RIDE UP, TWO TEENAGERS. AND WHEN HE HOLDS UP HIS HAND, THEY STOP INSTINCTIVELY. IT'S THERE IN HIS POSTURE, HIS VERY PHYSICALITY--COMMAND.
THEY TRY TO OPPOSE HIM, FOR EACH OTHER MORE THAN ANYTHING, "HEY, MAN, WHO THE HELL DO YOU THINK YOU ARE?"
WEST
MOTOR CLUB
"DO I NEED TO SAY IT?" HE SAYS.
AND JUST LIKE THAT, THEY BEND.
WATCHING IT ALL, I WONDER IF THIS IS A MOMENT THAT WILL SHAPE THEM, IF THE COURSES OF THEIR LIVES WILL CHANGE HAVING MET HIM, HAVING ENCOUNTERED AN ALLY IN OUTLAWRY.
I WANT TO TELL THEM TO TURN BACK. TO RUN HOME TO THEIR PARENTS. TO FORGET HIM AND ME AND ALL OF IT...

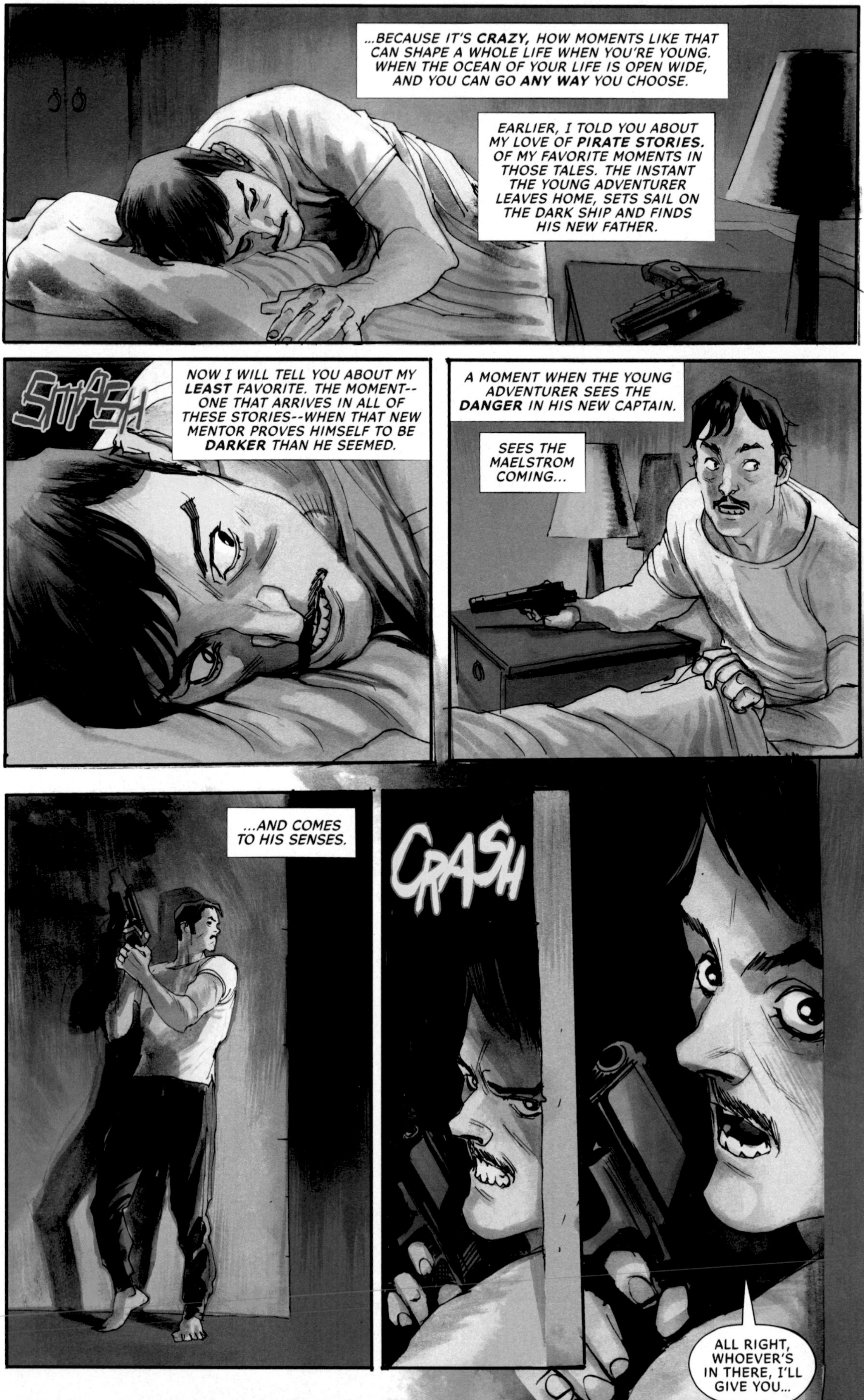
...BECAUSE IT'S CRAZY, HOW MOMENTS LIKE THAT CAN SHAPE A WHOLE LIFE WHEN YOU'RE YOUNG. WHEN THE OCEAN OF YOUR LIFE IS OPEN WIDE, AND YOU CAN GO ANY WAY YOU CHOOSE.
EARLIER, I TOLD YOU ABOUT MY LOVE OF PIRATE STORIES. OF MY FAVORITE MOMENTS IN THOSE TALES. THE INSTANT THE YOUNG ADVENTURER LEAVES HOME, SETS SAIL ON THE DARK SHIP AND FINDS HIS NEW FATHER.
SMASH
NOW I WILL TELL YOU ABOUT MY LEAST FAVORITE. THE MOMENT--ONE THAT ARRIVES IN ALL OF THESE STORIES--WHEN THAT NEW MENTOR PROVES HIMSELF TO BE DARKER THAN HE SEEMED.
A MOMENT WHEN THE YOUNG ADVENTURER SEES THE DANGER IN HIS NEW CAPTAIN.
SEES THE MAELSTROM COMING...
...AND COMES TO HIS SENSES.
CRASH
ALL RIGHT, WHOEVER'S IN THERE, I'LL GIVE YOU...

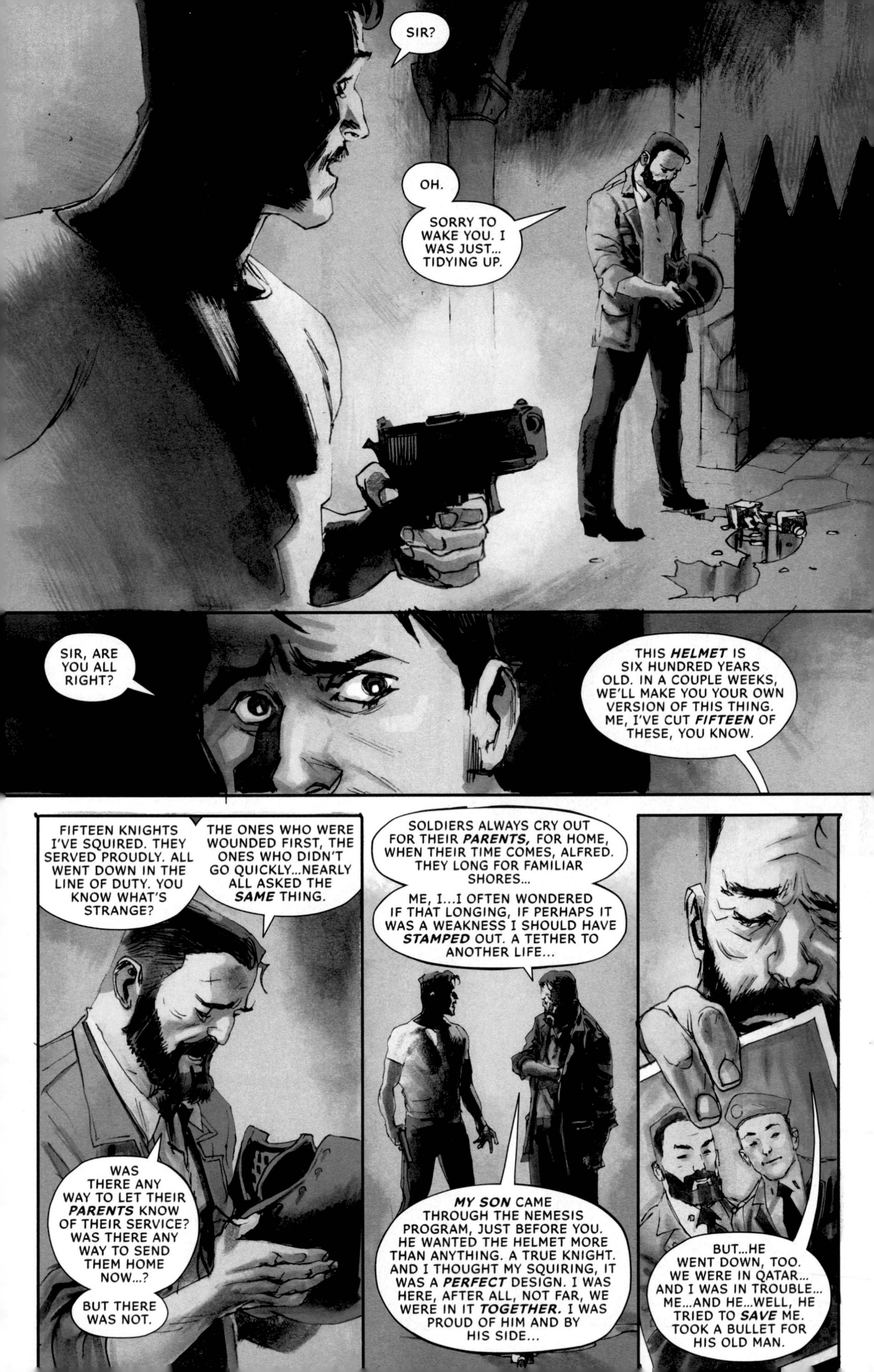
SIR?
OH.
SORRY TO WAKE YOU. I WAS JUST... TIDYING UP.
SIR, ARE YOU ALL RIGHT?
THIS HELMET IS SIX HUNDRED YEARS OLD. IN A COUPLE WEEKS, WE'LL MAKE YOU YOUR OWN VERSION OF THIS THING. ME, I'VE CUT FIFTEEN OF THESE, YOU KNOW.
FIFTEEN KNIGHTS I'VE SQUIRED. THEY SERVED PROUDLY. ALL WENT DOWN IN THE LINE OF DUTY. YOU KNOW WHAT'S STRANGE?
THE ONES WHO WERE WOUNDED FIRST, THE ONES WHO DIDN'T GO QUICKLY...NEARLY ALL ASKED THE SAME THING.
WAS THERE ANY WAY TO LET THEIR PARENTS KNOW OF THEIR SERVICE? WAS THERE ANY WAY TO SEND THEM HOME NOW...?
BUT THERE WAS NOT.
SOLDIERS ALWAYS CRY OUT FOR THEIR PARENTS, FOR HOME, WHEN THEIR TIME COMES, ALFRED. THEY LONG FOR FAMILIAR SHORES...
ME, I...I OFTEN WONDERED IF THAT LONGING, IF PERHAPS IT WAS A WEAKNESS I SHOULD HAVE STAMPED OUT. A TETHER TO ANOTHER LIFE...
MY SON CAME THROUGH THE NEMESIS PROGRAM, JUST BEFORE YOU. HE WANTED THE HELMET MORE THAN ANYTHING. A TRUE KNIGHT. AND I THOUGHT MY SQUIRING, IT WAS A PERFECT DESIGN. I WAS HERE, AFTER ALL, NOT FAR, WE WERE IN IT TOGETHER. I WAS PROUD OF HIM AND BY HIS SIDE...
BUT...HE WENT DOWN, TOO. WE WERE IN QATAR... AND I WAS IN TROUBLE... ME...AND HE...WELL, HE TRIED TO SAVE ME. TOOK A BULLET FOR HIS OLD MAN.

AND SO HE'S HERE.

BRIAR--

THIS *MARK*. RIGHT HERE. THIS...THORN. I'D DO ANYTHING TO BRING HIM BACK, IF I COULD. HE WAS THE BEST I TRAINED...UNTIL YOU.

GET OFF ME!

NOW YOU LISTEN...WHEN YOU PASS TRAINING, WHEN YOU PUT THAT *MASK* ON, THINGS NEED TO CHANGE. THAT'S WHAT I'VE LEARNED. THE BEST WAY I CAN HELP YOU IS TO *CUT YOU LOOSE.*

NO ONE TO FALL BACK ON. IF YOU CAN'T DO IT YOURSELF, SO BE IT. IT'S HOW I CAN BE YOUR BEST, *FIRST ALLY.* TO MAKE SURE YOU HAVE NO ONE TO CRY OUT FOR IN THE NIGHT.

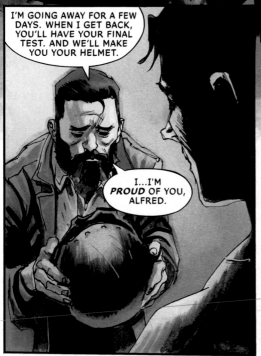

I'M GOING AWAY FOR A FEW DAYS. WHEN I GET BACK, YOU'LL HAVE YOUR FINAL TEST. AND WE'LL MAKE YOU YOUR HELMET.

I...I'M *PROUD* OF YOU, ALFRED.

I WISH I HAD GONE AFTER HIM...

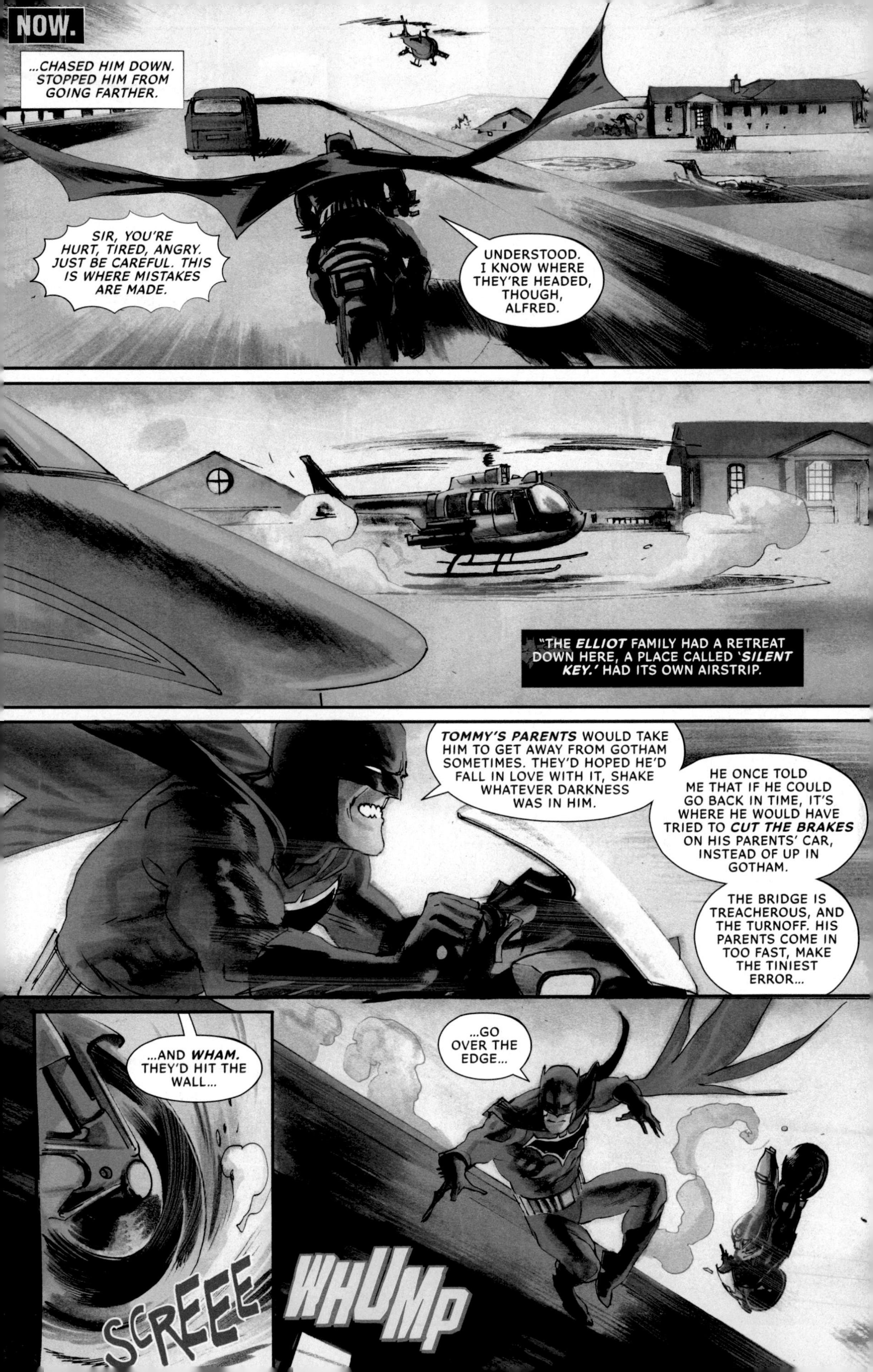
NOW.
...CHASED HIM DOWN. STOPPED HIM FROM GOING FARTHER.
SIR, YOU'RE HURT, TIRED, ANGRY. JUST BE CAREFUL. THIS IS WHERE MISTAKES ARE MADE.
UNDERSTOOD. I KNOW WHERE THEY'RE HEADED, THOUGH, ALFRED.
"THE *ELLIOT* FAMILY HAD A RETREAT DOWN HERE, A PLACE CALLED *'SILENT KEY.'* HAD ITS OWN AIRSTRIP.
TOMMY'S PARENTS WOULD TAKE HIM TO GET AWAY FROM GOTHAM SOMETIMES. THEY'D HOPED HE'D FALL IN LOVE WITH IT, SHAKE WHATEVER DARKNESS WAS IN HIM.
HE ONCE TOLD ME THAT IF HE COULD GO BACK IN TIME, IT'S WHERE HE WOULD HAVE TRIED TO ***CUT THE BRAKES*** ON HIS PARENTS' CAR, INSTEAD OF UP IN GOTHAM.
THE BRIDGE IS TREACHEROUS, AND THE TURNOFF. HIS PARENTS COME IN TOO FAST, MAKE THE TINIEST ERROR...
...AND ***WHAM.*** THEY'D HIT THE WALL...
...GO OVER THE EDGE...
SCREEE
WHUMP

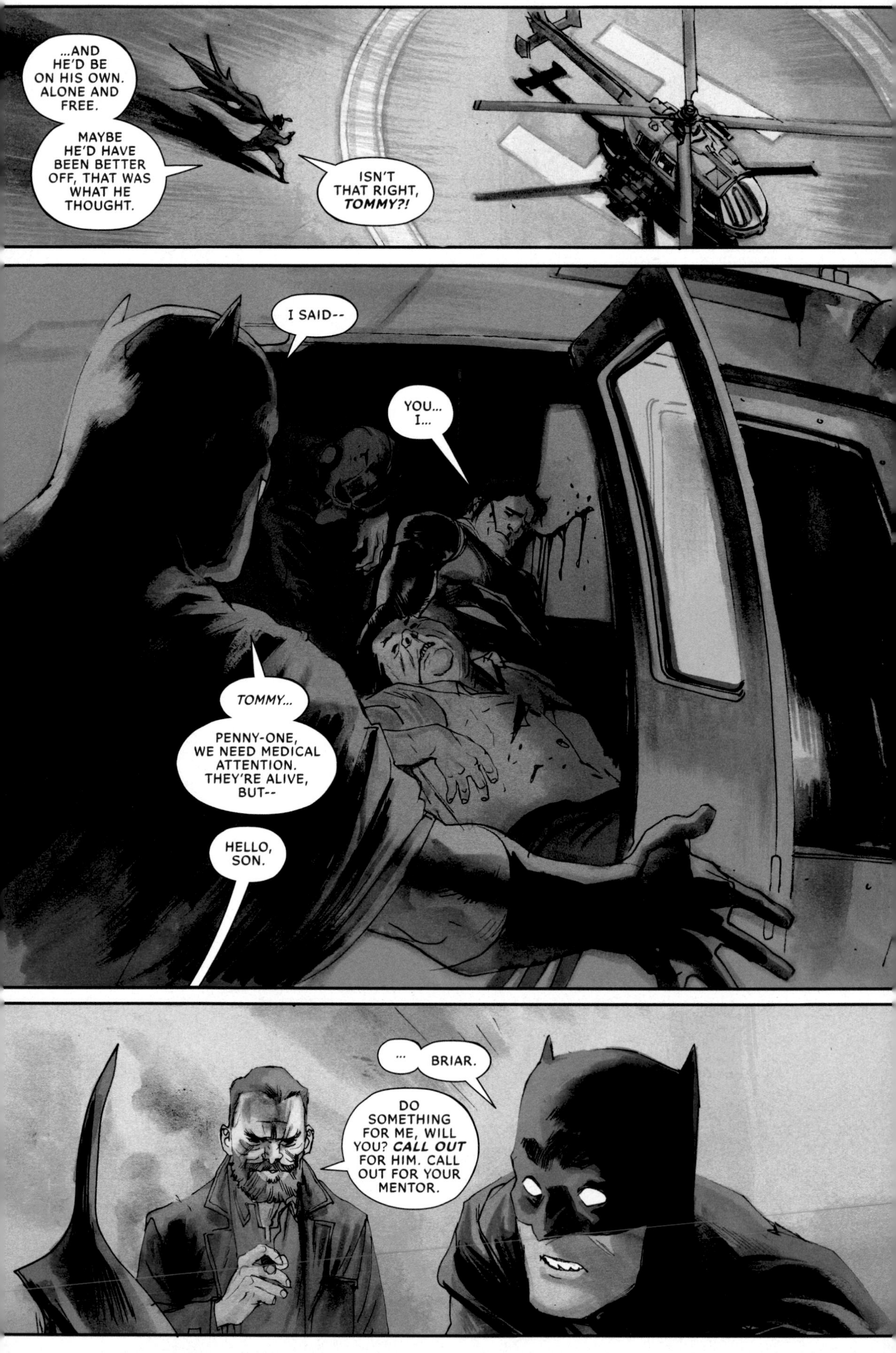
...AND HE'D BE ON HIS OWN. ALONE AND FREE.
MAYBE HE'D HAVE BEEN BETTER OFF, THAT WAS WHAT HE THOUGHT.
ISN'T THAT RIGHT, *TOMMY?!*
I SAID--
YOU... I...
TOMMY...
PENNY-ONE, WE NEED MEDICAL ATTENTION. THEY'RE ALIVE, BUT--
HELLO, SON.
...
BRIAR.
DO SOMETHING FOR ME, WILL YOU? ***CALL OUT*** FOR HIM. CALL OUT FOR YOUR MENTOR.

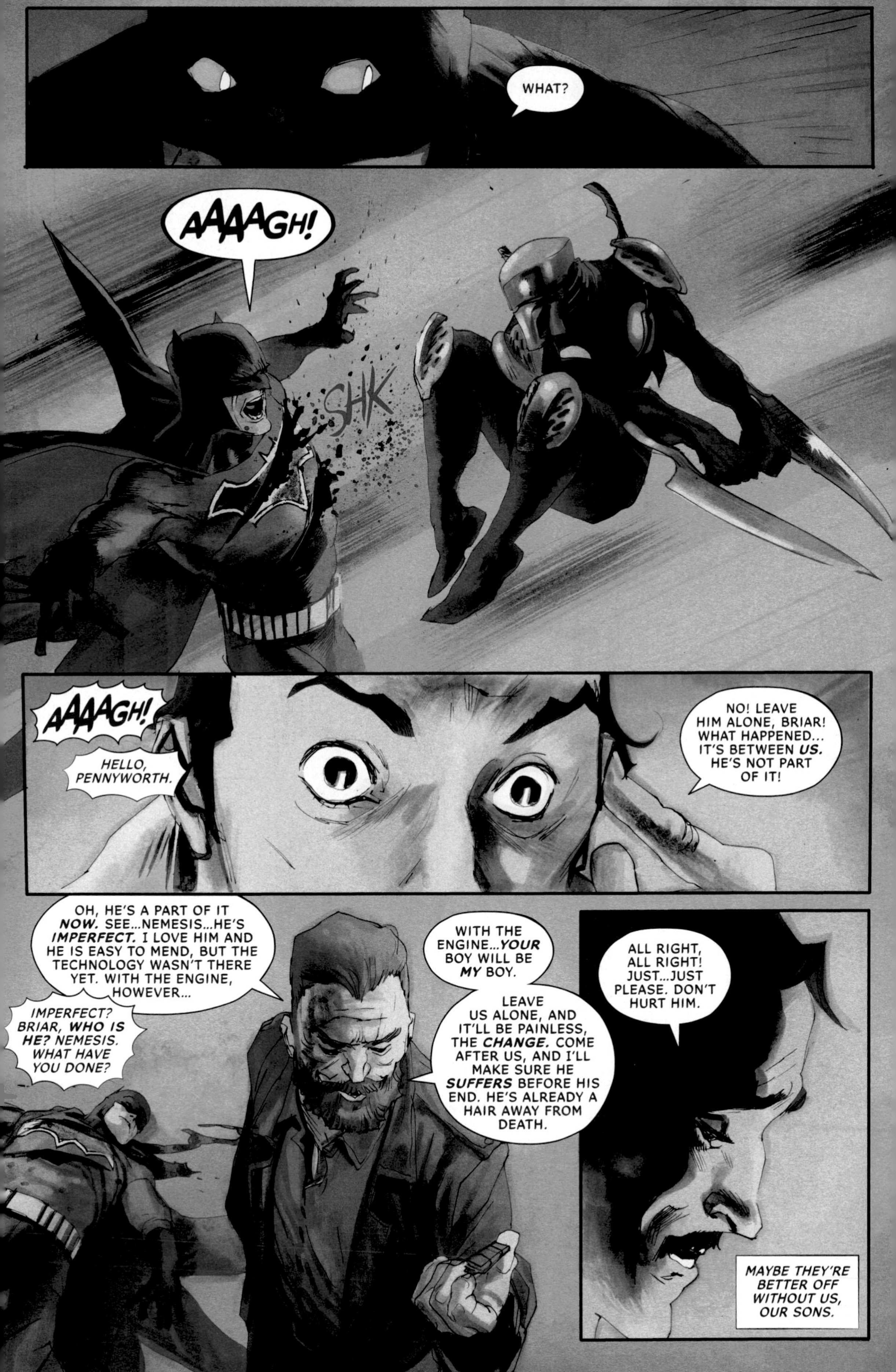
WHAT?
AAAAGH!
SHK
AAAAGH!
HELLO, PENNYWORTH.
NO! LEAVE HIM ALONE, BRIAR! WHAT HAPPENED... IT'S BETWEEN US. HE'S NOT PART OF IT!
OH, HE'S A PART OF IT NOW. SEE...NEMESIS...HE'S IMPERFECT. I LOVE HIM AND HE IS EASY TO MEND, BUT THE TECHNOLOGY WASN'T THERE YET. WITH THE ENGINE, HOWEVER...
IMPERFECT? BRIAR, WHO IS HE? NEMESIS. WHAT HAVE YOU DONE?
WITH THE ENGINE...YOUR BOY WILL BE MY BOY.
LEAVE US ALONE, AND IT'LL BE PAINLESS, THE CHANGE. COME AFTER US, AND I'LL MAKE SURE HE SUFFERS BEFORE HIS END. HE'S ALREADY A HAIR AWAY FROM DEATH.
ALL RIGHT, ALL RIGHT! JUST...JUST PLEASE. DON'T HURT HIM.
MAYBE THEY'RE BETTER OFF WITHOUT US, OUR SONS.

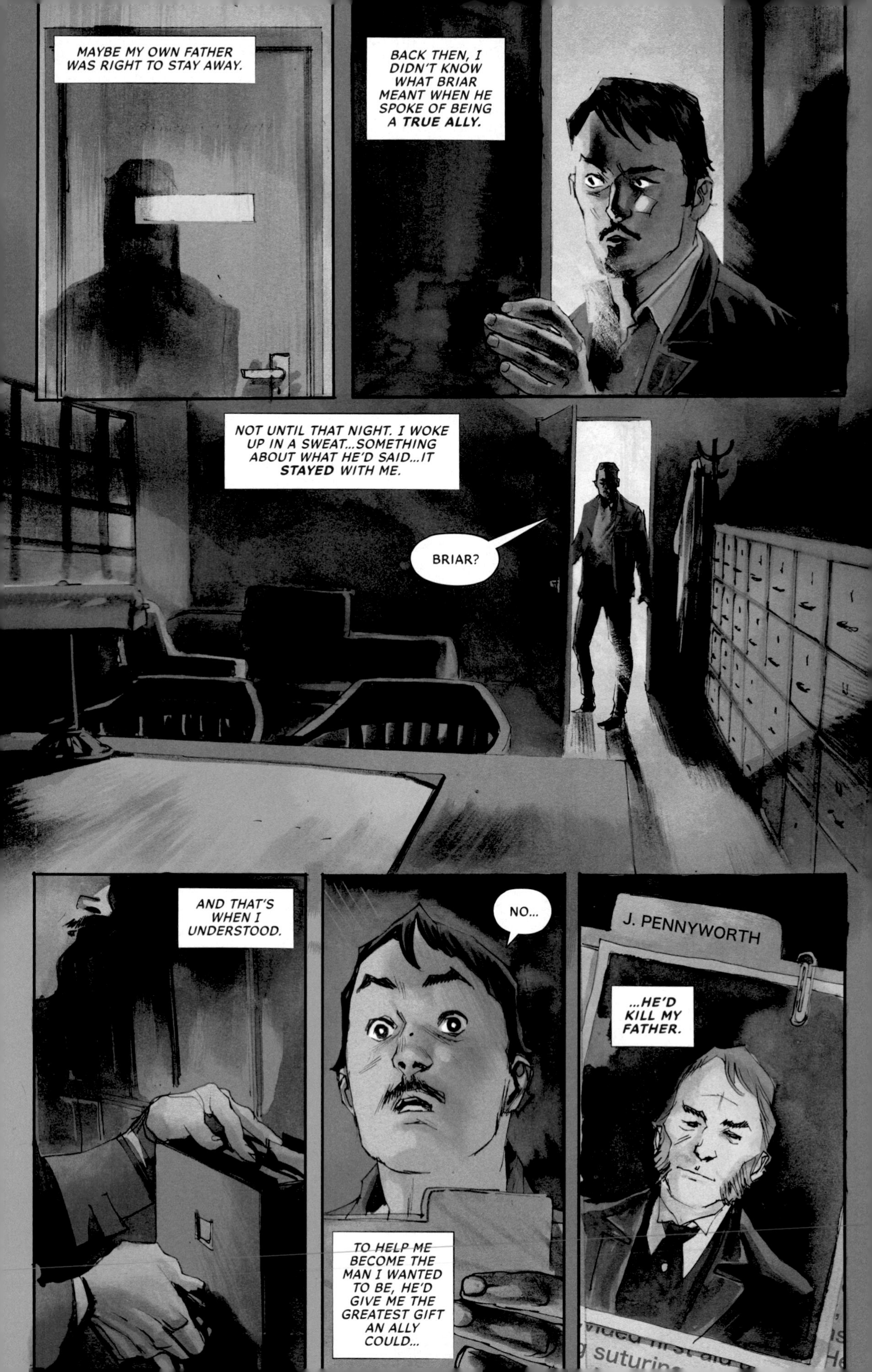

MAYBE MY OWN FATHER WAS RIGHT TO STAY AWAY.
BACK THEN, I DIDN'T KNOW WHAT BRIAR MEANT WHEN HE SPOKE OF BEING A **TRUE ALLY.**
NOT UNTIL THAT NIGHT. I WOKE UP IN A SWEAT...SOMETHING ABOUT WHAT HE'D SAID...IT **STAYED** WITH ME.
BRIAR?
AND THAT'S WHEN I UNDERSTOOD.
NO...
TO HELP ME BECOME THE MAN I WANTED TO BE, HE'D GIVE ME THE GREATEST GIFT AN ALLY COULD...
J. PENNYWORTH
...HE'D KILL MY FATHER.

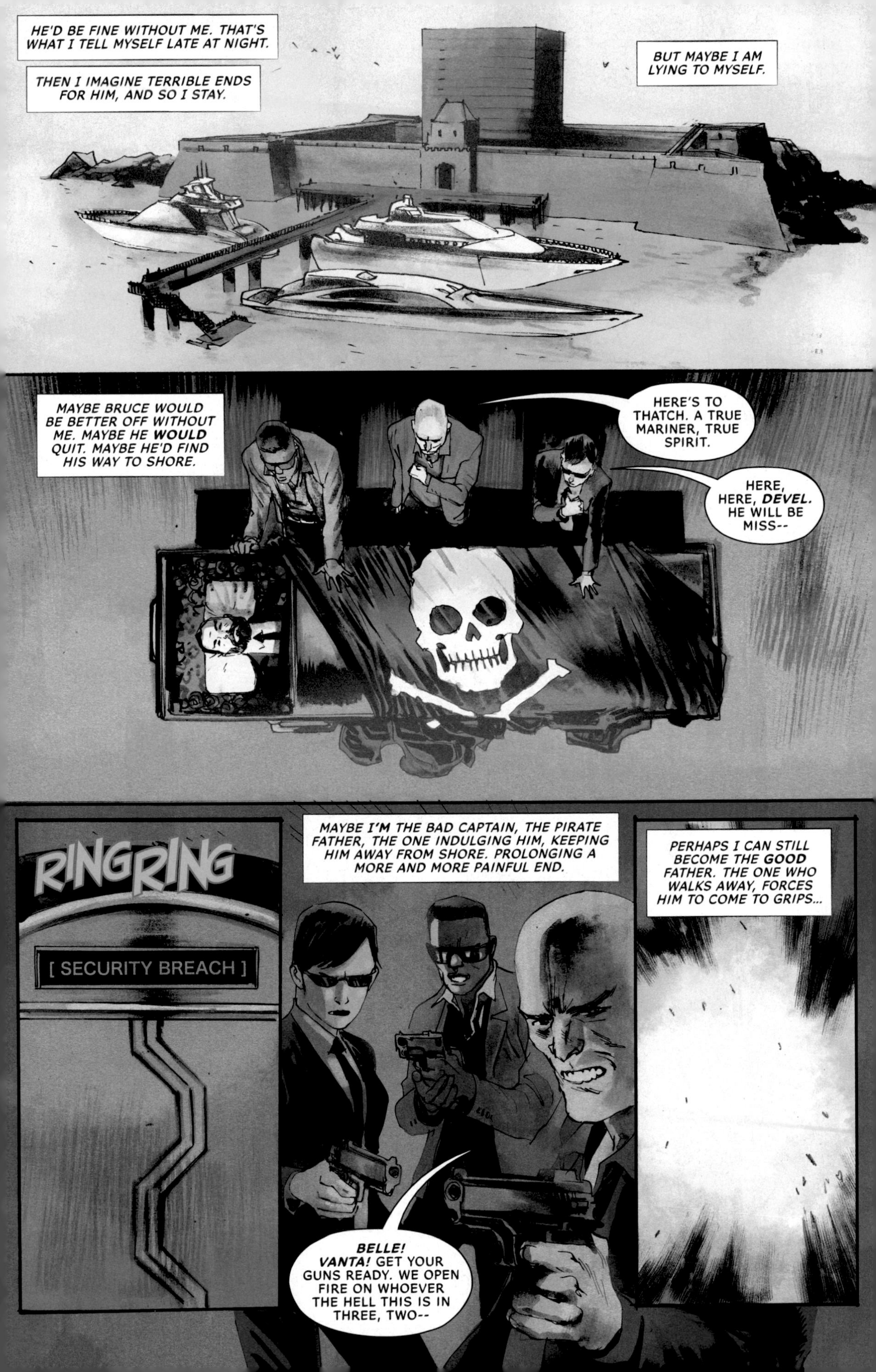
HE'D BE FINE WITHOUT ME. THAT'S WHAT I TELL MYSELF LATE AT NIGHT.
THEN I IMAGINE TERRIBLE ENDS FOR HIM, AND SO I STAY.
BUT MAYBE I AM LYING TO MYSELF.
MAYBE BRUCE WOULD BE BETTER OFF WITHOUT ME. MAYBE HE **WOULD** QUIT. MAYBE HE'D FIND HIS WAY TO SHORE.
HERE'S TO THATCH. A TRUE MARINER, TRUE SPIRIT.
HERE, HERE, **DEVEL.** HE WILL BE MISS--
RINGRING
[SECURITY BREACH]
MAYBE **I'M** THE BAD CAPTAIN, THE PIRATE FATHER, THE ONE INDULGING HIM, KEEPING HIM AWAY FROM SHORE. PROLONGING A MORE AND MORE PAINFUL END.
PERHAPS I CAN STILL BECOME THE **GOOD** FATHER. THE ONE WHO WALKS AWAY, FORCES HIM TO COME TO GRIPS...
BELLE! VANTA! GET YOUR GUNS READY. WE OPEN FIRE ON WHOEVER THE HELL THIS IS IN THREE, TWO--

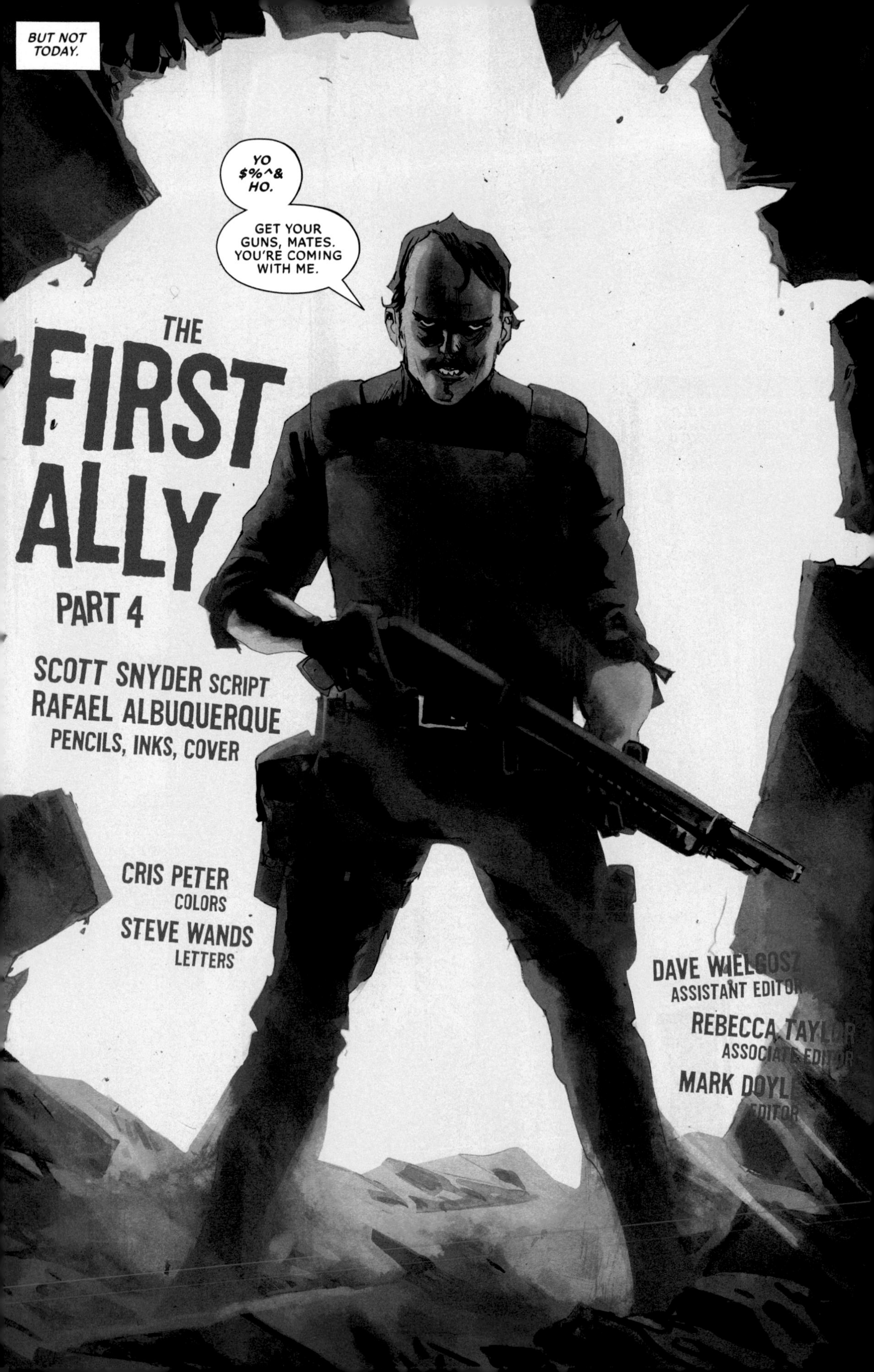
BUT NOT TODAY.
YO $%^& HO.
GET YOUR GUNS, MATES. YOU'RE COMING WITH ME.
THE FIRST ALLY
PART 4
SCOTT SNYDER SCRIPT
RAFAEL ALBUQUERQUE PENCILS, INKS, COVER
CRIS PETER COLORS
STEVE WANDS LETTERS
DAVE WIELGOSZ ASSISTANT EDITOR
REBECCA TAYLOR ASSOCIATE EDITOR
MARK DOYLE EDITOR

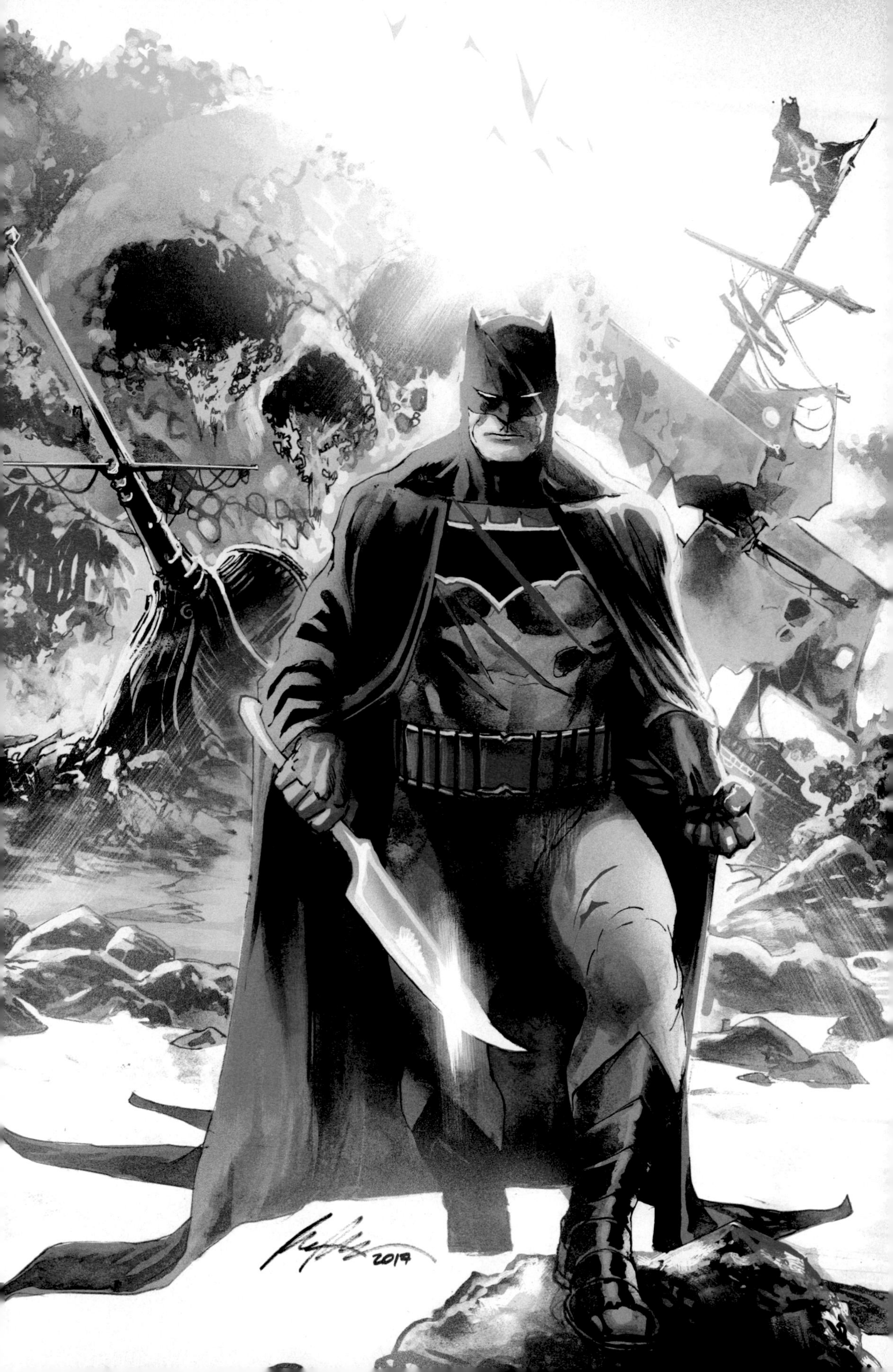

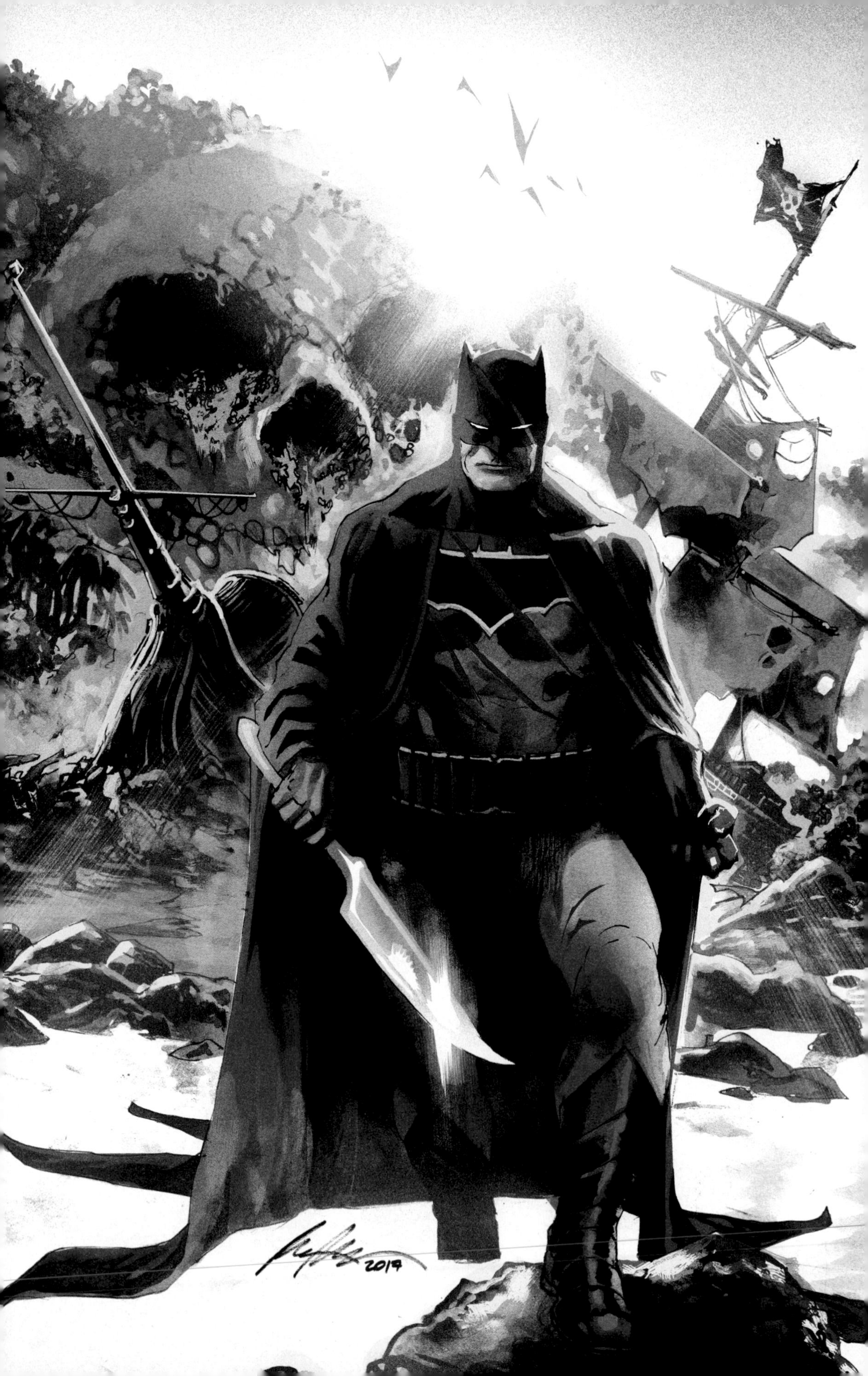

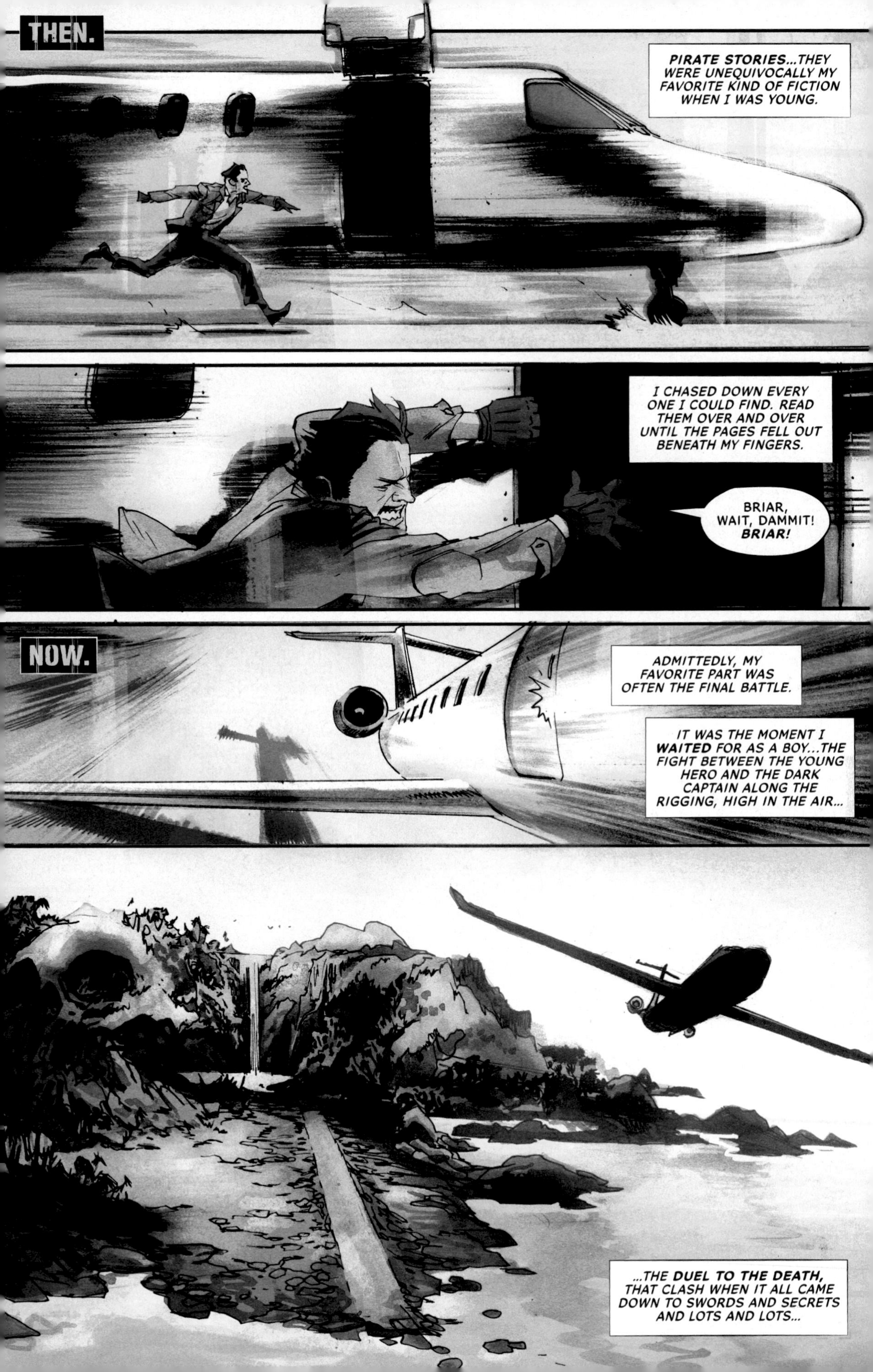
THEN.
PIRATE STORIES...THEY WERE UNEQUIVOCALLY MY FAVORITE KIND OF FICTION WHEN I WAS YOUNG.
I CHASED DOWN EVERY ONE I COULD FIND. READ THEM OVER AND OVER UNTIL THE PAGES FELL OUT BENEATH MY FINGERS.
BRIAR, WAIT, DAMMIT! BRIAR!
NOW.
ADMITTEDLY, MY FAVORITE PART WAS OFTEN THE FINAL BATTLE.
IT WAS THE MOMENT I WAITED FOR AS A BOY...THE FIGHT BETWEEN THE YOUNG HERO AND THE DARK CAPTAIN ALONG THE RIGGING, HIGH IN THE AIR...
...THE DUEL TO THE DEATH, THAT CLASH WHEN IT ALL CAME DOWN TO SWORDS AND SECRETS AND LOTS AND LOTS...

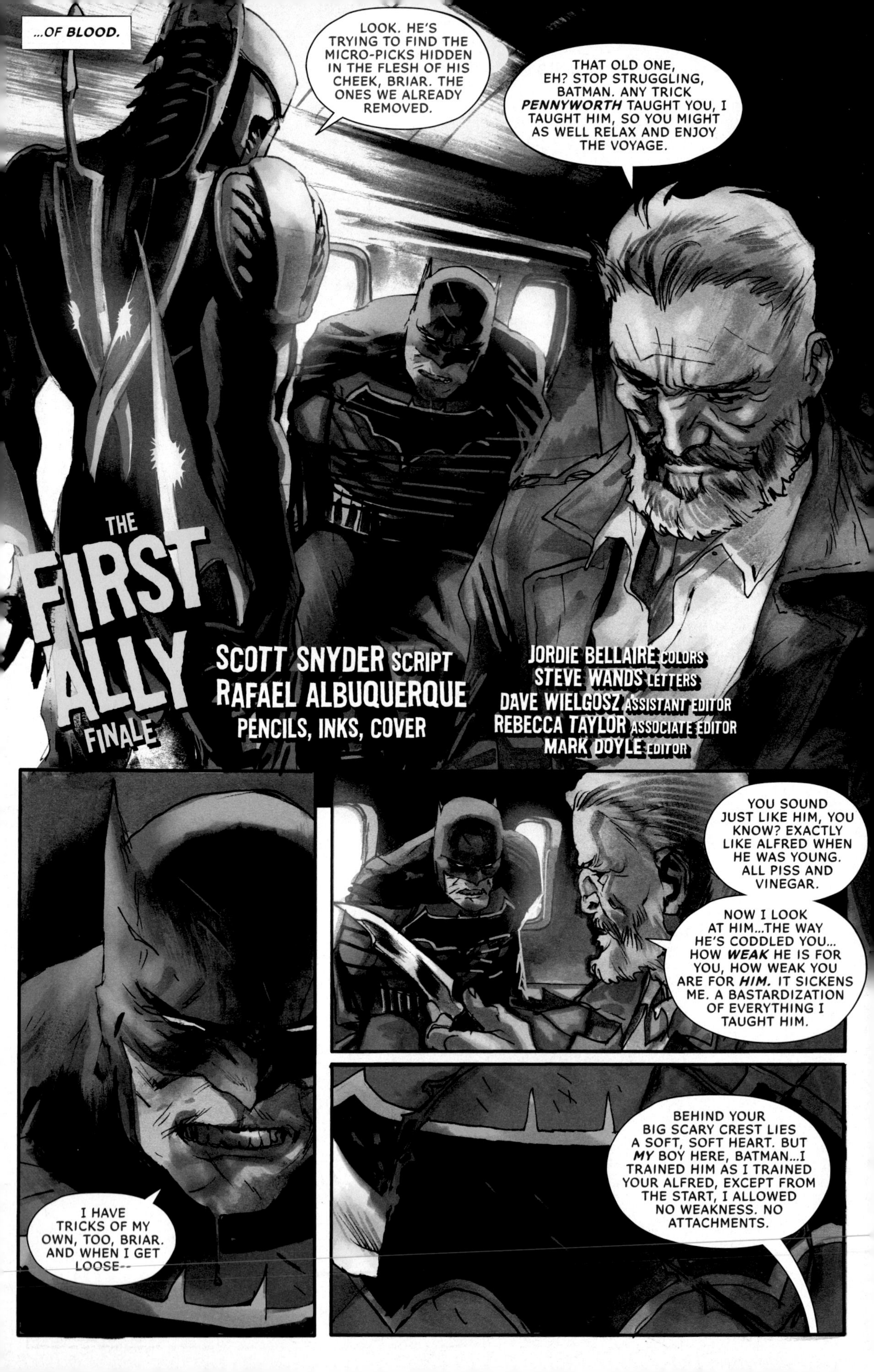
...OF BLOOD.
LOOK. HE'S TRYING TO FIND THE MICRO-PICKS HIDDEN IN THE FLESH OF HIS CHEEK, BRIAR. THE ONES WE ALREADY REMOVED.
THAT OLD ONE, EH? STOP STRUGGLING, BATMAN. ANY TRICK PENNYWORTH TAUGHT YOU, I TAUGHT HIM, SO YOU MIGHT AS WELL RELAX AND ENJOY THE VOYAGE.
THE FIRST ALLY FINALE
SCOTT SNYDER SCRIPT
RAFAEL ALBUQUERQUE PENCILS, INKS, COVER
JORDIE BELLAIRE COLORS
STEVE WANDS LETTERS
DAVE WIELGOSZ ASSISTANT EDITOR
REBECCA TAYLOR ASSOCIATE EDITOR
MARK DOYLE EDITOR
I HAVE TRICKS OF MY OWN, TOO, BRIAR. AND WHEN I GET LOOSE--
YOU SOUND JUST LIKE HIM, YOU KNOW? EXACTLY LIKE ALFRED WHEN HE WAS YOUNG. ALL PISS AND VINEGAR.
NOW I LOOK AT HIM...THE WAY HE'S CODDLED YOU... HOW WEAK HE IS FOR YOU, HOW WEAK YOU ARE FOR HIM. IT SICKENS ME. A BASTARDIZATION OF EVERYTHING I TAUGHT HIM.
BEHIND YOUR BIG SCARY CREST LIES A SOFT, SOFT HEART. BUT MY BOY HERE, BATMAN...I TRAINED HIM AS I TRAINED YOUR ALFRED, EXCEPT FROM THE START, I ALLOWED NO WEAKNESS. NO ATTACHMENTS.

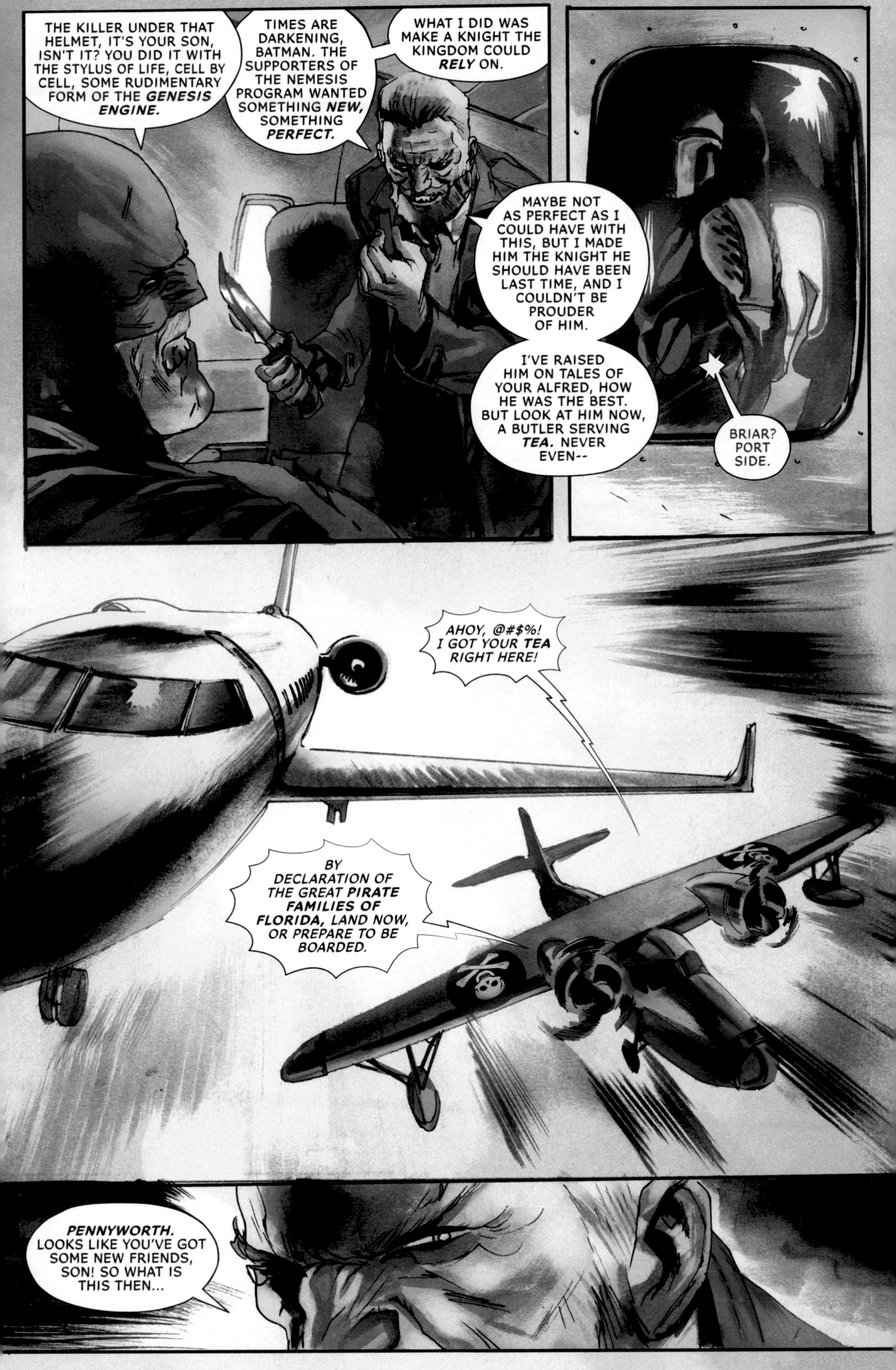

THE KILLER UNDER THAT HELMET, IT'S YOUR SON, ISN'T IT? YOU DID IT WITH THE STYLUS OF LIFE, CELL BY CELL, SOME RUDIMENTARY FORM OF THE GENESIS ENGINE.
TIMES ARE DARKENING, BATMAN. THE SUPPORTERS OF THE NEMESIS PROGRAM WANTED SOMETHING NEW, SOMETHING PERFECT.
WHAT I DID WAS MAKE A KNIGHT THE KINGDOM COULD RELY ON.
MAYBE NOT AS PERFECT AS I COULD HAVE WITH THIS, BUT I MADE HIM THE KNIGHT HE SHOULD HAVE BEEN LAST TIME, AND I COULDN'T BE PROUDER OF HIM.
I'VE RAISED HIM ON TALES OF YOUR ALFRED, HOW HE WAS THE BEST. BUT LOOK AT HIM NOW, A BUTLER SERVING TEA. NEVER EVEN--
BRIAR? PORT SIDE.
AHOY, @#$%! I GOT YOUR TEA RIGHT HERE!
BY DECLARATION OF THE GREAT PIRATE FAMILIES OF FLORIDA, LAND NOW, OR PREPARE TO BE BOARDED.
PENNYWORTH. LOOKS LIKE YOU'VE GOT SOME NEW FRIENDS, SON! SO WHAT IS THIS THEN...

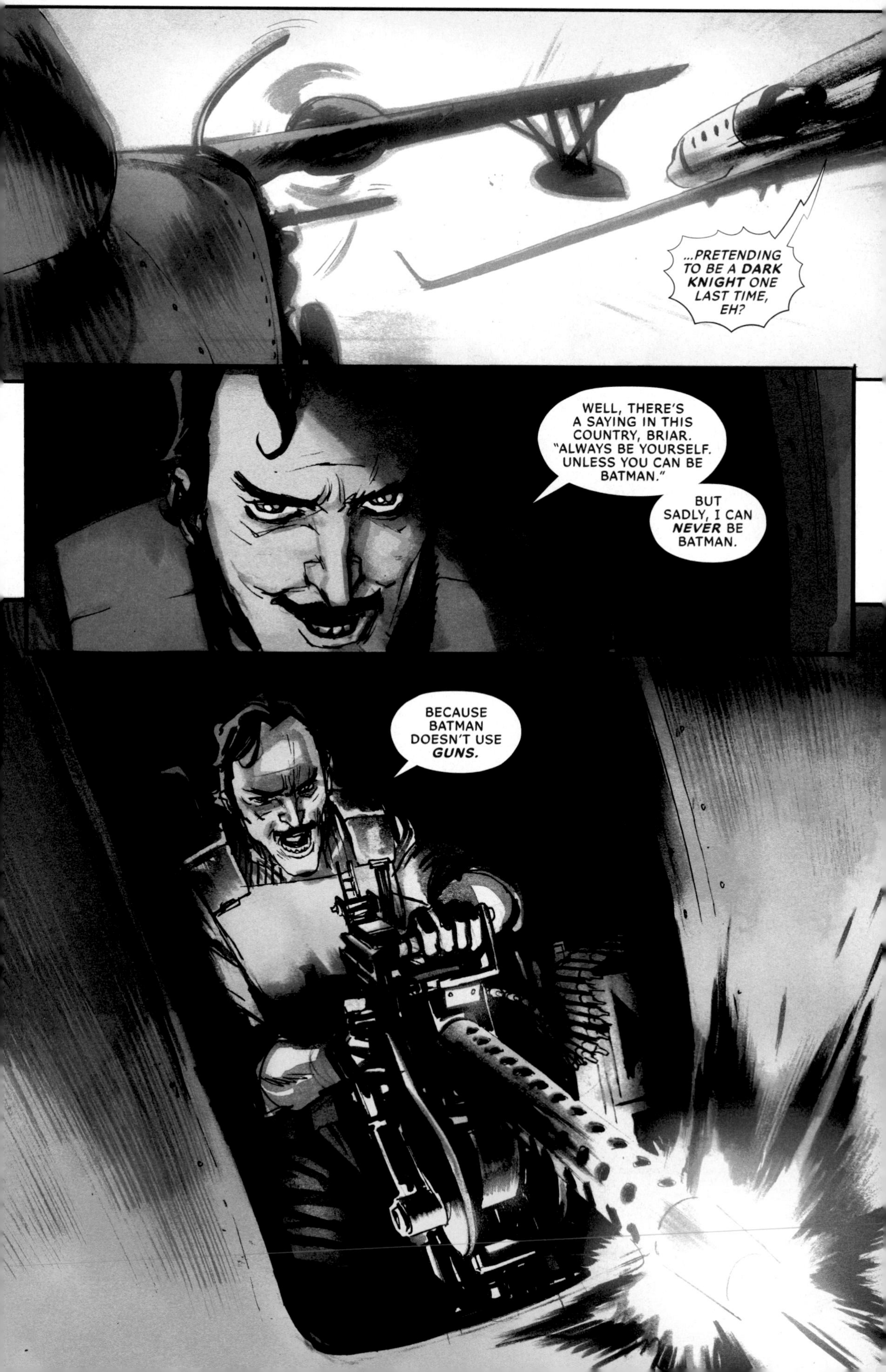

...PRETENDING TO BE A **DARK KNIGHT** ONE LAST TIME, EH?
WELL, THERE'S A SAYING IN THIS COUNTRY, BRIAR. "ALWAYS BE YOURSELF. UNLESS YOU CAN BE BATMAN."
BUT SADLY, I CAN ***NEVER*** BE BATMAN.
BECAUSE BATMAN DOESN'T USE ***GUNS.***

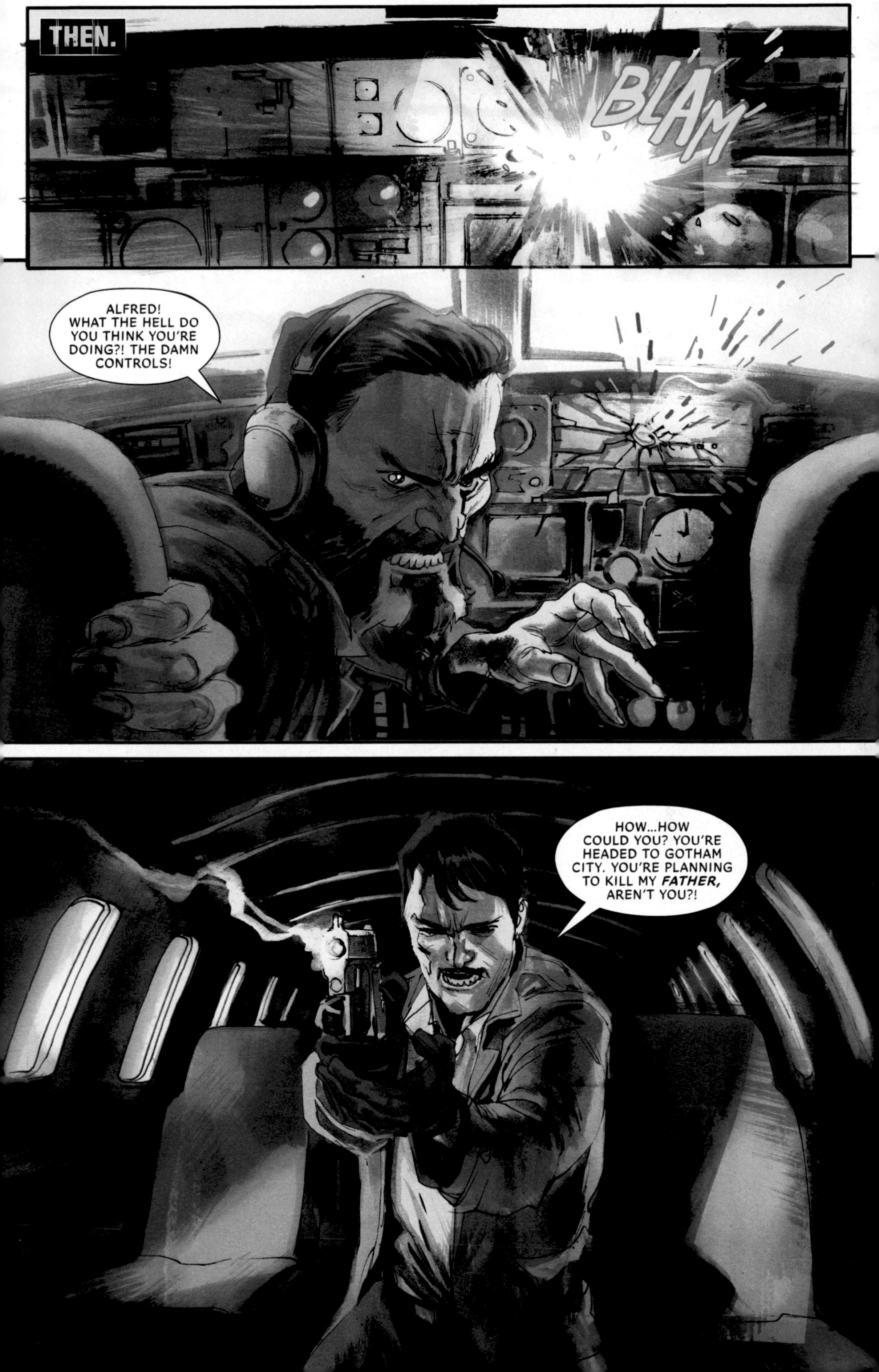
THEN.
BLAM
ALFRED! WHAT THE HELL DO YOU THINK YOU'RE DOING?! THE DAMN CONTROLS!
HOW...HOW COULD YOU? YOU'RE HEADED TO GOTHAM CITY. YOU'RE PLANNING TO KILL MY *FATHER,* AREN'T YOU?!

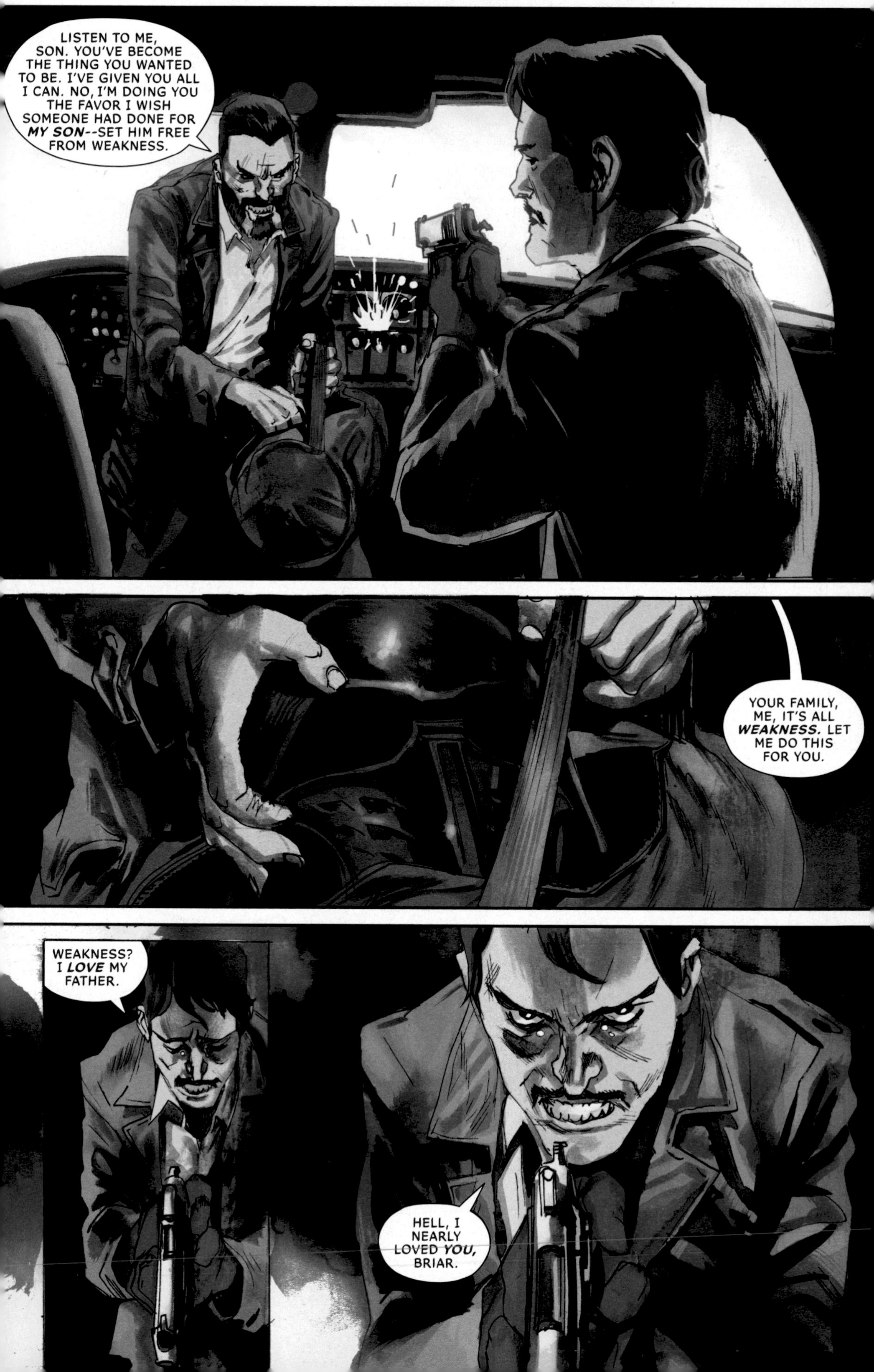
LISTEN TO ME, SON. YOU'VE BECOME THE THING YOU WANTED TO BE. I'VE GIVEN YOU ALL I CAN. NO, I'M DOING YOU THE FAVOR I WISH SOMEONE HAD DONE FOR *MY SON*--SET HIM FREE FROM WEAKNESS.
YOUR FAMILY, ME, IT'S ALL *WEAKNESS.* LET ME DO THIS FOR YOU.
WEAKNESS? I *LOVE* MY FATHER.
HELL, I NEARLY LOVED *YOU,* BRIAR.

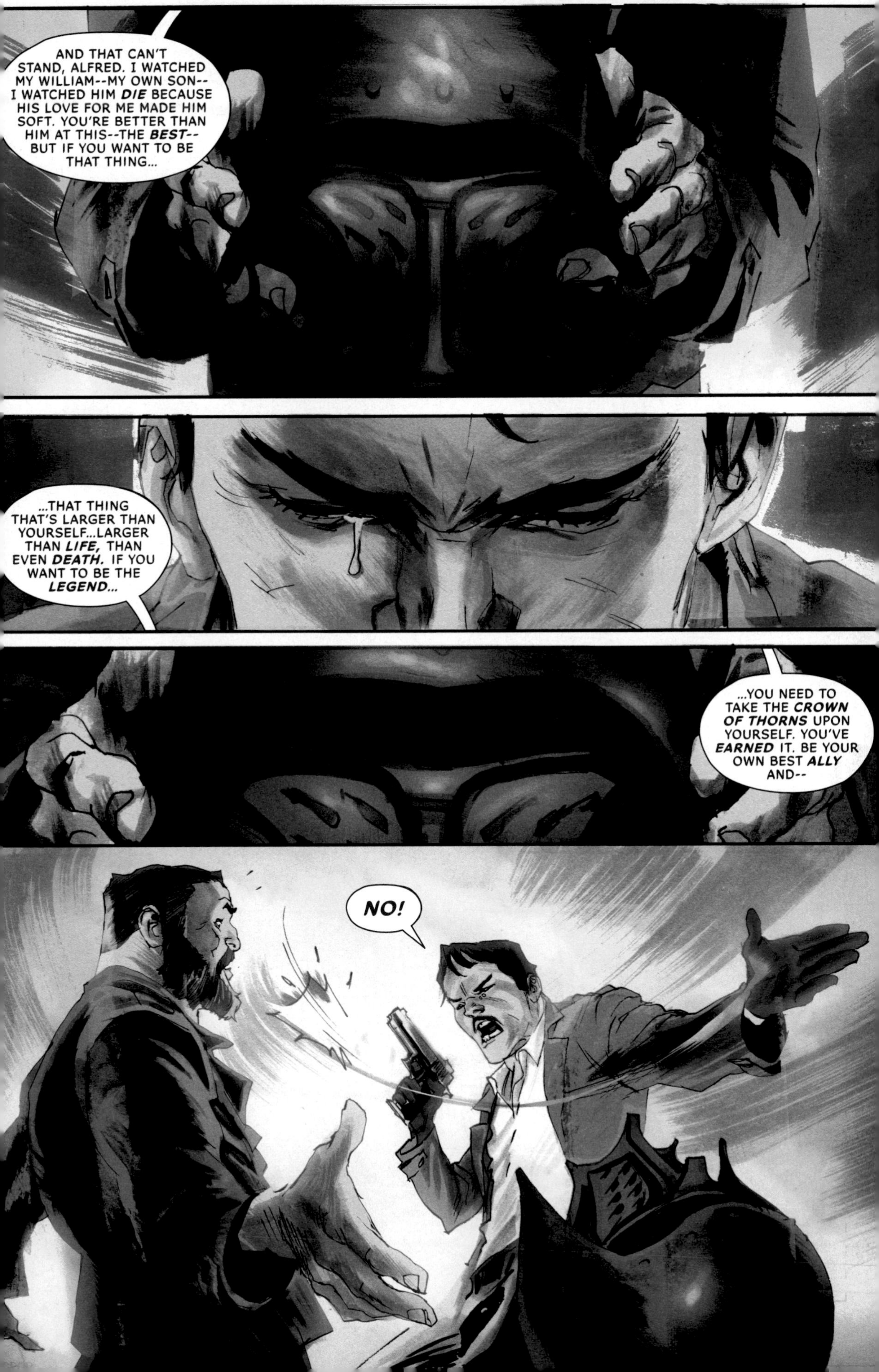
AND THAT CAN'T STAND, ALFRED. I WATCHED MY WILLIAM--MY OWN SON-- I WATCHED HIM DIE BECAUSE HIS LOVE FOR ME MADE HIM SOFT. YOU'RE BETTER THAN HIM AT THIS--THE BEST-- BUT IF YOU WANT TO BE THAT THING...
...THAT THING THAT'S LARGER THAN YOURSELF...LARGER THAN LIFE, THAN EVEN DEATH. IF YOU WANT TO BE THE LEGEND...
...YOU NEED TO TAKE THE CROWN OF THORNS UPON YOURSELF. YOU'VE EARNED IT. BE YOUR OWN BEST ALLY AND--
NO!

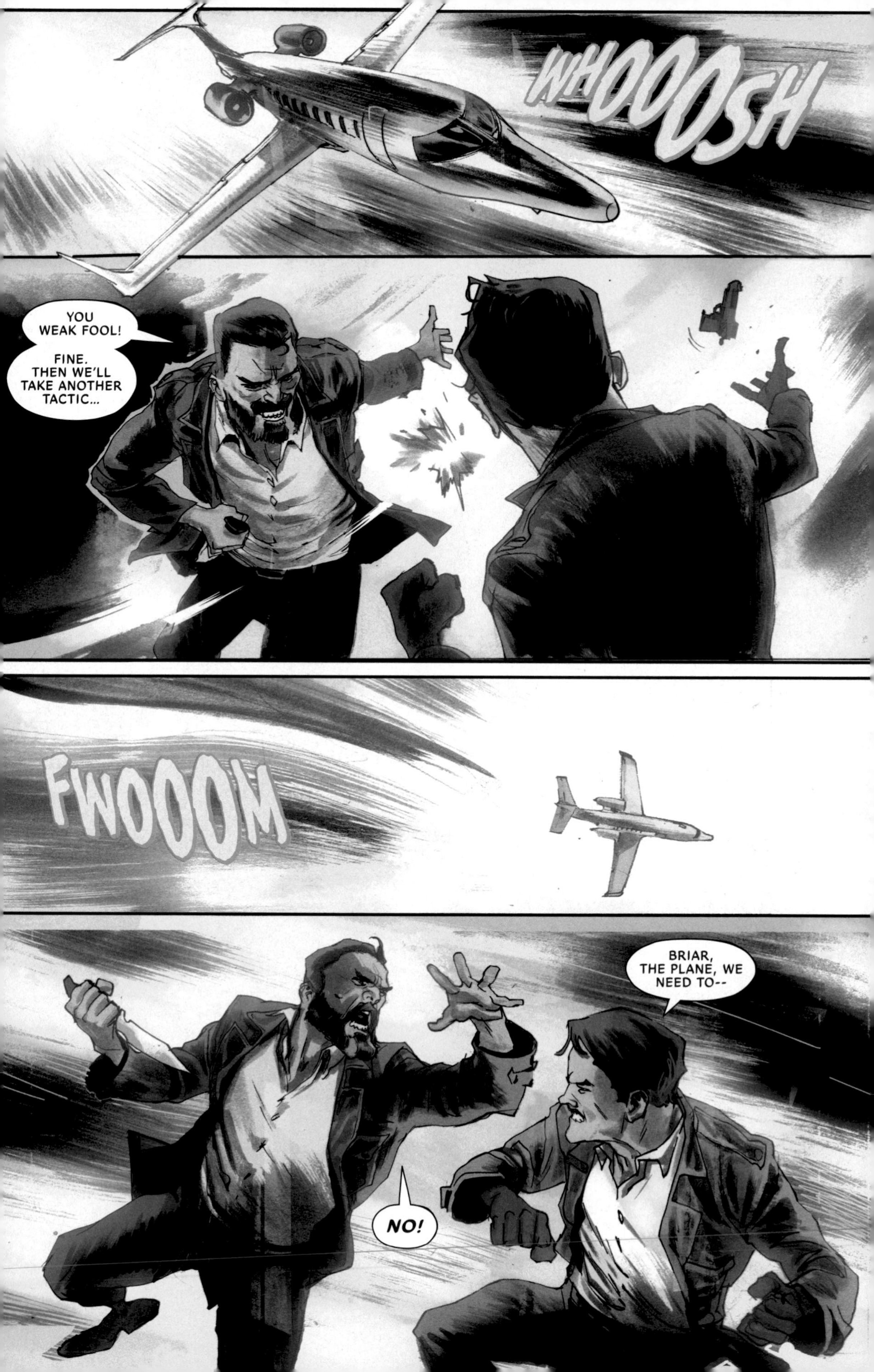
WHOOOOSH
YOU WEAK FOOL!
FINE. THEN WE'LL TAKE ANOTHER TACTIC...
FWOOOM
BRIAR, THE PLANE, WE NEED TO--
NO!

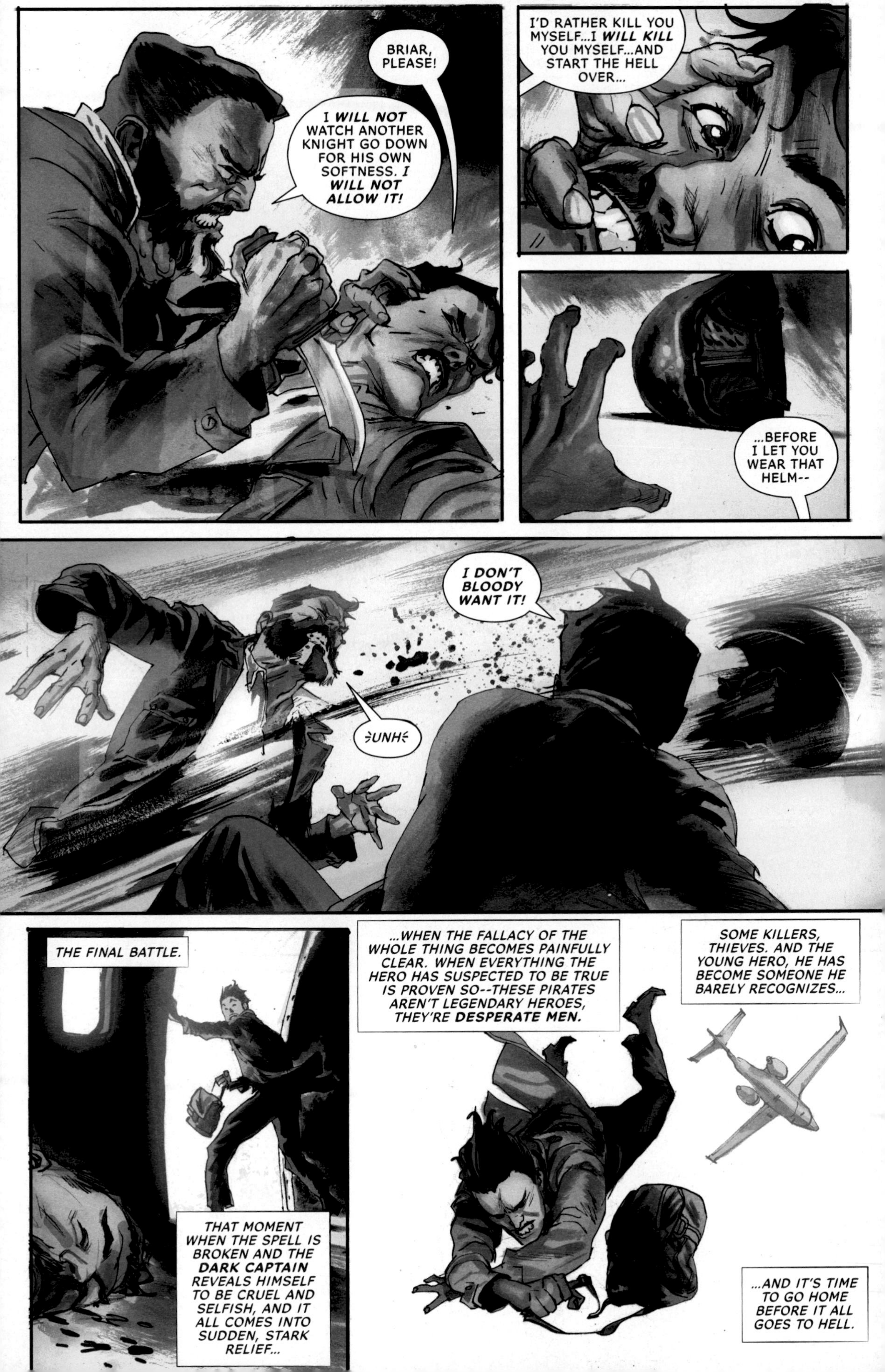
BRIAR, PLEASE!
I WILL NOT WATCH ANOTHER KNIGHT GO DOWN FOR HIS OWN SOFTNESS. I WILL NOT ALLOW IT!
I'D RATHER KILL YOU MYSELF...I WILL KILL YOU MYSELF...AND START THE HELL OVER...
...BEFORE I LET YOU WEAR THAT HELM--
I DON'T BLOODY WANT IT!
UNH
THE FINAL BATTLE.
THAT MOMENT WHEN THE SPELL IS BROKEN AND THE DARK CAPTAIN REVEALS HIMSELF TO BE CRUEL AND SELFISH, AND IT ALL COMES INTO SUDDEN, STARK RELIEF...
...WHEN THE FALLACY OF THE WHOLE THING BECOMES PAINFULLY CLEAR. WHEN EVERYTHING THE HERO HAS SUSPECTED TO BE TRUE IS PROVEN SO--THESE PIRATES AREN'T LEGENDARY HEROES, THEY'RE DESPERATE MEN.
SOME KILLERS, THIEVES. AND THE YOUNG HERO, HE HAS BECOME SOMEONE HE BARELY RECOGNIZES...
...AND IT'S TIME TO GO HOME BEFORE IT ALL GOES TO HELL.

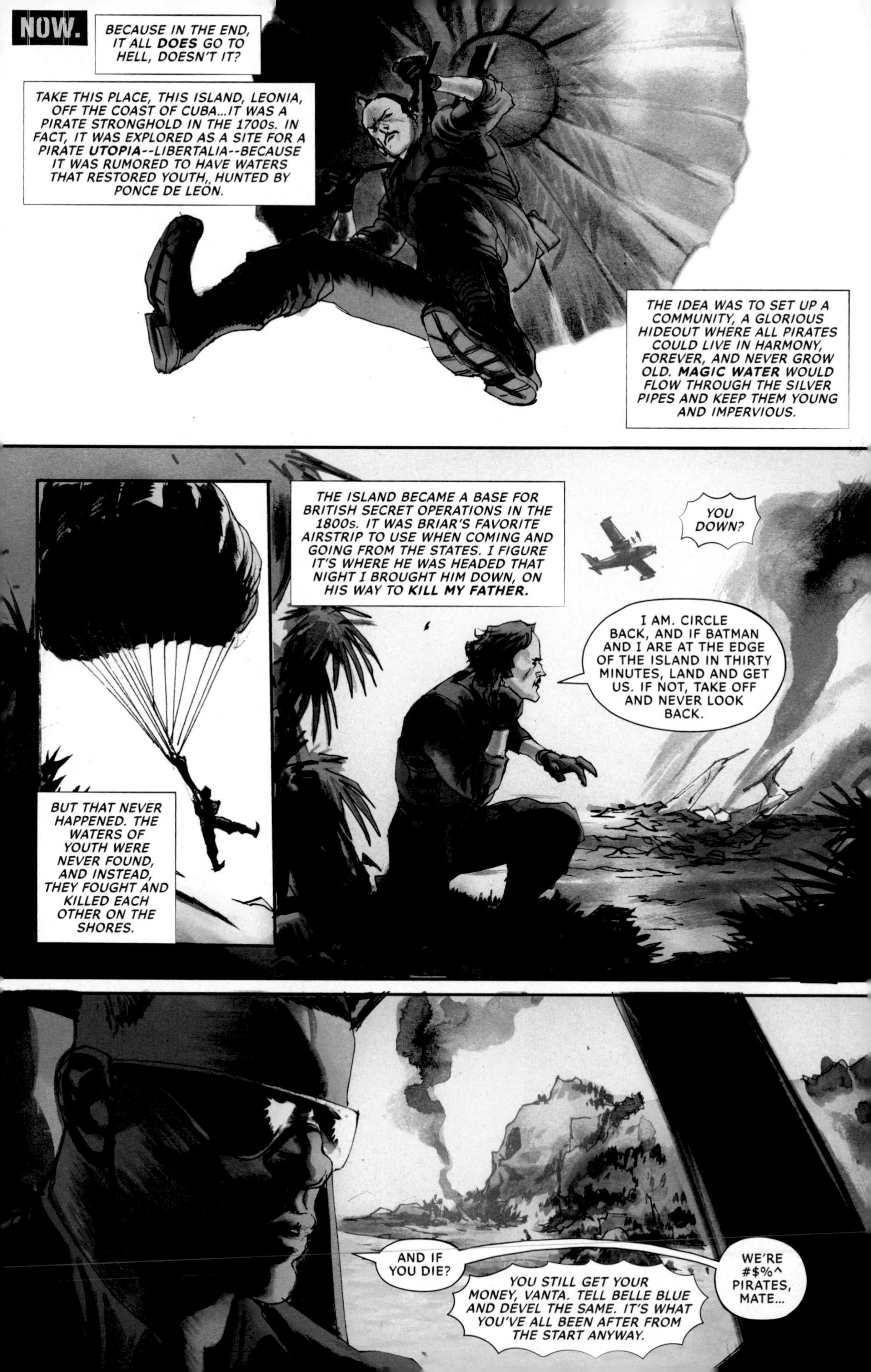
NOW.
BECAUSE IN THE END, IT ALL DOES GO TO HELL, DOESN'T IT?
TAKE THIS PLACE, THIS ISLAND, LEONIA, OFF THE COAST OF CUBA...IT WAS A PIRATE STRONGHOLD IN THE 1700s. IN FACT, IT WAS EXPLORED AS A SITE FOR A PIRATE UTOPIA--LIBERTALIA--BECAUSE IT WAS RUMORED TO HAVE WATERS THAT RESTORED YOUTH,, HUNTED BY PONCE DE LEÓN.
THE IDEA WAS TO SET UP A COMMUNITY, A GLORIOUS HIDEOUT WHERE ALL PIRATES COULD LIVE IN HARMONY, FOREVER, AND NEVER GROW OLD. MAGIC WATER WOULD FLOW THROUGH THE SILVER PIPES AND KEEP THEM YOUNG AND IMPERVIOUS.
BUT THAT NEVER HAPPENED. THE WATERS OF YOUTH WERE NEVER FOUND, AND INSTEAD, THEY FOUGHT AND KILLED EACH OTHER ON THE SHORES.
THE ISLAND BECAME A BASE FOR BRITISH SECRET OPERATIONS IN THE 1800s. IT WAS BRIAR'S FAVORITE AIRSTRIP TO USE WHEN COMING AND GOING FROM THE STATES. I FIGURE IT'S WHERE HE WAS HEADED THAT NIGHT I BROUGHT HIM DOWN, ON HIS WAY TO KILL MY FATHER.
YOU DOWN?
I AM. CIRCLE BACK, AND IF BATMAN AND I ARE AT THE EDGE OF THE ISLAND IN THIRTY MINUTES, LAND AND GET US. IF NOT, TAKE OFF AND NEVER LOOK BACK.
AND IF YOU DIE?
YOU STILL GET YOUR MONEY, VANTA. TELL BELLE BLUE AND DEVEL THE SAME. IT'S WHAT YOU'VE ALL BEEN AFTER FROM THE START ANYWAY.
WE'RE #$%^ PIRATES, MATE...

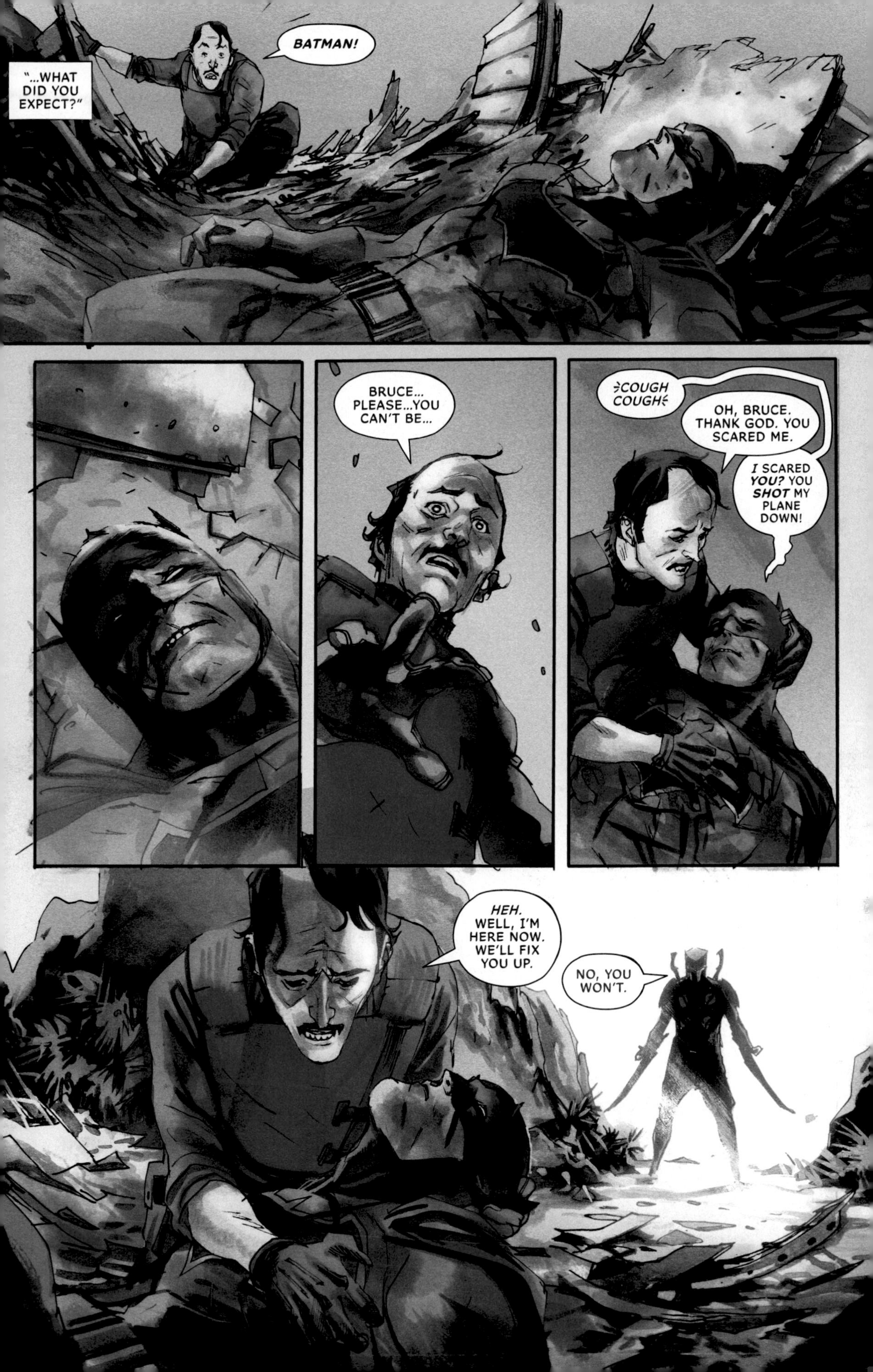
"...WHAT DID YOU EXPECT?"
BATMAN!
BRUCE... PLEASE...YOU CAN'T BE...
COUGH COUGH
OH, BRUCE. THANK GOD. YOU SCARED ME.
I SCARED YOU? YOU SHOT MY PLANE DOWN!
HEH. WELL, I'M HERE NOW. WE'LL FIX YOU UP.
NO, YOU WON'T.

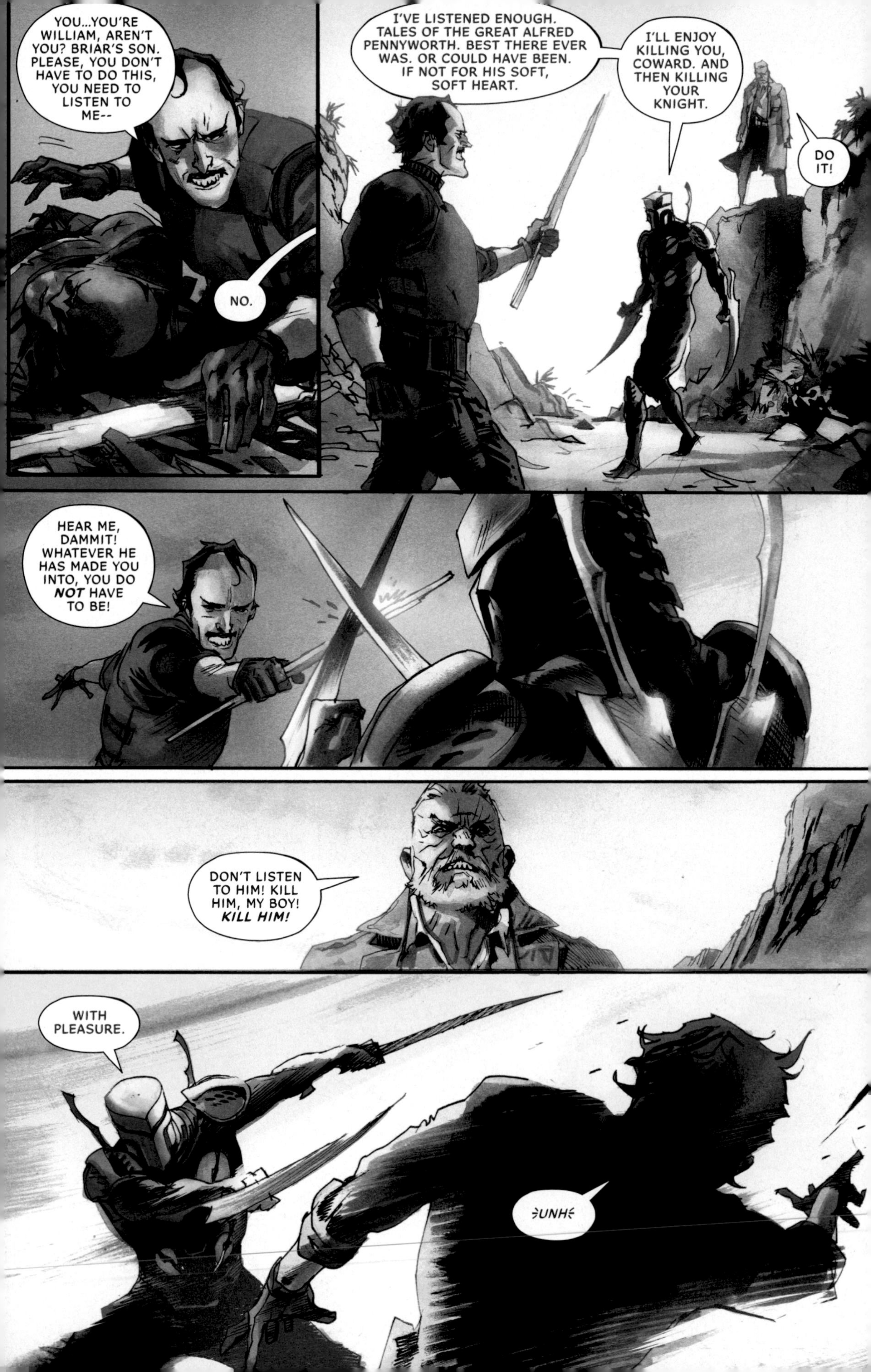
YOU...YOU'RE WILLIAM, AREN'T YOU? BRIAR'S SON. PLEASE, YOU DON'T HAVE TO DO THIS, YOU NEED TO LISTEN TO ME--
NO.
I'VE LISTENED ENOUGH. TALES OF THE GREAT ALFRED PENNYWORTH. BEST THERE EVER WAS. OR COULD HAVE BEEN. IF NOT FOR HIS SOFT, SOFT HEART.
I'LL ENJOY KILLING YOU, COWARD. AND THEN KILLING YOUR KNIGHT.
DO IT!
HEAR ME, DAMMIT! WHATEVER HE HAS MADE YOU INTO, YOU DO ***NOT*** HAVE TO BE!
DON'T LISTEN TO HIM! KILL HIM, MY BOY! ***KILL HIM!***
WITH PLEASURE.
UNH

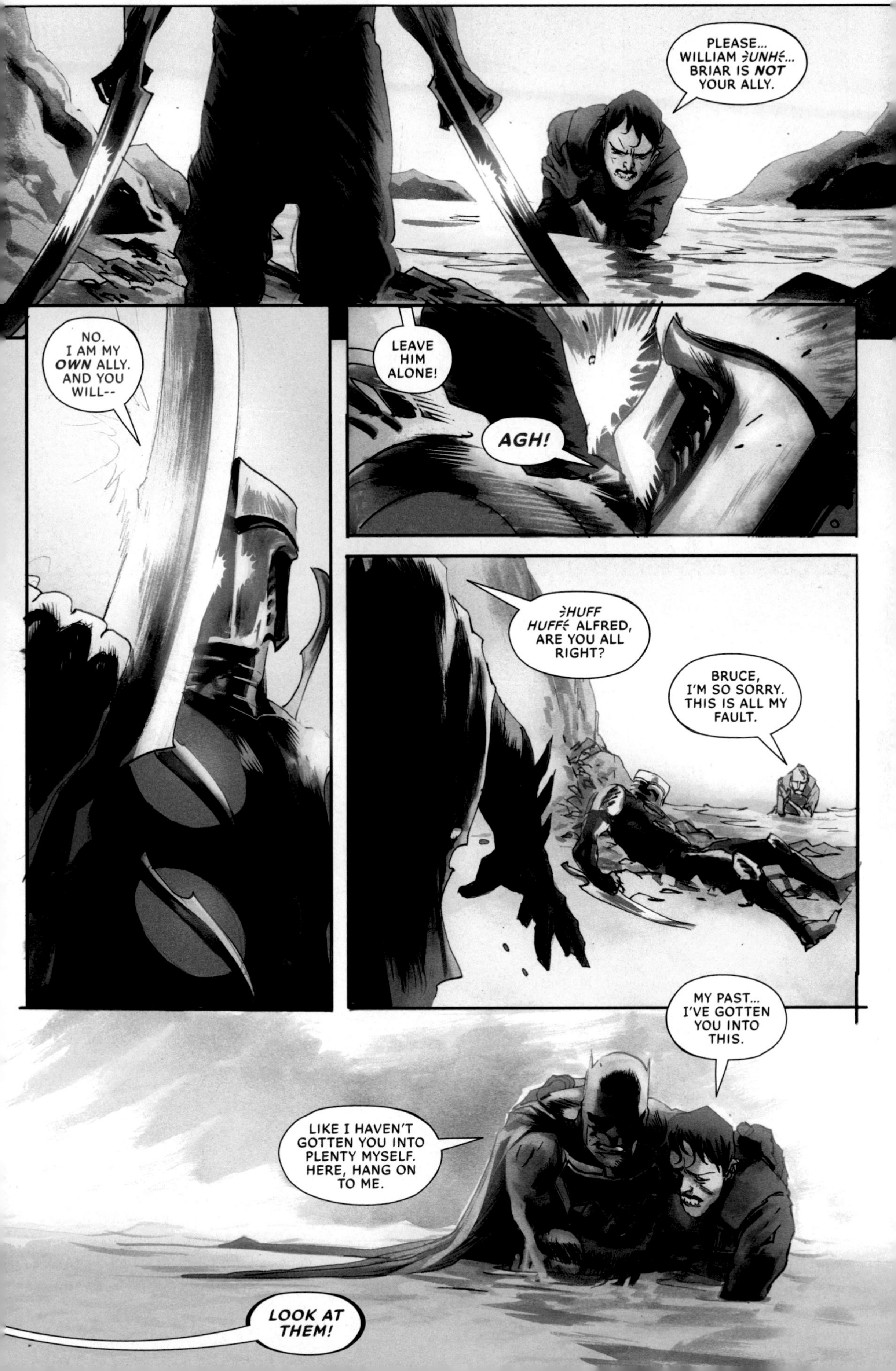
PLEASE... WILLIAM ⁓UNH⁓... BRIAR IS NOT YOUR ALLY.
NO. I AM MY OWN ALLY. AND YOU WILL--
LEAVE HIM ALONE!
AGH!
⁓HUFF HUFF⁓ ALFRED, ARE YOU ALL RIGHT?
BRUCE, I'M SO SORRY. THIS IS ALL MY FAULT.
MY PAST... I'VE GOTTEN YOU INTO THIS.
LIKE I HAVEN'T GOTTEN YOU INTO PLENTY MYSELF. HERE, HANG ON TO ME.
LOOK AT THEM!

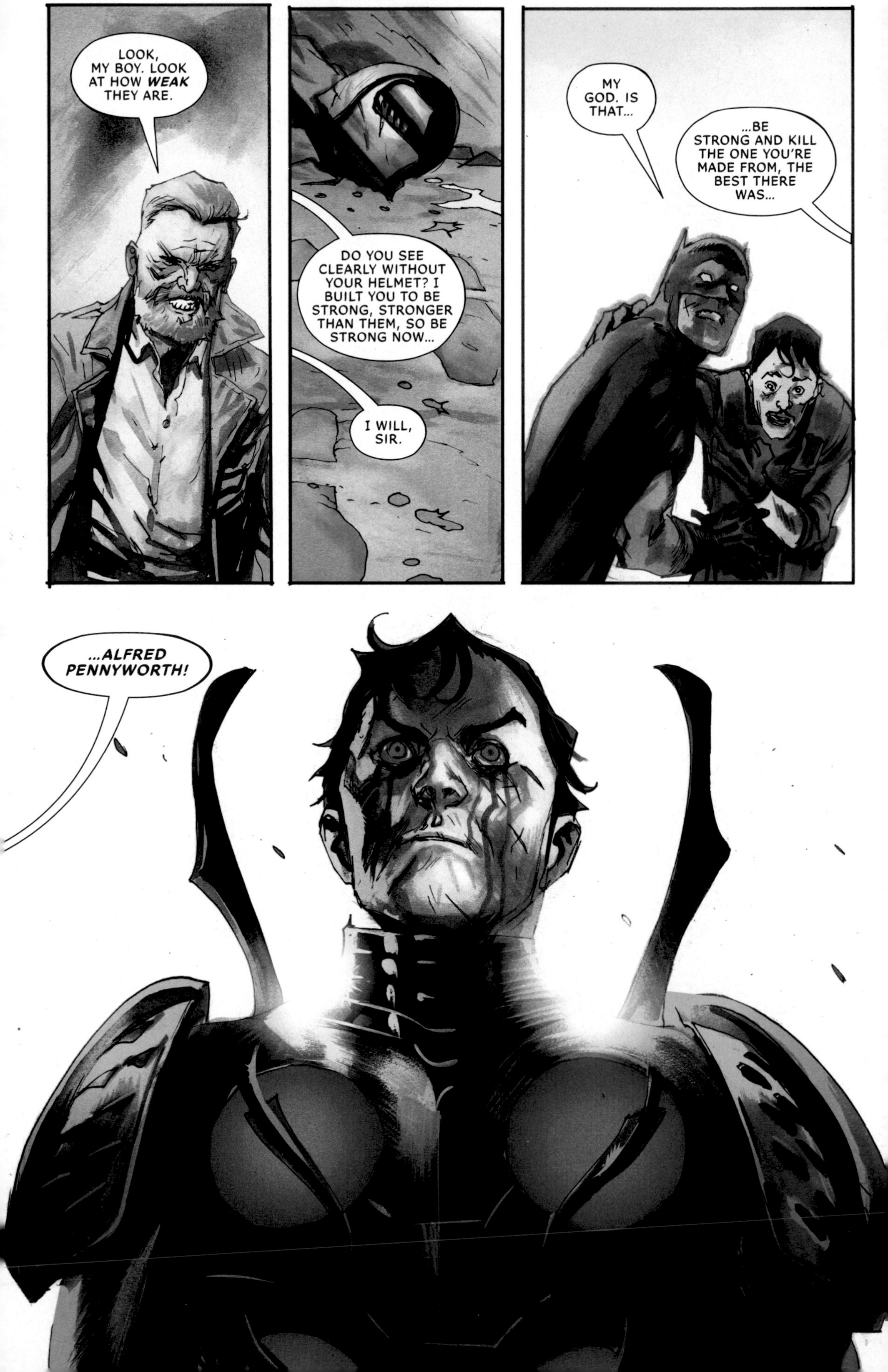
LOOK, MY BOY. LOOK AT HOW *WEAK* THEY ARE.
DO YOU SEE CLEARLY WITHOUT YOUR HELMET? I BUILT YOU TO BE STRONG, STRONGER THAN THEM, SO BE STRONG NOW...
I WILL, SIR.
MY GOD. IS THAT...
...BE STRONG AND KILL THE ONE YOU'RE MADE FROM, THE BEST THERE WAS...
...ALFRED PENNYWORTH!

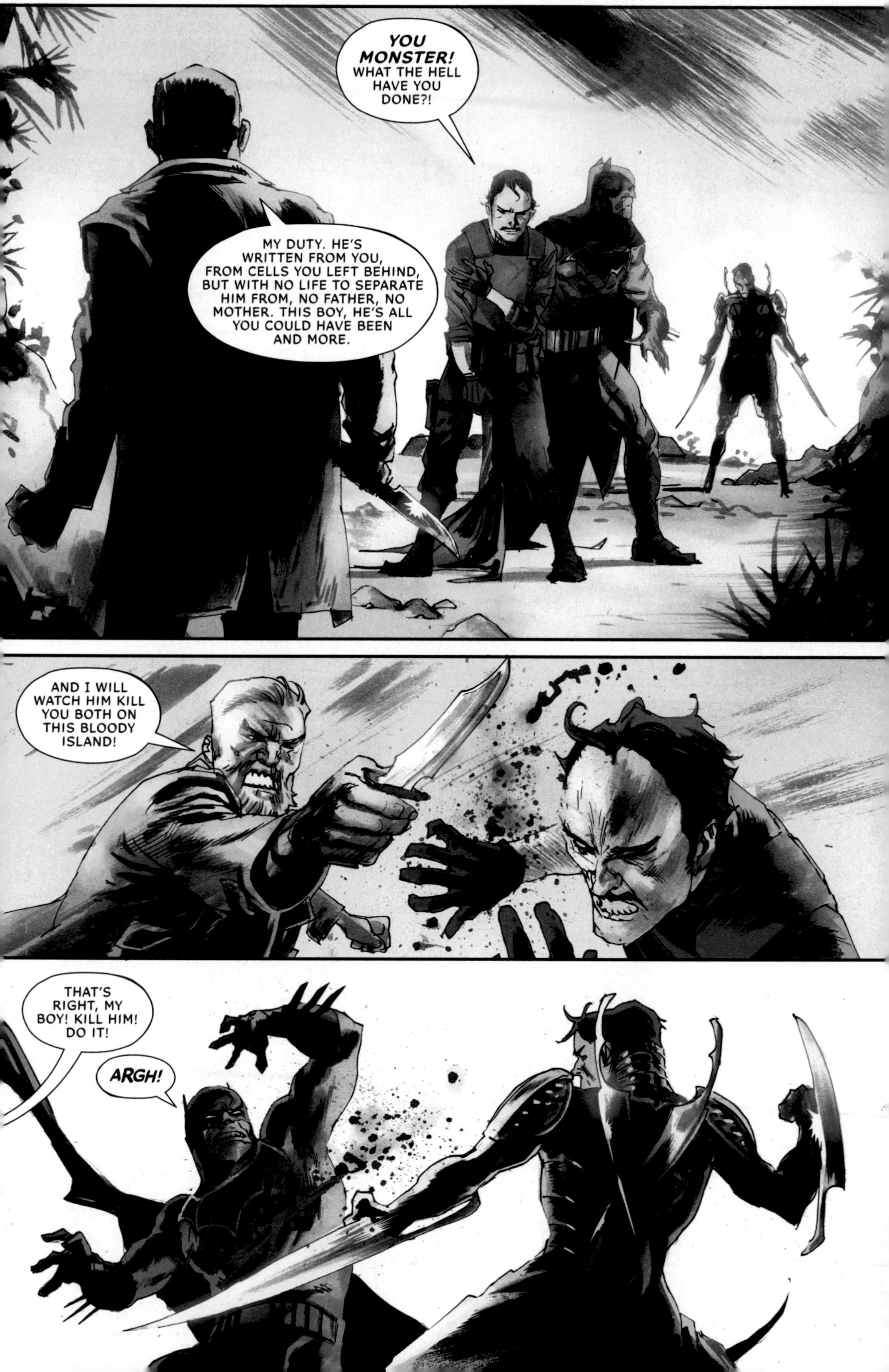
YOU MONSTER! WHAT THE HELL HAVE YOU DONE?!
MY DUTY. HE'S WRITTEN FROM YOU, FROM CELLS YOU LEFT BEHIND, BUT WITH NO LIFE TO SEPARATE HIM FROM, NO FATHER, NO MOTHER. THIS BOY, HE'S ALL YOU COULD HAVE BEEN AND MORE.
AND I WILL WATCH HIM KILL YOU BOTH ON THIS BLOODY ISLAND!
THAT'S RIGHT, MY BOY! KILL HIM! DO IT!
ARGH!

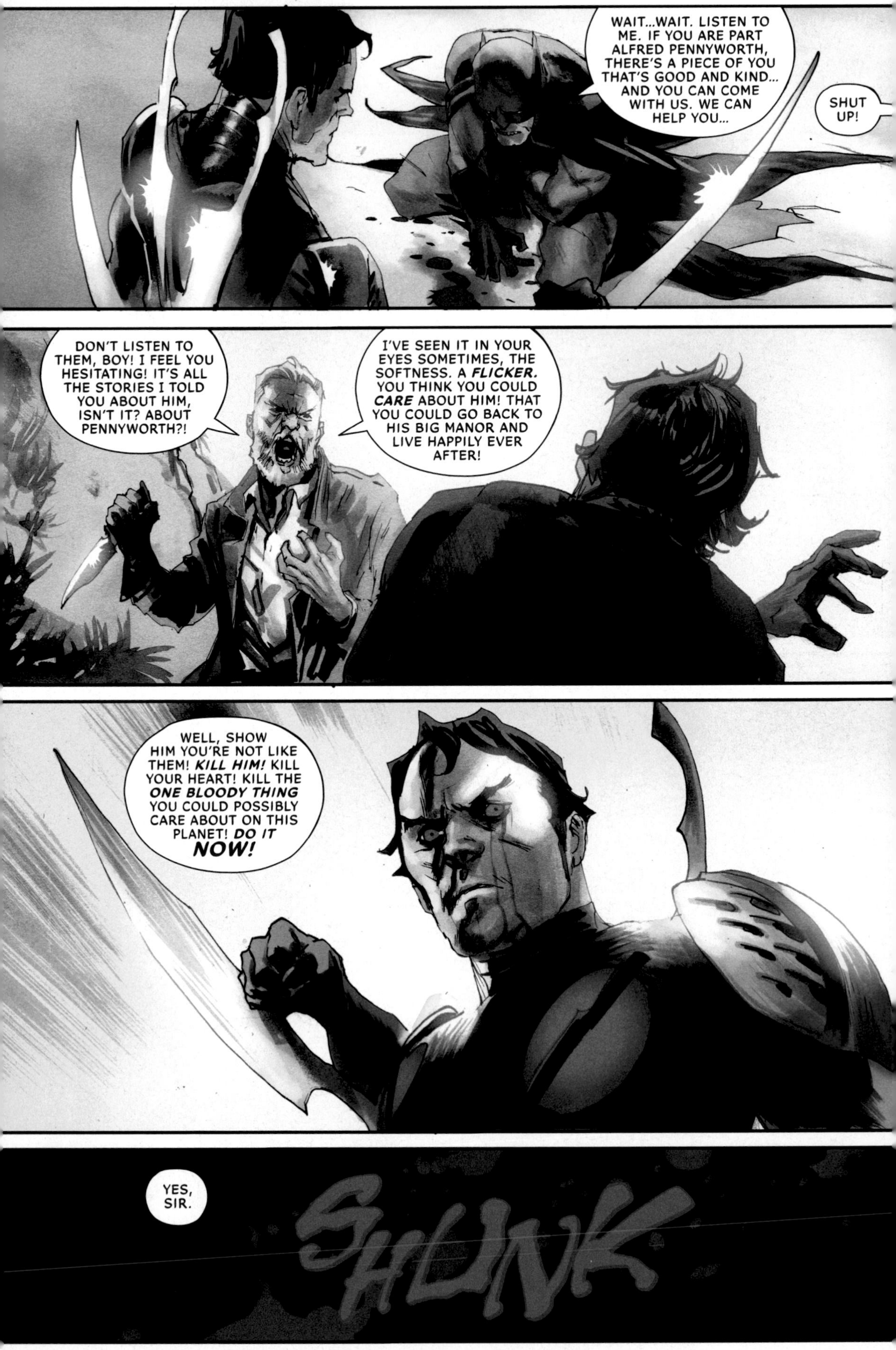
WAIT...WAIT. LISTEN TO ME. IF YOU ARE PART ALFRED PENNYWORTH, THERE'S A PIECE OF YOU THAT'S GOOD AND KIND... AND YOU CAN COME WITH US. WE CAN HELP YOU...
SHUT UP!
DON'T LISTEN TO THEM, BOY! I FEEL YOU HESITATING! IT'S ALL THE STORIES I TOLD YOU ABOUT HIM, ISN'T IT? ABOUT PENNYWORTH?!
I'VE SEEN IT IN YOUR EYES SOMETIMES, THE SOFTNESS. A *FLICKER.* YOU THINK YOU COULD *CARE* ABOUT HIM! THAT YOU COULD GO BACK TO HIS BIG MANOR AND LIVE HAPPILY EVER AFTER!
WELL, SHOW HIM YOU'RE NOT LIKE THEM! ***KILL HIM!*** KILL YOUR HEART! KILL THE ***ONE BLOODY THING*** YOU COULD POSSIBLY CARE ABOUT ON THIS PLANET! ***DO IT NOW!***
YES, SIR.
SHUNK

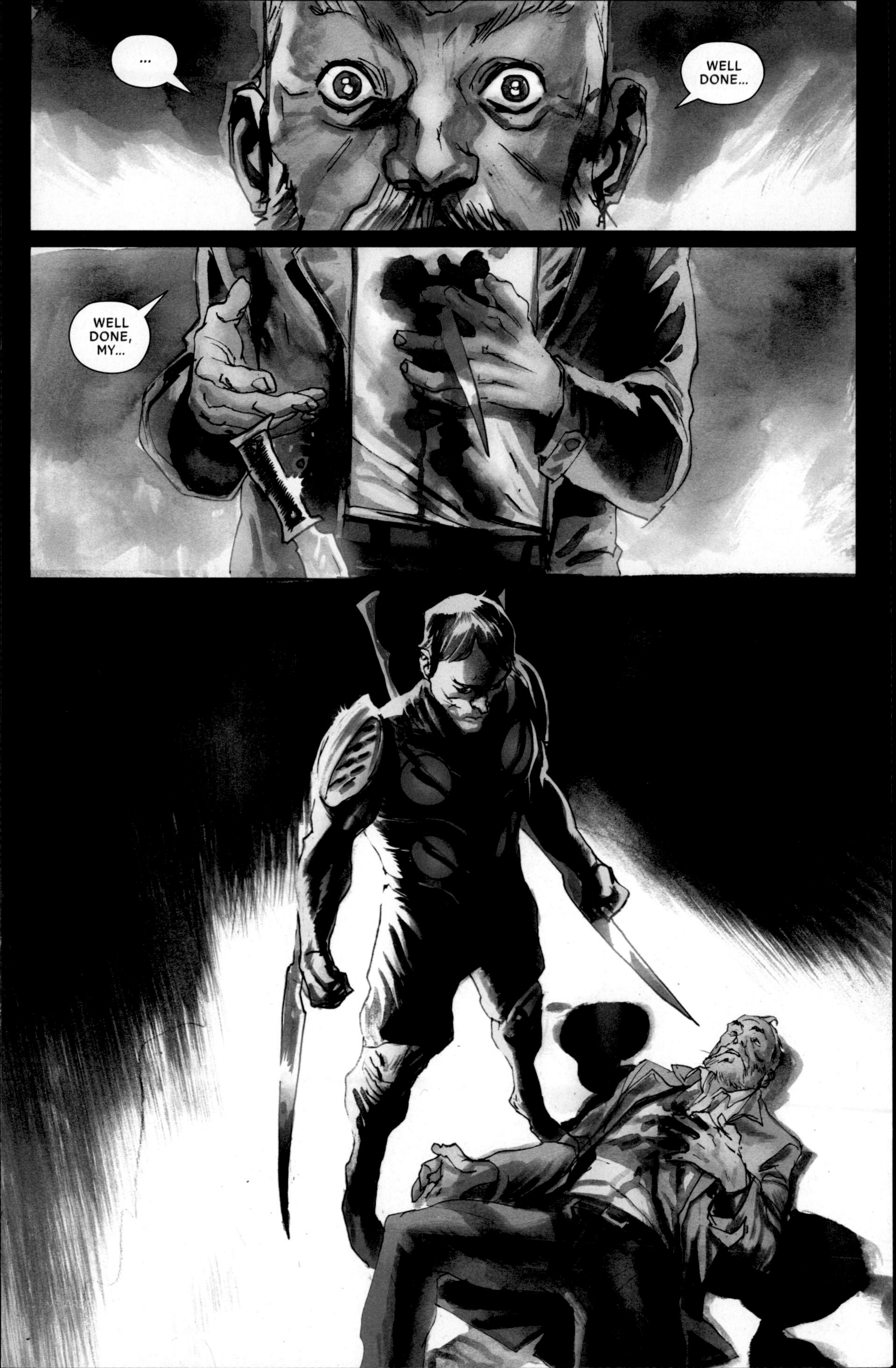
...
WELL DONE...
WELL DONE, MY...

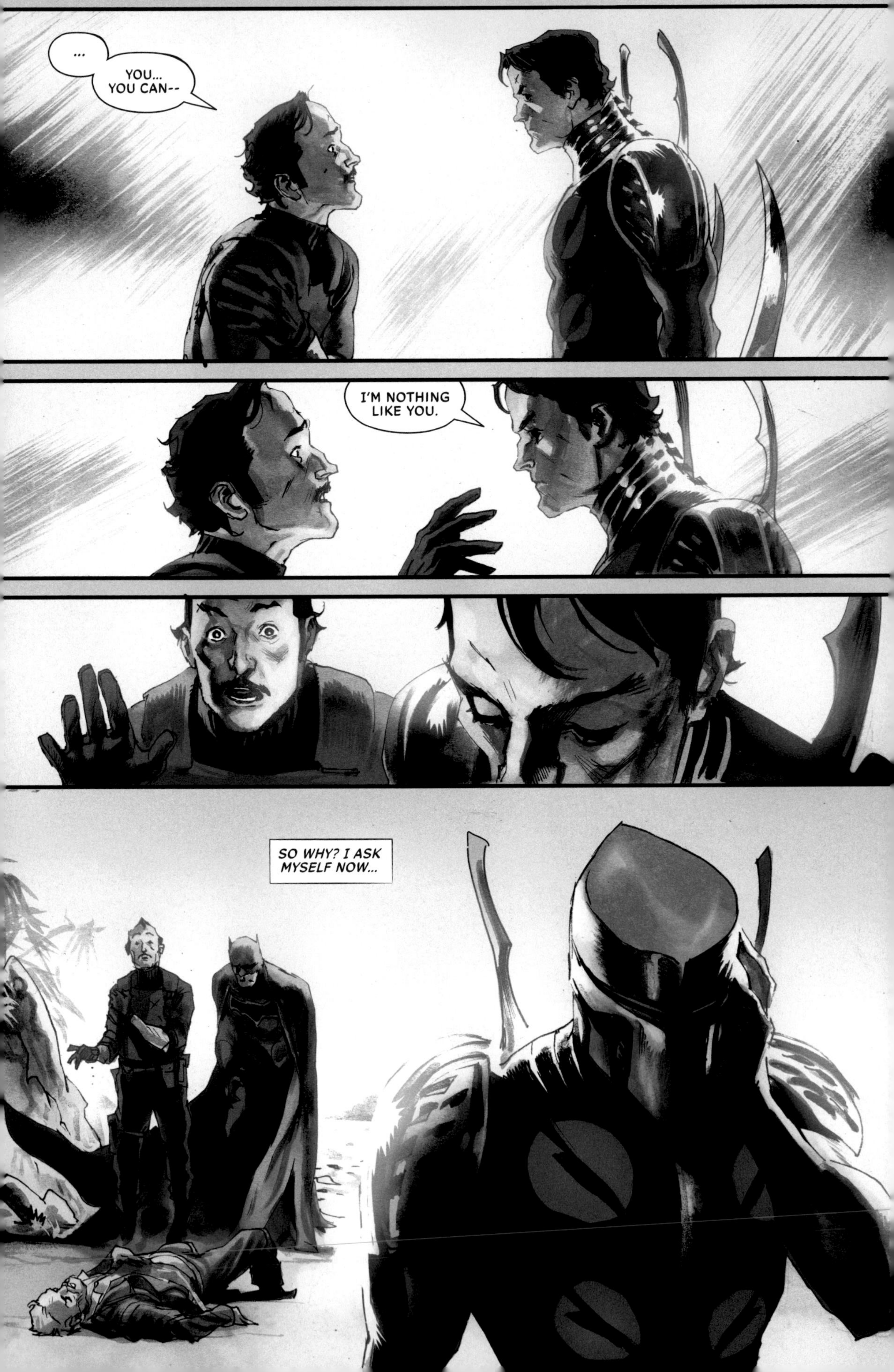
...
YOU... YOU CAN--
I'M NOTHING LIKE YOU.
SO WHY? I ASK MYSELF NOW...

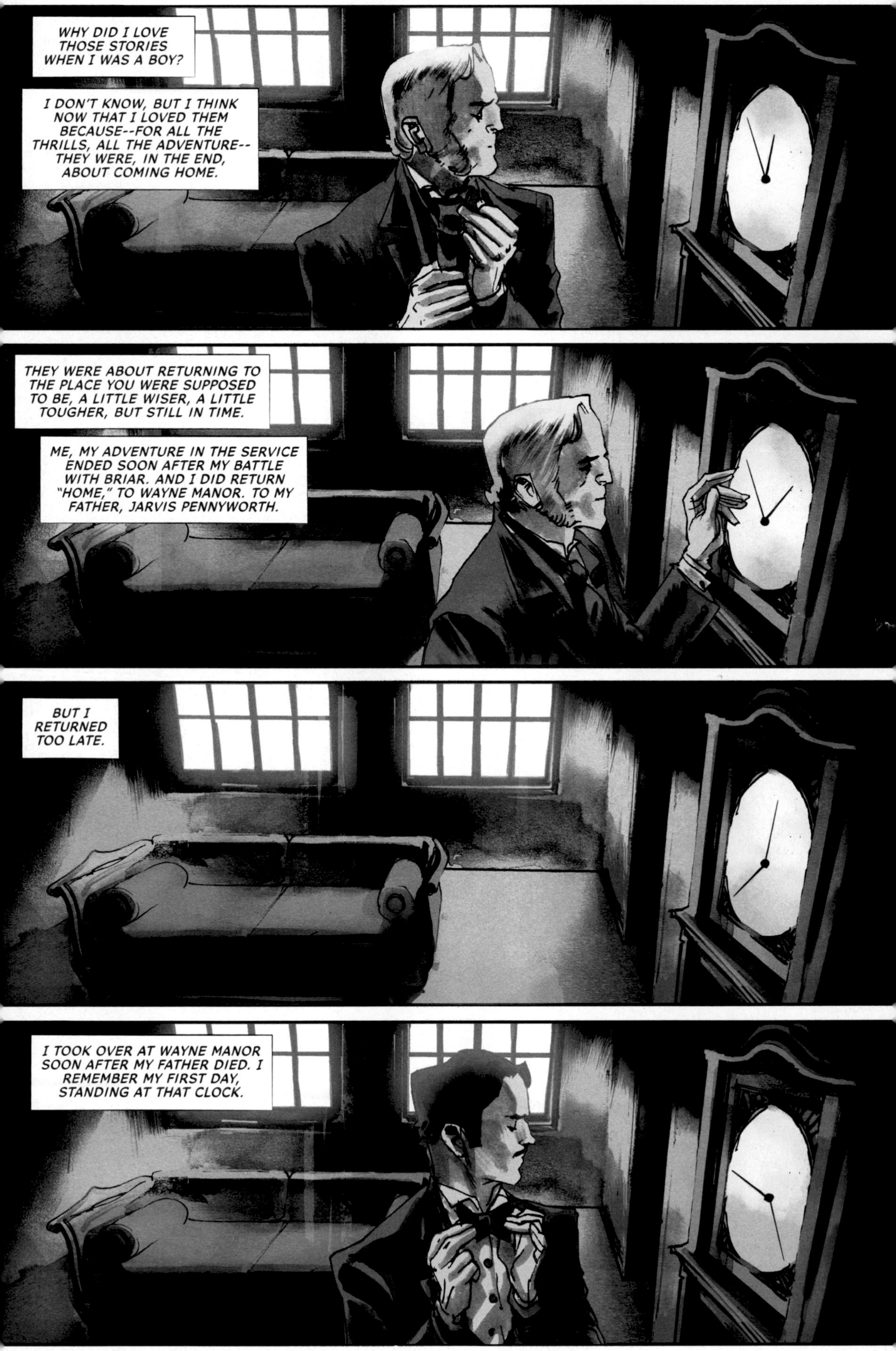
WHY DID I LOVE THOSE STORIES WHEN I WAS A BOY?
I DON'T KNOW, BUT I THINK NOW THAT I LOVED THEM BECAUSE--FOR ALL THE THRILLS, ALL THE ADVENTURE--THEY WERE, IN THE END, ABOUT COMING HOME.
THEY WERE ABOUT RETURNING TO THE PLACE YOU WERE SUPPOSED TO BE, A LITTLE WISER, A LITTLE TOUGHER, BUT STILL IN TIME.
ME, MY ADVENTURE IN THE SERVICE ENDED SOON AFTER MY BATTLE WITH BRIAR. AND I DID RETURN "HOME," TO WAYNE MANOR. TO MY FATHER, JARVIS PENNYWORTH.
BUT I RETURNED TOO LATE.
I TOOK OVER AT WAYNE MANOR SOON AFTER MY FATHER DIED. I REMEMBER MY FIRST DAY, STANDING AT THAT CLOCK.

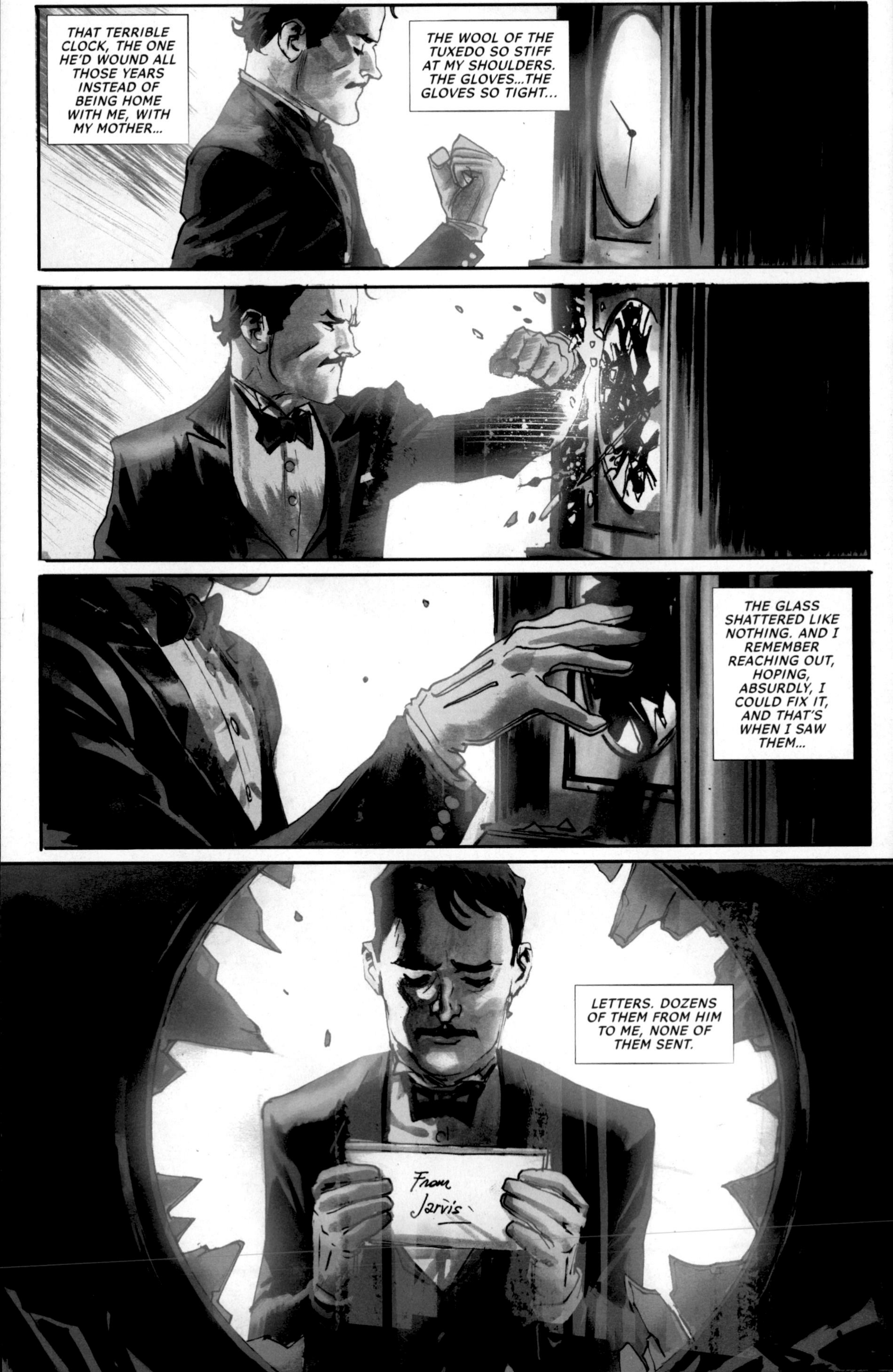
THAT TERRIBLE CLOCK, THE ONE HE'D WOUND ALL THOSE YEARS INSTEAD OF BEING HOME WITH ME, WITH MY MOTHER...
THE WOOL OF THE TUXEDO SO STIFF AT MY SHOULDERS. THE GLOVES...THE GLOVES SO TIGHT...
THE GLASS SHATTERED LIKE NOTHING. AND I REMEMBER REACHING OUT, HOPING, ABSURDLY, I COULD FIX IT, AND THAT'S WHEN I SAW THEM...
LETTERS. DOZENS OF THEM FROM HIM TO ME, NONE OF THEM SENT.
From Jarvis

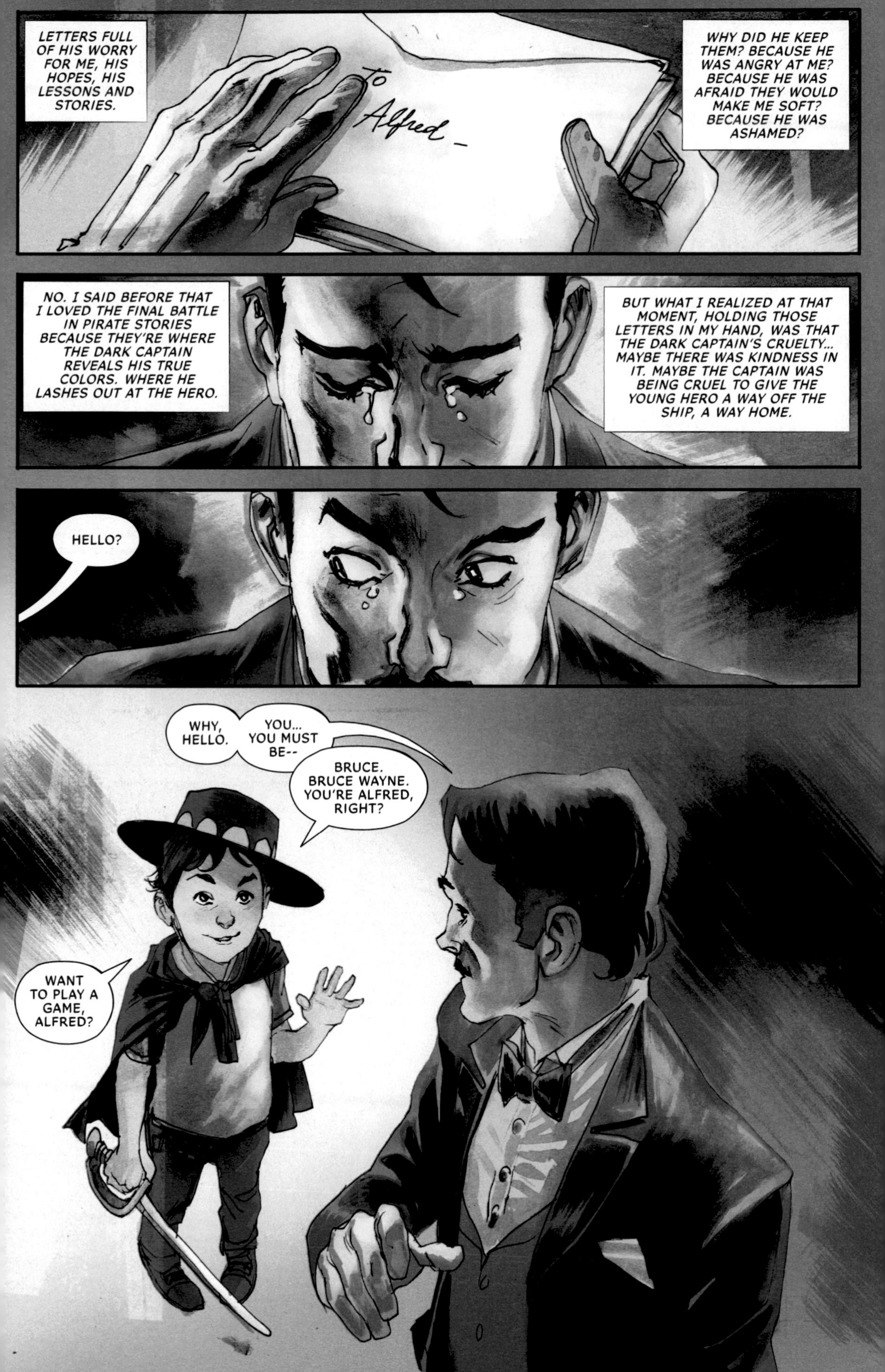
LETTERS FULL OF HIS WORRY FOR ME, HIS HOPES, HIS LESSONS AND STORIES.
To Alfred -
WHY DID HE KEEP THEM? BECAUSE HE WAS ANGRY AT ME? BECAUSE HE WAS AFRAID THEY WOULD MAKE ME SOFT? BECAUSE HE WAS ASHAMED?
NO. I SAID BEFORE THAT I LOVED THE FINAL BATTLE IN PIRATE STORIES BECAUSE THEY'RE WHERE THE DARK CAPTAIN REVEALS HIS TRUE COLORS. WHERE HE LASHES OUT AT THE HERO.
BUT WHAT I REALIZED AT THAT MOMENT, HOLDING THOSE LETTERS IN MY HAND, WAS THAT THE DARK CAPTAIN'S CRUELTY... MAYBE THERE WAS KINDNESS IN IT. MAYBE THE CAPTAIN WAS BEING CRUEL TO GIVE THE YOUNG HERO A WAY OFF THE SHIP, A WAY HOME.
HELLO?
WHY, HELLO.
YOU... YOU MUST BE--
BRUCE. BRUCE WAYNE. YOU'RE ALFRED, RIGHT?
WANT TO PLAY A GAME, ALFRED?

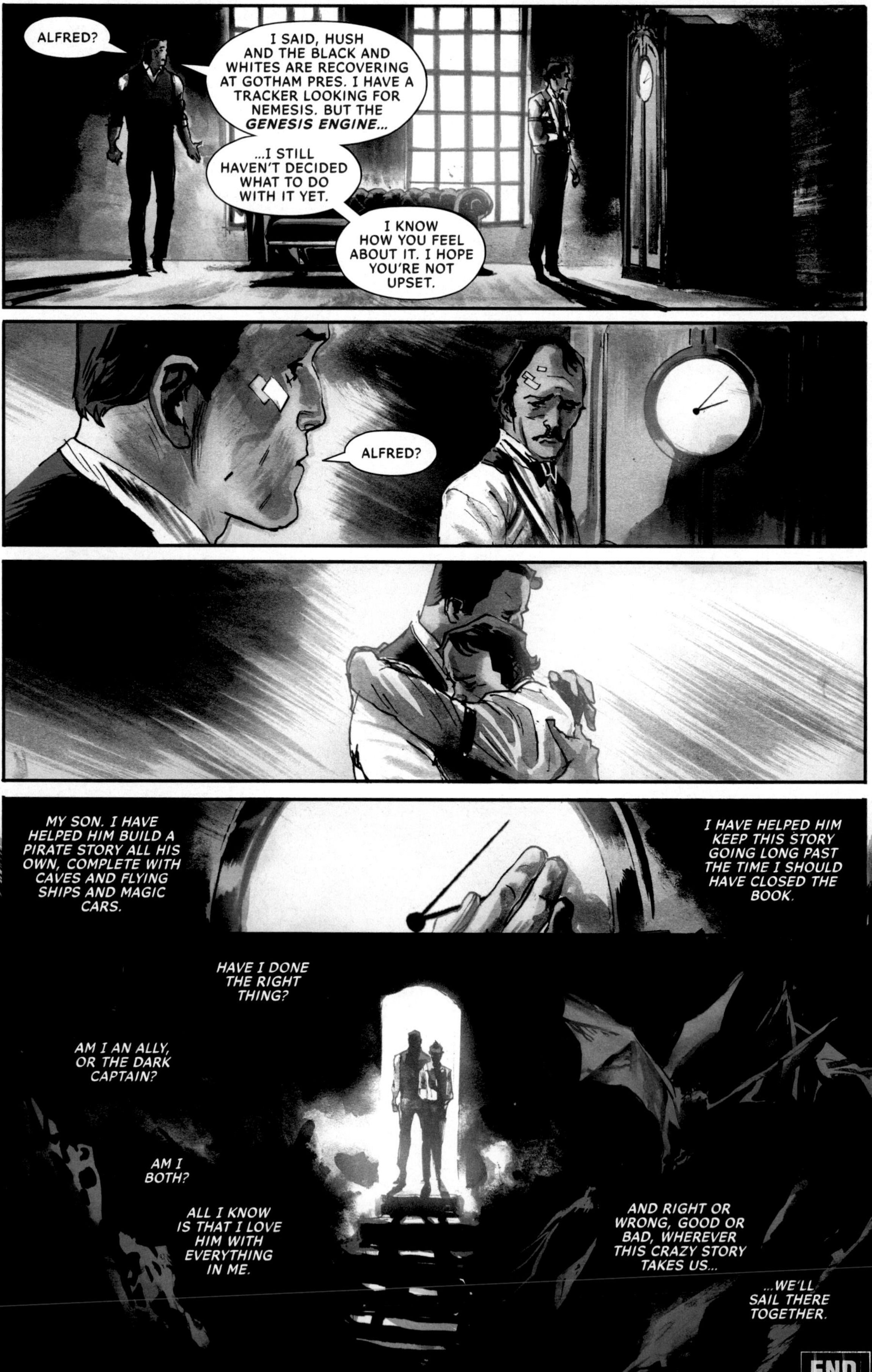
ALFRED?
I SAID, HUSH AND THE BLACK AND WHITES ARE RECOVERING AT GOTHAM PRES. I HAVE A TRACKER LOOKING FOR NEMESIS. BUT THE *GENESIS ENGINE...*
...I STILL HAVEN'T DECIDED WHAT TO DO WITH IT YET.
I KNOW HOW YOU FEEL ABOUT IT. I HOPE YOU'RE NOT UPSET.
ALFRED?
MY SON. I HAVE HELPED HIM BUILD A PIRATE STORY ALL HIS OWN, COMPLETE WITH CAVES AND FLYING SHIPS AND MAGIC CARS.
I HAVE HELPED HIM KEEP THIS STORY GOING LONG PAST THE TIME I SHOULD HAVE CLOSED THE BOOK.
HAVE I DONE THE RIGHT THING?
AM I AN ALLY, OR THE DARK CAPTAIN?
AM I BOTH?
ALL I KNOW IS THAT I LOVE HIM WITH EVERYTHING IN ME.
AND RIGHT OR WRONG, GOOD OR BAD, WHEREVER THIS CRAZY STORY TAKES US...
...WE'LL SAIL THERE TOGETHER.
END

MY NAME IS ALEXEY NOKAUT, BUT YOU CAN CALL ME *KNOCKOUT*-- OUTTA *RESPECT.*

I GREW UP AROUND TROUBLE-- MOSTLY CAUSING IT.

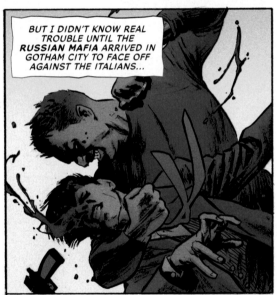

BUT I DIDN'T KNOW REAL TROUBLE UNTIL THE **RUSSIAN MAFIA** ARRIVED IN GOTHAM CITY TO FACE OFF AGAINST THE ITALIANS...

...AND TAKE THEIR SHARE.

SO I JOINED MY COUSINS IN "THE BROTHERHOOD."

ALSO KNOWN AS "THIEVES-IN-LAW."

I DID REALLY GOOD WORK FOR THEM--I HAD A **TALENT** FOR IT.

AND I LOVED IT.

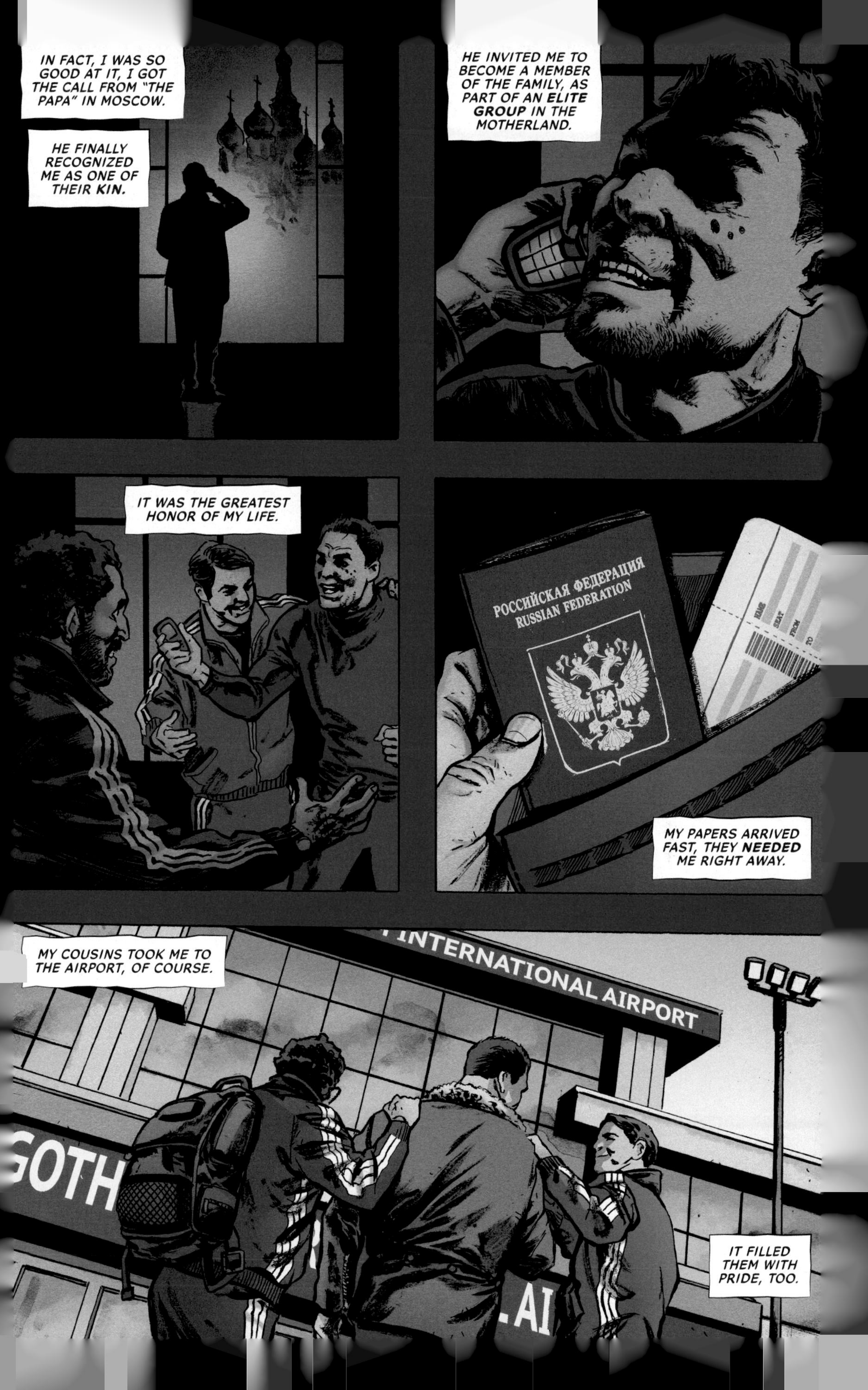
IN FACT, I WAS SO GOOD AT IT, I GOT THE CALL FROM "THE PAPA" IN MOSCOW.
HE FINALLY RECOGNIZED ME AS ONE OF THEIR KIN.
HE INVITED ME TO BECOME A MEMBER OF THE FAMILY, AS PART OF AN ELITE GROUP IN THE MOTHERLAND.
IT WAS THE GREATEST HONOR OF MY LIFE.
РОССИЙСКАЯ ФЕДЕРАЦИЯ
RUSSIAN FEDERATION
MY PAPERS ARRIVED FAST, THEY NEEDED ME RIGHT AWAY.
MY COUSINS TOOK ME TO THE AIRPORT, OF COURSE.
INTERNATIONAL AIRPORT
GOTH
IT FILLED THEM WITH PRIDE, TOO.

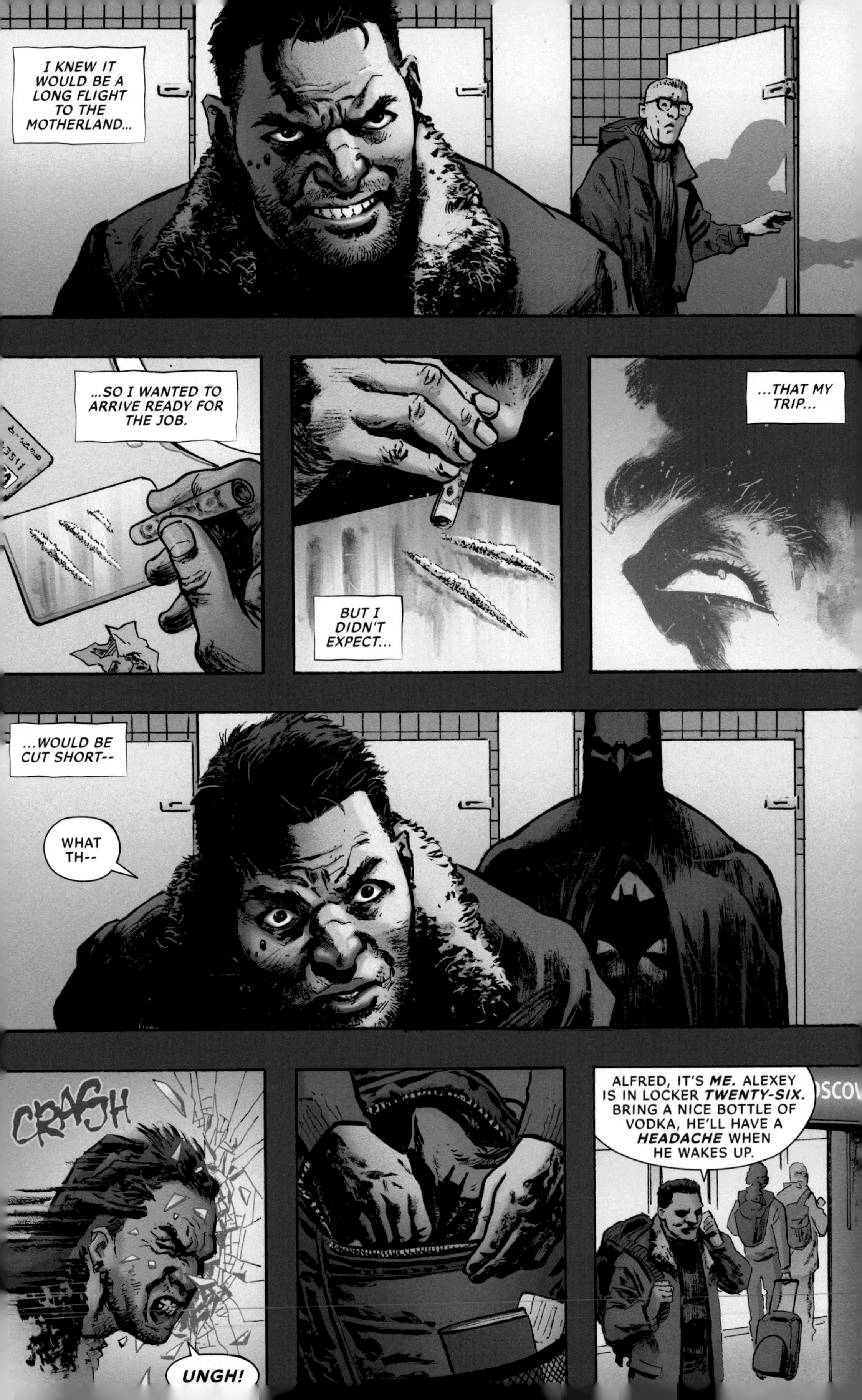
I KNEW IT WOULD BE A LONG FLIGHT TO THE MOTHERLAND...
...SO I WANTED TO ARRIVE READY FOR THE JOB.
BUT I DIDN'T EXPECT...
...THAT MY TRIP...
...WOULD BE CUT SHORT--
WHAT TH--
CRASH
UNGH!
ALFRED, IT'S ME. ALEXEY IS IN LOCKER TWENTY-SIX. BRING A NICE BOTTLE OF VODKA, HE'LL HAVE A HEADACHE WHEN HE WAKES UP.

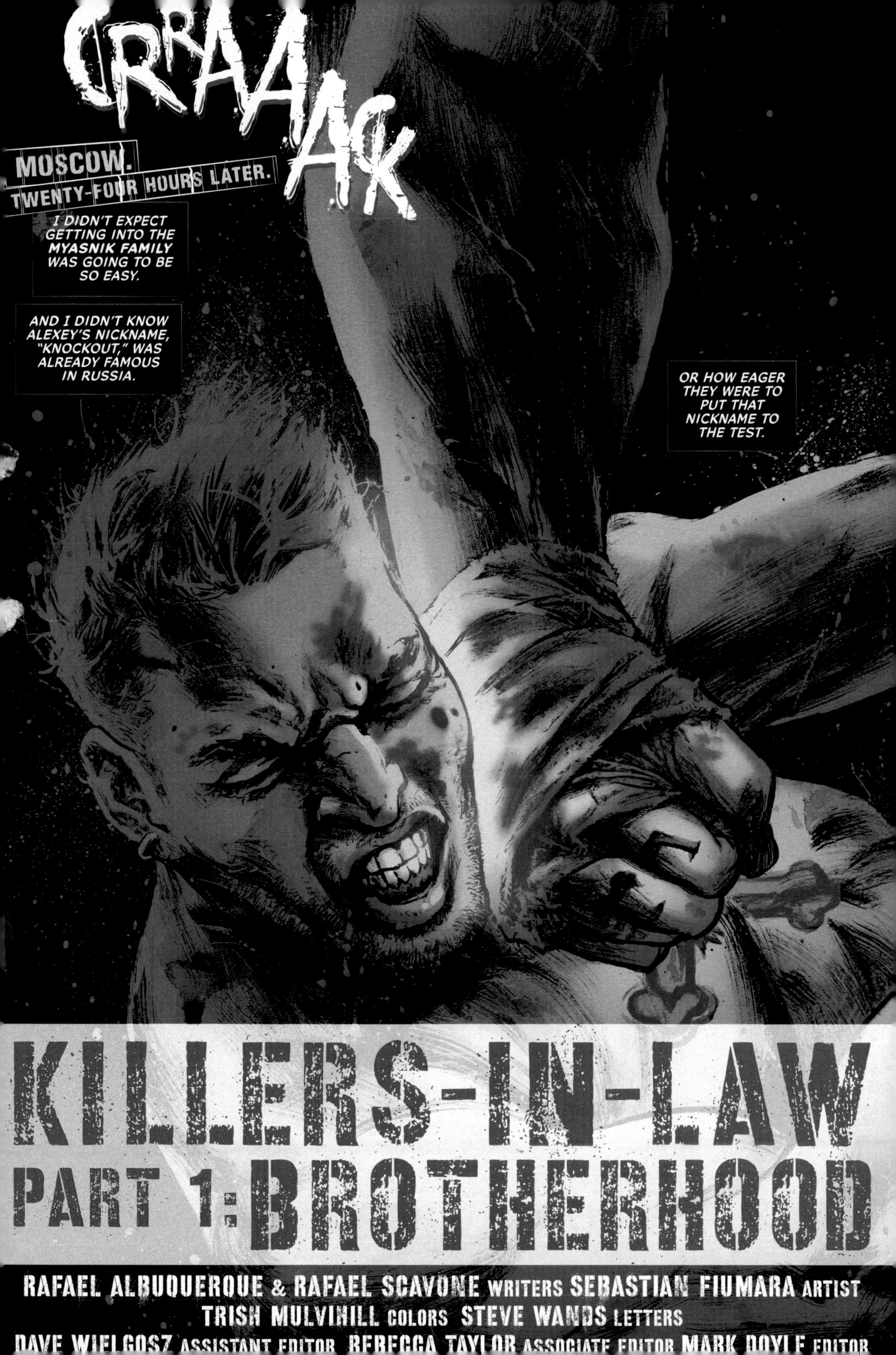
CRRAAACK
MOSCOW.
TWENTY-FOUR HOURS LATER.
I DIDN'T EXPECT GETTING INTO THE MYASNIK FAMILY WAS GOING TO BE SO EASY.
AND I DIDN'T KNOW ALEXEY'S NICKNAME, "KNOCKOUT," WAS ALREADY FAMOUS IN RUSSIA.
OR HOW EAGER THEY WERE TO PUT THAT NICKNAME TO THE TEST.
KILLERS-IN-LAW
PART 1: BROTHERHOOD
RAFAEL ALBUQUERQUE & RAFAEL SCAVONE WRITERS SEBASTIAN FIUMARA ARTIST
TRISH MULVIHILL COLORS STEVE WANDS LETTERS
DAVE WIELGOSZ ASSISTANT EDITOR REBECCA TAYLOR ASSOCIATE EDITOR MARK DOYLE EDITOR

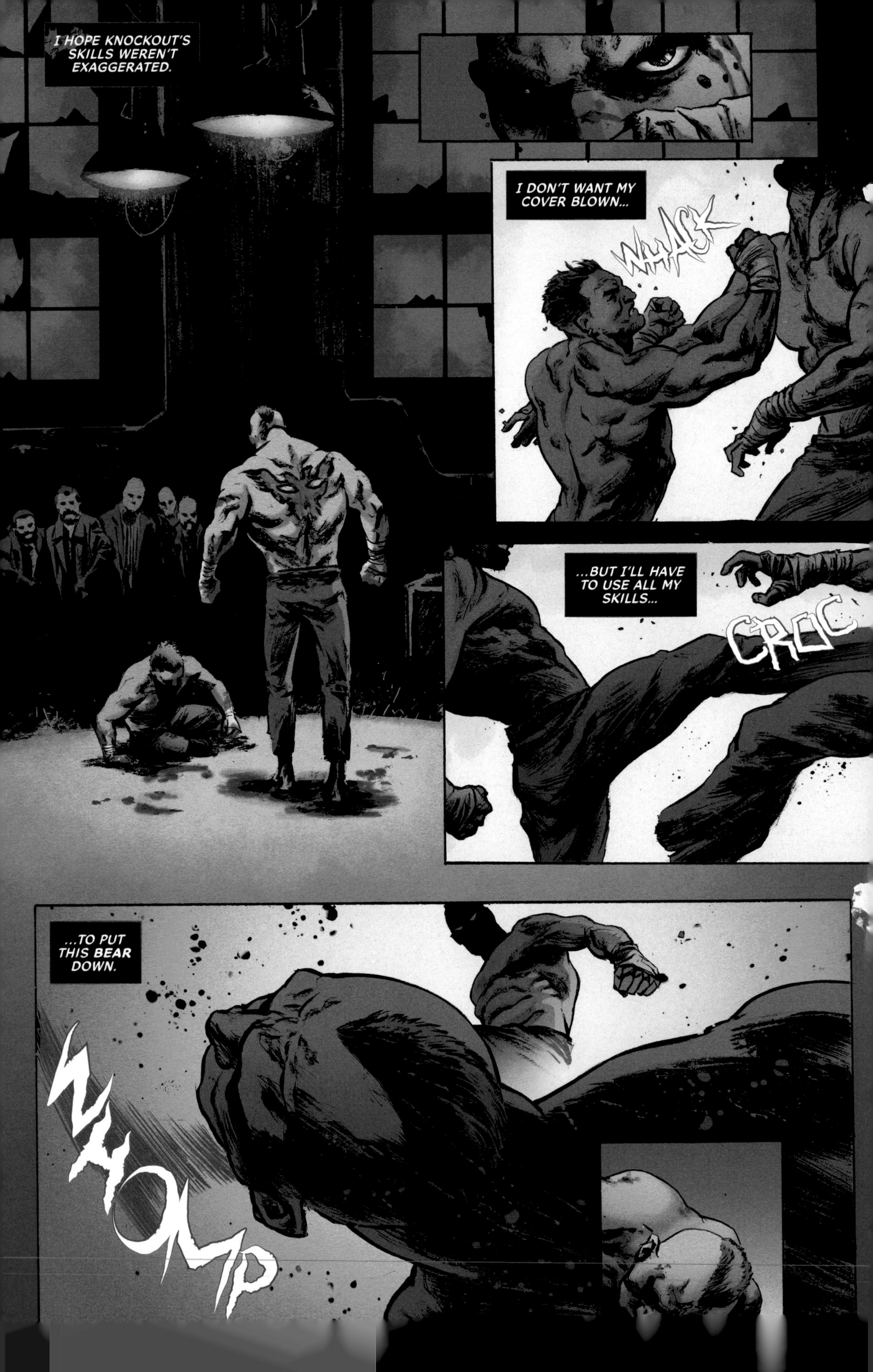
I HOPE KNOCKOUT'S SKILLS WEREN'T EXAGGERATED.
I DON'T WANT MY COVER BLOWN...
WHACK
...BUT I'LL HAVE TO USE ALL MY SKILLS...
CROC
...TO PUT THIS BEAR DOWN.
WHOMP

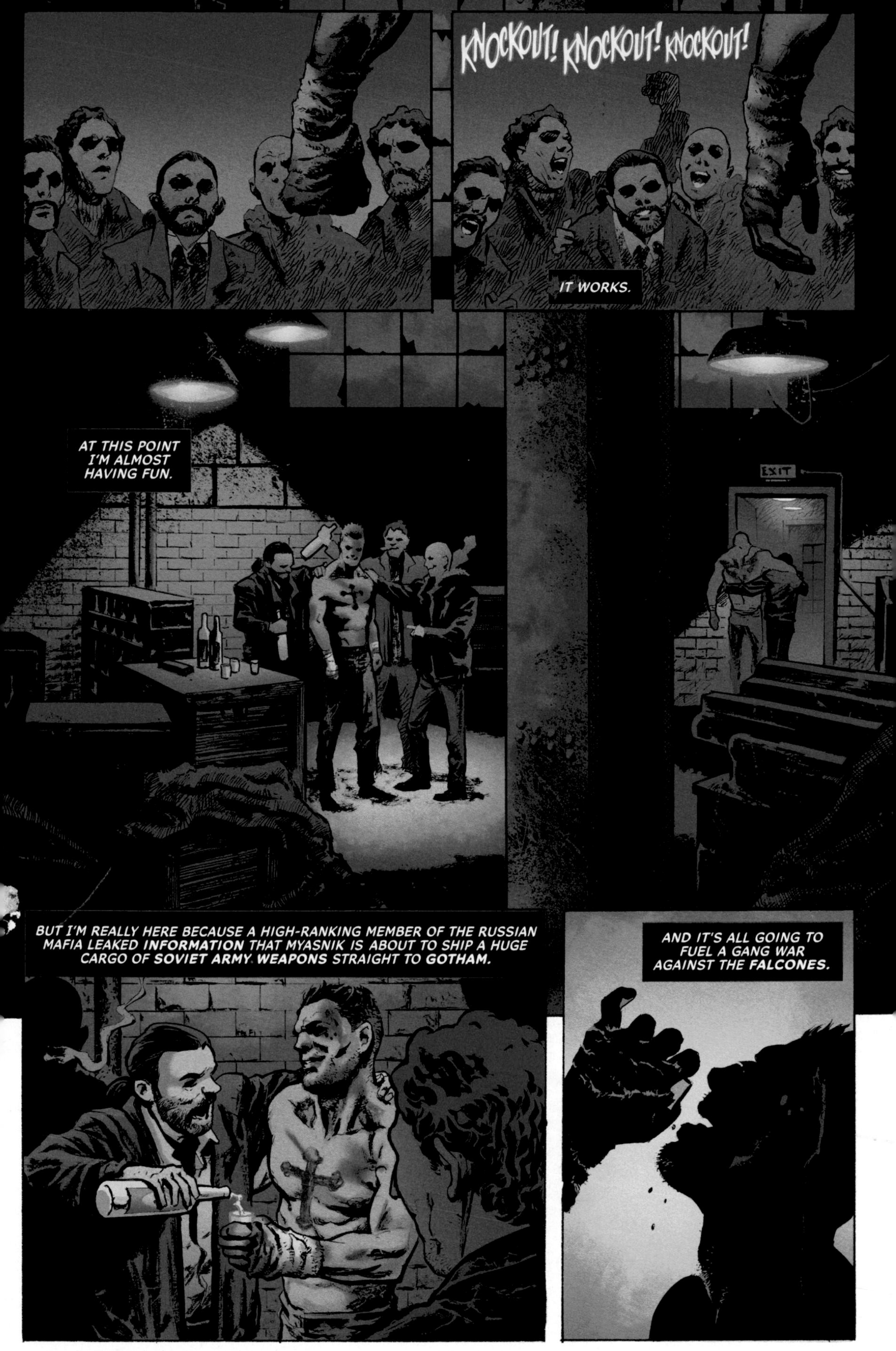
KNOCKOUT! KNOCKOUT! KNOCKOUT!
IT WORKS.
AT THIS POINT I'M ALMOST HAVING FUN.
EXIT
BUT I'M REALLY HERE BECAUSE A HIGH-RANKING MEMBER OF THE RUSSIAN MAFIA LEAKED INFORMATION THAT MYASNIK IS ABOUT TO SHIP A HUGE CARGO OF SOVIET ARMY WEAPONS STRAIGHT TO GOTHAM.
AND IT'S ALL GOING TO FUEL A GANG WAR AGAINST THE FALCONES.

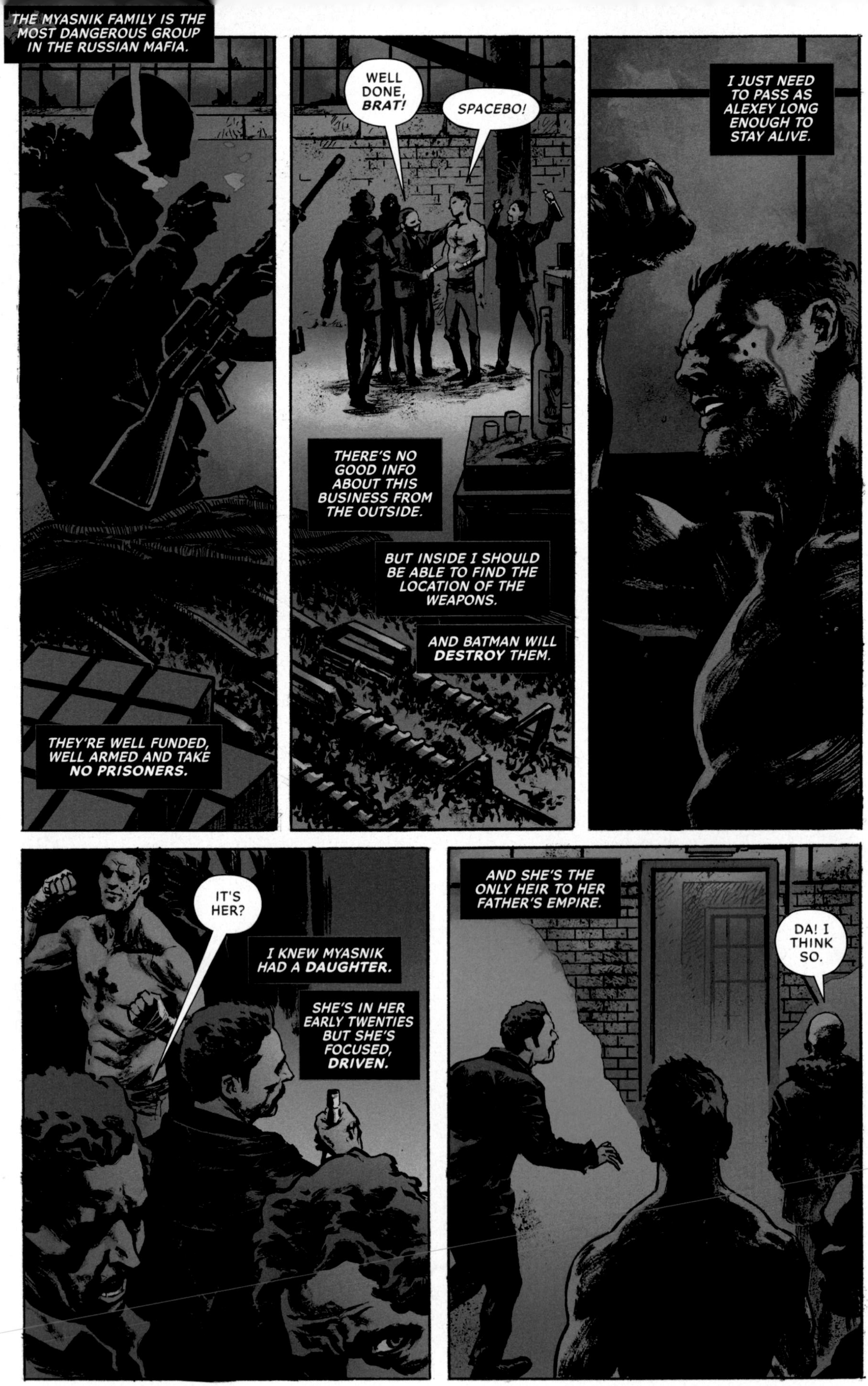
THE MYASNIK FAMILY IS THE MOST DANGEROUS GROUP IN THE RUSSIAN MAFIA.
THEY'RE WELL FUNDED, WELL ARMED AND TAKE NO PRISONERS.
WELL DONE, BRAT!
SPACEBO!
THERE'S NO GOOD INFO ABOUT THIS BUSINESS FROM THE OUTSIDE.
BUT INSIDE I SHOULD BE ABLE TO FIND THE LOCATION OF THE WEAPONS.
AND BATMAN WILL DESTROY THEM.
I JUST NEED TO PASS AS ALEXEY LONG ENOUGH TO STAY ALIVE.
IT'S HER?
I KNEW MYASNIK HAD A DAUGHTER.
SHE'S IN HER EARLY TWENTIES BUT SHE'S FOCUSED, DRIVEN.
AND SHE'S THE ONLY HEIR TO HER FATHER'S EMPIRE.
DA! I THINK SO.

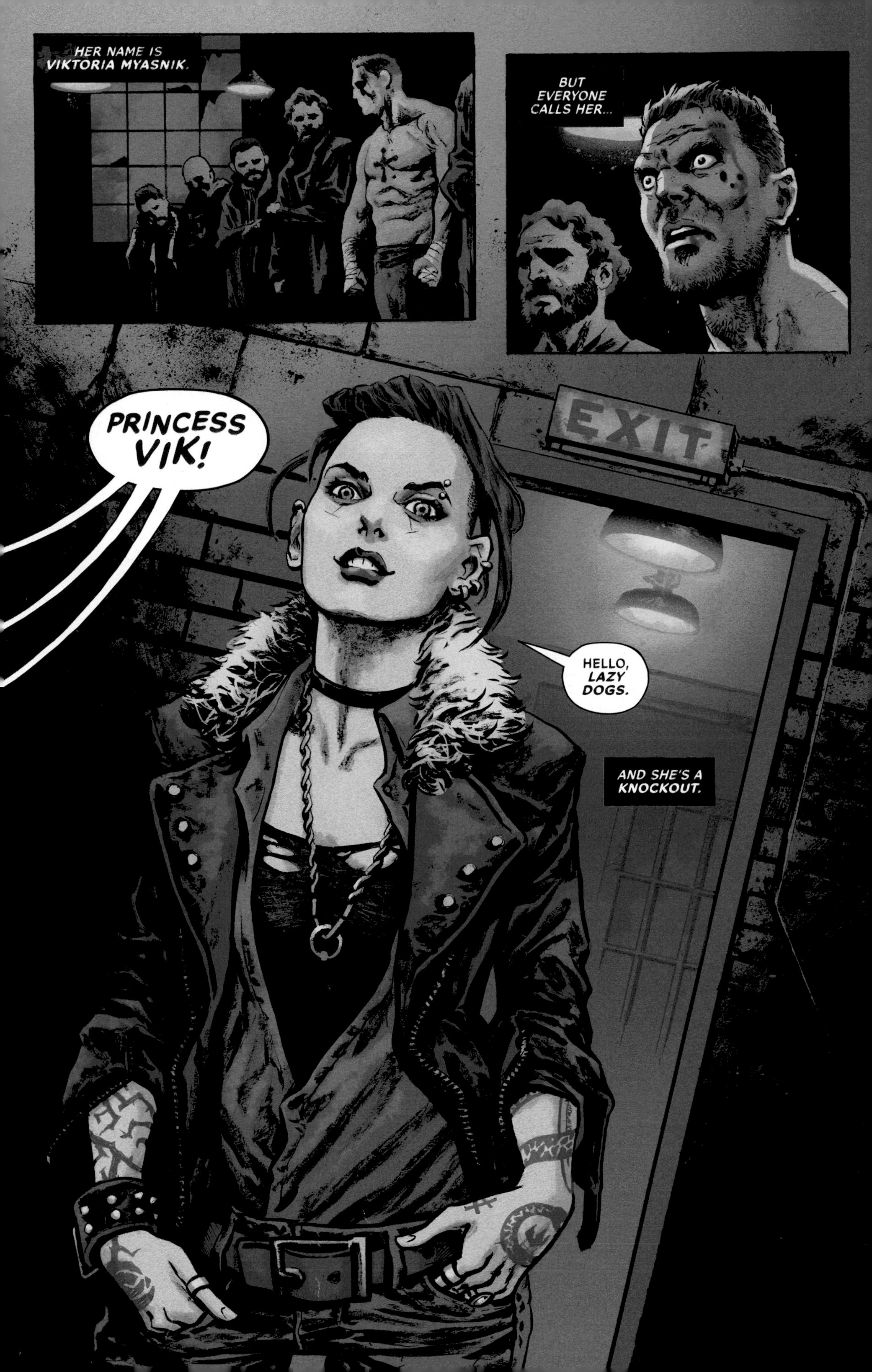
HER NAME IS VIKTORIA MYASNIK.
BUT EVERYONE CALLS HER...
PRINCESS VIK!
HELLO, LAZY DOGS.
AND SHE'S A KNOCKOUT.

I THOUGHT PEOPLE WERE EXAGGERATING WHEN THEY SAID RUSSIA COULD GET JUST AS STRANGE AS GOTHAM CITY.

I WAS *WRONG.*

IT'S A FROZEN EARLY MORNING IN MOSCOW. INSTEAD OF PATROLLING THE STREETS OF GOTHAM I'M HERE INFILTRATING RUSSIA'S MOST VIOLENT MAFIA FAMILY: *THE MYASNIKS.*

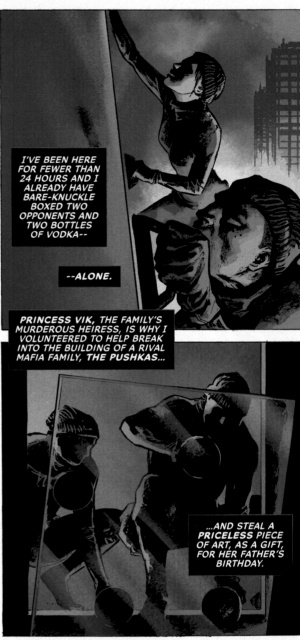

I'VE BEEN HERE FOR FEWER THAN 24 HOURS AND I ALREADY HAVE BARE-KNUCKLE BOXED TWO OPPONENTS AND TWO BOTTLES OF VODKA--

--ALONE.

PRINCESS VIK, THE FAMILY'S MURDEROUS HEIRESS, IS WHY I VOLUNTEERED TO HELP BREAK INTO THE BUILDING OF A RIVAL MAFIA FAMILY, *THE PUSHKAS...*

...AND STEAL A *PRICELESS* PIECE OF ART, AS A GIFT, FOR HER FATHER'S BIRTHDAY.

I THOUGHT IT WOULD HELP MY COVER AS ALEXEY *"KNOCKOUT"* NOKAUT.

AGAIN, I WAS WRONG.

WOO-WOO-WOO

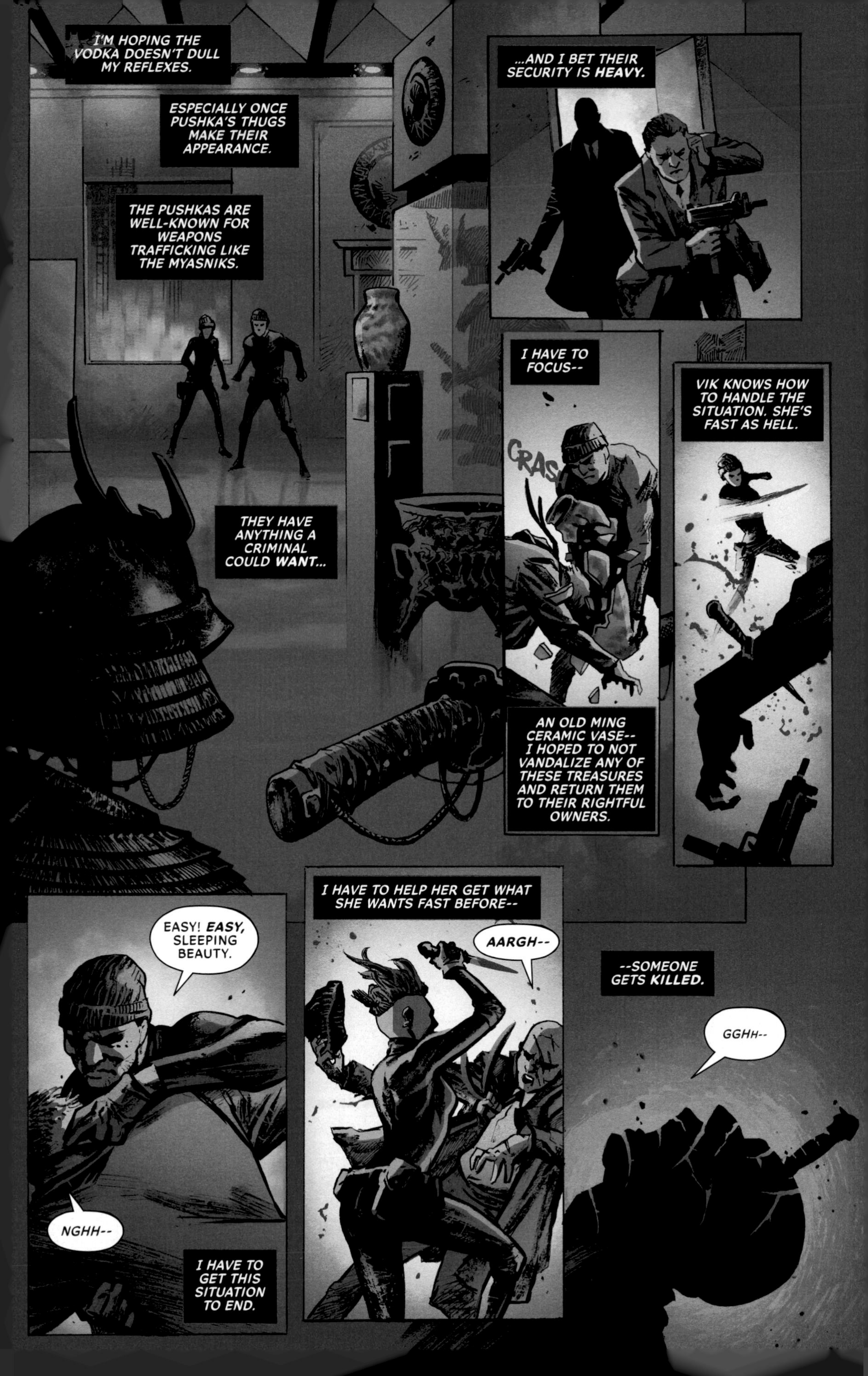
I'M HOPING THE VODKA DOESN'T DULL MY REFLEXES.
ESPECIALLY ONCE PUSHKA'S THUGS MAKE THEIR APPEARANCE.
THE PUSHKAS ARE WELL-KNOWN FOR WEAPONS TRAFFICKING LIKE THE MYASNIKS.
THEY HAVE ANYTHING A CRIMINAL COULD WANT...
...AND I BET THEIR SECURITY IS HEAVY.
I HAVE TO FOCUS--
CRASH
AN OLD MING CERAMIC VASE-- I HOPED TO NOT VANDALIZE ANY OF THESE TREASURES AND RETURN THEM TO THEIR RIGHTFUL OWNERS.
VIK KNOWS HOW TO HANDLE THE SITUATION. SHE'S FAST AS HELL.
EASY! EASY, SLEEPING BEAUTY.
NGHH--
I HAVE TO GET THIS SITUATION TO END.
I HAVE TO HELP HER GET WHAT SHE WANTS FAST BEFORE--
AARGH--
--SOMEONE GETS KILLED.
GGHH--

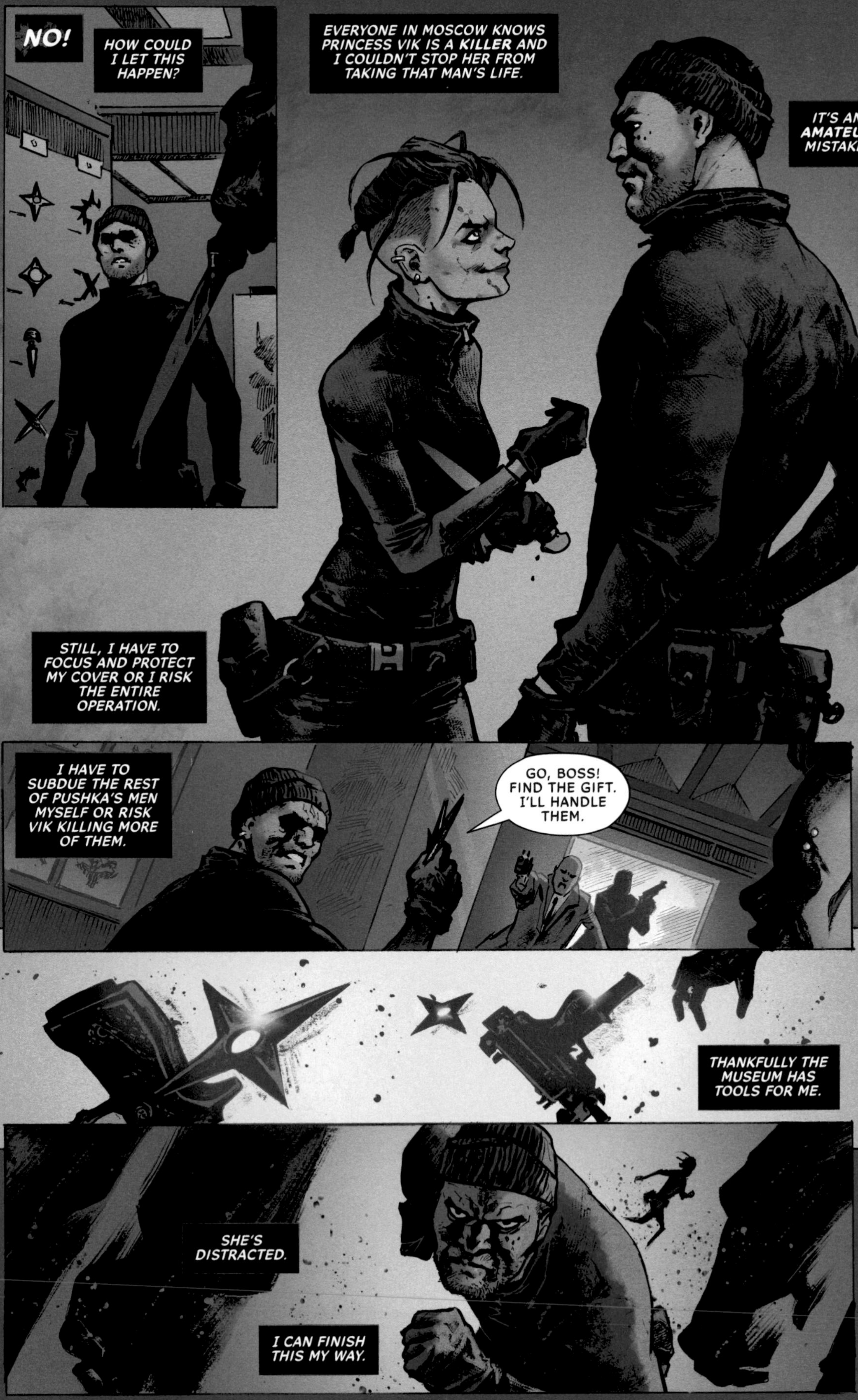
NO!
HOW COULD I LET THIS HAPPEN?
EVERYONE IN MOSCOW KNOWS PRINCESS VIK IS A KILLER AND I COULDN'T STOP HER FROM TAKING THAT MAN'S LIFE.
IT'S AN AMATEUR MISTAKE.
STILL, I HAVE TO FOCUS AND PROTECT MY COVER OR I RISK THE ENTIRE OPERATION.
I HAVE TO SUBDUE THE REST OF PUSHKA'S MEN MYSELF OR RISK VIK KILLING MORE OF THEM.
GO, BOSS! FIND THE GIFT. I'LL HANDLE THEM.
THANKFULLY THE MUSEUM HAS TOOLS FOR ME.
SHE'S DISTRACTED.
I CAN FINISH THIS MY WAY.

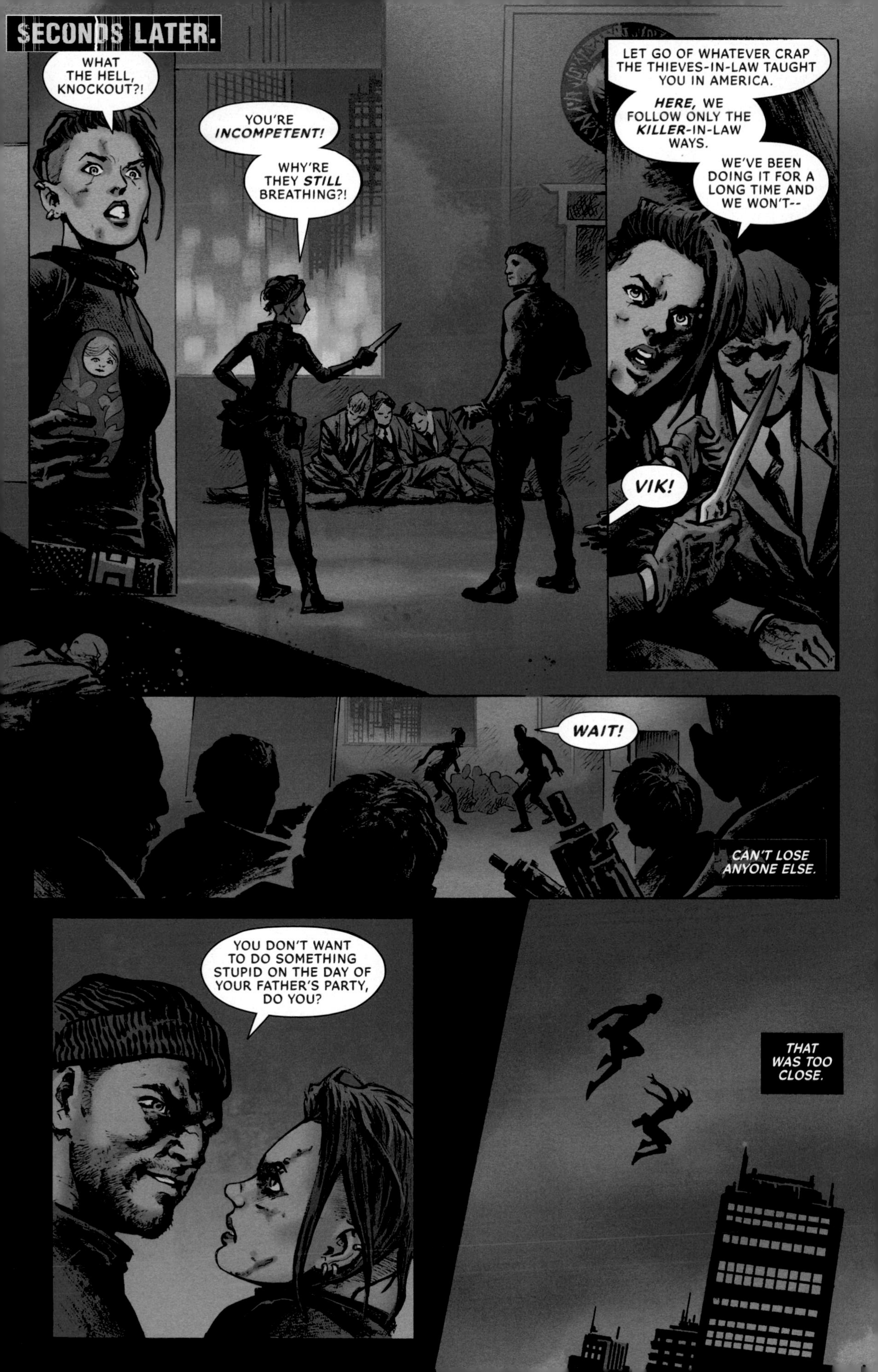
SECONDS LATER.
WHAT THE HELL, KNOCKOUT?!
YOU'RE *INCOMPETENT!*
WHY'RE THEY *STILL* BREATHING?!
LET GO OF WHATEVER CRAP THE THIEVES-IN-LAW TAUGHT YOU IN AMERICA.
HERE, WE FOLLOW ONLY THE *KILLER*-IN-LAW WAYS.
WE'VE BEEN DOING IT FOR A LONG TIME AND WE WON'T--
VIK!
WAIT!
CAN'T LOSE ANYONE ELSE.
YOU DON'T WANT TO DO SOMETHING STUPID ON THE DAY OF YOUR FATHER'S PARTY, DO YOU?
THAT WAS TOO CLOSE.

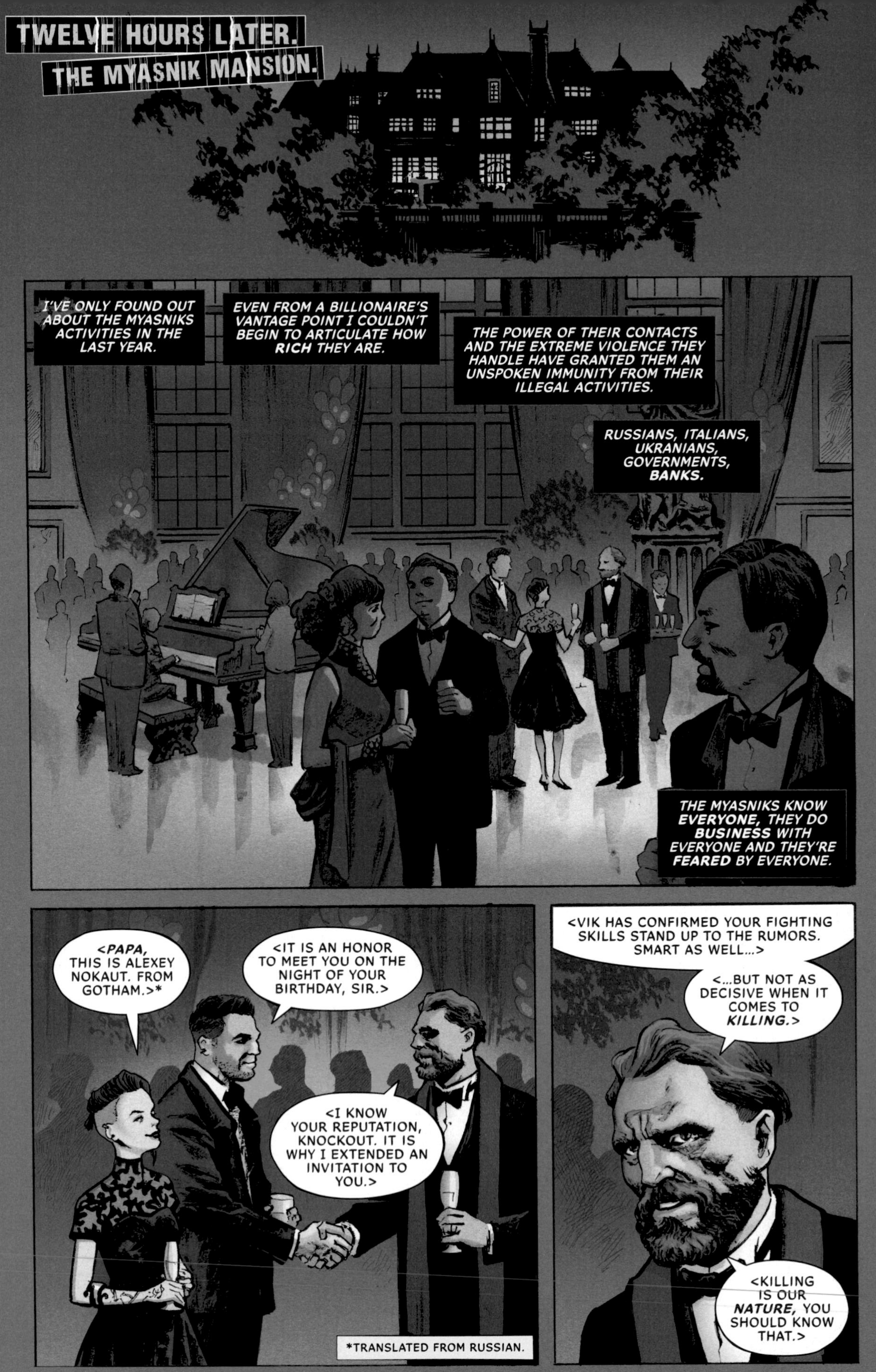
TWELVE HOURS LATER.
THE MYASNIK MANSION.
I'VE ONLY FOUND OUT ABOUT THE MYASNIKS ACTIVITIES IN THE LAST YEAR.
EVEN FROM A BILLIONAIRE'S VANTAGE POINT I COULDN'T BEGIN TO ARTICULATE HOW RICH THEY ARE.
THE POWER OF THEIR CONTACTS AND THE EXTREME VIOLENCE THEY HANDLE HAVE GRANTED THEM AN UNSPOKEN IMMUNITY FROM THEIR ILLEGAL ACTIVITIES.
RUSSIANS, ITALIANS, UKRANIANS, GOVERNMENTS, BANKS.
THE MYASNIKS KNOW EVERYONE, THEY DO BUSINESS WITH EVERYONE AND THEY'RE FEARED BY EVERYONE.
<PAPA, THIS IS ALEXEY NOKAUT. FROM GOTHAM.>*
<IT IS AN HONOR TO MEET YOU ON THE NIGHT OF YOUR BIRTHDAY, SIR.>
<I KNOW YOUR REPUTATION, KNOCKOUT. IT IS WHY I EXTENDED AN INVITATION TO YOU.>
*TRANSLATED FROM RUSSIAN.
<VIK HAS CONFIRMED YOUR FIGHTING SKILLS STAND UP TO THE RUMORS. SMART AS WELL...>
<...BUT NOT AS DECISIVE WHEN IT COMES TO KILLING.>
<KILLING IS OUR NATURE, YOU SHOULD KNOW THAT.>

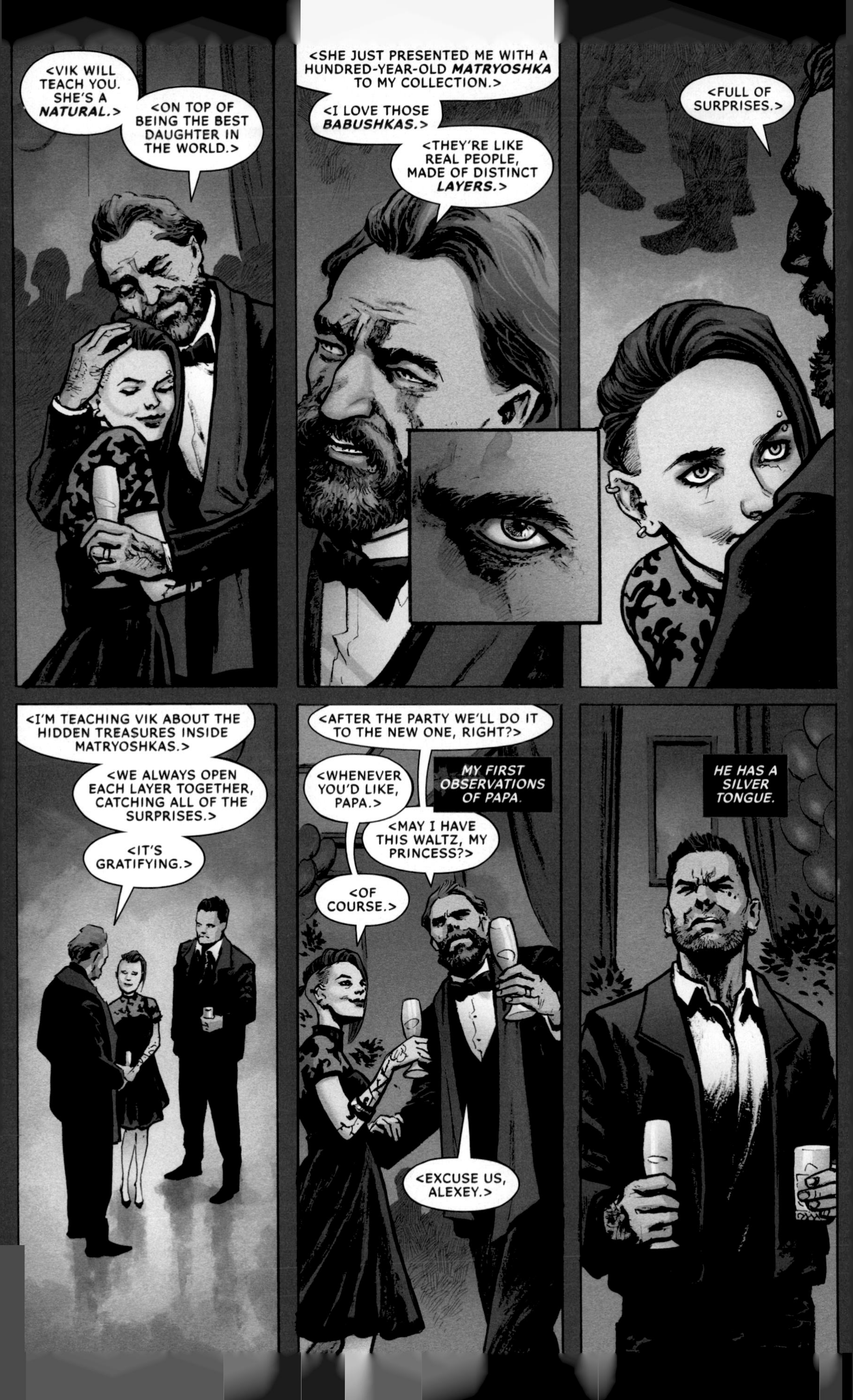
<VIK WILL TEACH YOU. SHE'S A *NATURAL.*>
<ON TOP OF BEING THE BEST DAUGHTER IN THE WORLD.>
<SHE JUST PRESENTED ME WITH A HUNDRED-YEAR-OLD *MATRYOSHKA* TO MY COLLECTION.>
<I LOVE THOSE *BABUSHKAS.*>
<THEY'RE LIKE REAL PEOPLE, MADE OF DISTINCT *LAYERS.*>
<FULL OF SURPRISES.>
<I'M TEACHING VIK ABOUT THE HIDDEN TREASURES INSIDE MATRYOSHKAS.>
<WE ALWAYS OPEN EACH LAYER TOGETHER, CATCHING ALL OF THE SURPRISES.>
<IT'S GRATIFYING.>
<AFTER THE PARTY WE'LL DO IT TO THE NEW ONE, RIGHT?>
MY FIRST OBSERVATIONS OF PAPA.
<WHENEVER YOU'D LIKE, PAPA.>
<MAY I HAVE THIS WALTZ, MY PRINCESS?>
<OF COURSE.>
<EXCUSE US, ALEXEY.>
HE HAS A SILVER TONGUE.

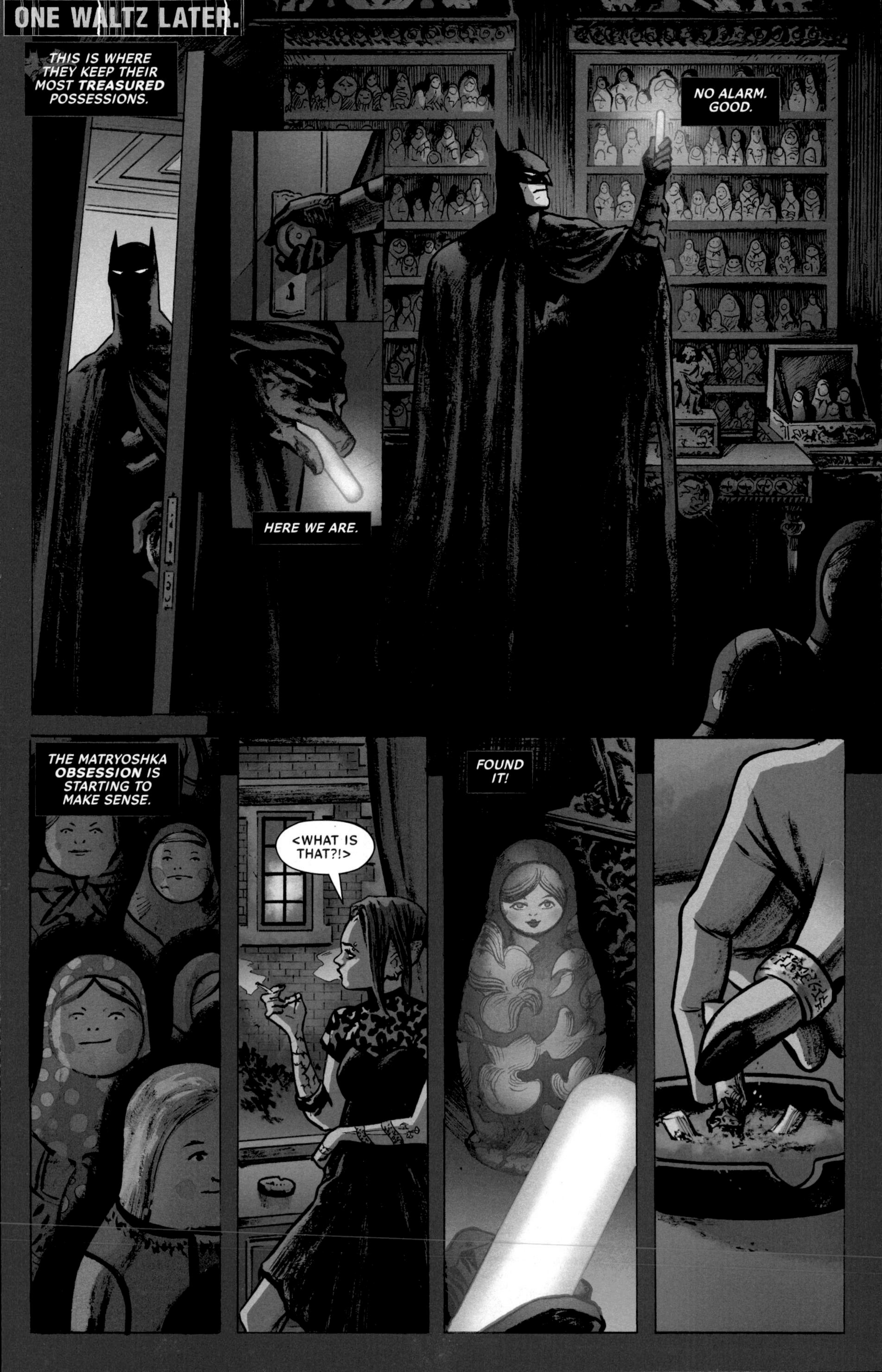
ONE WALTZ LATER.
THIS IS WHERE THEY KEEP THEIR MOST TREASURED POSSESSIONS.
NO ALARM. GOOD.
HERE WE ARE.
THE MATRYOSHKA OBSESSION IS STARTING TO MAKE SENSE.
<WHAT IS THAT?!>
FOUND IT!

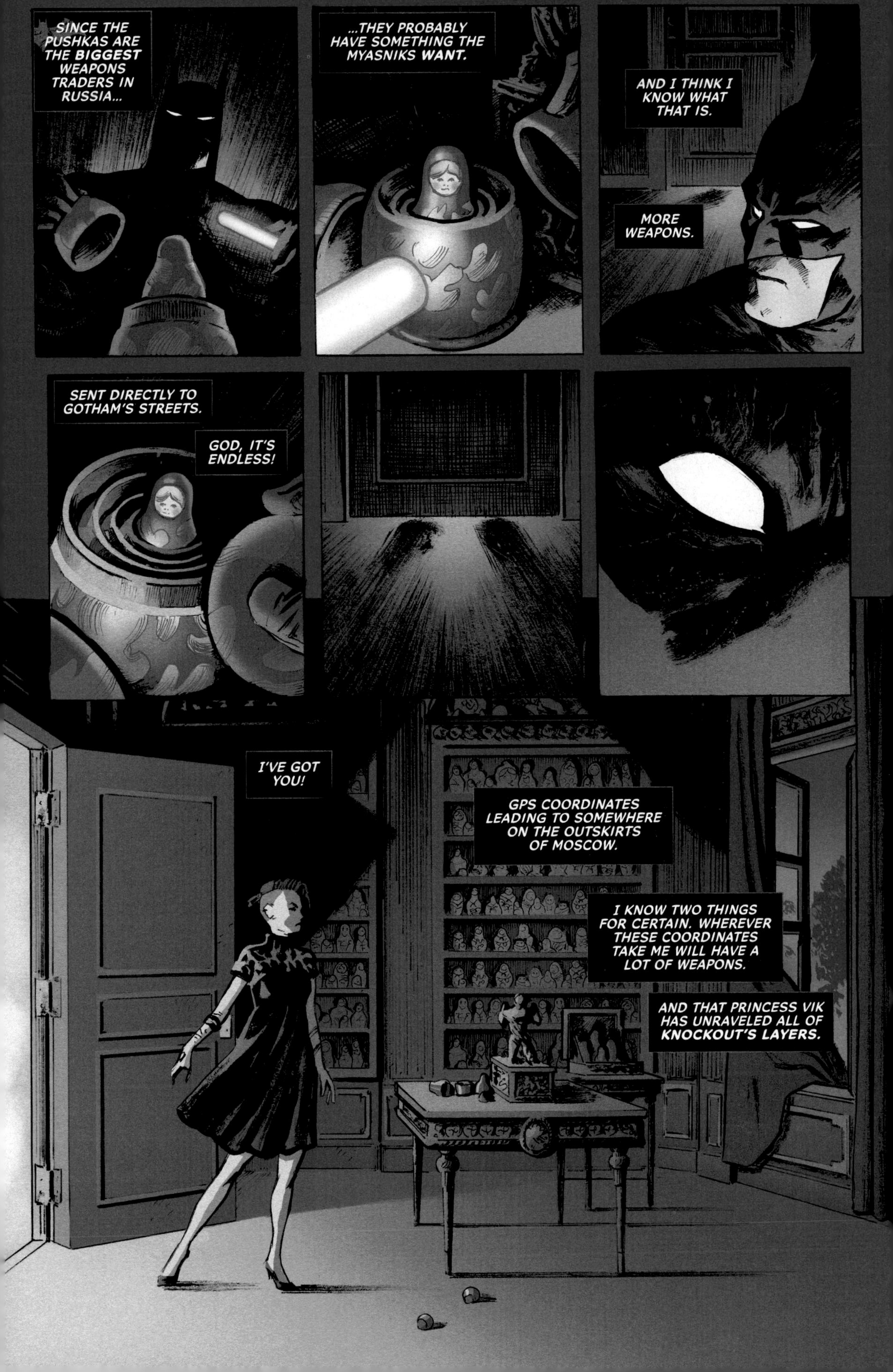
SINCE THE PUSHKAS ARE THE **BIGGEST** WEAPONS TRADERS IN RUSSIA...
...THEY PROBABLY HAVE SOMETHING THE MYASNIKS **WANT.**
AND I THINK I KNOW WHAT THAT IS.
MORE WEAPONS.
SENT DIRECTLY TO GOTHAM'S STREETS.
GOD, IT'S ENDLESS!
I'VE GOT YOU!
GPS COORDINATES LEADING TO SOMEWHERE ON THE OUTSKIRTS OF MOSCOW.
I KNOW TWO THINGS FOR CERTAIN. WHEREVER THESE COORDINATES TAKE ME WILL HAVE A LOT OF WEAPONS.
AND THAT PRINCESS VIK HAS UNRAVELED ALL OF **KNOCKOUT'S LAYERS.**

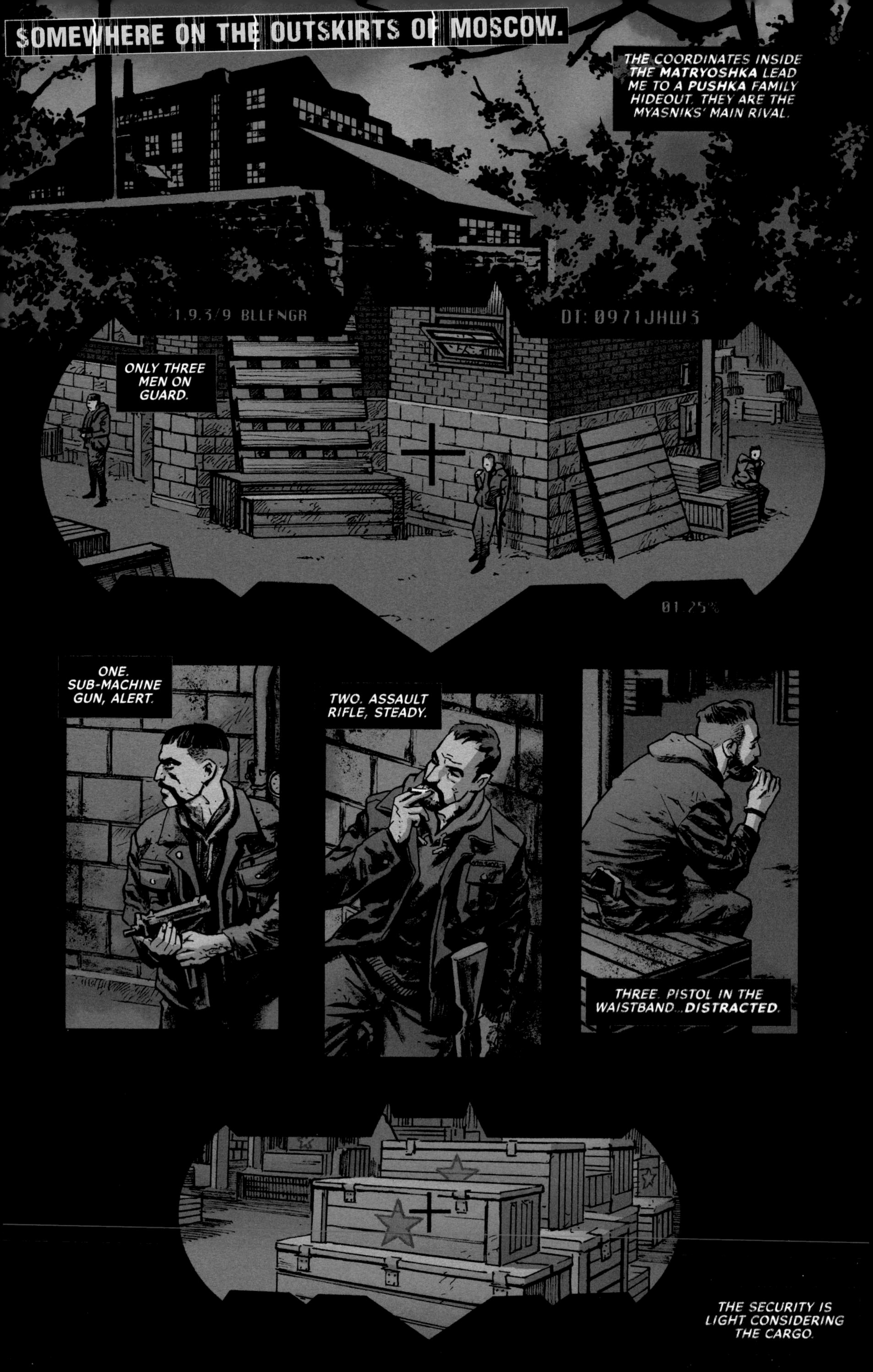
SOMEWHERE ON THE OUTSKIRTS OF MOSCOW.
THE COORDINATES INSIDE THE MATRYOSHKA LEAD ME TO A PUSHKA FAMILY HIDEOUT. THEY ARE THE MYASNIKS' MAIN RIVAL.
DT: 0971JHW3
ONLY THREE MEN ON GUARD.
01.25%
ONE. SUB-MACHINE GUN, ALERT.
TWO. ASSAULT RIFLE, STEADY.
THREE. PISTOL IN THE WAISTBAND...DISTRACTED.
THE SECURITY IS LIGHT CONSIDERING THE CARGO.

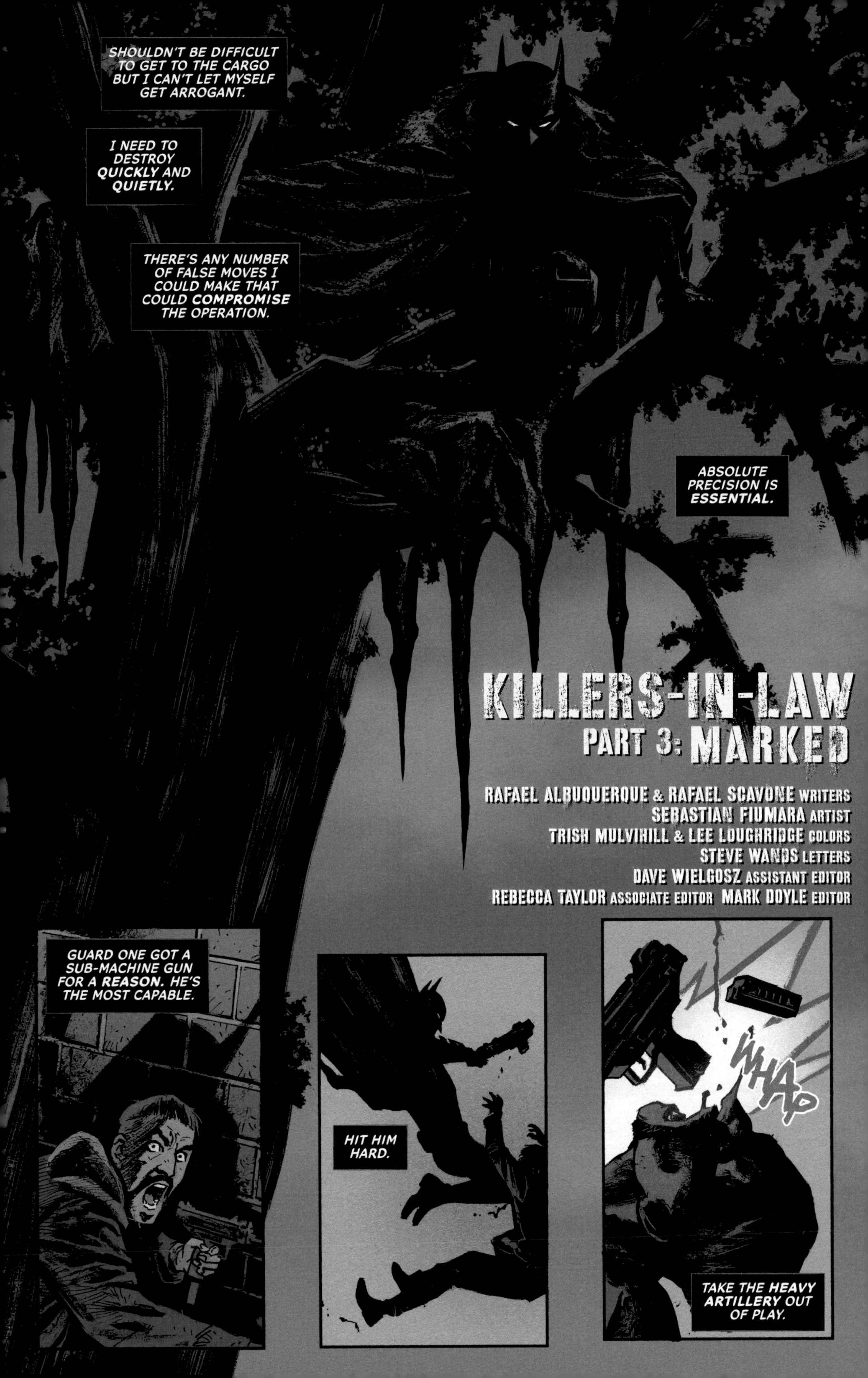
SHOULDN'T BE DIFFICULT TO GET TO THE CARGO BUT I CAN'T LET MYSELF GET ARROGANT.
I NEED TO DESTROY QUICKLY AND QUIETLY.
THERE'S ANY NUMBER OF FALSE MOVES I COULD MAKE THAT COULD COMPROMISE THE OPERATION.
ABSOLUTE PRECISION IS ESSENTIAL.
KILLERS-IN-LAW
PART 3: MARKED
RAFAEL ALBUQUERQUE & RAFAEL SCAVONE WRITERS
SEBASTIAN FIUMARA ARTIST
TRISH MULVIHILL & LEE LOUGHRIDGE COLORS
STEVE WANDS LETTERS
DAVE WIELGOSZ ASSISTANT EDITOR
REBECCA TAYLOR ASSOCIATE EDITOR MARK DOYLE EDITOR
GUARD ONE GOT A SUB-MACHINE GUN FOR A REASON. HE'S THE MOST CAPABLE.
HIT HIM HARD.
WHAP
TAKE THE HEAVY ARTILLERY OUT OF PLAY.

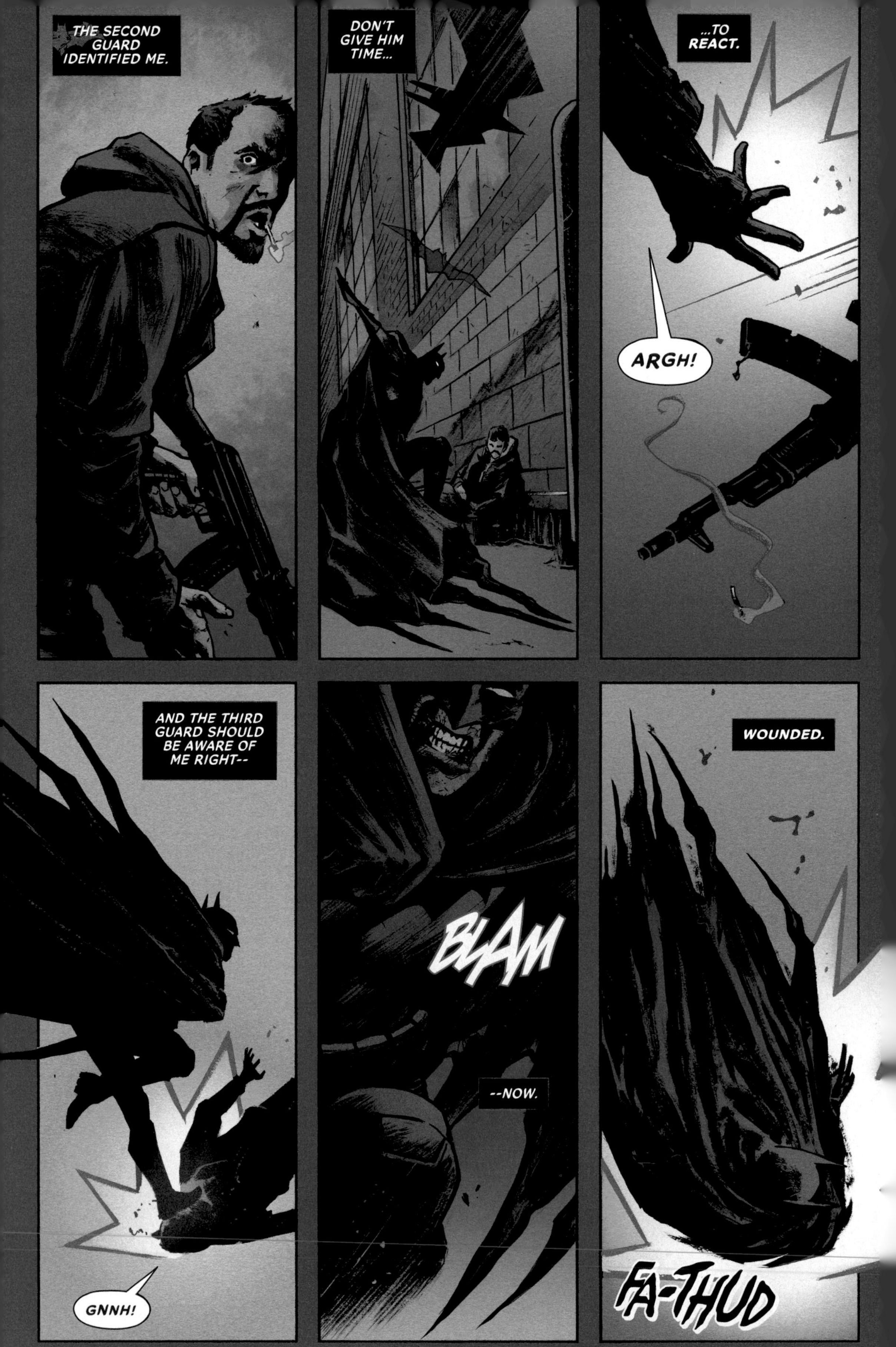
THE SECOND GUARD IDENTIFIED ME.
DON'T GIVE HIM TIME...
...TO REACT.
ARGH!
AND THE THIRD GUARD SHOULD BE AWARE OF ME RIGHT--
GNNH!
BLAM
--NOW.
WOUNDED.
FA-THUD

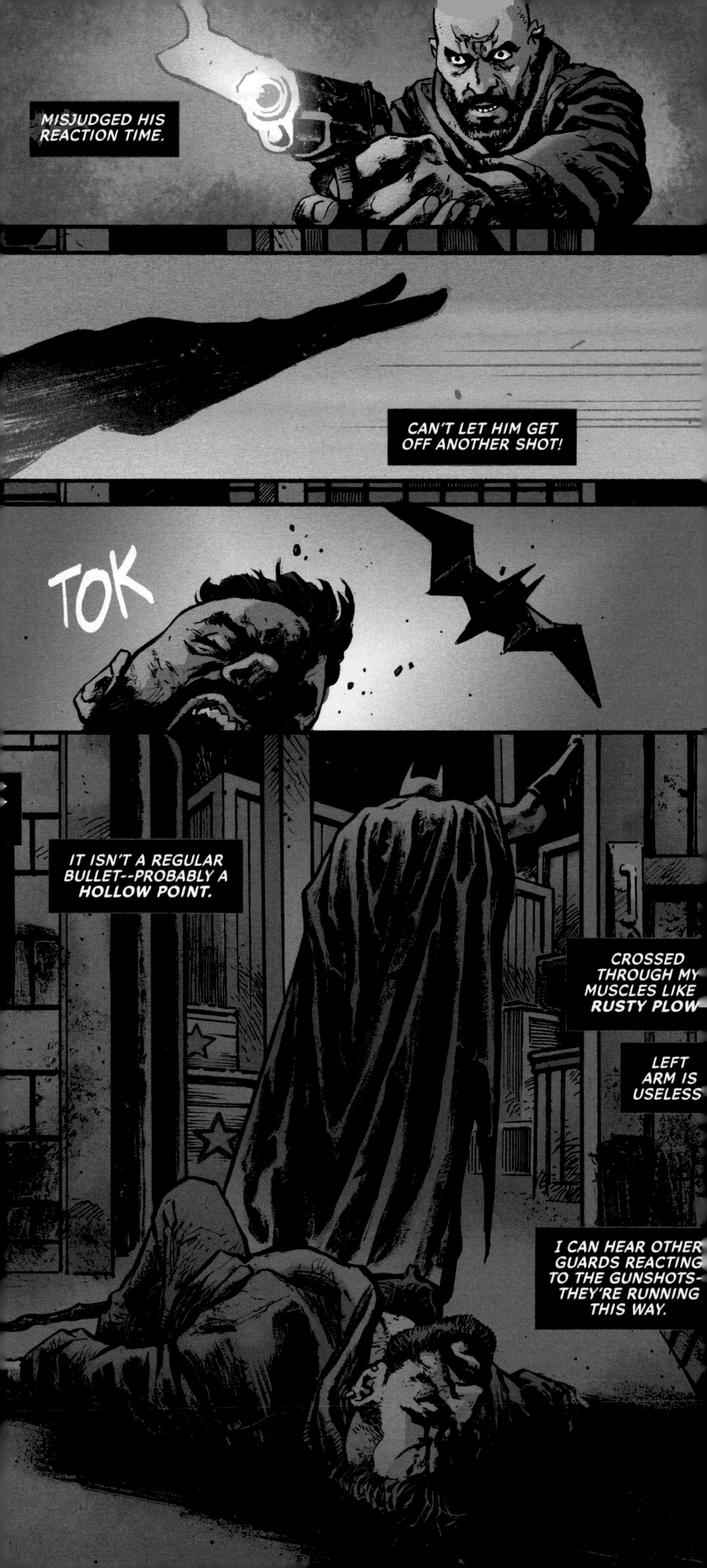
MISJUDGED HIS REACTION TIME.
CAN'T LET HIM GET OFF ANOTHER SHOT!
TOK
IT ISN'T A REGULAR BULLET--PROBABLY A HOLLOW POINT.
CROSSED THROUGH MY MUSCLES LIKE RUSTY PLOW
LEFT ARM IS USELESS
I CAN HEAR OTHER GUARDS REACTING TO THE GUNSHOTS- THEY'RE RUNNING THIS WAY.

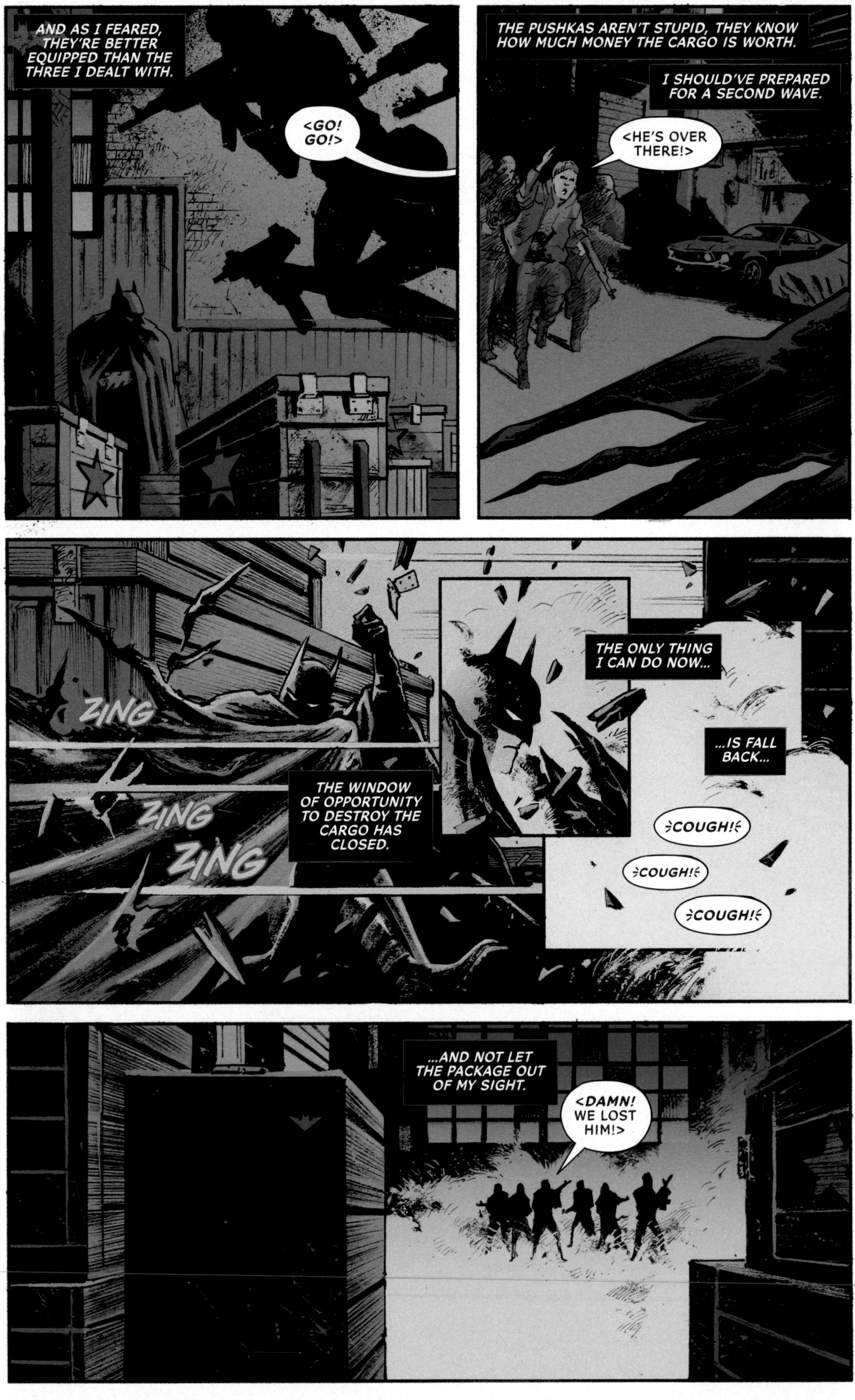

AND AS I FEARED, THEY'RE BETTER EQUIPPED THAN THE THREE I DEALT WITH.
<GO! GO!>
THE PUSHKAS AREN'T STUPID, THEY KNOW HOW MUCH MONEY THE CARGO IS WORTH.
I SHOULD'VE PREPARED FOR A SECOND WAVE.
<HE'S OVER THERE!>
ZING
ZING
ZING
THE WINDOW OF OPPORTUNITY TO DESTROY THE CARGO HAS CLOSED.
THE ONLY THING I CAN DO NOW...
...IS FALL BACK...
COUGH!
COUGH!
COUGH!
...AND NOT LET THE PACKAGE OUT OF MY SIGHT.
<DAMN! WE LOST HIM!>

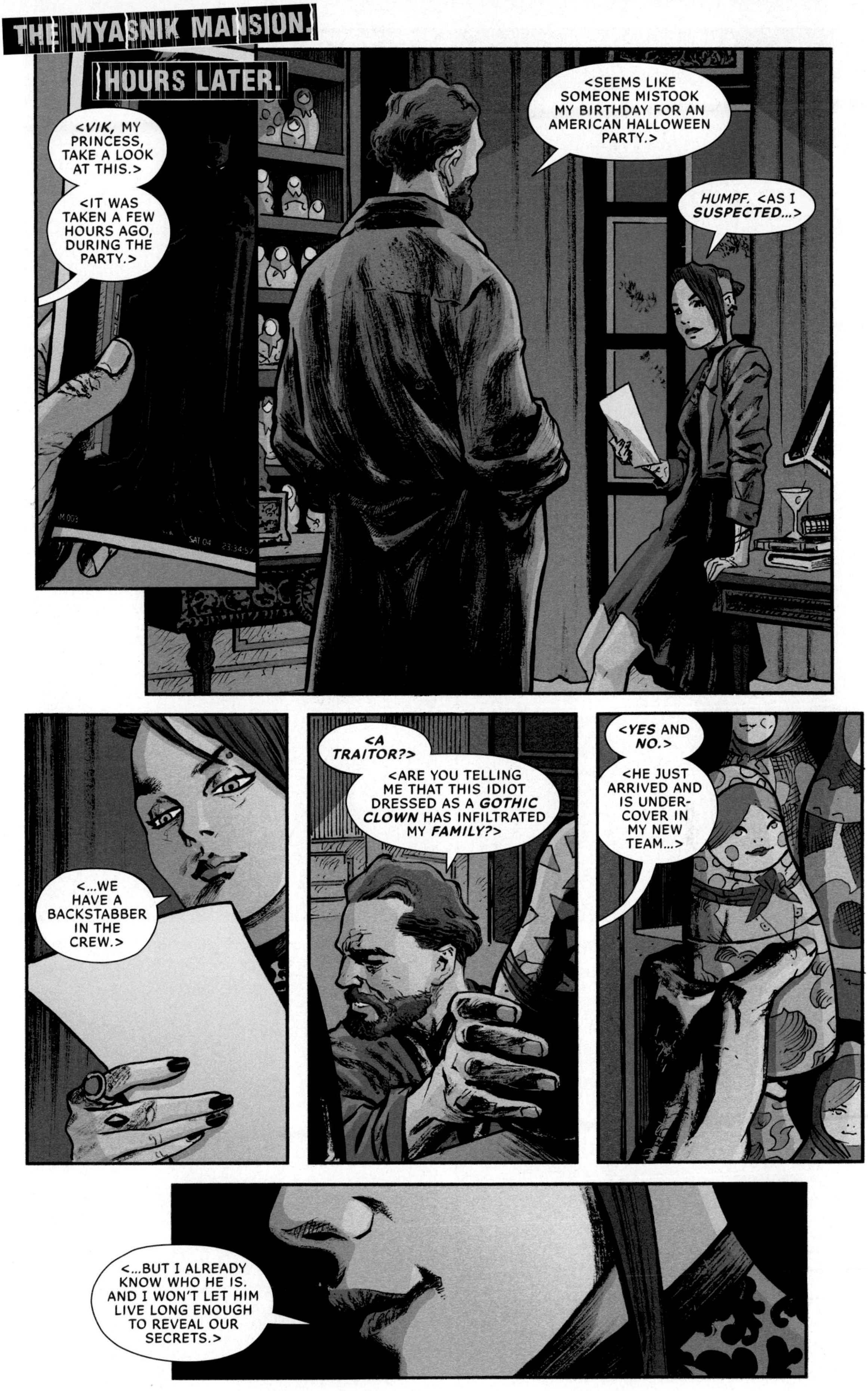
THE MYASNIK MANSION.
HOURS LATER.
<VIK, MY PRINCESS, TAKE A LOOK AT THIS.>
<IT WAS TAKEN A FEW HOURS AGO, DURING THE PARTY.>
SAT 04 23:34:57
<SEEMS LIKE SOMEONE MISTOOK MY BIRTHDAY FOR AN AMERICAN HALLOWEEN PARTY.>
HUMPF. <AS I SUSPECTED...>
<...WE HAVE A BACKSTABBER IN THE CREW.>
<A TRAITOR?>
<ARE YOU TELLING ME THAT THIS IDIOT DRESSED AS A GOTHIC CLOWN HAS INFILTRATED MY FAMILY?>
<YES AND NO.>
<HE JUST ARRIVED AND IS UNDER-COVER IN MY NEW TEAM...>
<...BUT I ALREADY KNOW WHO HE IS. AND I WON'T LET HIM LIVE LONG ENOUGH TO REVEAL OUR SECRETS.>

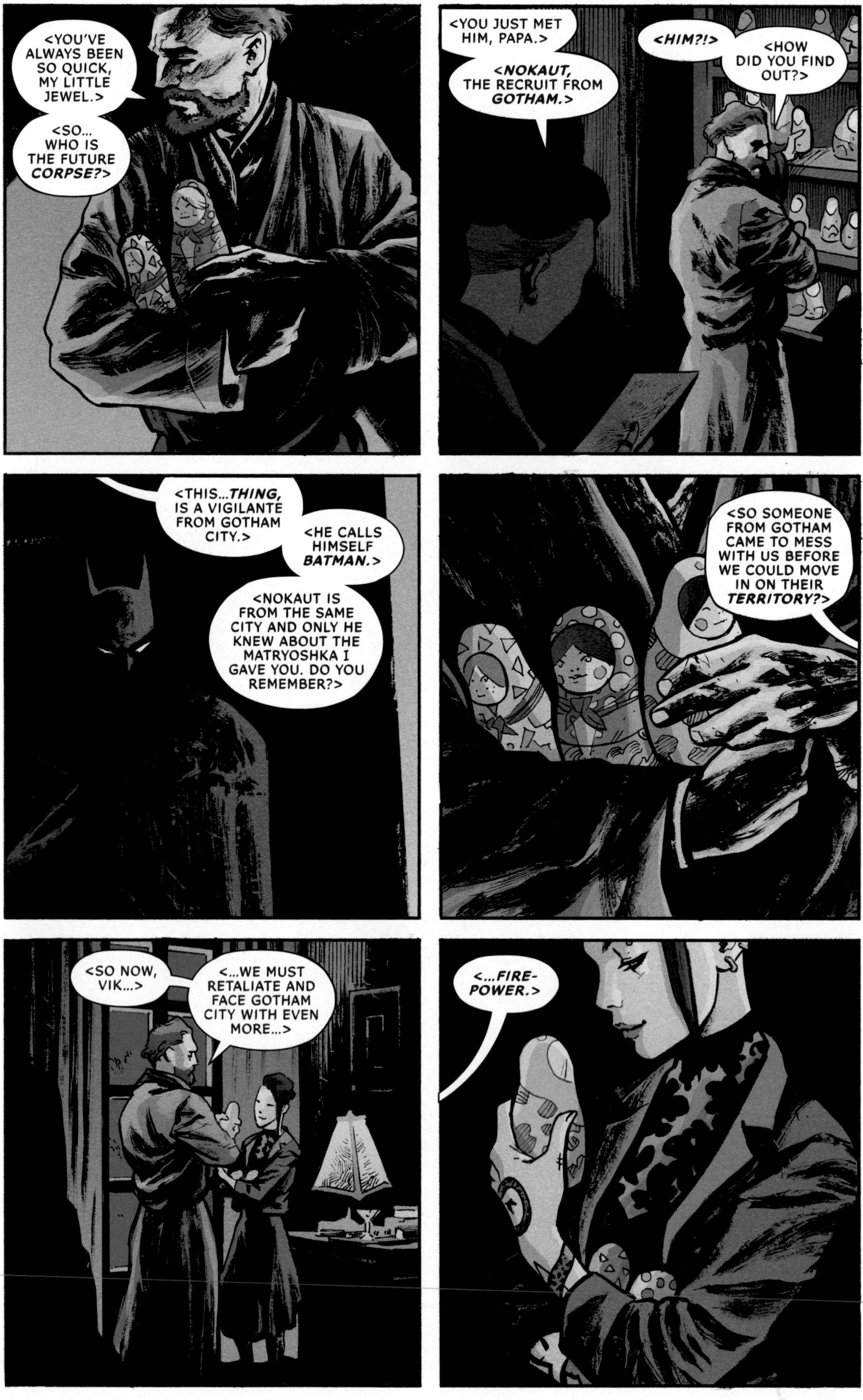
<YOU'VE ALWAYS BEEN SO QUICK, MY LITTLE JEWEL.>
<SO... WHO IS THE FUTURE *CORPSE?*>
<YOU JUST MET HIM, PAPA.>
<*NOKAUT,* THE RECRUIT FROM *GOTHAM.*>
<*HIM?!*>
<HOW DID YOU FIND OUT?>
<THIS...*THING,* IS A VIGILANTE FROM GOTHAM CITY.>
<HE CALLS HIMSELF *BATMAN.*>
<NOKAUT IS FROM THE SAME CITY AND ONLY HE KNEW ABOUT THE MATRYOSHKA I GAVE YOU. DO YOU REMEMBER?>
<SO SOMEONE FROM GOTHAM CAME TO MESS WITH US BEFORE WE COULD MOVE IN ON THEIR *TERRITORY?*>
<SO NOW, VIK...>
<...WE MUST RETALIATE AND FACE GOTHAM CITY WITH EVEN MORE...>
<*...FIRE-POWER.*>

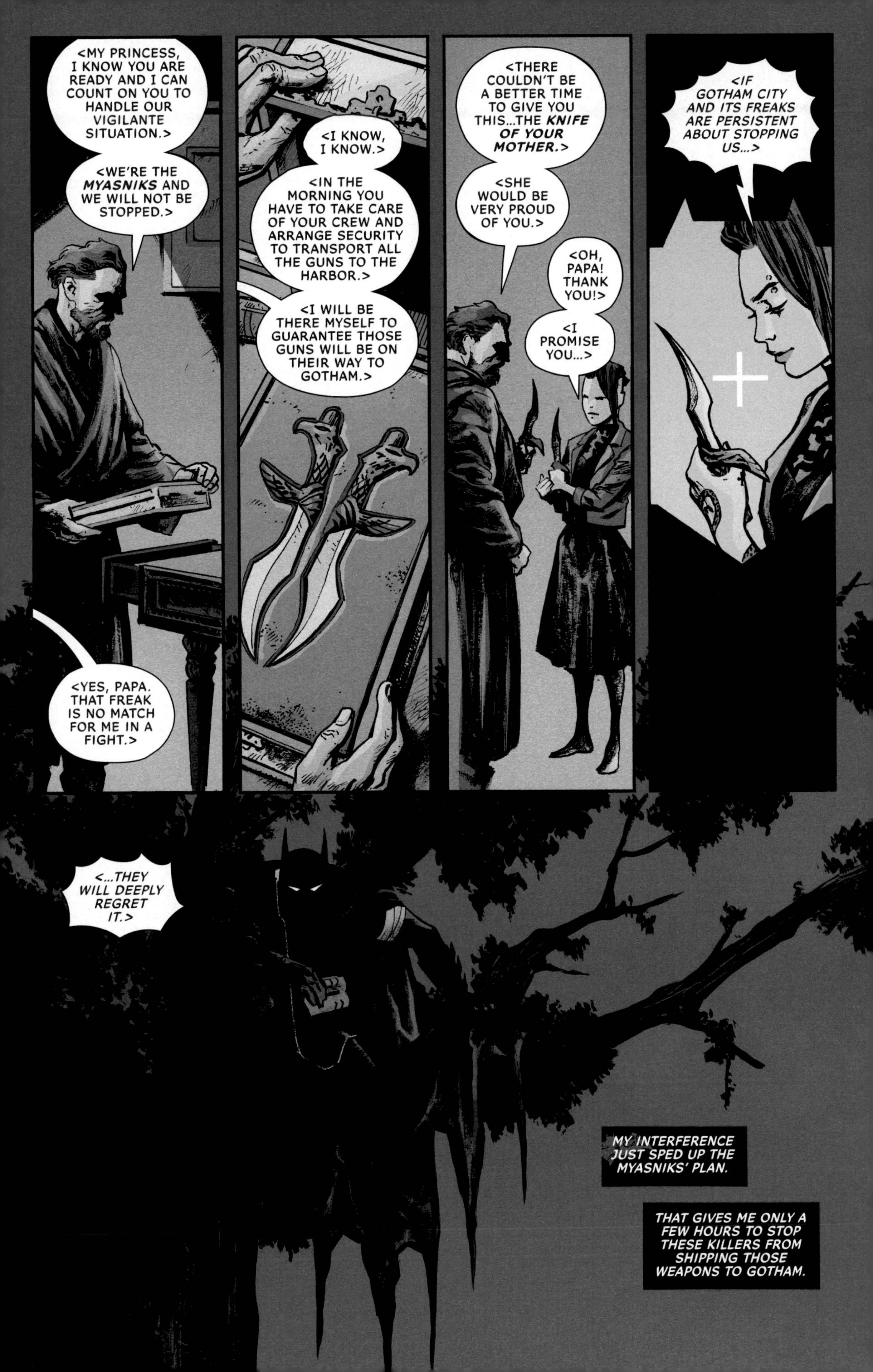

<MY PRINCESS, I KNOW YOU ARE READY AND I CAN COUNT ON YOU TO HANDLE OUR VIGILANTE SITUATION.>
<WE'RE THE *MYASNIKS* AND WE WILL NOT BE STOPPED.>
<YES, PAPA. THAT FREAK IS NO MATCH FOR ME IN A FIGHT.>
<I KNOW, I KNOW.>
<IN THE MORNING YOU HAVE TO TAKE CARE OF YOUR CREW AND ARRANGE SECURITY TO TRANSPORT ALL THE GUNS TO THE HARBOR.>
<I WILL BE THERE MYSELF TO GUARANTEE THOSE GUNS WILL BE ON THEIR WAY TO GOTHAM.>
<THERE COULDN'T BE A BETTER TIME TO GIVE YOU THIS...THE ***KNIFE OF YOUR MOTHER.***>
<SHE WOULD BE VERY PROUD OF YOU.>
<OH, PAPA! THANK YOU!>
<I PROMISE YOU...>
<IF GOTHAM CITY AND ITS FREAKS ARE PERSISTENT ABOUT STOPPING US...>
<...THEY WILL DEEPLY REGRET IT.>
MY INTERFERENCE JUST SPED UP THE MYASNIKS' PLAN.
THAT GIVES ME ONLY A FEW HOURS TO STOP THESE KILLERS FROM SHIPPING THOSE WEAPONS TO GOTHAM.

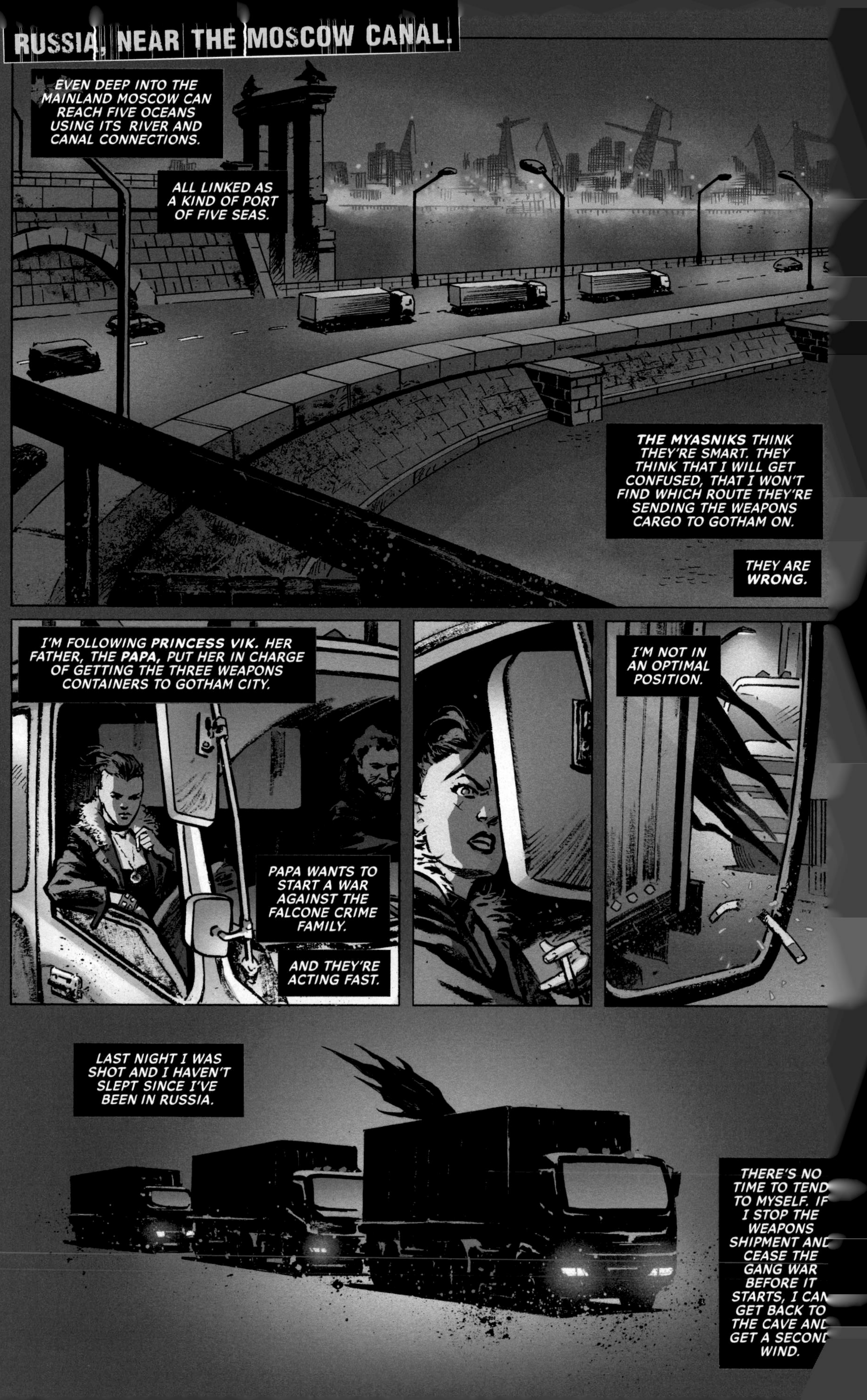

RUSSIA, NEAR THE MOSCOW CANAL.
EVEN DEEP INTO THE MAINLAND MOSCOW CAN REACH FIVE OCEANS USING ITS RIVER AND CANAL CONNECTIONS.
ALL LINKED AS A KIND OF PORT OF FIVE SEAS.
THE MYASNIKS THINK THEY'RE SMART. THEY THINK THAT I WILL GET CONFUSED, THAT I WON'T FIND WHICH ROUTE THEY'RE SENDING THE WEAPONS CARGO TO GOTHAM ON.
THEY ARE WRONG.
I'M FOLLOWING PRINCESS VIK. HER FATHER, THE PAPA, PUT HER IN CHARGE OF GETTING THE THREE WEAPONS CONTAINERS TO GOTHAM CITY.
PAPA WANTS TO START A WAR AGAINST THE FALCONE CRIME FAMILY.
AND THEY'RE ACTING FAST.
I'M NOT IN AN OPTIMAL POSITION.
LAST NIGHT I WAS SHOT AND I HAVEN'T SLEPT SINCE I'VE BEEN IN RUSSIA.
THERE'S NO TIME TO TEND TO MYSELF. IF I STOP THE WEAPONS SHIPMENT AND CEASE THE GANG WAR BEFORE IT STARTS, I CAN GET BACK TO THE CAVE AND GET A SECOND WIND.

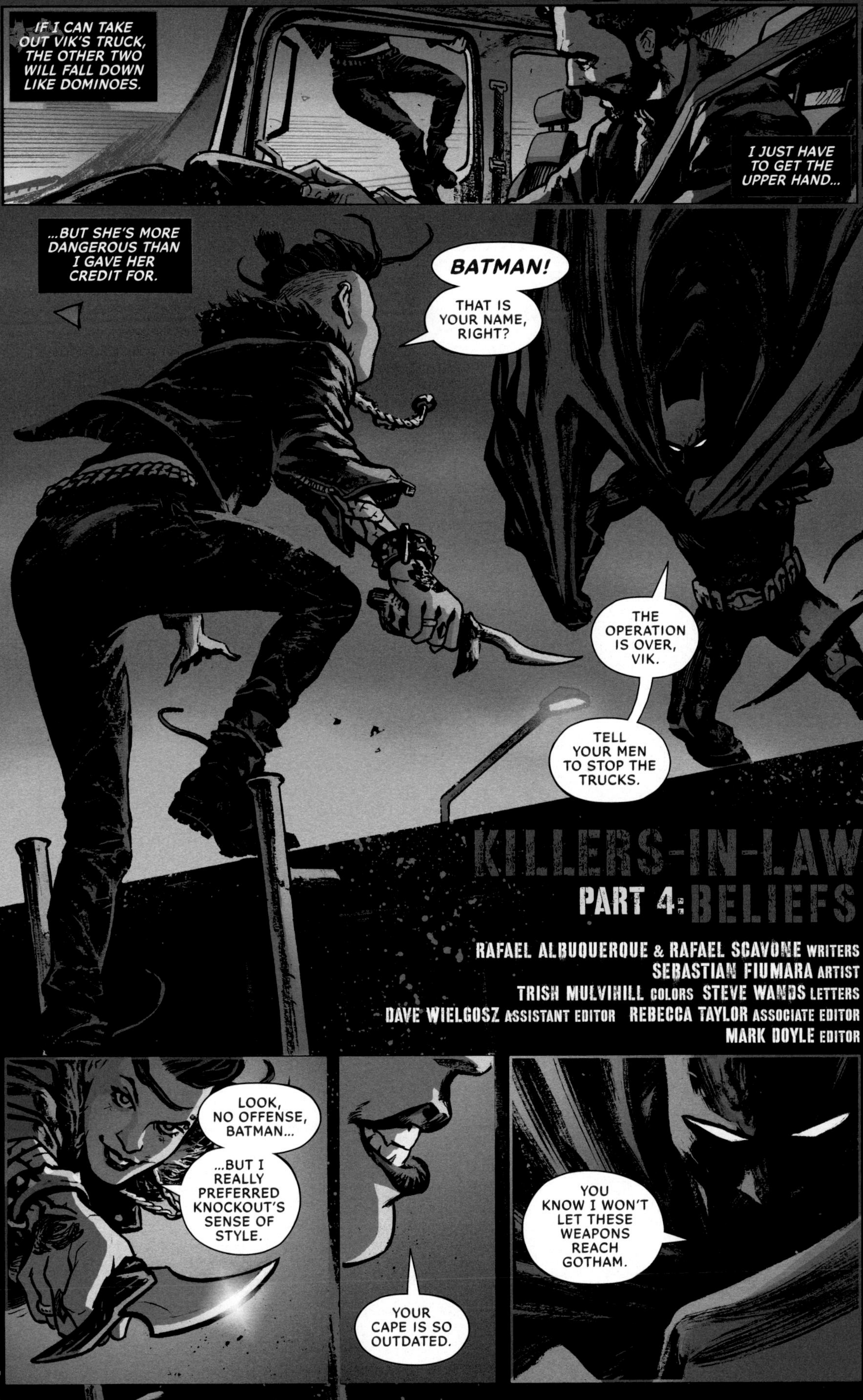
IF I CAN TAKE OUT VIK'S TRUCK, THE OTHER TWO WILL FALL DOWN LIKE DOMINOES.
I JUST HAVE TO GET THE UPPER HAND...
...BUT SHE'S MORE DANGEROUS THAN I GAVE HER CREDIT FOR.
BATMAN!
THAT IS YOUR NAME, RIGHT?
THE OPERATION IS OVER, VIK.
TELL YOUR MEN TO STOP THE TRUCKS.
KILLERS-IN-LAW
PART 4: BELIEFS
RAFAEL ALBUQUERQUE & RAFAEL SCAVONE WRITERS
SEBASTIAN FIUMARA ARTIST
TRISH MULVIHILL COLORS STEVE WANDS LETTERS
DAVE WIELGOSZ ASSISTANT EDITOR REBECCA TAYLOR ASSOCIATE EDITOR
MARK DOYLE EDITOR
LOOK, NO OFFENSE, BATMAN...
...BUT I REALLY PREFERRED KNOCKOUT'S SENSE OF STYLE.
YOUR CAPE IS SO OUTDATED.
YOU KNOW I WON'T LET THESE WEAPONS REACH GOTHAM.

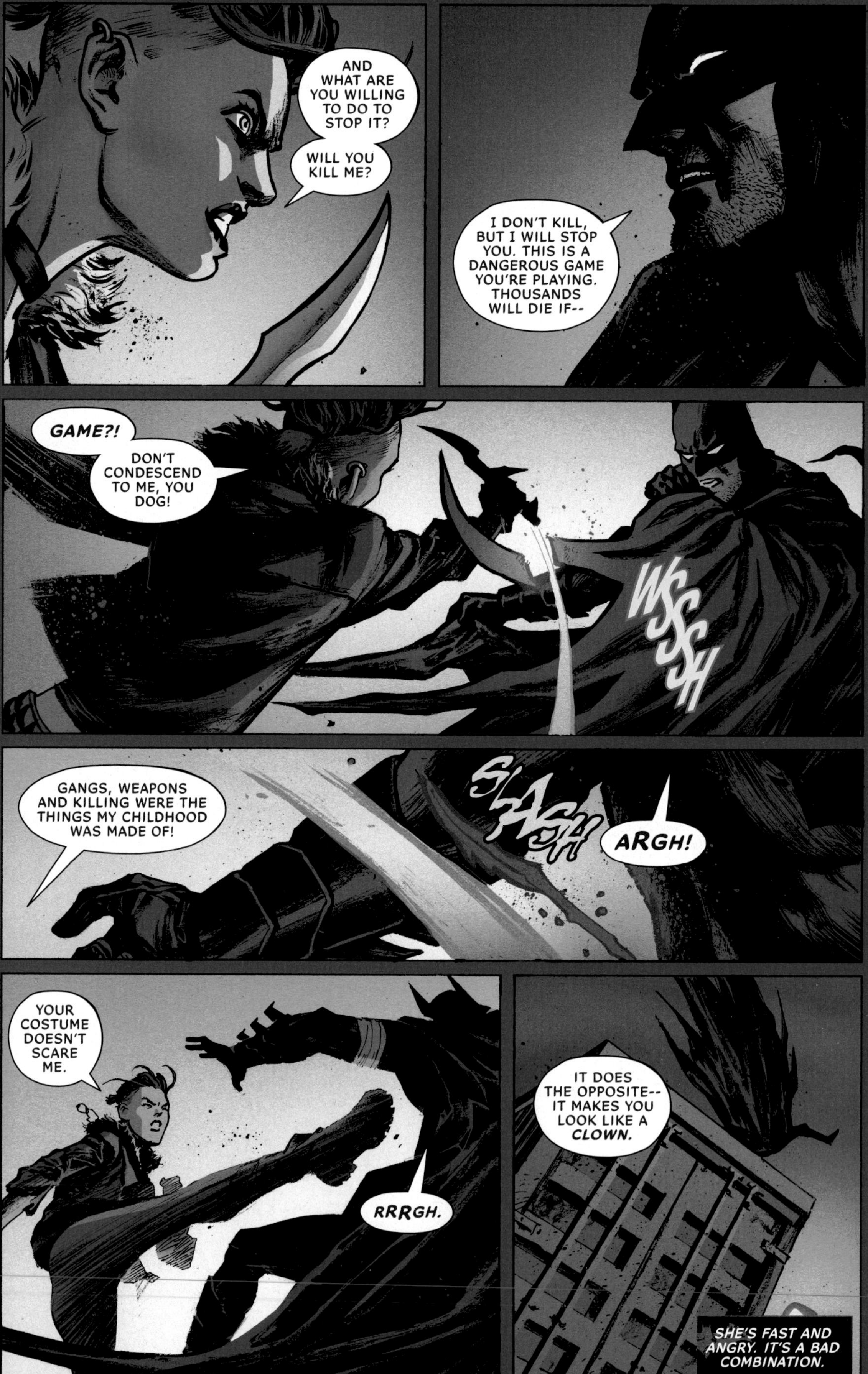
AND WHAT ARE YOU WILLING TO DO TO STOP IT?
WILL YOU KILL ME?
I DON'T KILL, BUT I WILL STOP YOU. THIS IS A DANGEROUS GAME YOU'RE PLAYING. THOUSANDS WILL DIE IF--
GAME?!
DON'T CONDESCEND TO ME, YOU DOG!
WSSSH
GANGS, WEAPONS AND KILLING WERE THE THINGS MY CHILDHOOD WAS MADE OF!
SLASH!
ARGH!
YOUR COSTUME DOESN'T SCARE ME.
RRRGH.
IT DOES THE OPPOSITE-- IT MAKES YOU LOOK LIKE A CLOWN.
SHE'S FAST AND ANGRY. IT'S A BAD COMBINATION.

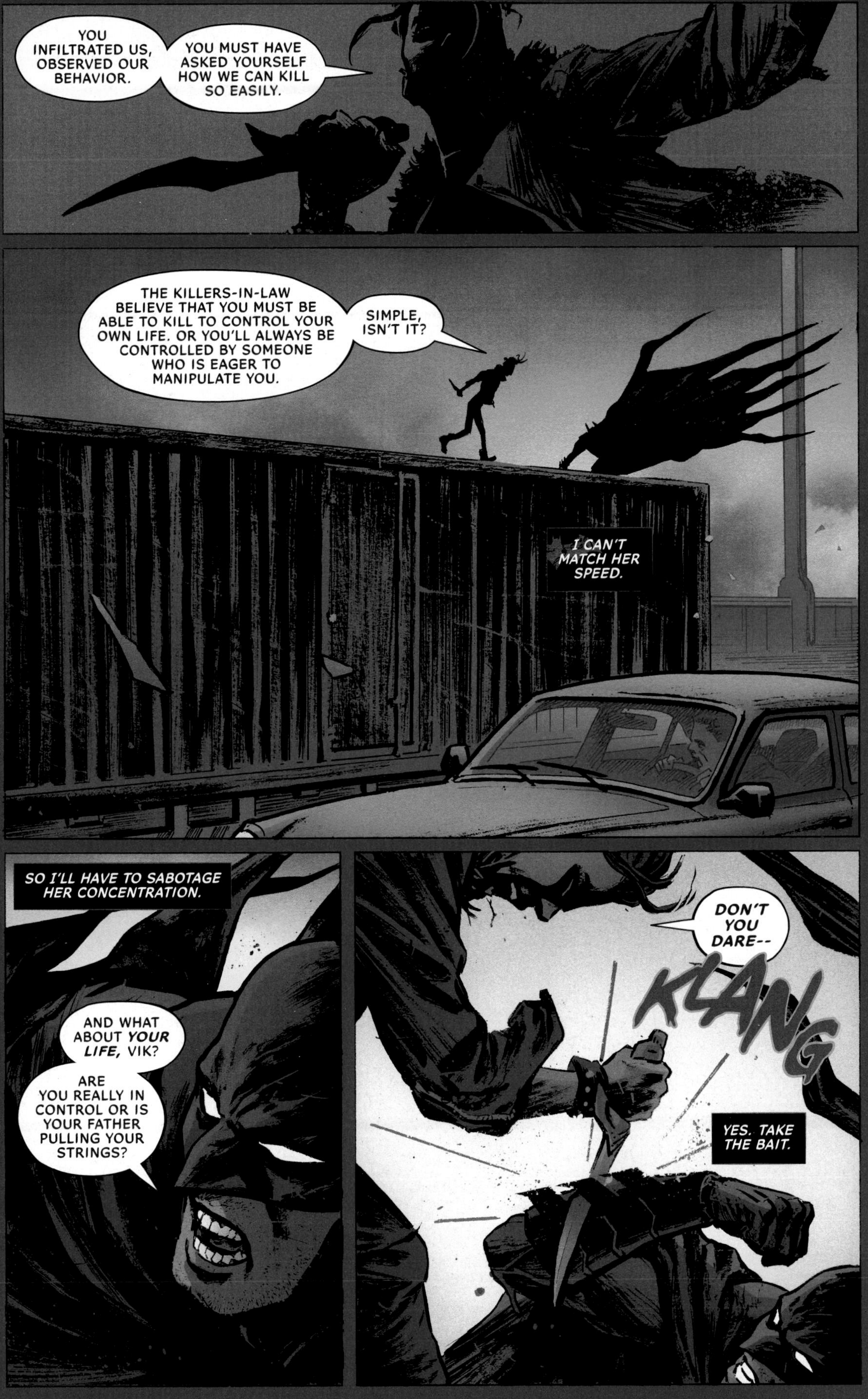

YOU INFILTRATED US, OBSERVED OUR BEHAVIOR.
YOU MUST HAVE ASKED YOURSELF HOW WE CAN KILL SO EASILY.
THE KILLERS-IN-LAW BELIEVE THAT YOU MUST BE ABLE TO KILL TO CONTROL YOUR OWN LIFE. OR YOU'LL ALWAYS BE CONTROLLED BY SOMEONE WHO IS EAGER TO MANIPULATE YOU.
SIMPLE, ISN'T IT?
I CAN'T MATCH HER SPEED.
SO I'LL HAVE TO SABOTAGE HER CONCENTRATION.
AND WHAT ABOUT *YOUR LIFE,* VIK?
ARE YOU REALLY IN CONTROL OR IS YOUR FATHER PULLING YOUR STRINGS?
DON'T YOU DARE--
KLANG
YES. TAKE THE BAIT.

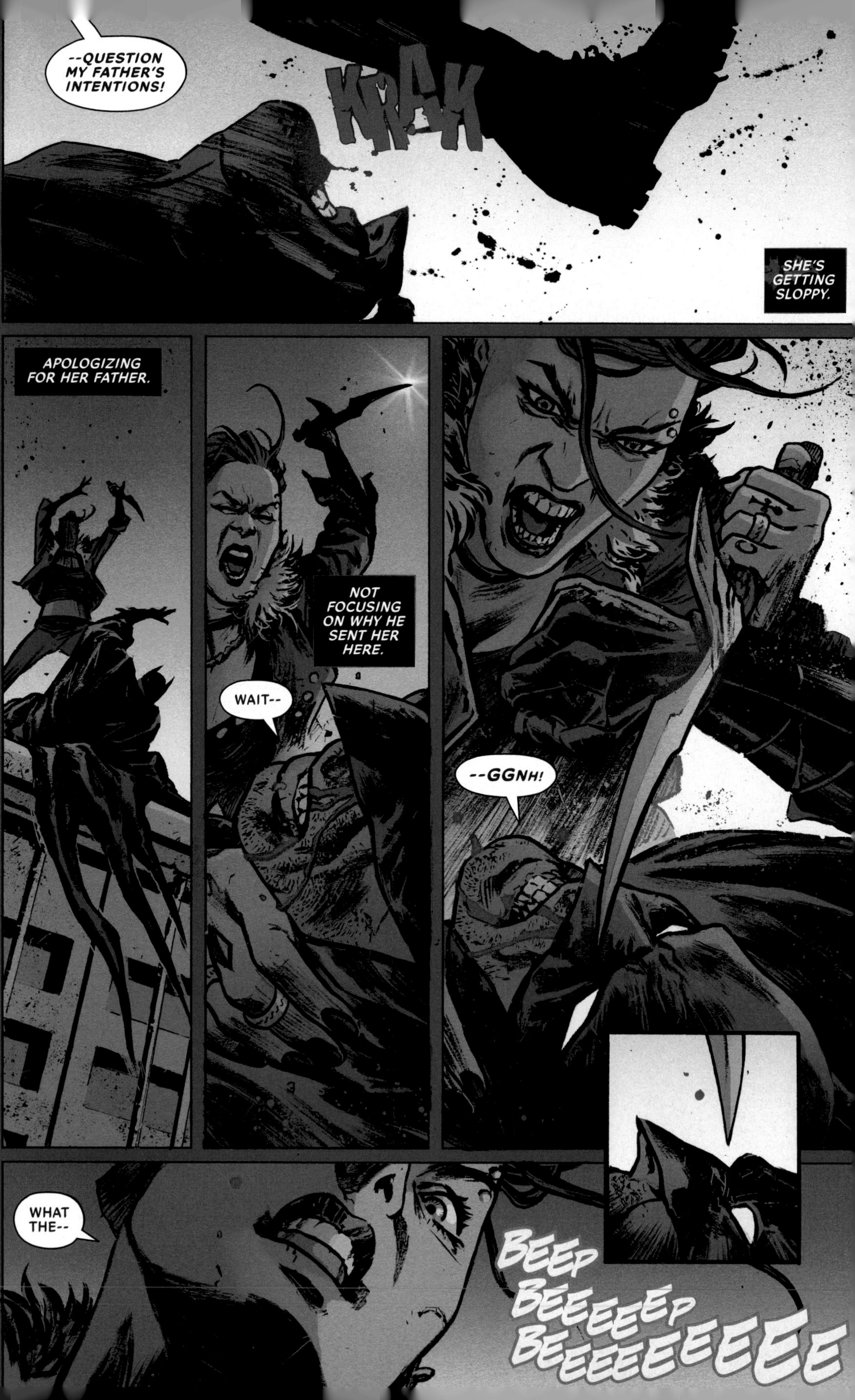
--QUESTION MY FATHER'S INTENTIONS!
KRAK
SHE'S GETTING SLOPPY.
APOLOGIZING FOR HER FATHER.
NOT FOCUSING ON WHY HE SENT HER HERE.
WAIT--
--GGNH!
WHAT THE--
BEEP
BEEEEEEP
BEEEEEEEEEE

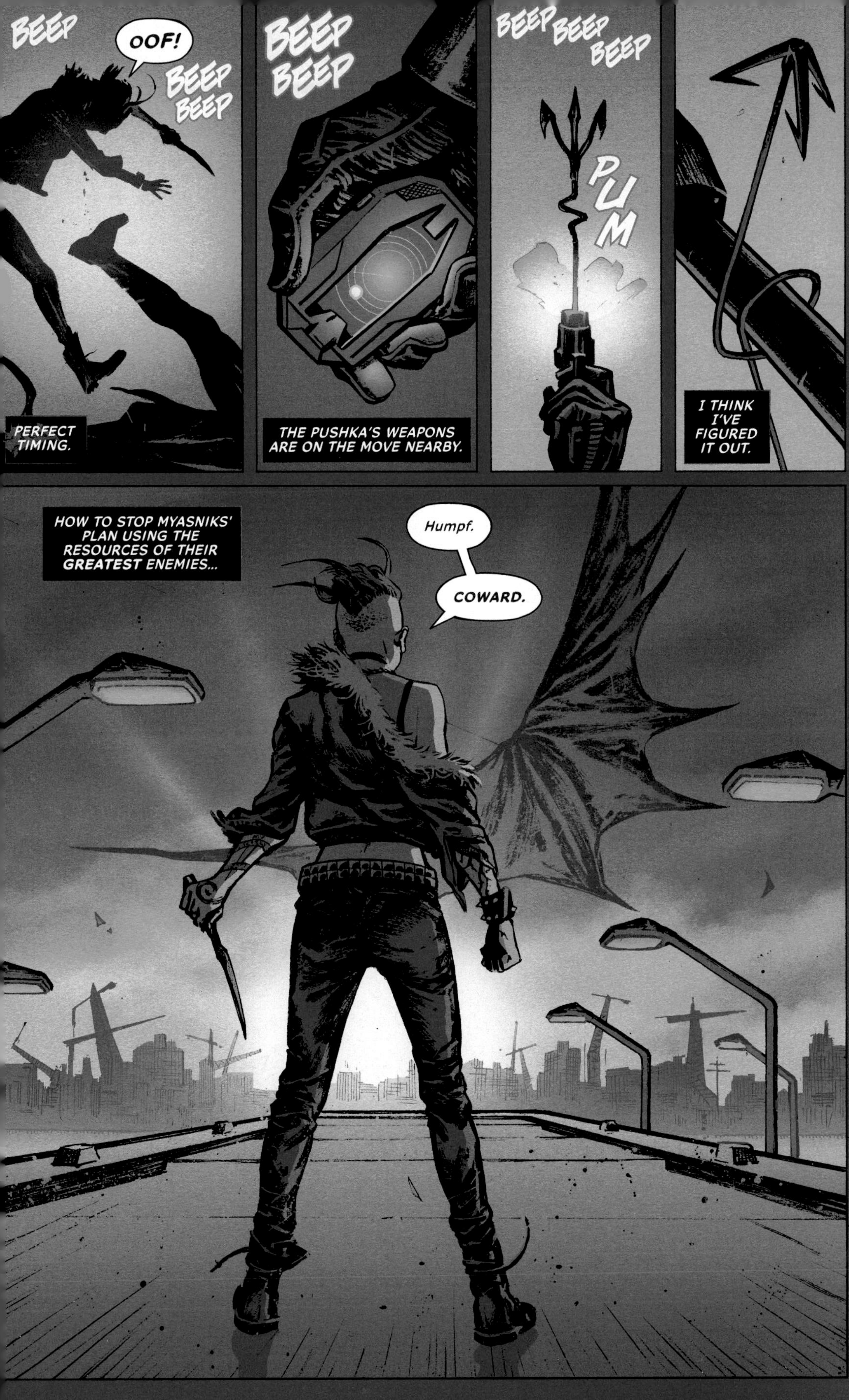
BEEP
OOF!
BEEP BEEP
PERFECT TIMING.
BEEP BEEP
THE PUSHKA'S WEAPONS ARE ON THE MOVE NEARBY.
BEEP BEEP BEEP
PUM
I THINK I'VE FIGURED IT OUT.
HOW TO STOP MYASNIKS' PLAN USING THE RESOURCES OF THEIR GREATEST ENEMIES...
Humpf.
COWARD.

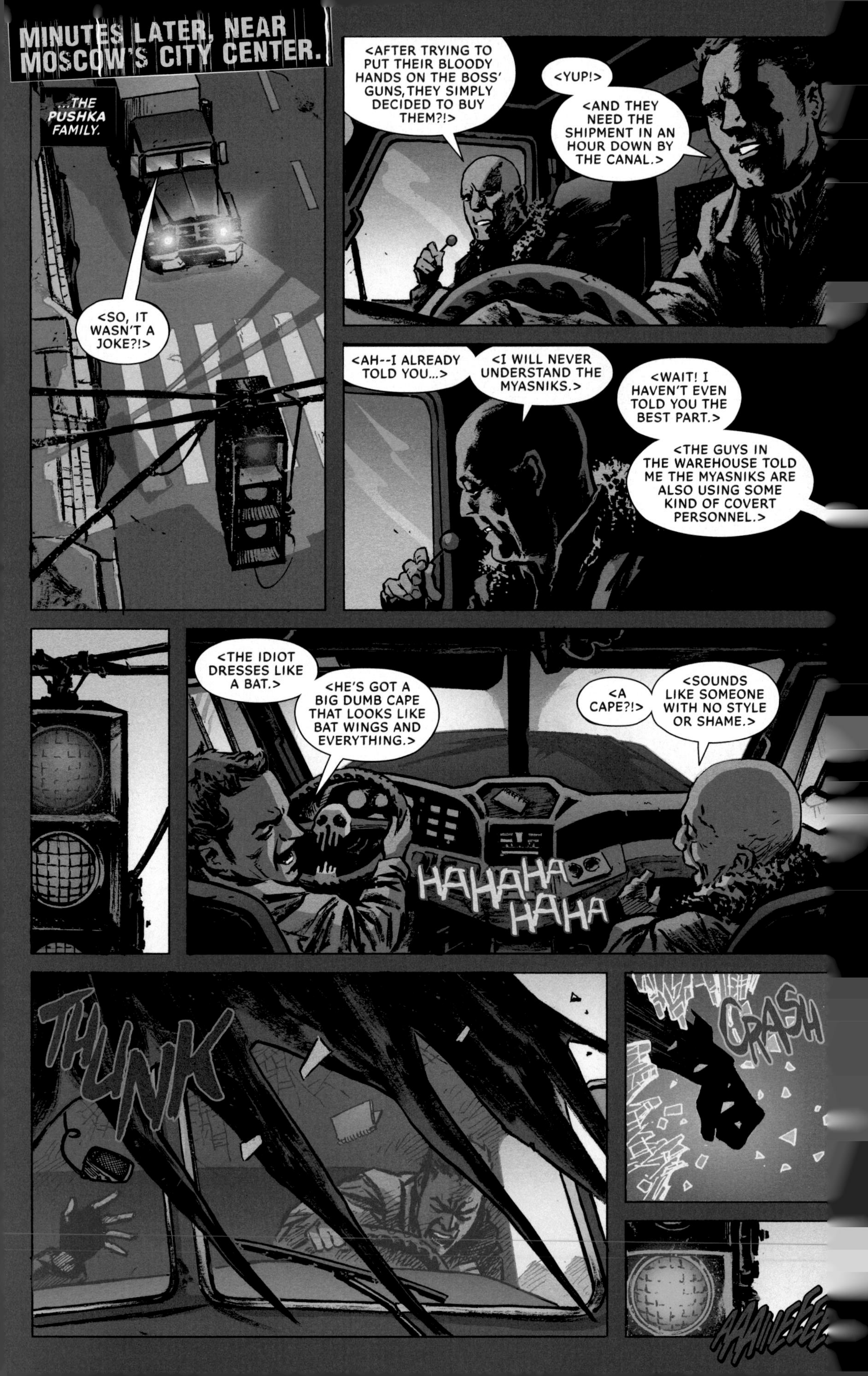
MINUTES LATER, NEAR MOSCOW'S CITY CENTER.
...THE PUSHKA FAMILY.
<SO, IT WASN'T A JOKE?!>
<AFTER TRYING TO PUT THEIR BLOODY HANDS ON THE BOSS' GUNS, THEY SIMPLY DECIDED TO BUY THEM?!>
<YUP!>
<AND THEY NEED THE SHIPMENT IN AN HOUR DOWN BY THE CANAL.>
<AH--I ALREADY TOLD YOU...>
<I WILL NEVER UNDERSTAND THE MYASNIKS.>
<WAIT! I HAVEN'T EVEN TOLD YOU THE BEST PART.>
<THE GUYS IN THE WAREHOUSE TOLD ME THE MYASNIKS ARE ALSO USING SOME KIND OF COVERT PERSONNEL.>
<THE IDIOT DRESSES LIKE A BAT.>
<HE'S GOT A BIG DUMB CAPE THAT LOOKS LIKE BAT WINGS AND EVERYTHING.>
<A CAPE?!>
<SOUNDS LIKE SOMEONE WITH NO STYLE OR SHAME.>
HAHAHA HAHA
THUNK
CRASH
AAAIIEEEE

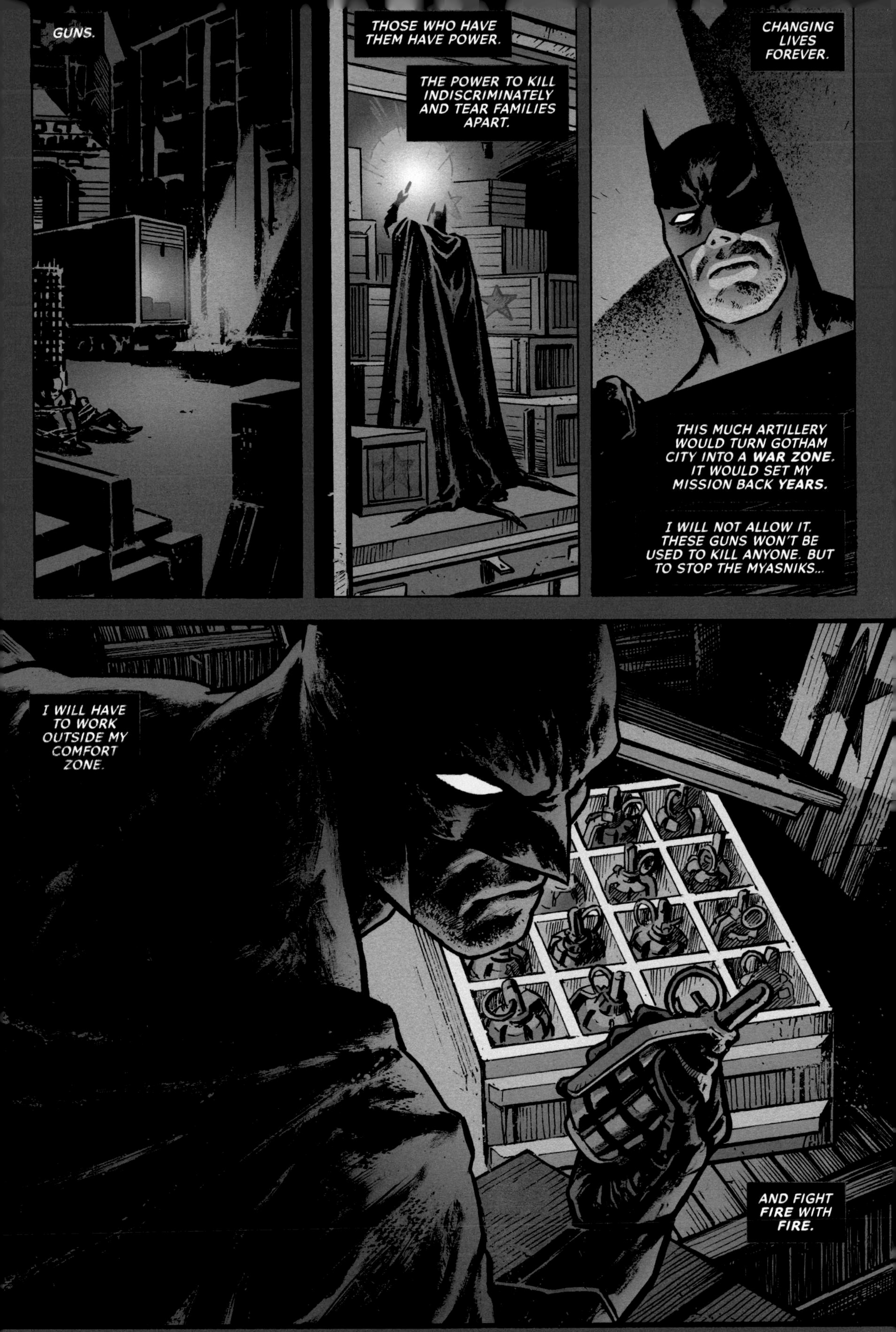
GUNS.
THOSE WHO HAVE THEM HAVE POWER.
THE POWER TO KILL INDISCRIMINATELY AND TEAR FAMILIES APART.
CHANGING LIVES FOREVER.
THIS MUCH ARTILLERY WOULD TURN GOTHAM CITY INTO A **WAR ZONE**. IT WOULD SET MY MISSION BACK **YEARS**.
I WILL NOT ALLOW IT. THESE GUNS WON'T BE USED TO KILL ANYONE. BUT TO STOP THE MYASNIKS...
I WILL HAVE TO WORK OUTSIDE MY COMFORT ZONE.
AND FIGHT **FIRE** WITH **FIRE**.

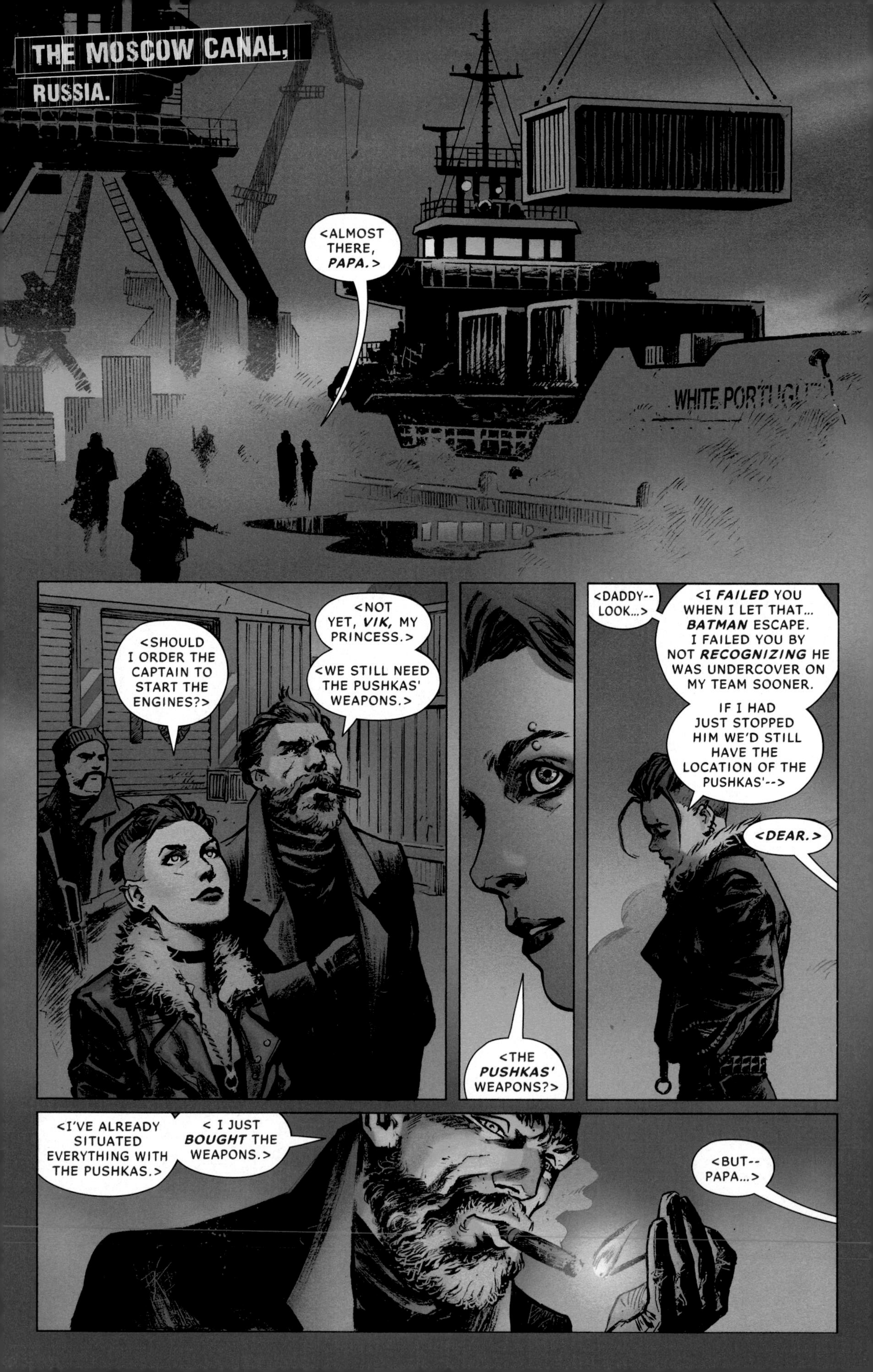
THE MOSCOW CANAL,
RUSSIA.
<ALMOST THERE, *PAPA.*>
WHITE PORTUG
<SHOULD I ORDER THE CAPTAIN TO START THE ENGINES?>
<NOT YET, *VIK,* MY PRINCESS.>
<WE STILL NEED THE PUSHKAS' WEAPONS.>
<THE *PUSHKAS'* WEAPONS?>
<DADDY-- LOOK...>
<I *FAILED* YOU WHEN I LET THAT... *BATMAN* ESCAPE. I FAILED YOU BY NOT *RECOGNIZING* HE WAS UNDERCOVER ON MY TEAM SOONER.
IF I HAD JUST STOPPED HIM WE'D STILL HAVE THE LOCATION OF THE PUSHKAS'-->
<DEAR.>
<I'VE ALREADY SITUATED EVERYTHING WITH THE PUSHKAS.>
< I JUST *BOUGHT* THE WEAPONS.>
<BUT-- PAPA...>

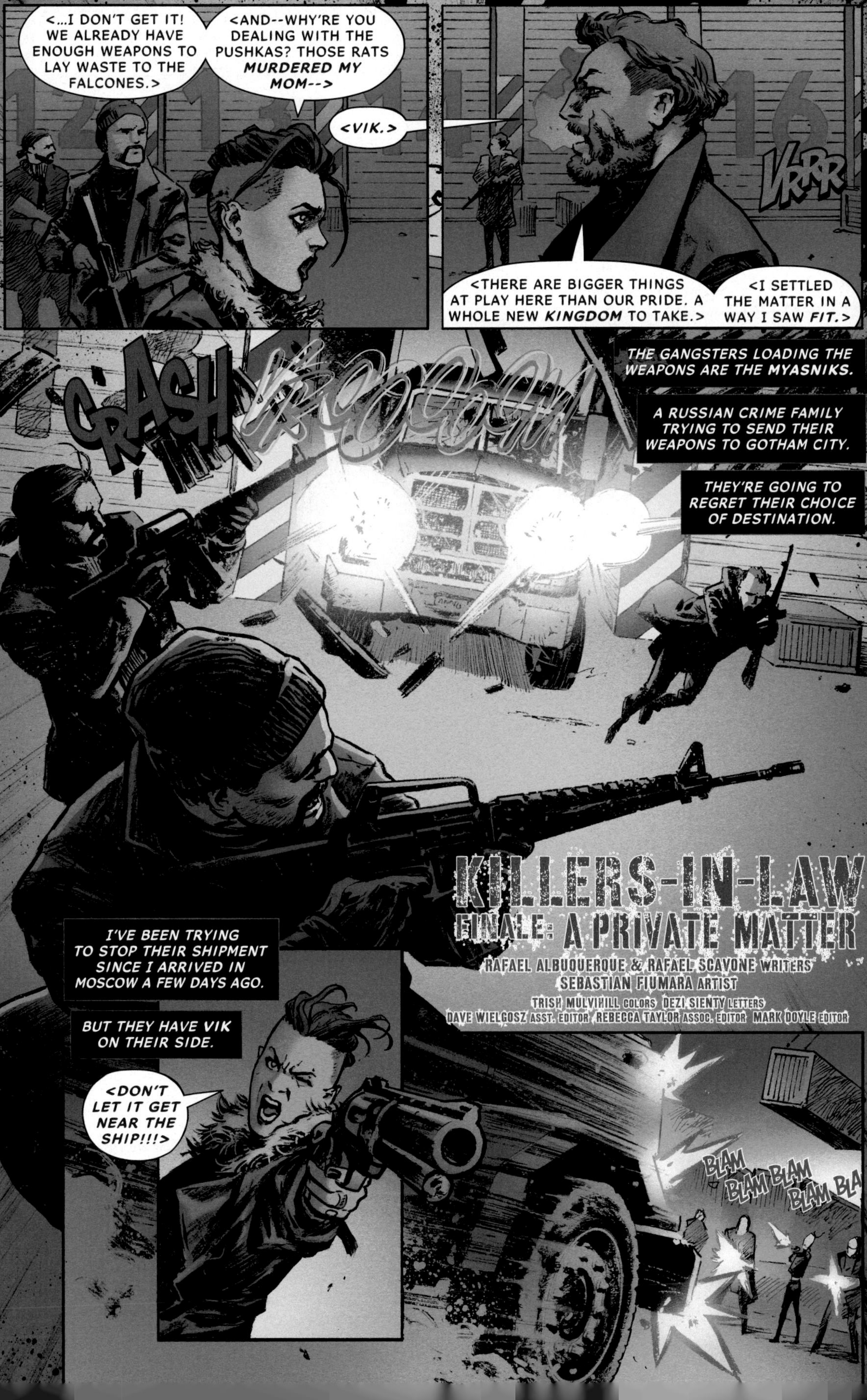
<...I DON'T GET IT! WE ALREADY HAVE ENOUGH WEAPONS TO LAY WASTE TO THE FALCONES.>
<AND--WHY'RE YOU DEALING WITH THE PUSHKAS? THOSE RATS MURDERED MY MOM-->
<VIK.>
VRRR
<THERE ARE BIGGER THINGS AT PLAY HERE THAN OUR PRIDE. A WHOLE NEW KINGDOM TO TAKE.>
<I SETTLED THE MATTER IN A WAY I SAW FIT.>
CRASH
THE GANGSTERS LOADING THE WEAPONS ARE THE MYASNIKS.
A RUSSIAN CRIME FAMILY TRYING TO SEND THEIR WEAPONS TO GOTHAM CITY.
THEY'RE GOING TO REGRET THEIR CHOICE OF DESTINATION.
KILLERS-IN-LAW
FINALE: A PRIVATE MATTER
RAFAEL ALBUQUERQUE & RAFAEL SCAVONE WRITERS
SEBASTIAN FIUMARA ARTIST
TRISH MULVIHILL COLORS DEZI SIENTY LETTERS
DAVE WIELGOSZ ASST. EDITOR REBECCA TAYLOR ASSOC. EDITOR MARK DOYLE EDITOR
I'VE BEEN TRYING TO STOP THEIR SHIPMENT SINCE I ARRIVED IN MOSCOW A FEW DAYS AGO.
BUT THEY HAVE VIK ON THEIR SIDE.
<DON'T LET IT GET NEAR THE SHIP!!!>
BLAM BLAM BLAM BLAM BLA

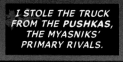

I STOLE THE TRUCK FROM THE PUSHKAS, THE MYASNIKS' PRIMARY RIVALS.
IT'S FULLY LOADED WITH SOVIET ARMS THEY WERE ANTICIPATING BEING DELIVERED. BUT NOT BY ME.
BLAM
ZING
ZING
BLAM
GOING IN AGAINST THAT MANY ARMED MEN HEAD ON WOULD BE A MISTAKE.
I HAVE A BULLET WOUND REMINDING ME OF THAT.
GOTHAM CAN'T AFFORD ANOTHER ONE OF MY ERRORS.
I SENT IN THE TRUCK.
POW
ALFRED TAUGHT ME THAT TRICK.
A SIMPLE DECOY.
THAT'S RIGHT. YOU EXPECTED THE PUSHKAS TO DOUBLE-CROSS YOU. FOCUS ON WHERE THE ATTACK CAME FROM.
SCRAAAAAAAATCH
DON'T LOOK WHERE IT COUNTS.

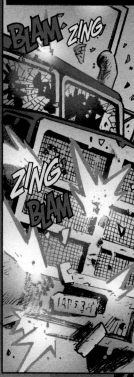

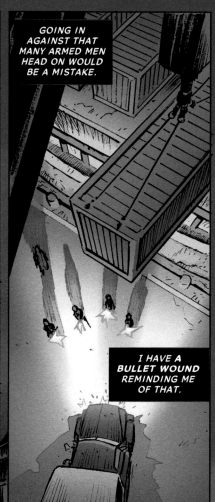

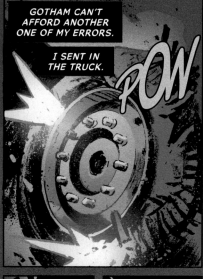

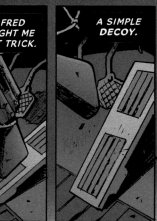

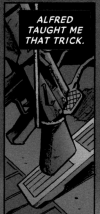

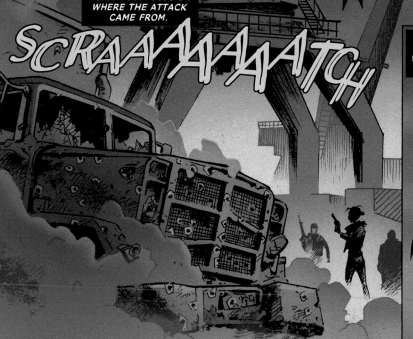

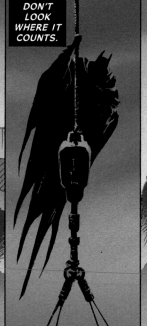

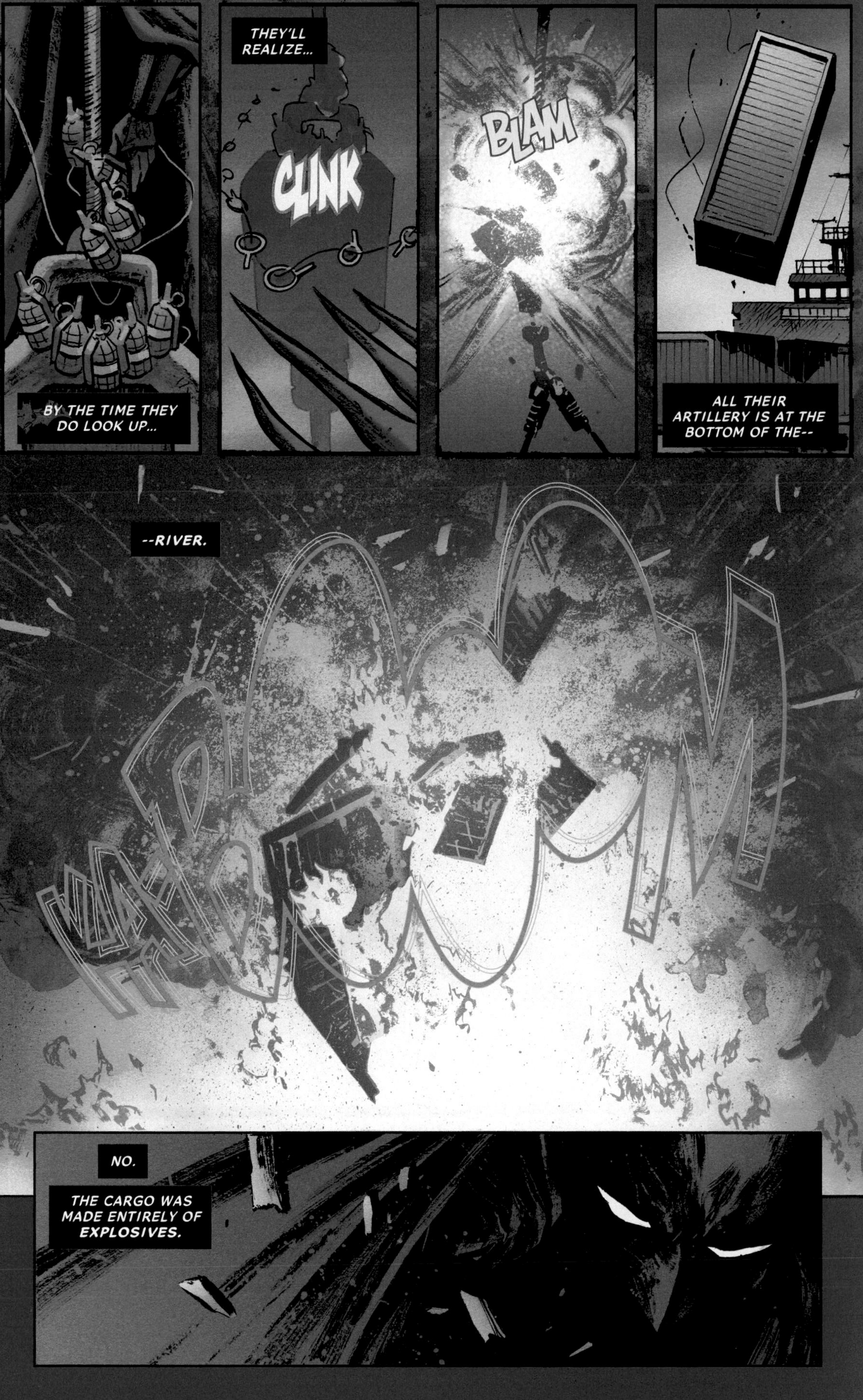
BY THE TIME THEY DO LOOK UP...
THEY'LL REALIZE...
CLINK
BLAM
ALL THEIR ARTILLERY IS AT THE BOTTOM OF THE--
--RIVER.
NO.
THE CARGO WAS MADE ENTIRELY OF EXPLOSIVES.

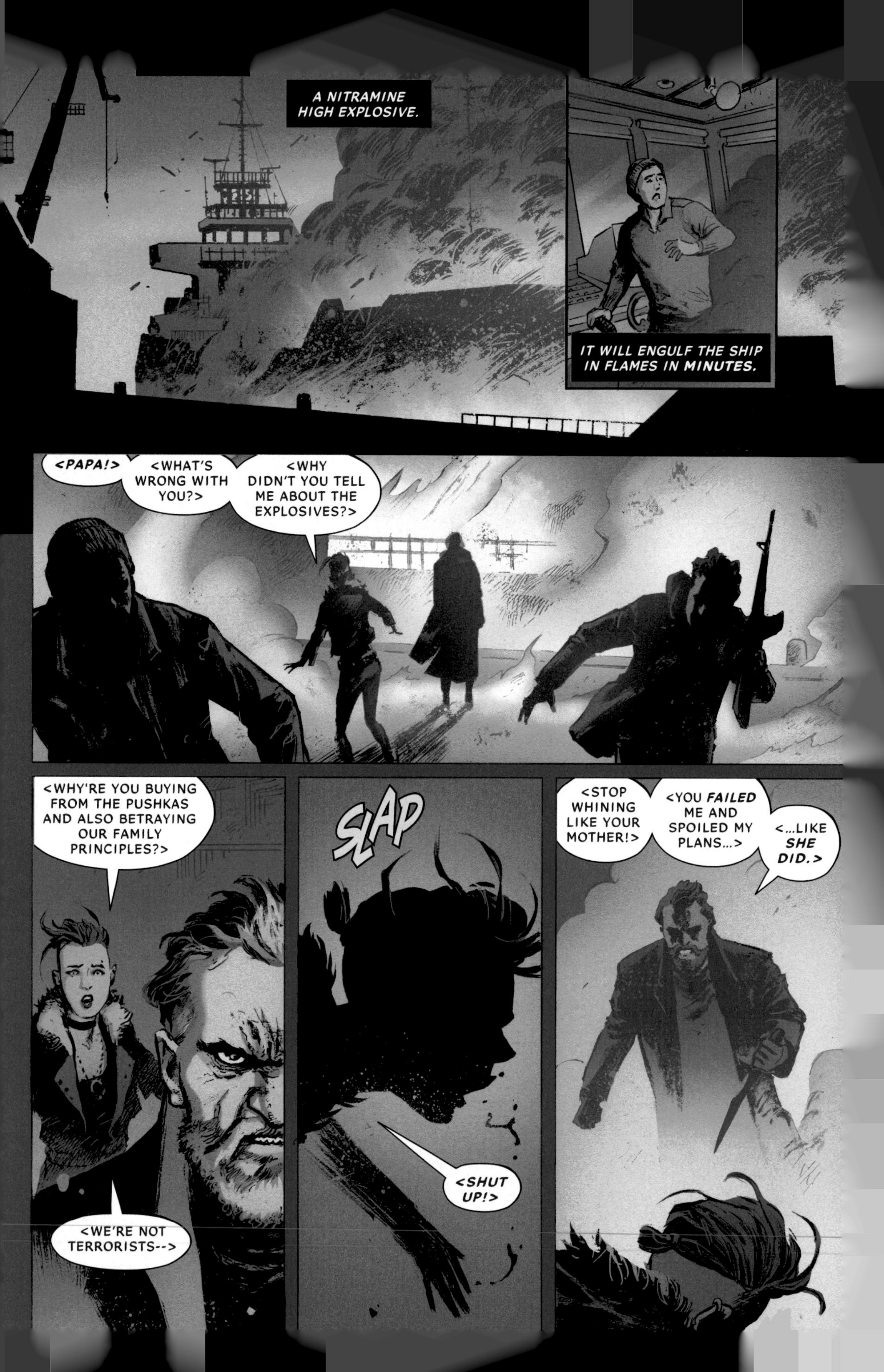
A NITRAMINE HIGH EXPLOSIVE.
IT WILL ENGULF THE SHIP IN FLAMES IN MINUTES.
<PAPA!>
<WHAT'S WRONG WITH YOU?>
<WHY DIDN'T YOU TELL ME ABOUT THE EXPLOSIVES?>
<WHY'RE YOU BUYING FROM THE PUSHKAS AND ALSO BETRAYING OUR FAMILY PRINCIPLES?>
<WE'RE NOT TERRORISTS-->
SLAP
<SHUT UP!>
<STOP WHINING LIKE YOUR MOTHER!>
<YOU FAILED ME AND SPOILED MY PLANS...>
<...LIKE SHE DID.>

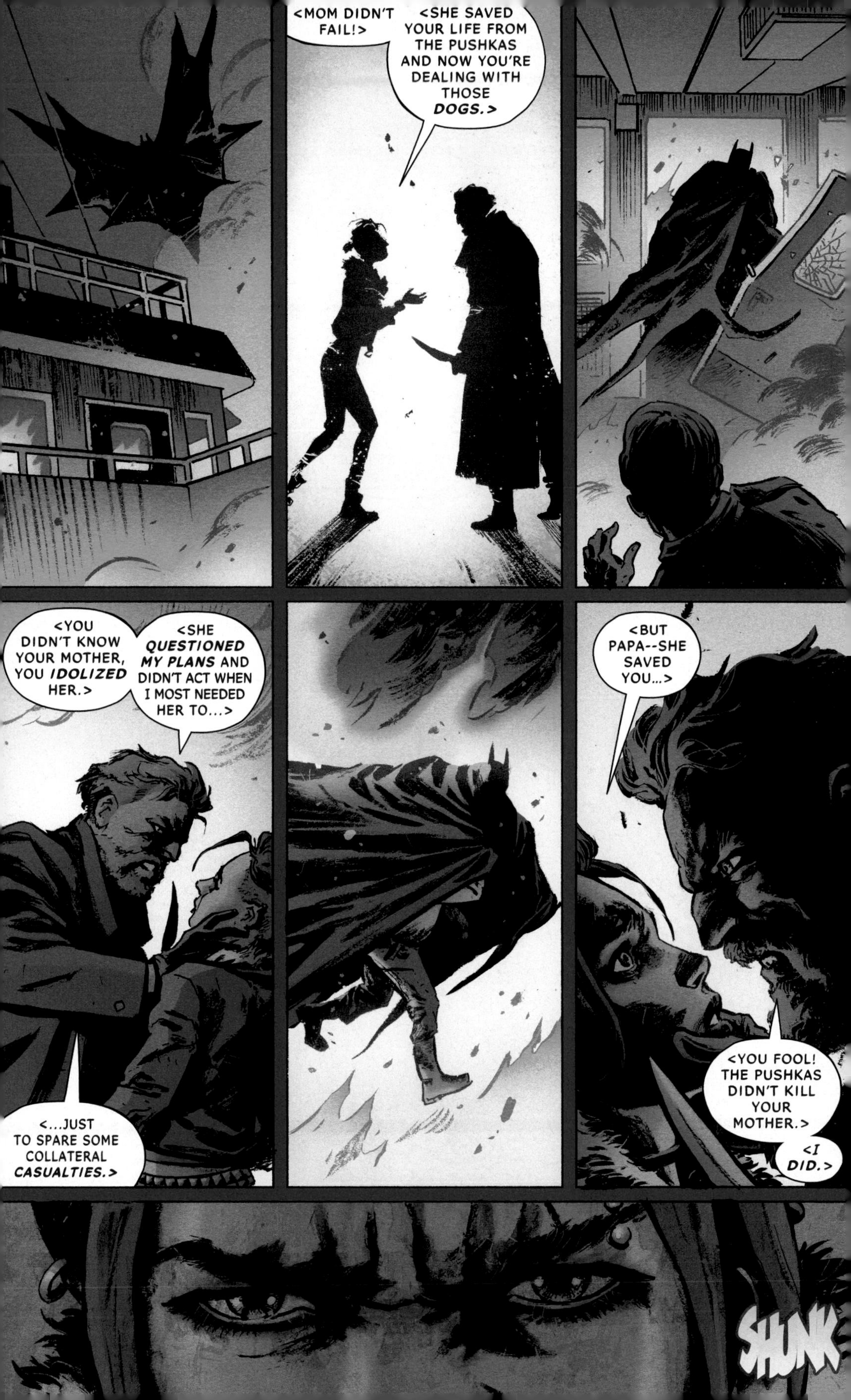

<MOM DIDN'T FAIL!>
<SHE SAVED YOUR LIFE FROM THE PUSHKAS AND NOW YOU'RE DEALING WITH THOSE DOGS.>
<YOU DIDN'T KNOW YOUR MOTHER, YOU IDOLIZED HER.>
<SHE QUESTIONED MY PLANS AND DIDN'T ACT WHEN I MOST NEEDED HER TO...>
<...JUST TO SPARE SOME COLLATERAL CASUALTIES.>
<BUT PAPA--SHE SAVED YOU...>
<YOU FOOL! THE PUSHKAS DIDN'T KILL YOUR MOTHER.>
<I DID.>
SHUNK

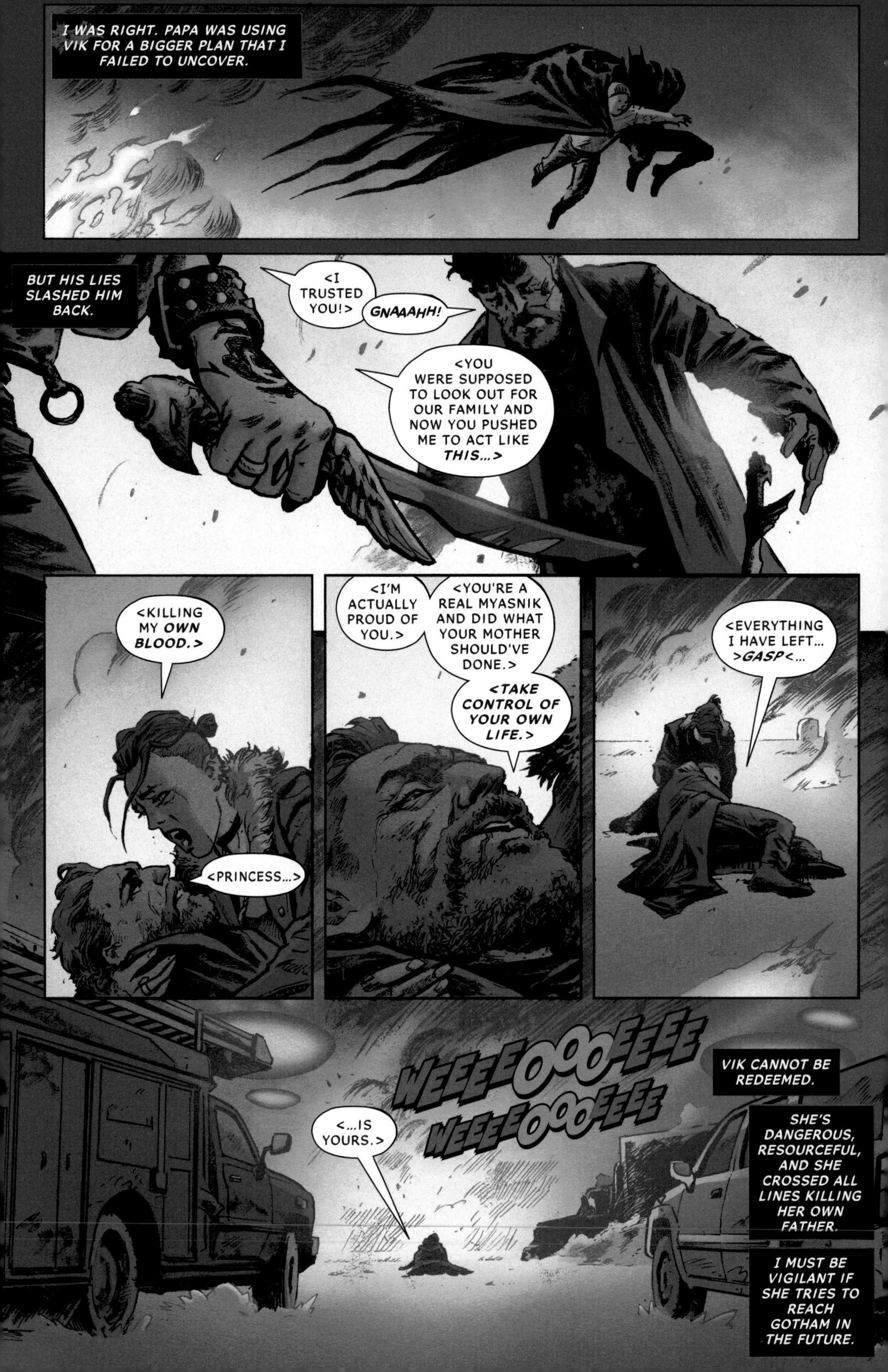
I WAS RIGHT. PAPA WAS USING VIK FOR A BIGGER PLAN THAT I FAILED TO UNCOVER.
BUT HIS LIES SLASHED HIM BACK.
<I TRUSTED YOU!>
GNAAAHH!
<YOU WERE SUPPOSED TO LOOK OUT FOR OUR FAMILY AND NOW YOU PUSHED ME TO ACT LIKE THIS...>
<KILLING MY OWN BLOOD.>
<PRINCESS...>
<I'M ACTUALLY PROUD OF YOU.>
<YOU'RE A REAL MYASNIK AND DID WHAT YOUR MOTHER SHOULD'VE DONE.>
<TAKE CONTROL OF YOUR OWN LIFE.>
<EVERYTHING I HAVE LEFT... >GASP<...
<...IS YOURS.>
WEEEEOOOEEEE
WEEEEOOOEEEE
VIK CANNOT BE REDEEMED.
SHE'S DANGEROUS, RESOURCEFUL, AND SHE CROSSED ALL LINES KILLING HER OWN FATHER.
I MUST BE VIGILANT IF SHE TRIES TO REACH GOTHAM IN THE FUTURE.

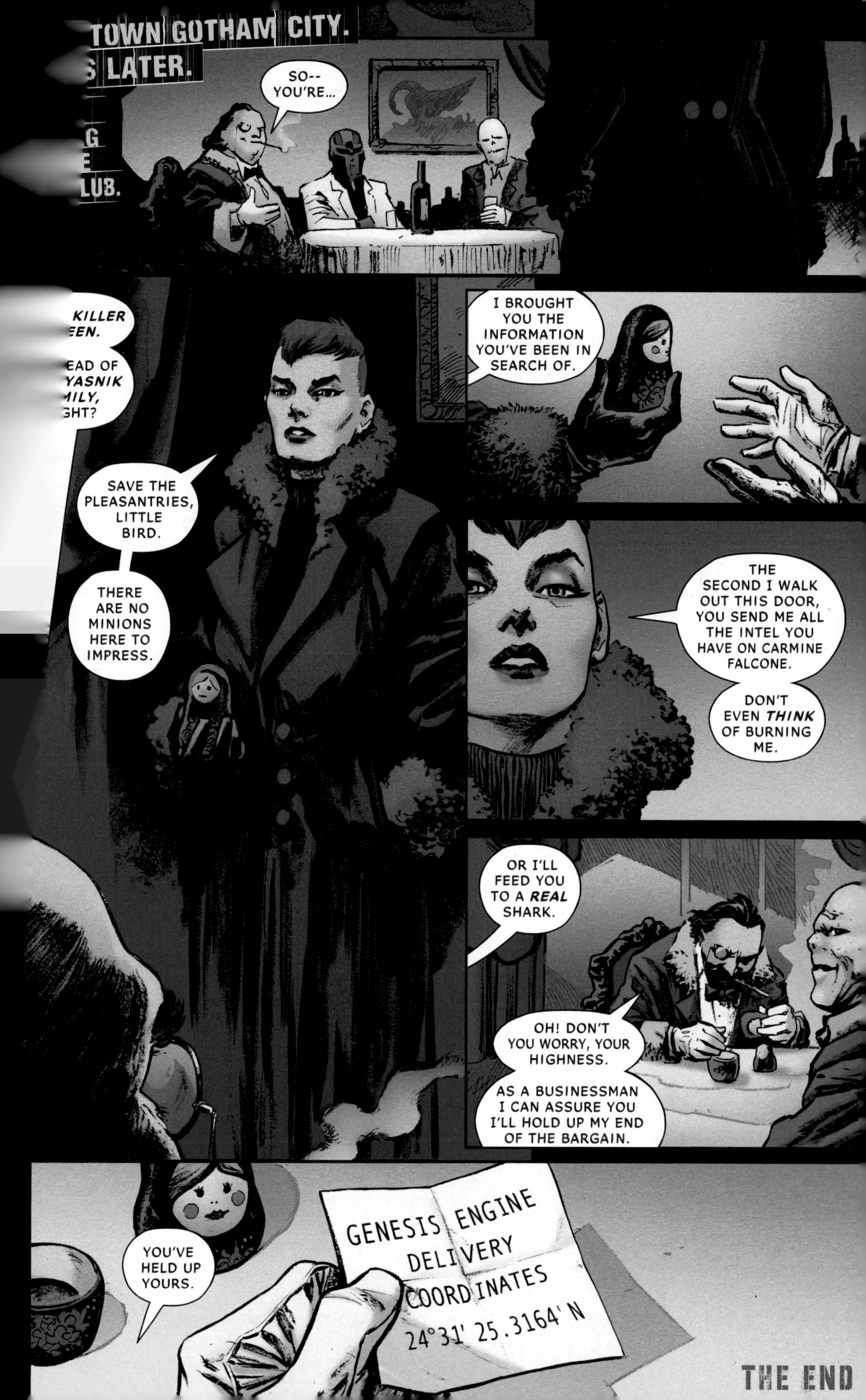
TOWN GOTHAM CITY.
LATER.
SO-- YOU'RE...
KILLER
SAVE THE PLEASANTRIES, LITTLE BIRD.
THERE ARE NO MINIONS HERE TO IMPRESS.
I BROUGHT YOU THE INFORMATION YOU'VE BEEN IN SEARCH OF.
THE SECOND I WALK OUT THIS DOOR, YOU SEND ME ALL THE INTEL YOU HAVE ON CARMINE FALCONE.
DON'T EVEN *THINK* OF BURNING ME.
OR I'LL FEED YOU TO A *REAL* SHARK.
OH! DON'T YOU WORRY, YOUR HIGHNESS.
AS A BUSINESSMAN I CAN ASSURE YOU I'LL HOLD UP MY END OF THE BARGAIN.
YOU'VE HELD UP YOURS.
GENESIS ENGINE DELIVERY COORDINATES 24°31' 25.3164' N
THE END

ALL★STAR BATMAN

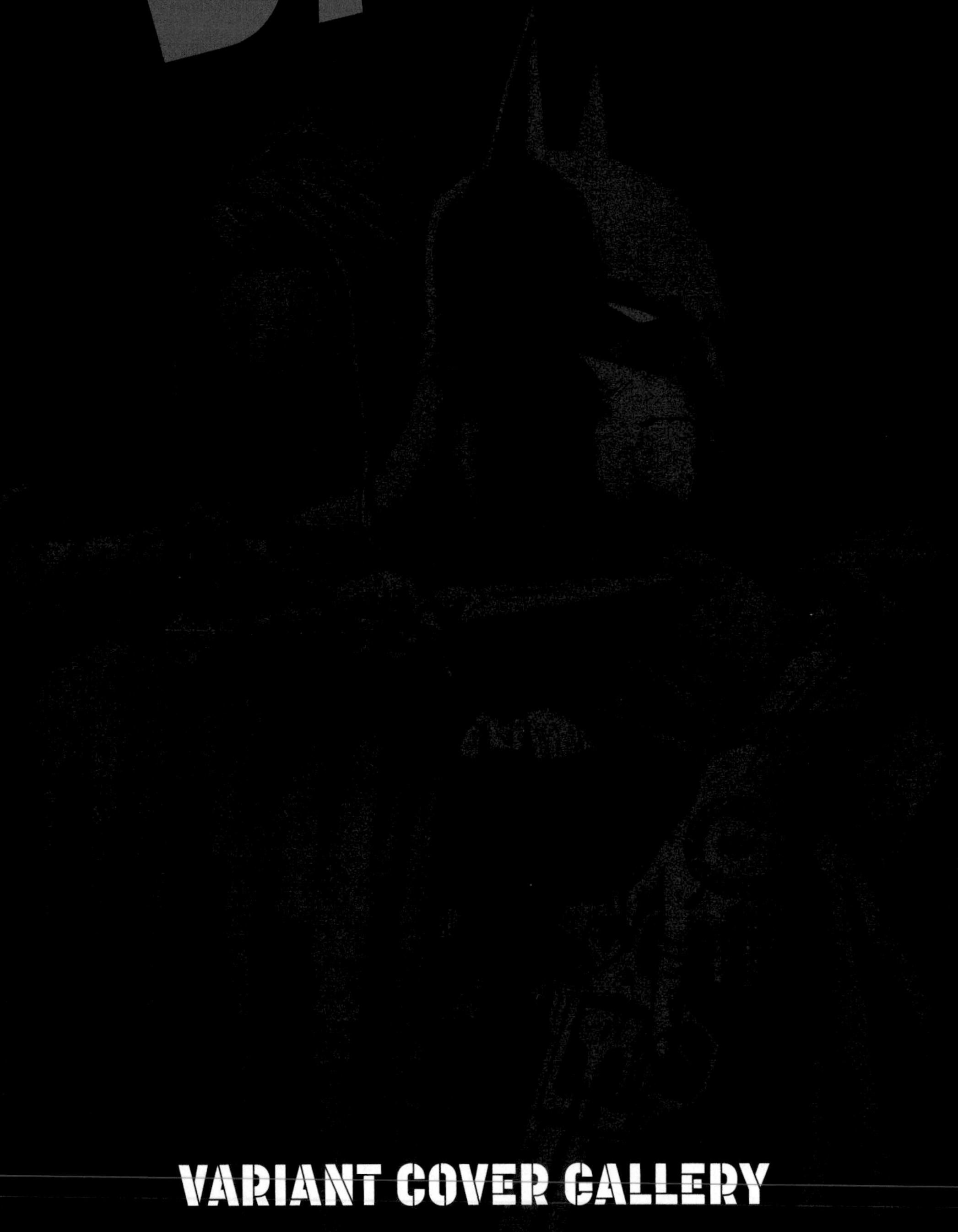

VARIANT COVER GALLERY

ALL-STAR BATMAN #10 variant by Rafael Albuquerque

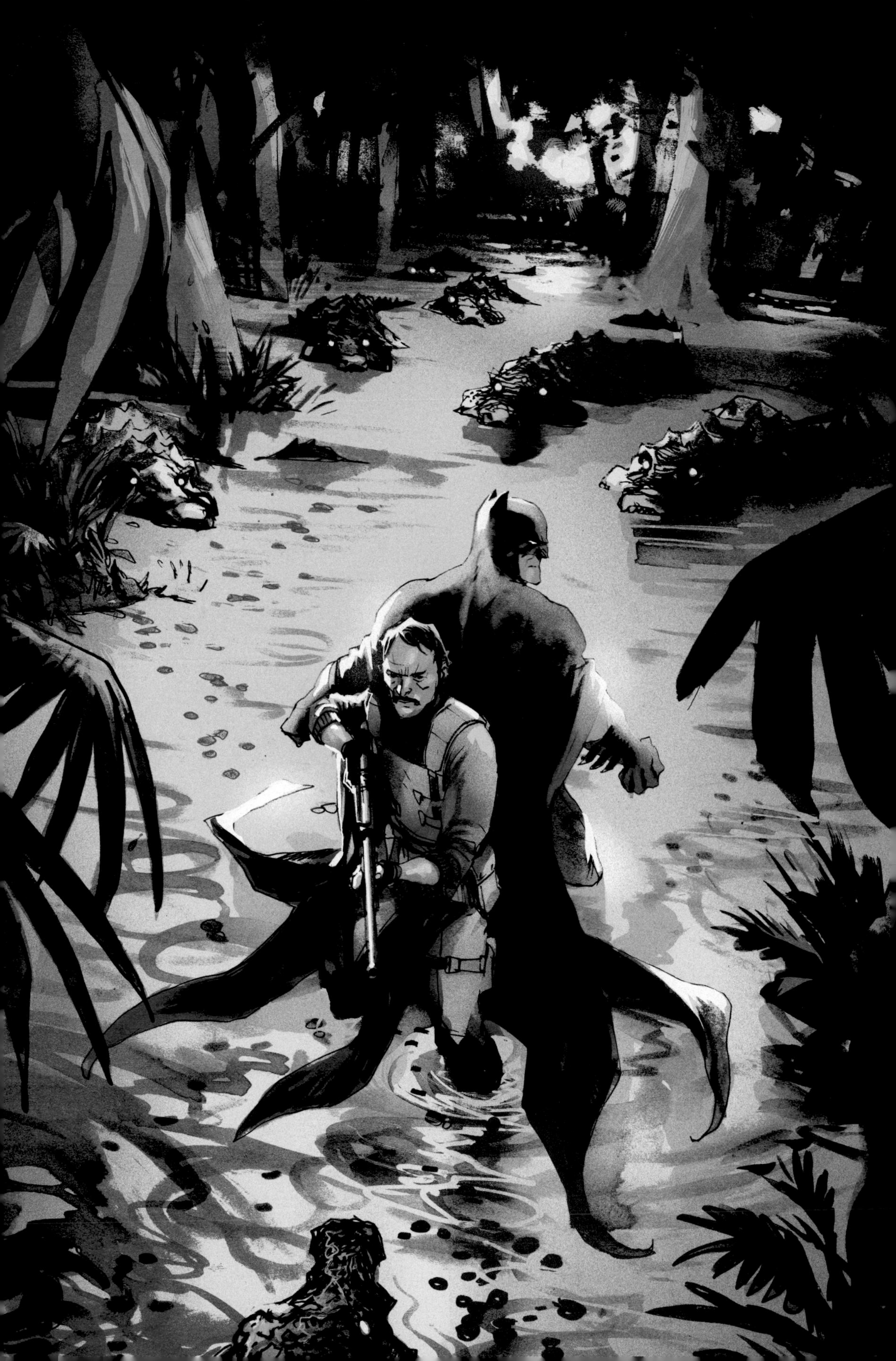

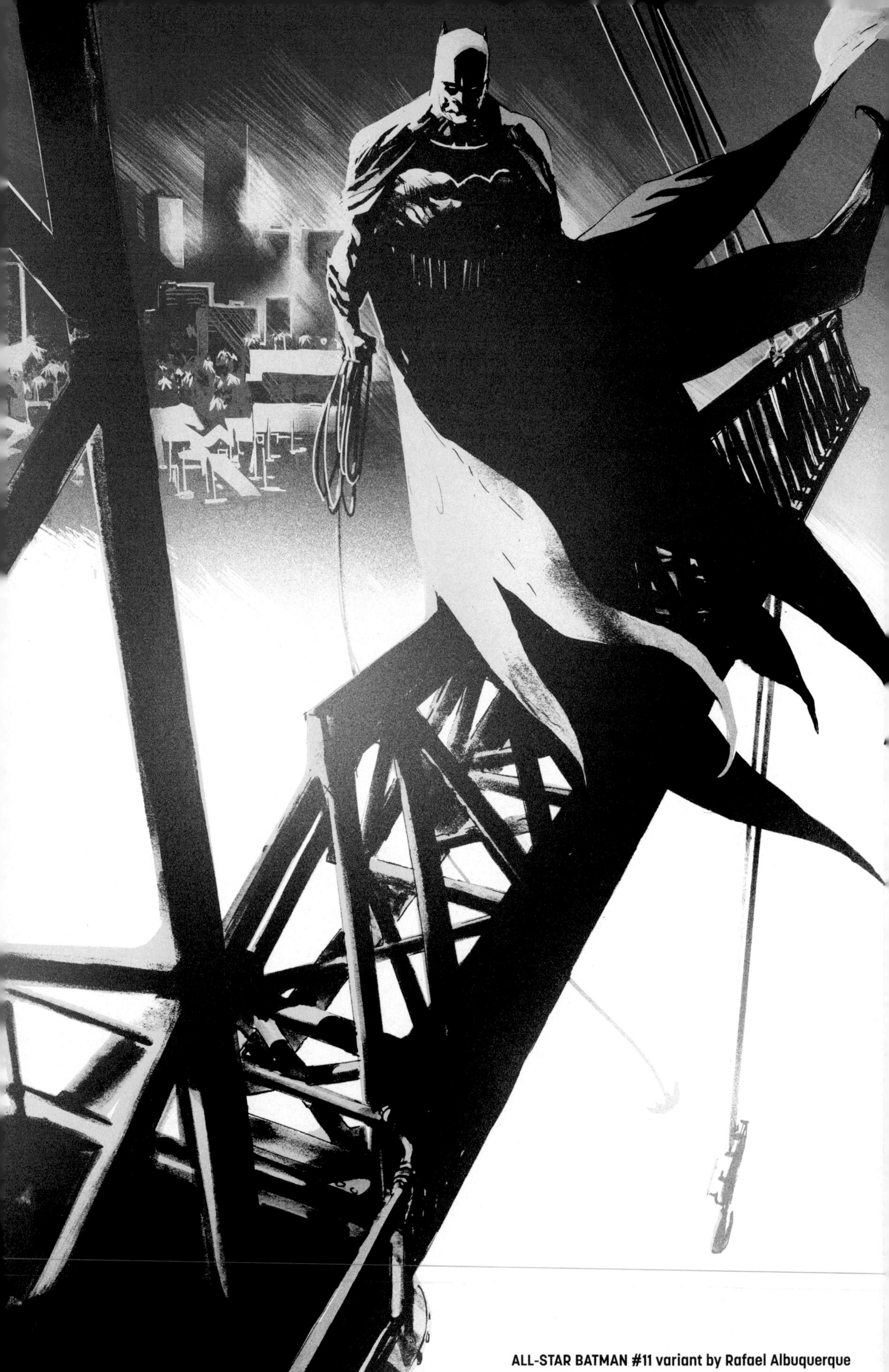

ALL-STAR BATMAN #11 variant by Rafael Albuquerque

ALL-STAR BATMAN #12 variant by Rafael Albuquerque

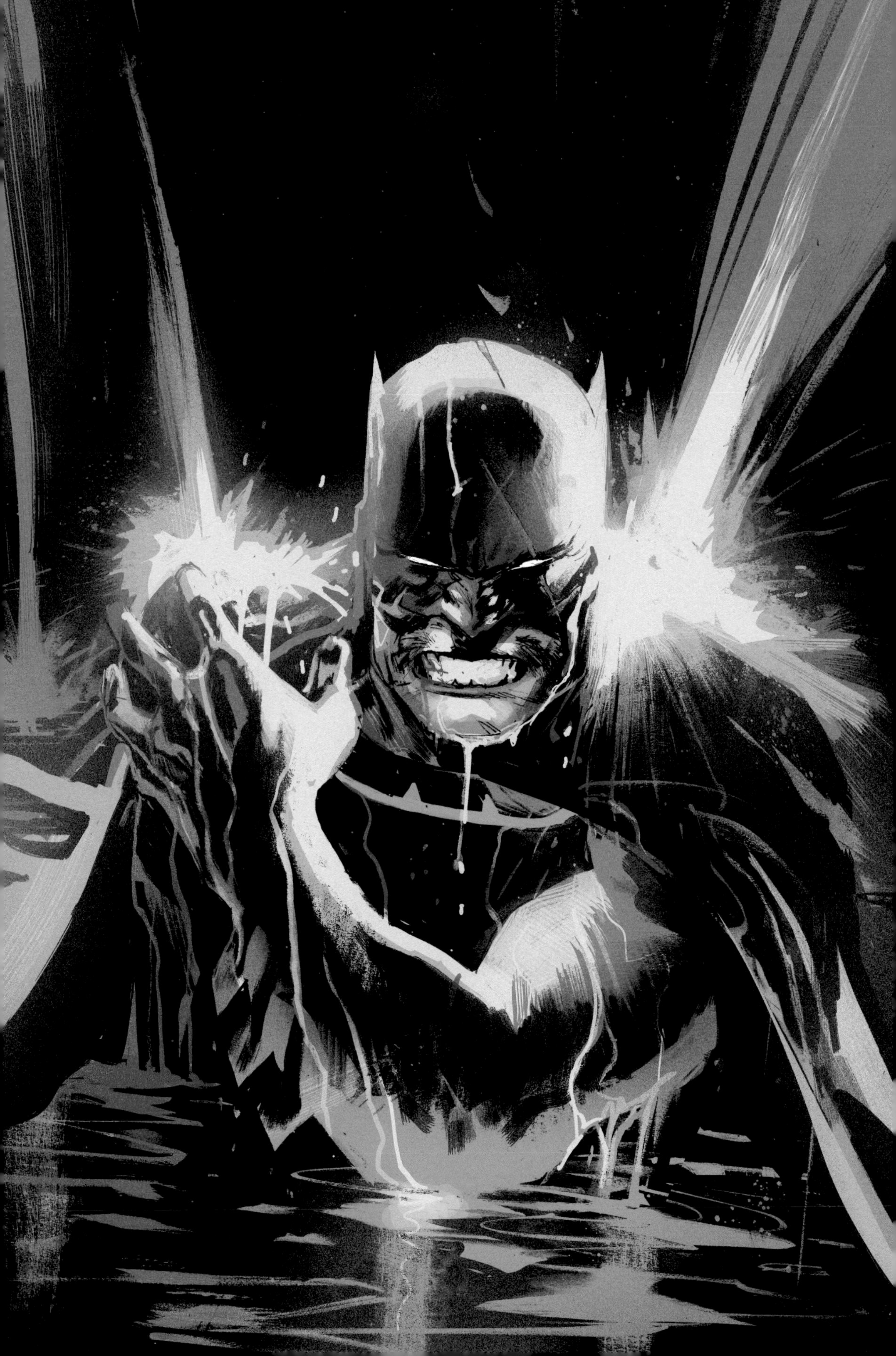

ALL-STAR BATMAN #13 variant by Rafael Albuquerque

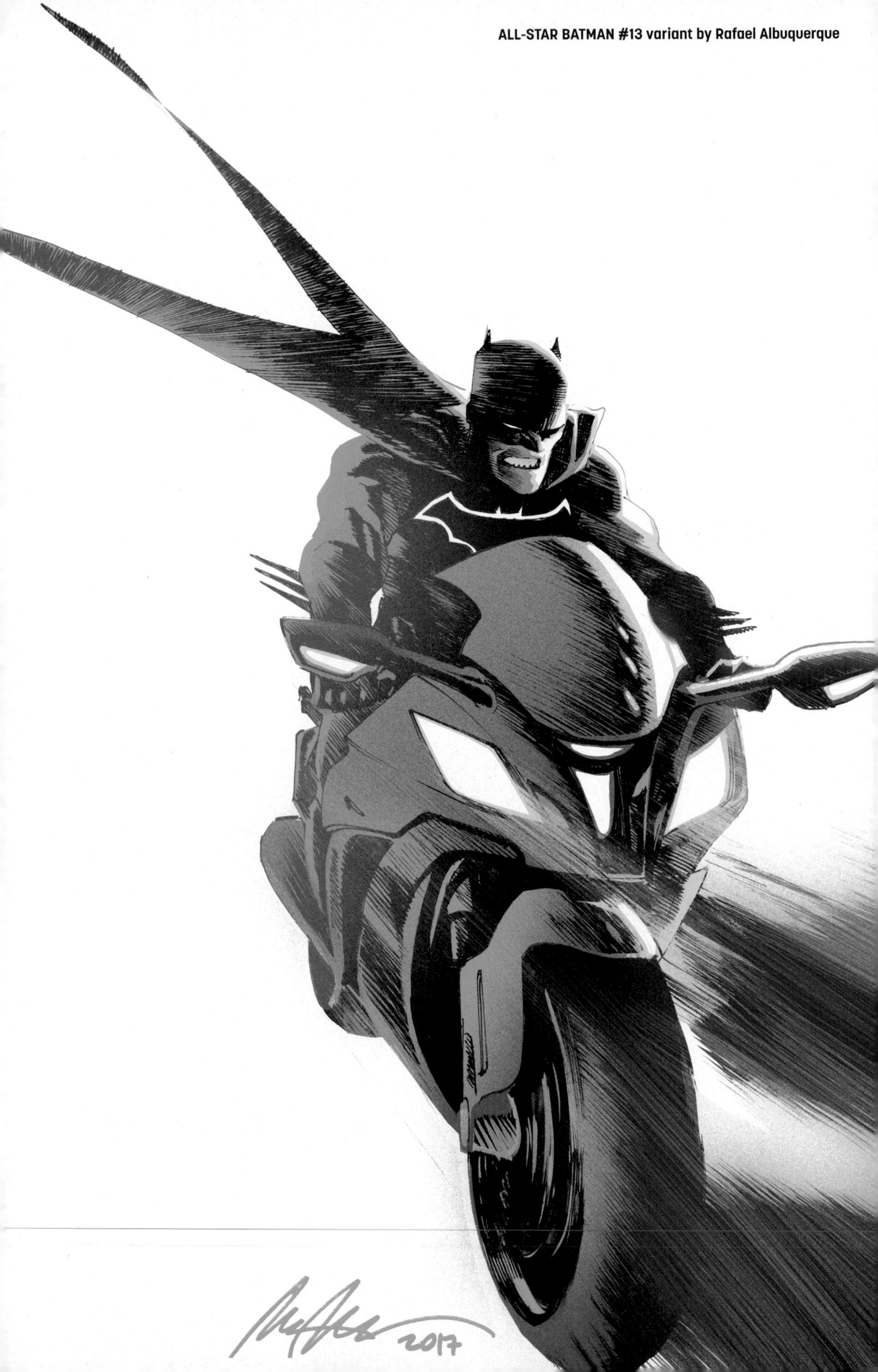

ALL-STAR BATMAN #14 variant by Rafael Albuquerque

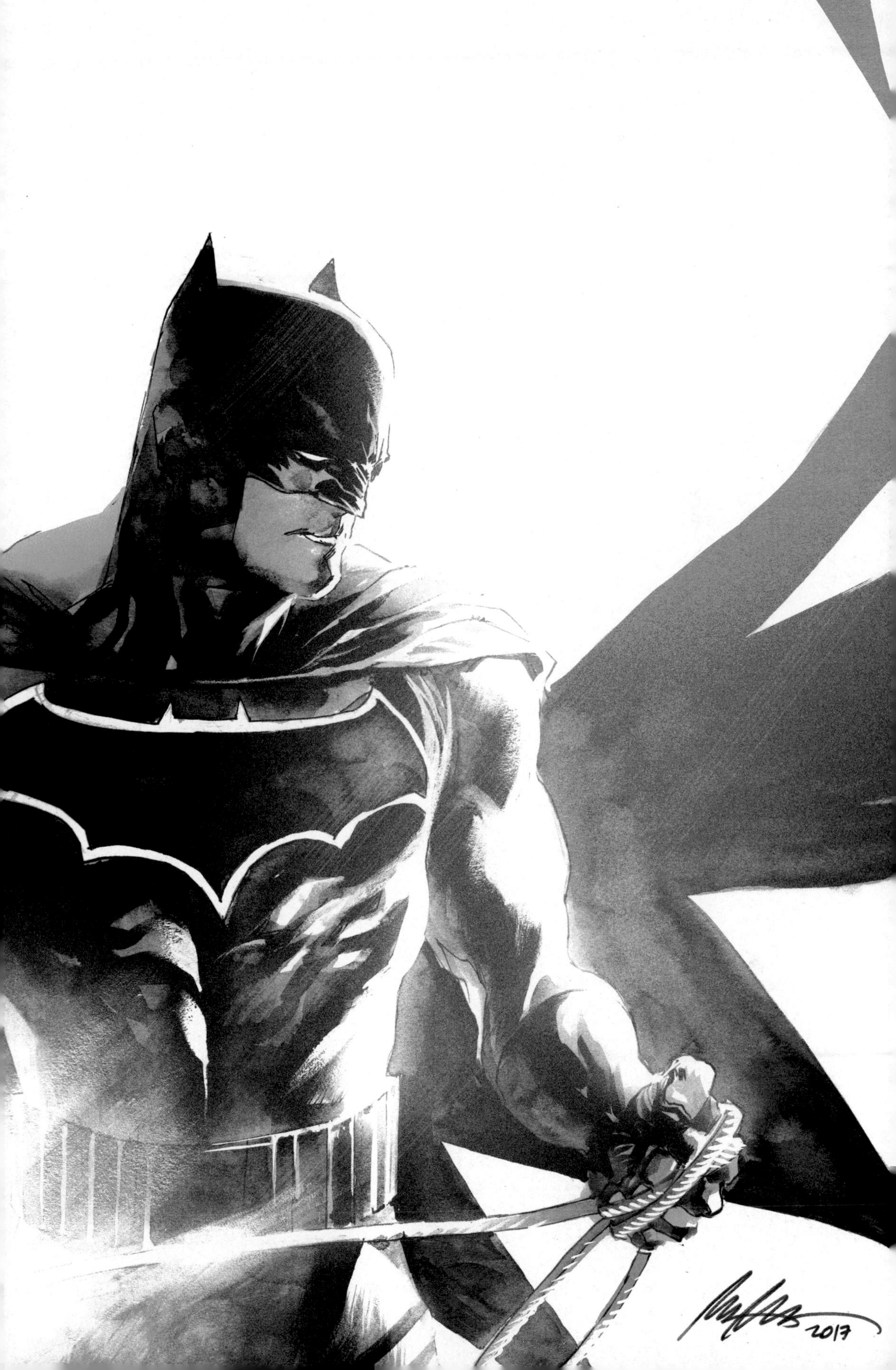
2017

ALL-STAR BATMAN #10 variant by Sebastian Fiumara

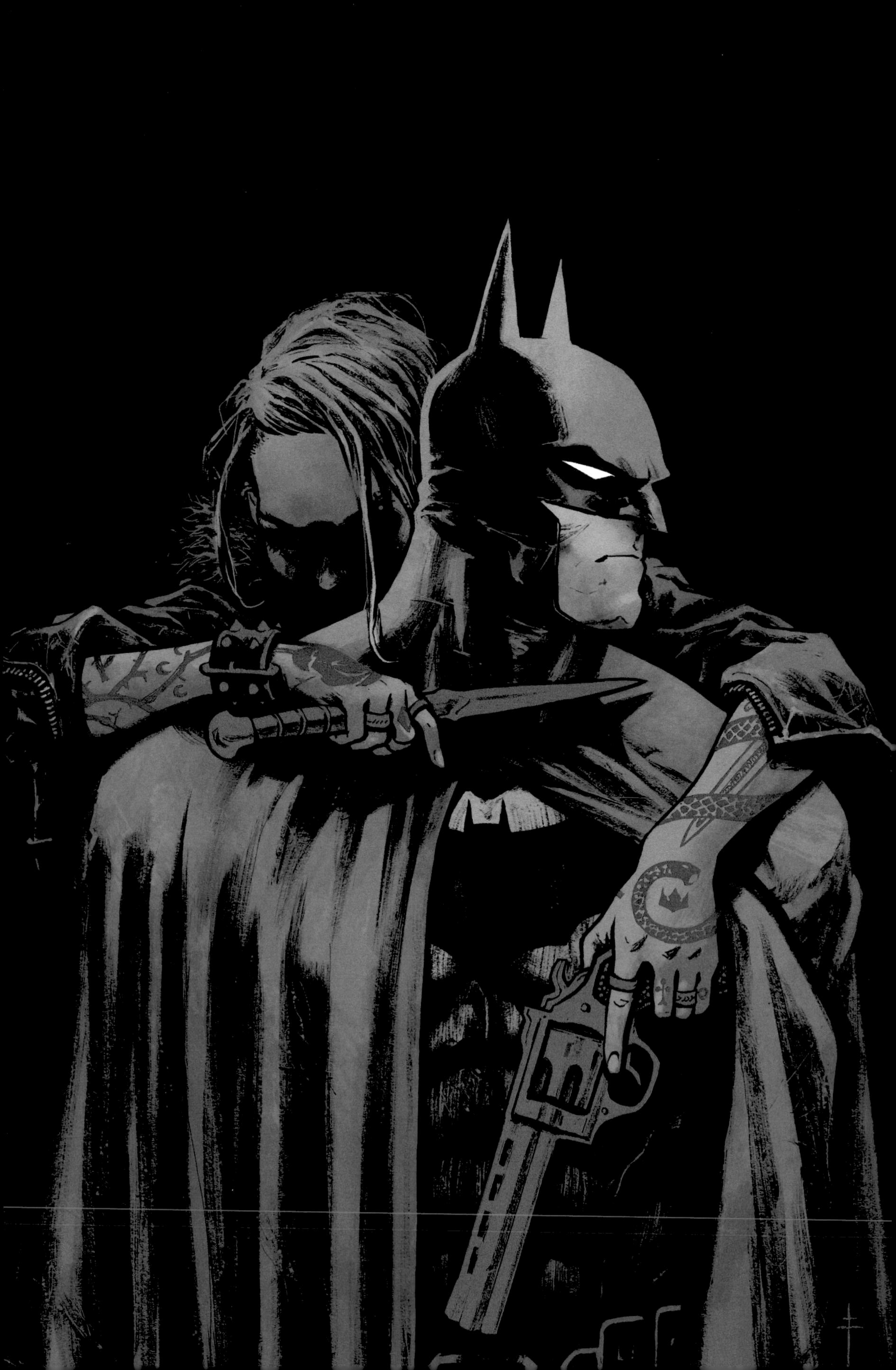

ALL-STAR BATMAN #11 variant by Sebastian Fiumara

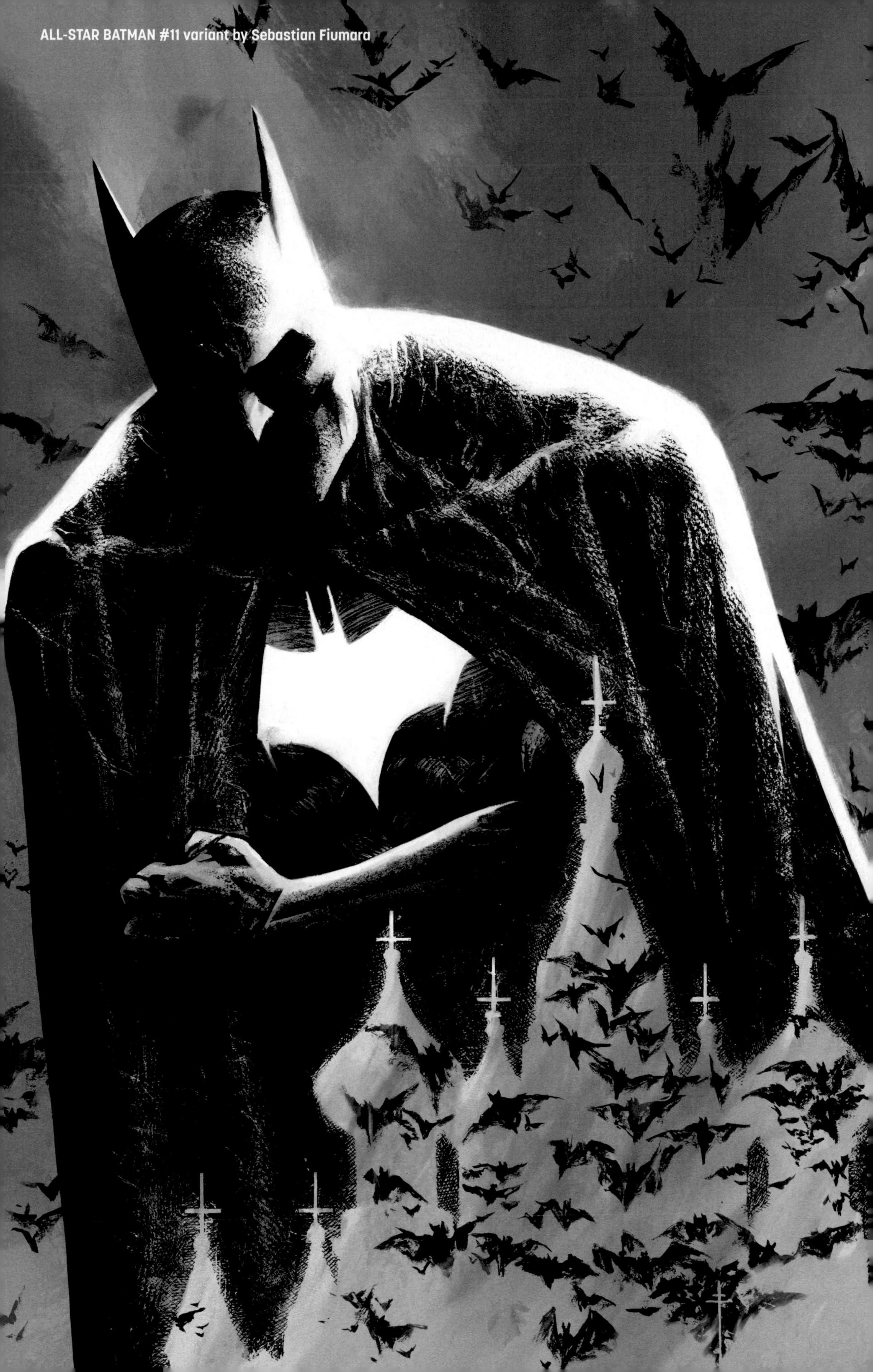

ALL-STAR BATMAN #12 variant by Sebastian Fiumara

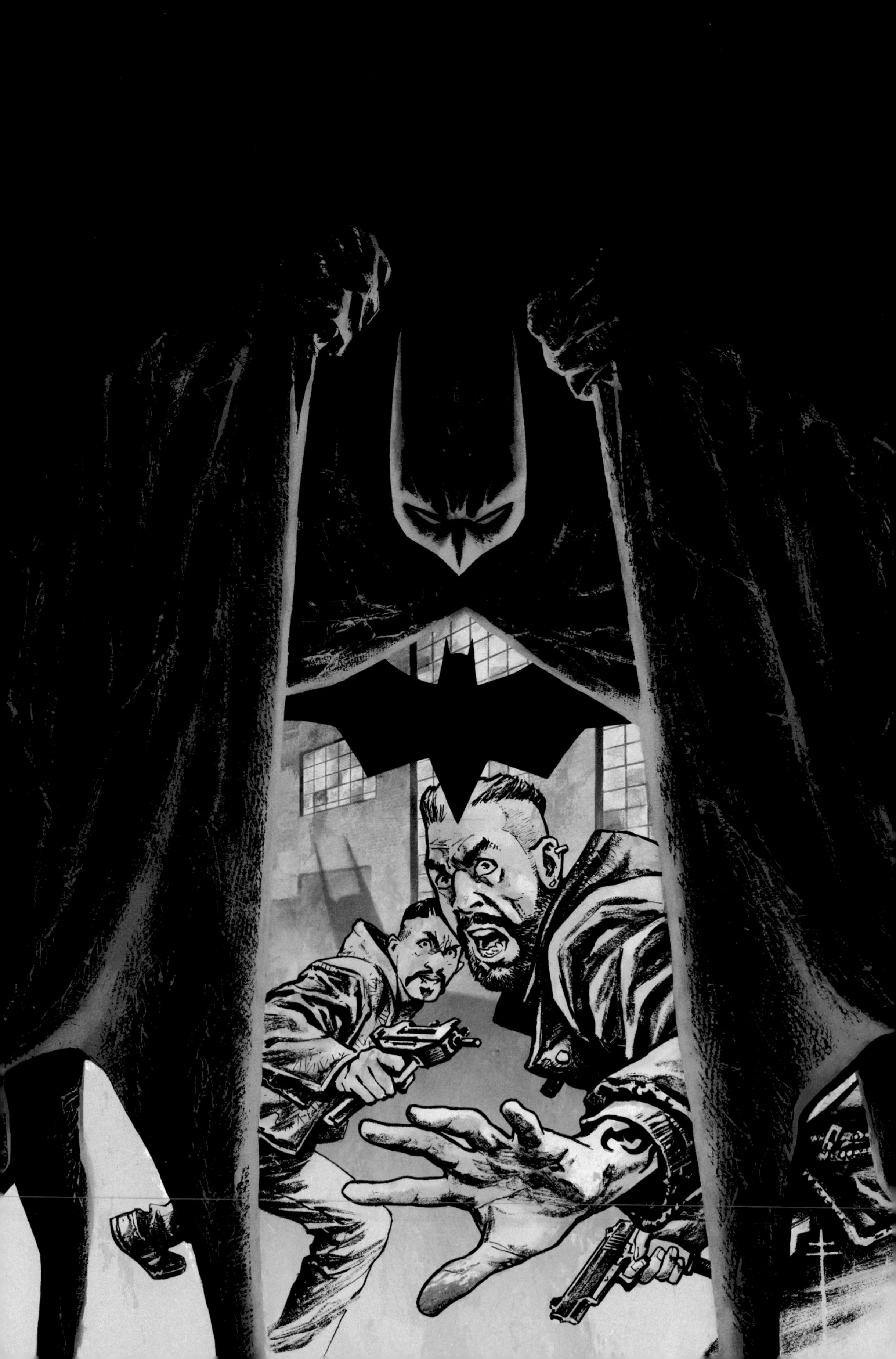

ALL-STAR BATMAN #13 variant by Sebastian Fiumara

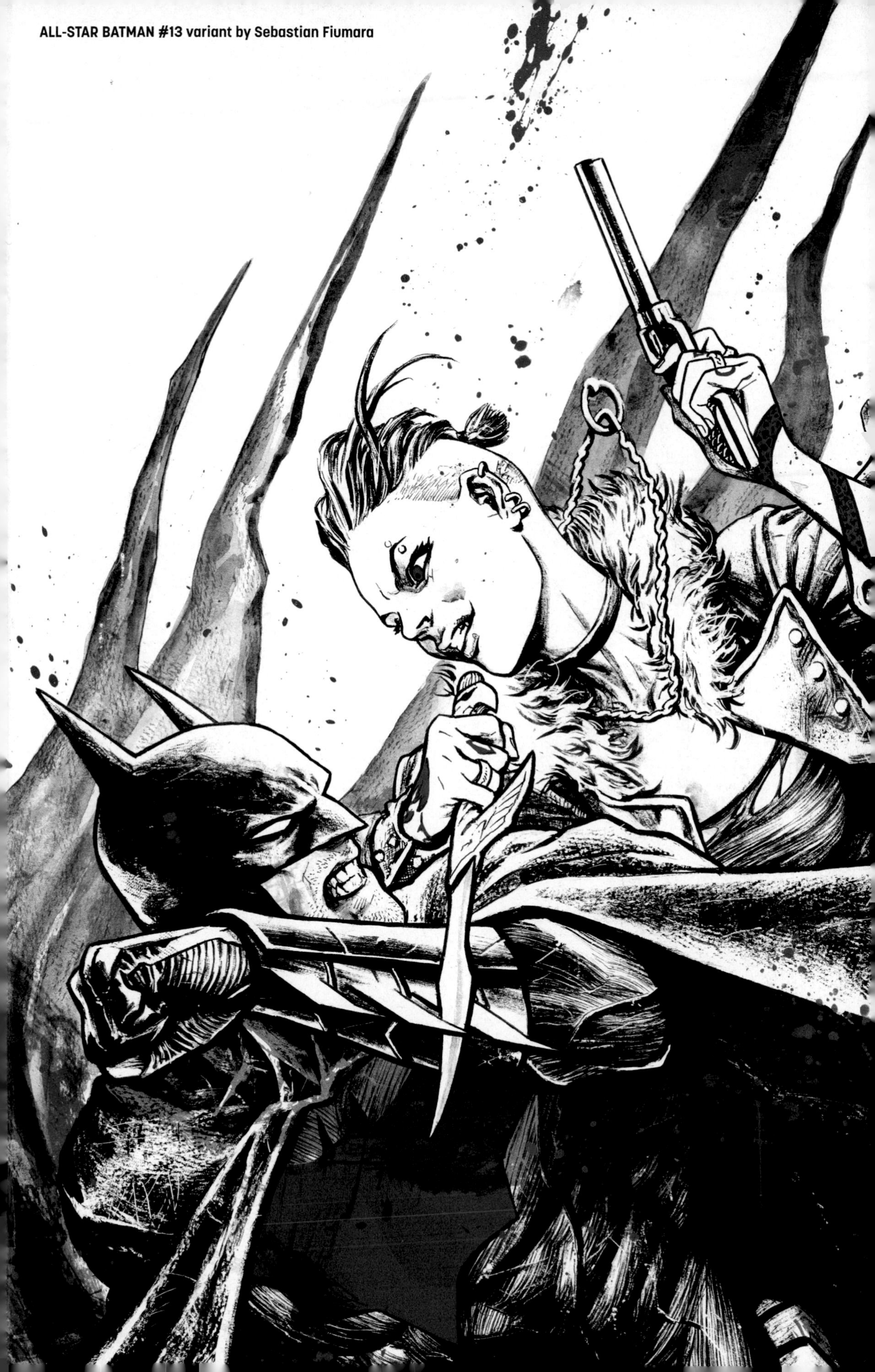

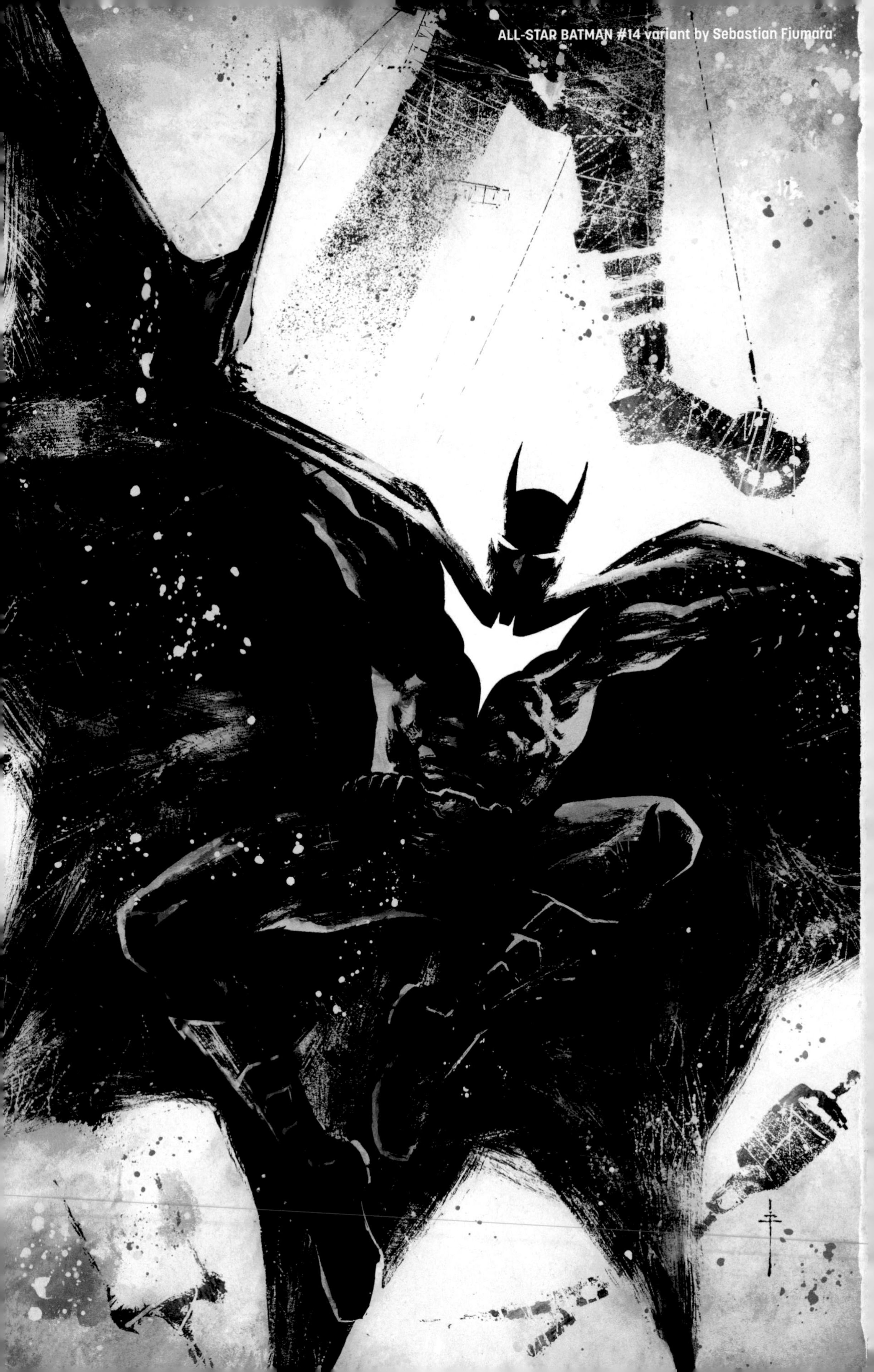

ALL-STAR BATMAN #14 variant by Sebastian Fiumara